GHETTO
IN FLAMES

YITZHAK ARAD

GHETTO IN FLAMES

THE STRUGGLE AND DESTRUCTION
OF THE JEWS IN VILNA
IN THE HOLOCAUST

HOLOCAUST LIBRARY
NEW YORK

Library of Congress Catalogue Card Number: 80-50198

Copyright © 1982 by Yitzhak Arad and Yad Vashem

ISBN 0-89604-043-7

Cover Design by Michael Meyerowitz
Printed in the United States

To my parents

Haya and Israel Moshe Rudnicki
who were murdered with the Jews
of Warsaw,
date of death unknown

CONTENTS

FOREWORD

From the end of the fifteenth century a large and flourishing community existed in Vilna. The large number of rabbinic scholars, writers, and centers of learning and Torah studies in Vilna assured the city a central place in the cultural life of Lithuanian Jewry. In the Jewish world at large Vilna was known as "Jerusalem of Lithuania."

Throughout her history Vilna was ruled successively by the Lithuanians, the Poles, the Russians, and, during World War I, even the Germans. Between the two world wars Vilna was under Polish domination. The Polish Government conducted a policy of "Polonization" of the city and surrounding area. The Poles ousted the Jews from a variety of economic footholds, both in industry and commerce, and, as a result, the Jews' economic position deteriorated.

In contrast to the economic decline of Vilna Jewry, a lively and flourishing cultural life developed. Zionist, religious, and Yiddishist groups were active in preserving the Jewish character of the community and in fostering Jewish consciousness through the network of educational and cultural establishments. The great majority of Jewish children were educated in elementary schools in which the language of instruction was Yiddish or Hebrew.

The Yiddish schools were conducted by the Central Committee for Education. Hebrew schools were operated by the Tarbut

[1]

network. Each of these educational systems had its own secondary schools and teacher-training college. The Yavneh religious elementary schools were run by the Mizrachi and Talmud Torah of the Orthodox Jewish circles. Vilna had two Jewish secondary schools and several vocational training establishments. Jews were discriminated against in government schools. The number of Jews admitted into the government technical colleges was limited to a mere 5 percent, and the *numerus clausus* was actively applied at the University of Vilna.

Vilna Jewry had many institutions in which the treasures of Jewish culture found their repository. Prominent among the large libraries was "Straszun," founded in 1893, which contained some 35,000 volumes: half the collection was rabbinical literature. It also possessed manuscripts dating to the fifteenth century. The Jewish Historical and Ethnographical Society, established in 1903, collected rare Jewish material in the fields of history, folklore, literature, drama, music, and art. Its library preserved original Yiddish and Hebrew manuscripts by renowned authors. The Jewish Scientific Institute, YIVO (Yiddisher Visnshaftlecher Institut), founded in 1924, dealt in the collection of cultural riches and in research work. YIVO possessed a collection of about 20,000 books, Yiddish newspapers published in all parts of the world, and rare paintings and musical compositions by Jewish artists. Several Jewish publishing houses were active in the city, and five daily newspapers and periodicals were published regularly.

A Jewish community council of twenty-five members, representing nine Zionist and non-Zionist parties and groups, was elected on July 29, 1928. Dr. Jacob Wygodzki (Zionist) was chosen as head of the council, which had an executive committee of twelve members. The council decided that all its official publications would be in Yiddish and Hebrew.

The Polish authorities, which had in the meantime assumed a semi-dictatorial character, did not favor democratic elections out of fear that this would arouse public demands for more democracy in other spheres. After two years, the elected Jewish council was dispersed, and the government appointed a Jewish council. This situation continued until 1934, when, under the pressure of public opinion, elections to the community council were held with the participation of all parties. The lawyer S. Milkonovicki, representing Po'alei Zion, was elected chairman of the council.

Throughout the period of Polish rule, a struggle for control of the "Jewish Street" was waged between the Zionist parties and the Bund. The Zionist groups were predominant in the community council, while the Bund wielded the strongest influence over the Jewish labor unions. The Jews in Vilna initiated their own independent welfare institutions, as well as social, religious, medical, economic, and sports organizations. In all they embraced every area of communal life.

During the final years of Polish rule, anti-Semitism and discrimination against the Jews became rampant in all spheres of life and assumed a violent form. Jews were attacked, and a bomb exploded in a synagogue at the beginning of February 1935. The anti-Jewish campaign was particularly rife on the University of Vilna campus. Separate seating for Jewish students, on the left side of the classrooms, was introduced in all universities in Poland in the fall of 1937. Mounting anti-Semitism and discriminatory practices continued almost until the very outbreak of the Germano-Polish war on September 1, 1939.

During the year of Soviet rule in Vilna, between June 1940 and June 1941, all Jewish organizations and institutions were disbanded. Therefore, when the Germans invaded the U.S.S.R. there was no recognized Jewish organization to deal with them.

This study focuses upon the life, struggle, and annihilation of the Jews of Vilna in the period between June 22, 1941—the day of the German attack upon the Soviet Union—and July 13, 1944, when Vilna was liberated by the Soviet Army. This treatise is limited to the events in one city and describes in detail what occurred there—the forces at work, the key personalities and their influence — in order to examine those events and developments in depth. The German administrative structure

[3]

and the anti-Jewish policy on the local level in Vilna are also described in order to demonstrate how the policy and general directives issued by the upper echelons of the ruling hierarchy in Germany were implemented by the local authorities. The German administrative organization in Vilna and the powers and functions given to those departments that dealt with the Jews constitute a sample of the German system of government and activity in the occupied territories in the East.

During the Holocaust the Jews of Vilna endured most of the edicts and persecutions that the Germans inflicted upon Jewry at large—expropriation of property, wearing the yellow badge, forced labor, abductions, humiliation and massacre by the Einsatzgruppen, confinement within the ghetto, deportations to forced-labor and death-camps. Faced with these eventualities, their problem was how to organize, how to conduct themselves, in order to survive.

The operating forces in the "Jewish Street" were the Judenrat and its institutions, existing political groups as well as those that came into being in the wake of ghetto conditions, the armed underground, and the Jewish public as a whole. The community suddenly found itself isolated from the rest of the Jewish world, a world with which it had, in the past, formed close ties and into which it was completely integrated. Its relationship with the non-Jewish environment, in whose midst it had existed for many generations, was radically transformed. In spite of the fact that, even in the past, the Jews had suffered enmity and much suffering at the hands of the local population, the eruption of savage, unrestrained hatred during the Nazi period came as a shock. The Jews were compelled to establish relations with an alien and hostile government that regarded them as subhuman and fit only for exploitation and extermination. The human values in which they believed and on which they had built their lives tottered and collapsed.

In this cruel reality, Vilna Jewry struggled to survive and seek rescue. The daily struggle was for life itself, to survive in the face of hunger and disease. Jewish Vilna embodied the majority

of hardships and torment that European Jewry at large under-
went during the Holocaust, and its responses sum up most of
the options that were available to the Jews during this tragic
epoch. Vilna Jewry was a microcosm of the fate of all Jewish
communities in Eastern Europe.

Part One

WORLD WAR II: THE CHANGED SITUATION

CHAPTER 1

THE JEWISH COMMUNITY IN VILNA FROM THE OUTBREAK OF WORLD WAR II UNTIL THE GERMAN INVASION

Political Fluctuations

World War II brought about far-reaching changes in Vilna's position. Control of the city, which was under Polish rule since October 9, 1920, changed hands four times during the period from the outbreak of the war on September 1, 1939, until the German invasion of the Soviet Union on June 22, 1941.

The Ribbentrop-Molotov agreement, signed in Moscow on August 23, 1939, contained a secret appendix relating to Lithuania and Vilna. Article 1 of this secret appendix provided that:

> In the event of territorial and political changes in the areas belonging to the Baltic countries (Finland, Estonia, Latvia, and Lithuania) the northern frontier of Lithuania shall constitute the frontier between the zones of influence of Germany and the U.S.S.R. Pursuant to that provision, the two parties (Germany and the U.S.S.R.) recognize the interests which Lithuania has in the Vilna region.

Other articles in the secret appendix relate to the division of spheres of influence in Poland and southeastern Europe. One week after the signing of the pact, on September 1, 1939, the Germans invaded Poland, and World War II began.

On September 17, 1939, the Red Army crossed the eastern frontier of Poland and began its conquest of western Belorussia and the western Ukraine. Two days later the Red Army entered

Vilna. At the end of September, all of Poland was under either German or Soviet rule.

On September 25, 1939, amendments were made to the Ribbentrop-Molotov pact concerning divisions and spheres of influence. The new agreement stated: "Article 1 of the appendix ... shall be thus amended: Lithuania shall henceforth be a sphere of Soviet influence ..." The new agreement gave the Soviet Union a free hand to operate in Lithuania as it saw fit and solely in accord with its own interests.

On October 10, 1939, the Lithuanian Foreign Minister, Urbsys, signed an agreement with the Soviet Union: "With a view to enhancing the friendship between the Soviet Union and Lithuania, the U.S.S.R. transfers to Lithuania the city of Vilna and the Vilna district, which will become an integral part of the State of Lithuania ..."

Other clauses of the agreement deal with a defense pact and the presence of Soviet troops in Lithuanian bases. Lithuania had received Vilna in exchange for these concessions.

The Jews of Vilna under Lithuanian Rule

Fear and apprehension gripped Vilna's Jews during the first days of the war. The advance of the German armies and the swift collapse of Poland confronted them with the threat of German occupation and all that it implied. Consequently, they joyously acclaimed the news that the Red Army had crossed the Polish frontier, and on September 19, 1939, they welcomed the Soviet vanguard that entered Vilna and dissipated the Nazi menace. As in all other areas of Poland that had been captured by the Red Army, Jewish fugitives from the areas occupied by German troops began to flock to Vilna. It was the first and comparatively limited tide of refugees fleeing from the German invaders.

On October 28, 1939, Vilna was taken over by the Lithuanians, marking a new era for the Jewish inhabitants of the city. With the transfer of Vilna to the Lithuanians, hundreds of Jewish youngsters left Vilna and crossed into the Soviet Union. They included communist activists and sympathizers, as well as those who had served in the Soviet militia.

The day that Vilna came under Lithuanian control was marked by anti-Jewish riots. One young man was killed, and a number of others were wounded. The rioting continued for several days, reaching a climax on Tuesday, October 31, when some 200 Jews were injured and Jewish shops were broken into and ransacked.

The outbreak of violence was unexpected. As to what exactly caused these disturbances there are several versions. The background was certainly the tension among the populace over the rise in food prices and the general uncertainty about the future. Long lines of angry people formed outside the bakeries and bread-shops while groups of communists—among them some Jews—bid farewell to the evacuating Soviet forces. Cries of "Down with the Lithuanians! Down with the Jews! Down with the Soviets!" rose from among the Poles thronging the streets. Anti-Semitic agitators inflamed feelings still further by blaming the Jews for the soaring prices and the disappearance of bread from the bakery shelves. In the midst of this tension, a rumor spread among the infuriated Polish mobs that the Jews had murdered a child and a Polish priest.

Groups of rioters began breaking into shops, grabbing everything in sight and assaulting Jews. The rioters overran various parts of the city and were joined by Lithuanian policemen, who beat up the Jewish victims instead of trying to quell the unrest. Jews who tried to defend themselves were arrested by the Lithuanian police.

Dr. Wygodzki and other Vilna Jewish leaders urged the Lithuanian commander and the Lithuanian Government delegate in Vilna, Merkys, to use force in putting down the anti-Jewish disturbances. When these appeals proved futile, they turned for aid to the Soviet garrison commander at Novo-Vileyka, pleading with him to restore order. Their pleas elicited a favorable response, and Soviet tanks rumbled into the streets of the city in a display of power. Order was in fact reinstated.[1]

The rioting, which lasted from October 28 to 31, 1939, was minimized by Lithuanian sources. An announcement issued by the official Lithuanian news agency stated:

> Clashes occurred yesterday in Vilna between groups of fanatical Polish youths and Jews. The police immediately restored order. Several people were arrested and certain rioters will be brought to trial. It should be stressed that hostility has been rife between Polish and Jewish youths for a long while, and it has been heightened by events during the present war and the change in regime. More-over, in Vilna there are considerable numbers of foreign elements, refugees frorm the different wars, including criminals who have been freed from prison... Quiet now prevails in Vilna and district...

After the riots on October 31, 1939, rumors spread among the Jews in the surrounding area that preparations were being made for a new wave of anti-Jewish violence scheduled for November 10–11. These were traditional dates for anti-Semitic assaults in Vilna ever since November 10, 1931, when a Polish youth was killed in a quarrel between Jews and Polish anti-Semitic mobs. On November 6, 1939, Dr. Wygodzki wrote to the Lithuanian Minister of the Interior warning of possible resumption of the "traditional" rioting on November 10–11, and urging that necessary security measures be invoked. The Lithuanian authorities promised to prevent any such recurrence.[2]

The Jews of Vilna no longer believed that they could rely on the protection of the Lithuanian authorities, and they began to organize their own self-defense. At a meeting of local Jewish leaders with representatives of refugee groups, it was decided

1 M. Balberyszski, *Shtarker fun ayzn,* Tel Aviv, 1967, p. 74. L. Rann, *Ash fun Yerushalayim de-Lite,* New York, 1959, pp. 274, 279, 289, 291-292, 297; I. Cohen, *Vilna,* Philadelphia, 1943, p. 473.
2 Rann, *op. cit.,* pp. 292–295.

to organize their own self-defense and simultaneously to request the Lithuanian Government delegate in Vilna to ensure that the authorities maintain order in the city. A proclamation was issued in the first days of November 1939 calling on Jewish workers in Vilna to undertake their own measures of self-defense.

The Lithuanian Government in Vilna was prepared to allocate arms to the Jews for their self-defense on condition that those receiving the weapons would obey Lithuanian orders. There was readiness among the Jews of Vilna to accept the offer of arms, but only within an autonomous Jewish framework and not on behalf of, or under orders from, the government.[3] The Jews wished to appear as an independent and neutral factor and not as an element veering towards any particular side in the controversy. Jews armed with weapons and appearing as a unit on behalf of the Lithuanian Government might be identified with the Lithuanians—something the Jews wished to avoid at any cost.

The days of November 10–11 passed quietly. The Lithuanian Government took appropriate preventive measures, and the Lithuanian Minister of Interior summoned the principals of the schools in Vilna and warned them that the Lithuanian police had received orders to shoot anyone disturbing the peace and demanded that they maintain law and order.[4]

Eight months of Lithuanian rule in Vilna were marked by increased Jewish activity—the final chapter in the history of "Jerusalem of Lithuania." Vilna had by then become the most active center in Eastern Europe; it likewise maintained communications with Eretz Israel, with other Jewish centers abroad, and with Jews in the occupied parts of Poland.[5]

---

3 *Ibid.*, pp. 298–299; J. Gilboa, *Lishmor La-nezah*, Tel Aviv, 1963, p. 21; *Sefer ha-Shomer ha-Za'ir*, Vol. I, Merhavia, 1956, p. 442.
4 Rann, *op. cit.*, pp. 295, 300.
5 Y. Helman, "Le-Reshita shel ha-Mahteret ha-Haluzit be-Polin ha-Kvusha," *Dappim le-Heker ha-Sho'ah ve-ha-Mered*, 2nd Series, Vol. I, Tel Aviv, 1969, p. 68. Appended to the article are 17 letters

The Jewish organizations that had existed during the period of Polish rule continued to function, including the community council. Vilna had in the past been institutionally linked with the Jewish centers in Warsaw, but in the changed situation it began to form ties with the organizations of Lithuanian Jewry. Dr. Moshe Kleinbaum (Sneh) tells of a ceremony transferring the Vilna branch of the Zionist Organization from the aegis of the Central Committee of Zionists in Poland to the Central Committee of Zionists in Lithuania.[6] Discussions were held on the amalgamation of the Zionist youth movements in Vilna with the youth movements in Lithuania with which they had an ideological affinity. The leadership of the Zionist youth movements and training groups (Hachshara) from Poland were concentrated in Vilna, and instructors were sent out into the towns and townships of Lithuania to strengthen and organize Zionist activity there.

As was true under Polish rule, a vigorous Jewish cultural life flourished in Vilna. Three Jewish daily papers appeared. A Jewish Historical Committee was set up to record testimony and gather material on anti-Jewish action in the German occupied areas of Poland.

The Refugees

The report of the annexation of Vilna to Lithuania served as a sign for thousands of Jews in the German zone of occupation in Poland and in the regions annexed to the U.S.S.R. to make their way to Vilna. Individuals, organized groups, Zionist youth movements, yeshiva students, party leaders, and others began to stream into the city. A He-Halutz member wrote at that time:

> Reports arrived concerning Vilna. This city, held by the
> Soviets, was about to be transferred to Lithuania. The

sent to Eretz Israel during that period, mainly from Vilna (hereafter: "17 letters").

6 Testimony of Dr. Moshe Kleinbaum (Sneh), Yad Vashem Archives (hereafter: YVA), 0–33/1237, p. 5.

rumor about Vilna spread like wildfire among the He-Halutz members and scores upon scores began to stream there. Our kibbutz in Vilna, which had a small number of members, began to increase daily... and became a kibbutz of 600 members by the time the Lithuanians entered.[7]

From October 10, 1939, until the city came under Lithuanian control, it was not difficult for Jews in Soviet-annexed Poland to reach Vilna. The city was still under Soviet rule and the roads to it were open. One of the refugees wrote:

At first instinctively and spontaneously, and thereafter in an organized way, masses of Jews moved to Vilna. The guiding thought was: To be able to get to it by train and free movement so long as it belonged to the Soviets and to remain there after their withdrawal. Indeed trains going to the city were crowded.[8]

This situation continued until Lithuania took over Vilna and the new borders between the U.S.S.R. and Lithuania were closed.

The illegal frontier crossings began in mid-November 1939. These movements took place under the most arduous conditions in a particularly severe winter in the area between Lida on the Soviet side and Ejszyszki (Eishishkes) on the Lithuanian side. They were carried out in an organized manner, under the aegis of the Zionist youth movements. The crossing was made on foot or in sleighs—depending on the topography and the activity of frontier patrols.

The He-Halutz Central Committee of Poland, which had left Warsaw before Nazi occupation, convened in Kovel (in the Soviet zone) and, upon learning of the agreement ceding Vilna to the Lithuanians, decided to concentrate the He-Halutz members from all sectors of occupied Poland there. He-Halutz emissaries went from Kovel to Warsaw and other centers in occupied

7 *Mi-Bifnim,* Vol. VI, Ein Harod, May 1941, p. 383.
8 Gilboa, p. 20.

Poland to transmit the Central Committee's decision. He-Halutz organized a special group, which was engaged in smuggling its members to Vilna, and operated on both sides of the border. The He-Halutz members came from all parts of occupied Poland to Lida, where they were provided with money, food, and guides, led Ejszyszki, and from there to Vilna.[9]

The leadership of Ha-Shomer ha-Za'ir moved from Warsaw to Rovno. With the publication of the agreement transferring Vilna to Lithuania, the Ha-Shomer ha-Za'ir leadership decided to concentrate its members there after becoming convinced that there was no prospect for operating legally under the Soviet regime.[10]

The Central Committee of Ha-No'ar ha-Ziyyoni in Poland, which arrived in Pinsk from Warsaw, also decided to relocate to Vilna and assemble its adherents there.[11] About 1,400 Halutzim from all Zionist movements arrived there after crossing the border, following the annexation of Vilna to Lithuania.[12]

The Betar movement also decided to gather its members in Vilna, where virtually the entire command of Betar in Poland had already assembled. Messengers were dispatched to the Soviet and German sectors of Poland to assemble the members at Vilna, and hundreds of them arrived after stealthily crossing the borders.[13]

In addition to the organized smuggling by Zionist youth movements, yeshiva students, individual Jews, and entire families managed to cross the border. Local peasants and professional smugglers were engaged in smuggling Jews across the border

---

9 *Sefer Dror*, Ein Harod, 1947, p. 383; *Mi-Bifnim*, Vol. VI, p. 60.

10 *Sefer ha-Shomer ha-Za'ir*, Vol. I, *op. cit.*, pp. 440–441.

11 Testimony of N. Reznik, YVA. 0–33/1238, p. 1.

12 Y. Bauer, "Rescue Operations Through Vilna," *Yad Vashem Studies*, Vol. IX, Jerusalem, 1973, p. 215. The figures are based on data in the archives of the American Joint Distribution Committee. See also: *Mi-Bifnim*, Vol. VI, p. 113.

13 I. Sheib, *Ma'aser Rishon, Tel Aviv*, 1950, p. 40. S. Skolski, "Betar be-Mahteret Rusyah," *Ha-Medina*, Tel Aviv, 1944, p 21.

for heavy payments. More than once these smugglers deserted the Jews in the frontier zones after taking their money.

Not all who tried to cross over were successful in their attempts. Hundreds were caught en route by Soviet or Lithuanian patrols; some were arrested, others returned. No small number met their end on these trails—either from the patrolmen's bullets or from the cold. When the snows melted in the spring, the bodies of Jewish youths who had died on the trek were revealed. Then, too, a large number reached Vilna with frozen limbs, and some perished from these afflictions after arrival.[14]

Toward the end of January 1940, the border smugglings ceased almost entirely due to the reinforced Soviet patrols and the particularly harsh winter. Small-scale smugglings went on for some months until Lithuania was annexed to the U.S.S.R. The number of Jewish refugees in Vilna reached approximately 14,000.[15]

Many leaders of Polish Jewry arrived in Vilna with the waves of refugees, among them Dr. M. Kleinbaum, chairman of the Zionist Organization in Poland; Dr. Z. Warhaftig, one of the leaders of Mizrachi–Ha-po'el ha-Mizrachi; A. Bialopolski, a Po'alei Zion leader; Menahem Begin, who had been Betar commander in Poland; S. Millman, a Bund leader, and others. The refugees who came as groups—the youth movements and yeshiva students — continued to maintain their former organizational structures.

A Central Refugee Committee functioned actively. The local Jewish community, led by Dr. Wygodzki, and the Jewish community of Lithuania were the first to extend aid to the thousands of Jewish refugees who reached Vilna. At a later stage the "Joint" took them under its wing. Soup kitchens were opened, clothing was distributed, and vocational training courses were started. The "Joint" channeled its assistance through the

---

14 *Sefer Dror*, p. 383; *Mi-Bifnim*, Vol. VI, p. 113. Reznik's testimony, 0–33/1238; Sheib, *op. cit.*, p. 40.
15 Bauer, *op. cit.*, p. 215.

Refugee Committee. Notwithstanding this aid, the refugees' plight was very severe, especially the Hachshara groups who had assembled in Vilna and could not find employment.

The "He-Halutz Concentration" in Vilna comprised about 2,000 members of pioneer youth movements.[16] The Zionist movements in Vilna sent emissaries to their organizations operating clandestinely in the occupied areas of Poland. They also kept in touch with their respective movements in Palestine and elsewhere abroad. The Vilna committee thus served as a connecting link between the movements in occupied Poland and Palestine.

The He-Halutz youth movements established a joint umbrella organization that dealt with establishing common enterprises, vocational training, and immigration to Palestine. This organization was given the title of "He-Halutz Coordination" and representatives of each movement served on its secretariat.[17]

Hundreds of Betar members were quartered in refugee reception hostels. The Etzel continued to conduct courses in the "use of arms."[18] About 2,440 yeshiva students and hundreds of rabbis congregated in Vilna, including those from the large yeshivot of Mir, Kamieniec, and Kleck. There were also small concentrations of kibbutzim from among the members of the Zionist religious youth movements. Another group in Vilna, comprised of some 400 refugees belonging to the Bund, had organized independently and did not join the Refugees Committee.[19]

In January 1940, the Lithuanian Government published an order whereby all refugees were required to leave Vilna and

16 "17 letters," pp. 81, 88, 94; *Mi-Bifnim*, Vol. VI, p. 113; Reznik's testimony, 0-33/1238, p. 2; *Sefer ha-Shomer ha-Za'ir*, pp. 442, 463. The 2,000 members were distributed as follows: 580 in the Gush (Ha-Kibbutz ha-Me'uhad); 600 — Ha-Shomer ha-Za'ir; close to 400 — Ha-No'ar ha-Ziyyoni; about 100 — Gordonia; and 85 in Akiva.

17 *Ibid.*, p. 444; Reznik's testimony, 0-33/1238, p. 3; *Mi-Bifnim*, Vol. VI, p. 116.

18 Skolski, *op. cit.*, p. 21; Sheib, *op. cit.*, pp. 40–41.

19 Bauer, *op. cit.*, pp. 215, 217; Balberyszski, *op. cit.*, p. 91.

proceed to the interior of the country. Consequently, some of the refugees, among them 600 Halutzim and several yeshivot left Vilna for various provincial towns of Lithuania.[20]

There was a strong desire among some of the Jews of Vilna, and particularly among the refugees and Zionist groups, to leave Vilna and Lithuania for Eretz Israel or other places in the free world. It was patently clear to Vilna Jewry that the period of relative tranquility, which they had enjoyed with the transfer of the city to the Lithuanians, would not long endure and that one day Lithuania would be annexed either by the U.S.S.R. or Nazi Germany. Furthermore, in spite of the aid given by the Jews of Vilna and Lithuania and the J.D.C. agencies to the Jewish fugitives from Poland, the position of these refugees was barely tolerable.

The Palestine Office was established in Vilna at the beginning of November 1939, several days after the city had been ceded to the Lithuanians. The initiative came from the Polish Zionist leaders then assembled in the city, among them Dr. M. Kleinbaum, chairman of the Central Committee of the Polish Zionist Organization. The Palestine Office had been formally recognized by the Jewish Agency in Jerusalem. Although the main purpose of the Palestine Office was to deal with immigration to Palestine, the very limited number of certificates available led it to seek other countries of refuge to which Jews could be sent temporarily until conditions became more suitable for emigration to Eretz Israel. The total number of immigration certificates granted during this period was about 400, and a bitter struggle ensued over their distribution.[21] The first group of

---

20 "17 letters," pp. 95, 205, 114; *Sefer ha-Shomer ha-Za'ir,* p. 447. Bauer, *op. cit.,* p. 216, writes that the steps taken by the Lithuanian administration were directed mainly against the Polish refugees in Vilna in an attempt to reduce the Polish population in Vilna.

21 Sneh's testimony, pp. 4–5, 7; Immigration File of the Palestine Office in Lithuania, in the Central Zionist Archives, Jerusalem, letter dated November 6, 1939, to the Immigration Office in Kovno.

emigrants for Palestine left Vilna in March 1940 and was followed by a number of other groups who went by way of Latvia, Sweden, Holland, France, and Italy. About 400 traveled to Eretz Israel by this route, while another 150 Jews went to the U.S.A. After May 1940, transit to Palestine via the Scandinavian countries was closed, as Western Europe was occupied by the German armies. It was essential to find alternate routes. During April–May 1940, for the first time the Dutch Consulate granted entry visas for Curaçao (Dutch West Indies) and Surinam (Dutch Guyana). Those holding visas for Curaçao were granted transit visas through Japan by the Japanese Minister in Kovno, and many of the Jewish refugees received these permits. But before the visas could be used, Lithuania lost its independence and became a Soviet Republic.[22]

The Jews of Vilna under Soviet Rule
The Lithuanian rule in Vilna lasted about six months, until mid-June 1940. The changes that occurred during this period on the map of Europe—the German conquests in Western Europe and Scandinavia, as well as the expansionist aims and intentions of Soviet policy—caused changes in Lithuania.

On June 14, 1940, the Soviet Union presented Lithuania with an ultimatum. Lithuania was charged with having kidnapped Soviet soldiers and of having entered into military pacts with Estonia and Latvia, which was considered a breach of the Soviet–Lithuanian defense pact of October 10, 1939. The ultimatum demanded that Lithuania would, among other things, establish a new government, friendly to the Soviet Union, and acquiesce to the entry of more Soviet army units. On June 15, 1940, without waiting for the reply of the Lithuanian Government to this ultimatum, Soviet units crossed the Lithuanian border, and, in coordination with those Soviet units already inside the country, took control. The president of Lithuania, A.

22   "17 letters," pp. 75, 82, 114, 117; Bauer, *op. cit.*, p. 1.

Smetona, and other high-ranking members of the government, fled to Germany.

On June 17, 1940, a popular government was set up in Lithuania under the Lithuanian Communist leader, Justas J. Paleckis. On July 1, 1940, an order was issued outlawing all parties and organizations except the Communist Party, which had of course been legalized. The non-Communist press was closed down entirely on July 11–12.

On July 14, 1940, elections were held for a "Liaudies Seimas" (People's Parliament). The Lithuanian Workers Union, in which the Communists were predominant, polled 99.19 percent of all votes cast, according to the official announcement. The Liaudies Seimas resolved to convert Lithuania into a Soviet Republic and to submit an application to the U.S.S.R. to admit Lithuania into that union. The Supreme Soviet approved the application on August 3, 1940.

The process of Sovietization in the country began at once. On July 26, 1940, the Liaudies Seimas agreed upon the nationalization of industrial and craft enterprises that employed more than ten workers, the nationalization of banks and commercial firms and the freezing of bank deposits, and proclaimed all land to be state property. On September 27 an order was enacted for the nationalization of private enterprises that had an annual turnover of more than 150,000 lit. (5 lit. = $1). On October 31 all private buildings were nationalized. All schools came under the jurisdiction of the Ministry of Education and were forbidden to teach religion.

The order proscribing activity by all organizations and parties, with the exception of the Communist Party, put to a formal end the legal functioning of the Jewish institutions, organizations, and parties. Jewish schools fell under government supervision; Yiddish remained the language of instruction, but the teaching of Hebrew, Bible, and Jewish history was forbidden. Jewish libraries were incorporated within municipal libraries after works which were not in accord with Soviet ideology had been eliminated. A Jewish state theater was established in Vilna.

A Yiddish daily, *Vilner Emes,* began appearing in August 1940, after the three Jewish newspapers were closed by government order.

The nationalization decrees for industries, crafts, shops, large residential buildings, and banks, which were enacted during the months of July–October 1940, struck hard at wide strata of the Jewish population. In Vilna, 102 factories and workshops of Jewish ownership were nationalized. Out of the 370 nationalized stores and businesses, 265 belonged to Jews.[23] As a result of the government's new taxation policy, small businessmen whose establishments had not been confiscated could not make a living, as they were unable to compete with state commerce. Most were compelled to liquidate their businesses and seek other means of earning their livelihood. Most of the artisans whose workshops were nationalized found employment in artisans' cooperatives, to which the government granted raw materials. Members of the liberal professions were forced to give up their private practice and seek employment, mainly in government establishments. Soviet economic policy thus seriously impaired Jewish traditional vocations.

The hired Jewish workers were in the best position; for the most part they continued in their previous places of employment and, in some cases, were even promoted. Jews were also admitted to posts in government institutions that, in the past, during Polish and Lithuanian rule, had been denied to them. Jews in considerable numbers were thus appointed to government, party, and militia posts.

The Zionist youth movements organized themselves for underground operation after they were declared illegal. He-Halutz ha-Za'ir–Dror decided to close its Hachshara groups outside Vilna and set up a clandestine organization divided into cells of five to ten members. The movement's seminar operated clandestinely at the agricultural farm at Wolokumpia (Valakampiai).[24]

---

23 J. Gar, *Azoy iz es geshen in Lite,* Tel Aviv, 1965, pp. 107, 115.
24 *Mi-Bifnim,* Vol. VI, p. 62; B. Klibanski, "The Underground

The Council of Ha-Shomer ha-Za'ir decided to dismantle the framework of the Hachshara trainee groups and to restructure into groups of four or five members who would live and work together. The Ha-Shomer ha-Za'ir agricultural farm at Michalin, which served as a center of activity for all of Lithuania, continued to exist until the Nazi invasion, and the Soviet authorities regarded the farm as a *kolkhoz*. A joint emergency leadership of the local Ha-Shomer ha-Za'ir and members from among the refugees was set up in Vilna, and the movement began holding its seminars in secret.[25]

The Ha-No'ar ha-Ziyyoni movement likewise went underground. The leadership decided to disperse the kibbutzim and organized their people into small groups. There were five members of the underground leadership who maintained contact with 250–300 members in various parts of Lithuania.[26] The pioneer youth movements continued to maintain connections within the framework of the "He-Halutz Coordination," which had been set up during the Lithuanian period, especially in seeking ways and means for *aliya*.

The final meeting of Betar, at which the dissolution of the movement was announced, took place at the beginning of July 1940. It marked the end of legal activity, but the Betar movement continued to function clandestinely. It reorganized itself into underground cells, each having five members, and dealt with forging the necessary certificates and documents in order to leave Lithuania. The Betar underground cells also offered training in arms during the initial months of Soviet rule in Lithuania.[27]

Archives of the Bialystok Ghetto," *Yad Vashem Studies*, Vol. II, 1958, pp. 304–305.

25 *Sefer ha-Shomer ha-Za'ir*, pp. 448–449, 451; Testimony of Abba Kovner, YVA, 0–33/1239, p. 1.

26 Reznik's testimony, 0–33/1238, p. 2.

27 *Ha-Medina*, pp. 22, 26; Testimony of Tzippora Kuperberg, Institute of Contemporary Jewry, (12) 161, pp. 3–5.

The Struggle for Emigration

The order to dismantle the various organizations also embraced the Palestine Office and all other Jewish bodies that aided Jews wishing to emigrate. The Soviet administration had announced the closing of the foreign diplomatic missions in Lithuania, so the immediate problem was how to get the most transit permits and entry visas possible in the short time available. During the few days that elapsed until the closing of the diplomatic missions, thousands of Jews indeed managed to get entry visas for Palestine from the British consul, entry visas into Curaçao from the Dutch consul, and transit permits from the Japanese consul. Many persons also retained special "attestations" from the British Consulate which testified that the holder had been granted permission by His Majesty's Government to enter Palestine.

Toward the end of July 1940, a Jewish deputation led by Dr. Z. Warhaftig called on the director-general of the Foreign Ministry of the Soviet Lithuanian Government, P. Glovackas, and described the plight of the thousands of refugees from the German occupied territories. These people had valid emigration passports but required Soviet exit and transit permits. The deputation urged the director-general to recommend to the central authorities in Moscow to grant these exit and transit documents for passage through U.S.S.R. territory. Simultaneously, contact was also established with the U.S.S.R. delegate in Lithuania, Pozdniakov, to whom the same problem was presented. Pozdniakov promised to take the matter up with Moscow and to recommend granting exit permits from the Soviet Union.

The chief rabbi of Eretz Israel, Dr. Isaac Halevy-Herzog, appealed to the Soviet ambassador in London, I. Maisky, to intervene with the Moscow authorities for permission for thousands of yeshiva students, refugees from Poland, to leave Lithuania.

Consent to issue exit permits to refugees holding entry visas for a number of overseas countries was received in September

[24]

1940.[28] According to established procedure, every refugee holding an entry visa for any country had to submit a personal application to the Soviet Emigration Office in Vilna or Kovno. After inquiries and the completion of sundry forms, most of the applicants received these permits.

Exit permits for Japan were given to those who held entry visas for Curaçao and Surinam and transit permits issued by the Japanese. Those who had immigration permits for Palestine (or British "attestations") were also given permission to travel to Persia or Turkey. Departures continued until the beginning of May 1941, when the issue of exit documents was terminated. The number of Jews who left Lithuania during the period of Lithuanian and Soviet rule between March 1940 and May 1941 was estimated at 6,500. This figure included several groups of yeshiva students and rabbis as well as workers' leaders and Bundists who were given entry visas for the United States.[29]

The Deportations

On November 28, 1940, the Commissar for Interior Affairs of the Lithuanian Republic (N.K.V.D.), A. Guzevicius, published an order requiring the preparation of a list of "unreliable elements." It comprised

> all persons who because of their social and political past, nationalist-chauvinist views, religious convictions, and moral or political instability, oppose the Socialist Order... All foreign citizens... persons who have personal ties and maintain correspondence with overseas, with foreign embassies and consulates... and refugees from Poland...[30]

28 Y. Idelstein, "Masa u-Mattan im Shiltonot Brit ha-Mo'azot al Yezi'at Yehudim," *Gesher,* Vol. I, No. 42, March 1965, pp. 79–80; Bauer, p. 221.
29 *Ibid.,* pp. 221–223; C. Barlas, "Mivza Aliyat Lita," *Dappim le-Heker ha-Sho'ah ve-ha-Mered,* 2nd Series, Vol. I, 1970, pp. 249, 254.
30 *An Appeal,* Lithuanian American Information Center, New York, August 1944, pp. 19–21 (hereafter: Lithuanian Center).

Thousands of refugees who held entry visas for overseas countries and maintained contact with foreign consulates and families abroad were thus on the list of anti-Soviet elements.

The N.K.V.D. district commissars submitted a report every five days in which "anti-Soviet elements" were listed according to nationality groupings. Clause 5 of the report specified Jewish anti-Soviet elements as follows:

(1) The leadership of all Zionist organizations and regular contributors to their publications;

(2) The leadership of the Bund and regular contributors to their publications;

(3) The leadership of Jewish military and Fascist organizations:

    a. The Jewish Association of Fighters for the Independence of Lithuania

    b. The Association of Jewish Fighters

    c. Betar and Etzel

    d. The Zionist-Revisionist Party.

Clause 9 of the report required the registration of refugees from Poland, who were mainly Jews.

Preparations for the deportation of "anti-Soviet elements" from Lithuania lasted for about six months; the expulsions were carried out on June 14 and 15, 1941. About 30,000 persons were expelled to the regions of Altai, Western Siberia, Kazakhstan and Karelia.

Among the deportees were also 5–6,000 Jews, some of them refugees from Poland, members of parties and of youth movements, and some who had not agreed to take out Soviet citizenship so as not to give up their prospects for leaving the U.S.S.R.[31]

These deportations aroused fear among the Lithuanian popu-

31 Gar, *op. cit.*, pp. 136, 140–146, 150; Lithuanian Center, pp. 22–28; N. Tenenbaum-Backer, *Ha-Adam ve-ha-Lohem,* Jerusalem, 1974, pp. 69–70.

BEFORE THE GERMAN INVASION

lation. Rumors were rife that the expulsions were only the beginning. The Soviet regime, which had always been unpopular,
now incurred even greater animosity. Although there were
thousands of Jews among those deported, the measures led to
an increase in hatred of the Jews, as they constituted a fairly
large proportion of those in local government and in the Communist party. During this period of alarm and fear over further
deportations and the growing rancor against the Soviet order
and the Jews, Germany invaded the Soviet Union.

The Population in Vilna on the Eve of the German Invasion
The last population census in Vilna prior to World War II had
been taken in 1931, during the period of Polish rule. The figures for 1931 showed the total population of Vilna as 195,100
persons: Poles constituted the majority — 128,600; Jews —
54,600; and Lithuanians — 2,000. The remaining 10,000 were
Belorussians, Russians, Ukrainians, and other minority groups.
The results of the census were tendentious and did not reflect
the true picture; Vilna was a bone of contention between Poland and Lithuania, and the Poles had an interest in proving
that the Lithuanians were a small minority in the city and in
magnifying the number of Polish inhabitants.

According to Lithuanian sources communicated to the Germans on their invasion of the U.S.S.R., the Lithuanians composed 30 percent of the civilian population; the Jews were close
to 40 percent; and the remaining 30 percent were Poles, Belorussians, Russians, etc.[32] The population of Vilna totaled about
200,000. According to the Lithuanian computation, the number
of Lithuanians was 60,000; Jews — 80,000; and the Poles and
the rest — 6,000. These Lithuanian figures are a gross exag-
geration in favor of their own people in the city.

The report given to the Germans was also distorted with regard to the number of Jews in Vilna. The Jewish community
there had been declining from the beginning of the century until

32 Einsatzgruppen Report (No. 17) of July 9, 1941, YVA, 0-51/57-1.

[27]

the last census in 1931. Its severance from Russia and Lithuania and the "Polonization" of Vilna after the end of World War I had played havoc with the Jewish economy and means of livelihood and led to a decline in the number of Jewish inhabitants. During the decade following the 1931 population census, there were demographic changes in the Jewish community caused by a combination of factors: natural increase, emigration to other countries, and the influx of Jews from provincial towns. Due to these changes it may be assumed that the number of Jews in Vilna grew between 1931 and 1939 from 55,000 to 58,000.[33]

The Jewish refugees who came to Vilna at the beginning of World War II from occupied areas of Poland increased the Jewish community to 67–70,000. Under the successive Lithuanian and Soviet regimes, about 6,500 Jews left for the free world; these were in large part refugees. In addition, some of the refugees who had come to Vilna left for other places in Lithuania. Several thousand Jews from Vilna were also expelled to the U.S.S.R. in mid-June 1941. It is therefore reasonable to estimate the number of Jews in Vilna at the outbreak of the war between Germany and the U.S.S.R. at approximately 60,000.

33 The number of Jews in Vilna in comparison with the general population of that city was as follows:

Year	Gen. Pop.	Jews	% Jews
1897	154,532	63,996	40.9
1916	140,840	61,263	43.5
1923	167,454	56,168	33.5
1931	193,337	55,007	28.5

(Cohen, *op. cit.*, pp. 403, 405).

Chapter 2

THE GERMAN INVASION

Vilna, June 22–24, 1941
The morning of June 22, 1941, began in Vilna as any other Sunday. It was a rest day: factories and offices were closed; people strolled through the streets; some went to church.

At 10 o'clock the sirens sounded. The roar of aircraft followed, and explosions were heard coming from the direction of the Porobanek Airport. Many believed that the aircraft were Soviet and that the sirens were sounding the air-raid precautionary drill announced the day before.

At 11 o'clock the Soviet Foreign Minister declared in a broadcast to the peoples of the U.S.S.R. that the Germans had attacked their country. The people of Vilna heard that war had broken out seven hours after the German invasion had already begun. By that time German tanks had advanced to the point of overcoming the bridges across the river Nieman (Nemunas) on their way to Vilna.

At 12 noon the German air force began to bomb the city and its suburbs. No directives had been issued by the authorities to the population as to how to behave. There was no guiding hand. The fact that the attack was launched on a Sunday, when government and municipal institutions were closed, added to the disorder and confusion. Nothing was known of the events at the front. The inhabitants had no information about the German advance.[1] Toward evening the bombing intensified.

1 G. Shur, "Vilna." This diary is in Russian, a sequence of fragments which to this date remains unedited. The order in which

For the Jews of Vilna, the first day of the war was marked by fear arising out of the obscurity of the situation and the uncertainty as to what the next day would bring. The general feeling of dread was augmented by the fact that the families of the Soviet army garrison, government officials and party members had started to leave the city. The Jews of Vilna had no idea of the gravity of the situation nor of the swift German advance toward the city. It was difficult to conceive that the mighty Soviet war machine had collapsed in a matter of a few hours and that the German Army would enter the city within two days. The Moscow radio announcement at 10 o'clock that night that the Red Army was repelling the Germans failed to clarify the situation.

The bombing of Vilna was resumed on Monday morning, June 23, 1941, and the gloomy picture of developments at the frontlines became evident. Rumors spread that the Germans had captured Kovno and were advancing on Vilna, and thousands of Jews began streaming out of the city. Throngs of people besieged the railway station. About 3,000 people, mostly Jews, managed to leave Vilna on the two trains that Monday.[2]

The government, party institutions, and the army were in possession of a limited number of trucks, which they used for their own evacuation purposes, and civilians were virtually unable to board them. Masses of people were forced to proceed eastward on foot. The majority of them traveled on the Vilna-Oshmyany (Ašmena) Minsk road under the incessant bombardment of the city and its environs.

the fragments appear on the microfilm (YVA, JM/2786) is the order in which they were donated by the author's daughter and is therefore somewhat arbitrary. The numbers in square brackets given throughout these notes refer to the frame numbers and form a system of temporary enumeration for reference purposes only [6]. See also Balberyszski, *op. cit.*, p. 112; A. Sutzkewer, *Getto Vilna*, Tel Aviv, 1947, p. 7.

2 H. Grossman, *Anshei ha-Mahteret*, Tel Aviv—Merhavia, 1965, p. 16. R. Korczak, *Lehavot ba-Efer*, Tel Aviv, 1946, p. 8. H. Kruk, *Togbuch fun vilner Geto*, New York, 1961, pp. 16–17.

The Soviet administration in Vilna did not publish any announcements on the situation nor did it issue directives to the population. The Jews who tried to leave Vilna did so on their own initiative. They tried to flee from Vilna out of fear of the persecution and maltreatment that they knew to be the lot of the Jews under the Nazi yoke. They knew nothing of the German extermination plans, so it was not to save their lives that they left the city. Consequently, many Vilna Jews were torn between remaining at home with their families, even under the oppressive Nazi rule, or abandoning everything and risking a perilous journey to some unknown destination.

Hermann Kruk describes their dilemma in an entry in his diary dated June 23, 1941:

> What to do? What to do with myself? Many people stood on the threshold of their houses and watched aimlessly... People were seen fleeing, this one going this way and that one going that way. What shall I do with myself? ... I lacked the strength to take up the wanderer's staff and start off on the way on foot, I remained ... It was clear that Vilna would be captured, that the Germans would carry out the Fascistization of the city, Jews would be enclosed in a ghetto — all this I would record ... I decided to keep an account of events in Vilna ...[3]

Faced by two alternatives, to depart or to remain, the greater majority of the 60,000 Jews in Vilna decided to stay. Their choice would undoubtedly have been different had they had any inkling of the fate that awaited them.

Several thousand went off on foot, in vehicles, and by rail. These were chiefly the Jews who were connected with the Soviet administration, party and Komsomol (Communist youth organization) members, intellectuals, and Jewish youths. Another group of those who left were Jewish refugees from Poland and members of Zionist youth movements living in Vilna. They had

3 *Ibid.*, pp. 3–4.

neither local nor family ties and were therefore more mobile.

The last of the Soviet government authorities left during the night of Monday, June 23, 1941, and no vestige of Soviet government remained in the city on the following day. Lithuanians perched in several places in the city fired at the Soviet soldiers as they retreated. Some of the sharpshooters were Lithuanian soldiers who had deserted the Soviet armed forces.[4]

With daybreak on Tuesday, June 24, 1941, the first German units, troops of the 7th Armored Division, entered Vilna. M. Balberyszski, an eyewitness, writes:

> We heard the noise of the approaching motorcycles. They sped by us like demons, two on each bike ... Then came the tanks with the large black Swastikas on them. Then the artillery moved in and finally—truckloads of soldiers ... All these were welcomed with enthusiastic shouts by scores of young Lithuanian "partisans" ... We stood at the windows and watched the endless army columns, leaving our lookout posts tired and frightened, each retreating to his own corner ...[5]

The thousands of Jews who had left Vilna by rail, car, and on foot tried to reach the Soviet Union interior before the advancing German forces could catch up with them. The attacking German airplanes compelled the escapees to scatter frequently and take cover. These swoops caused numerous casualties and slowed down their flight. Even without the attacking aircraft, the people on foot had little chance of reaching their destination. The Wehrmacht's mechanized units advanced far more quickly than any possible progress on foot.

The poet Abraham Sutzkewer, who left Vilna on the second day of the war, wrote:

> People carrying bundles streamed to the outskirts of the city ... Marching in the direction of Minsk ... the con-

---

4 H. Lazar, *Hurban u-Mered*, Tel Aviv, 1950, p. 19.
5 Balberyszski, *op. cit.*, p. 115.

gestion on the roads grew from minute to minute. Young, old, streamed eastwards—fleeing from the plague, the plague that pursued and caught up ... German airplanes sweeped like swarms of locusts. Our group scattered on the run ... At night, we stayed in the forest. Red Army soldiers warned us of German parachutists dressed in Soviet army uniforms ... The Germans caught up with us near Oshmyany... We turned back to the road we had fled on—and were once more back in the city.[6]

Most of the Jews who tried to flee suffered a similar fate. Some met their death on the roads when they were caught by peasants who turned them over to the Germans.

The fate of many of those who managed to board the trains was no different. Rail traffic was impeded and disrupted by the German air attacks. The train that left Vilna on Monday evening, June 23, reached the former U.S.S.R.-Polish frontier, a distance of no more than 160 miles, on Wednesday, forty hours later.

All those who succeeded, despite all obstacles, in arriving at the old Soviet–Polish frontier near the town of Radoszkowice encountered an additional difficulty—permission to cross over was withheld. Inhabitants of the areas annexed to the U.S.S.R. at the outset of World War II required special entry permits into other zones in the Soviet Union. This ban was not revoked after the German invasion. As a result of conditions in the first days of the war—the retreat of the Red Army and the withdrawal of the N.K.V.D. units which guarded the frontier posts on the main highways and railroads—there were many spots at which the old border could be crossed without special permits. But at many other points people without permits were detained at the frontier and prevented from entering the hinterland. Only those who had party-membership cards or special crossing permits were allowed to cross over, and these

6 Sutzkewer, *op. cit.*, p. 8.

permits were held by only a select few. Most of the train passengers were therefore compelled to return to Vilna.[7]

How many Jews who left Vilna succeeded in reaching the Soviet Union? It is impossible to offer a precise answer. In view of the conditions prevailing in the Soviet Union during the war years, the Soviet sources are unable to shed light on how many Jews left Vilna. Consequently, it is possible only to examine what conditions and opportunities to leave Vilna existed on June 22 and 23, 1941, and to arrive at some general estimate.

Jewish sources—books, diaries, and articles on the subject of the Jewish flight from Vilna on the two days in question — refer to the total in terms of "tens of thousands" or "thousands," and it is clear that these are only general estimates.[8]

The number of Jews who set out from Vilna and reached the interior of the U.S.S.R. was small. Conditions in the city, the limited time available to those wanting to leave, the absence of means of transport, the situation on the highways, and the pace of the German advance all contributed to reducing the number of those who left; and an even smaller number managed to enter the Soviet Union.

Ignorance of the situation and the absence of any information on the German advance created a situation in which many people failed to avail themselves of the opportunity to flee on the first day of the war. The number of those who did ranged from several hundred to 1,000, especially Jews who had held posts in the administration and party. It may be assumed that most of those who left on Sunday managed to reach the Soviet interior, as the government and party functionaries had means of transport.

The departures from Vilna on Monday, June 23, encompassed thousands. The number of Jews among the train passengers who entered the Soviet Union may be estimated at

7 Kruk, *op. cit.*, p. 16.
8 M. Dworzecki, *Yerushalayim de-Lita ba-Meri u-va-Sho'ah*, Tel Aviv, 1951, p. 18.

1,500–2,000. Several hundred other Jews were able to leave by conveyances belonging to the authorities.

The chances of the refugees on foot escaping the advancing Germans were very slim. Their rate of progress was no more than 15 to 30 miles per day, and by the time they came to Oshmyany, the German tanks were already there. By the evening of June 24, 1941, they had cut off all the main highways from Vilna to the East.

No more than 3,000 Jews were able to leave Vilna on June 22 and 23, 1941, and reach the interior of the Soviet Union — by any means of transportation. Thousands of others did not reach their destinations, and a part returned to the city. Some remained in the townships of Belorussia; others found their death on the highways under the German aerial bombardment.

Thus, only several thousand of the Jews in Vilna were able to save their lives by leaving before the German forces entered. The majority had no choice but to stay in the city and await their fate.

The German Invasion and the Lithuanians

The invading Germany Army was welcomed with great rejoicing by the majority of Lithuanians, in spite of the long history of dissension and wars between them. In March 1939, the Lithuanians had been compelled to cede the one and only port of Memel to the Germans. But since independent Lithuania became a Soviet republic on July 21, 1940, most Lithuanians regarded the Germans as potential allies. Many Lithuanian leaders fled to Germany and on November 17, 1940, founded the "Lithuanian Activists' Front" (L.A.F.), which was headed by K. Skirpa and included all the Lithuanian political parties except the Communists and Social Democrats. Within Lithuania itself armed underground anti-Soviet groups were organized. The Germans had encouraged these Lithuanian anti-Soviet activities.[9]

9 *Gitlerovskaya okupatsiya v Litve,* Sbornik statyei, Vilna, 1966,

The L.A.F. in Germany and its clandestine offshoots in Li-
thunia became anti-Jewish and disseminated anti-Semitic propaganda. Their written declarations, which appeared in Berlin,
called for the liquidation of the Jews of Lithuania. It was
stated in a manifesto published by the L.A.F. on March 19,
1941:

> As has been mentioned, the hour of Lithuania's liberation
> is close at hand. As soon as the campaign from the West
> starts you will be informed ... Local uprisings must break
> out in the occupied cities ... Local Communists and all
> other traitors in Lithuania must be detained at once ...
> (The traitors will be pardoned only if they provide cer-
> tain proof that every one of them has liquidated at least
> one Jew.) The Jews must be informed immediately that
> their fate has been decided upon ... At the decisive mo-
> ment, seize their property, so that nothing will be lost.

Another manifesto published in Berlin on the day of the German invasion (June 22, 1941), or close to that date, stated:

> The crucial day of reckoning has come for the Jews at
> last. Lithuania must be liberated not only from the yoke
> of Bolshevism but also from the long-protracted bur-
> den of the Jewish yoke ... The new State of Lithuania
> will be built by the Lithuanians themselves ... All Jews
> are to be excluded from Lithuania forever ... New Lithu-
> ania will not give any Jew civil rights nor possibility of
> existence ... [10]

With the outbreak of war on June 22, 1941, the Lithuanians
revolted. Units of Lithuanians organized clandestinely and were
joined by mutineering soldiers from the Lithuanian Corps of

---

p. 29 (hereafter: *Gitlerovskaya okupatsiya); Documents Accuse*, ed.,
E. Rozauskas, Vilna, 1970, pp. 43–44 (hereafter: *Documents Accuse*).
10 *Ibid.*, pp. 123–125.

the Red Army. Together they began attacking detachments of the retreating Red Army and murdering Jews.[11]

On June 23, 1941, at 11:30 A.M., after the Soviet authorities had fled Kovno, the Lithuanians announced over the radio that a Provisional Lithuanian Government had been formed under the premiership of Juozas Ambrazevicius. The radio announcer called on the populace "to fight to extirpate the Soviet regime in Lithuania and to set up an autonomous Lithuania." "Lithuanian Committees" were constituted in all districts and, with the disintegration of Soviet rule, seized the reins of power. A Lithuanian police force and military units were organized in conjunction with these committees.

Skirpa, who was then in Berlin, sought the permission of the German Government to leave for Lithuania in order to become the head of his government, but it was not granted. The Germans did not recognize the Provisional Lithuanian Government, nor were they ready to grant Lithuania independence. The Provisional Government continued to officiate until the inception of German civilian administration in Lithuania at the beginning of August 1941.

The aim of German policy was to render Lithuania, Latvia, and Estonia territories of the German Reich and prepare them for extensive German colonization. The directives for German policy in the Baltic countries were drawn up by Alfred Rosenberg before the invasion of the U.S.S.R. A document bearing the date of May 8, 1941, which Rosenberg prepared, stated:

> The *General Komissare* of Estonia, Latvia and Lithuania will take measures to establish a German Protectorate there, so that it will be possible in the future to annex these territories to the German Reich. The suitable elements among the population must be assimilated and the

11 These Lithuanian units consisted of citizens and deserters from the Lithuanian Corps No. 29, which was a part of the Red Army. According to Lithuanian sources (pro-German), some 100,000 Lithuanians participated in the anti-Soviet mutiny.

undesirable elements exterminated. The Baltic Sea must become an inland German lake, under the protection of Greater Germany.[12]

In line with this German policy there was no room for Lithuania as a national, independent state. It was this policy that dictated the actions of the German military administration vis-à-vis the Lithuanian national institutions that arose with the withdrawal of the Red Army and during the first phase of German occupation, as well as the actions of the German civil administration when it assumed direct control in Lithuania. On July 14, 1941, three days before Rosenberg was officially appointed *Reichsminister* for Eastern Territories, he signed an agreement with the Wehrmacht commanders that they would not recognize any government or army formed in the Baltic lands. This was to assure that the civilian administration would not confront any *faits accomplis* when it took over in the Eastern territories.[13]

The majority of Lithuanians had anticipated that Nazi Germany would grant them some form of political independence. They believed that their insurrection and fighting against the retreating Red Army, their volunteering for, and complicity in, the murder of Jews, justified their claims to independence and recognition of their Provisional Government. But disappointment awaited them. The Germans neither recognized their Provisional Government nor extended independence to Lithuania. Yet, in spite of this, when the war began, and in the first few months thereafter, before they became fully cognizant of German policy, the Lithuanians tendered their full sympathy to Nazi Germany and collaborated with the German administration—especially in its anti-Jewish policy and actions.

12 *Documents Accuse*, p. 28.
13 Nuremberg Documents, PS-1042 and 1043. (All Nuremberg documents cited herein can also be found in the YVA, TR collection).

Part Two

MASS EXTERMINATION

Chapter 3

THE FIRST STEPS OF LIQUIDATION

Joint German-Lithuanian Administration, June 24–July 2
German administration in Vilna began to function on June 24, 1941, the day on which the city fell to the German forces, and lasted until July 13, 1944, when the city was liberated by the Soviet Army.

With the entry of the Wehrmacht into the city, a military government was set up. During the five weeks of military government in Vilna, the military commanders were changed each time that the city passed from the control of one military command to another in the course of the German Army's advance eastward.

The period of German military administration in Vilna, between June 24 and August 1, 1941, may be divided into two phases: the first lasted until July 2; and the second was from July 3 to August 1. Characteristic of the first phase was the German-Lithuanian joint government in Vilna; whereas the predominant characteristic of the second phase was direct German military command, during which a number of Lithuanian institutions were abolished and a number of others were limited to municipal functions only.

The Lithuanians, though a minority in Vilna, possessed the power, organization, and means to take over the local administration upon the entry of the German Army. "The Committee of Lithuanian Activists," headed by S. Zakevicius, assumed control of Vilna and its surrounding area. A. Iskauskas was placed in charge of the Lithuanian police force. The Lithuanian Committee organized itself on the lines of a national sovereign administration with political functions and state institutions, subject to the Provisional Government constituted in Kovno. Their aim was to confront the Germans with the *fait accompli* of an autonomous Lithuanian administration.[1]

During the first few days of German rule in Vilna, the military government recognized the authority of the Lithuanians and the existence of a Lithuanian-German co-administration. Decree No. 1 of the German military government in the city, issued on June 24, 1941, was signed by S. Zakevicius as Chairman of the Vilna City Committee and Von Ostman, the military commander of the city. Article 1 of the decree stated: "All orders issued by me and which were approved by the Vilna City Committee shall be carried out in full." Other articles in this decree related to daily life in the city—functioning of services, hours of curfew, prices, transportation, fuel and the like. Article 5 declared: "... The police, patrols of the Lithuanian Army ... shall supervise the enactment of the order."[2] Von Ostman, the military governor of Vilna, thereby vested the Lithuanian Committee with the power of enforcing the decrees. It also referred to the existence of a "Lithuanian Army."

On June 27, 1941, "Order No. 1" was promulgated by the Acting Commissioner for Internal Affairs in the Vilna district, K. Kalendra, and the district head, B. Draugelis. The order directed all members of the police force and state employees in the Vilna district who had served until June 15, 1940 (when

---

1 Einsatzgruppen Report (No. 10) of July 2, 1941, describes the situation in Vilna as follows: "After the entry of the German Army, the Lithuanian nationalist leaders established an Urban Committee, headed by Zakevicius, recognized by the Army High Command. The leaders aspire to independence as a reward for the toll of blood which they paid." YVA, 0–51/57–1, Nuremberg Document, No. 2661).

2 *Documents Accuse,* p. 80; Balberyszski *op. cit.,* p. 122.

the Red Army overran Lithuania) to report for duty to their previous posts, to reorganize their offices, and to assume responsibility for the property belonging to state institutions. The same order stated that, until further notice, all such persons would act in accordance with the laws that were in force in independent Lithuania prior to June 15, 1940. On June 27, 1941, a further order was issued by the Lithuanian administration, bearing the signatures of Kalendra and the chief of Vilna police, Iskauskas. This order required all members of the Communist party, candidates for party membership, and Komsomol members to register at their neighborhood police-stations before 8 P.M. the next day, June 28, 1941.[3]

The Lithuanians in Vilna lacked the self-confidence that was evident in other parts of the country. Vilna had not been part of the independent state of Lithuania during the interwar period but had belonged to Poland, and most of its inhabitants were Polish. Therefore, the Lithuanians were not at all certain that Vilna in fact would be included within the Lithuanian state under German auspices.

The Lithuanians regarded the Poles as a potential danger to their authority in the city. They thus concentrated their main efforts toward imparting a Lithuanian character to Vilna and creating the impression in the German military command that the city had a stable Lithuanian administration complete with civilian, military, and police institutions. The Germans were aware of Lithuanian activities in Vilna and their intentions. The Operational Report No. 17 of July 9, 1941 states:

> ... An attempt is being made to create the impression among the German military establishments that the Lithuanian state apparatus is fully functional and a Lithuanian command has been set up under a Lithuanian commander. The German Army is tolerant of this development ... The Lithuanian activists are trying their utmost to exploit the

3 *Documents Accuse*, p. 83; *Gitlerovskaya okupatsiya*, p. 32.

unclear situation and especially to give a pure Lithuanian character to the city of Vilna, this by an impressive decoration of the city with Lithuanian national flags. Nevertheless, the Lithuanian element constitutes a minority in addition to the Poles, the Belorussians, the Russians and the Jews. Naturally, after many years of nationalist struggle, it is particularly active.

According to data furnished by the Lithuanians themselves, they constitute 30 percent of the total city population, the Jews close to 40 percent and the Poles, Belorussians and others 30 percent. The Lithuanian institutions, especially the police, made immediate attempts to halt the non-Lithuanian groupings (Belorussian and Polish) in their efforts to play down the Lithuanian character of the city.

According to information from the Lithuanian political police which is still functioning, there is increasing coalescence by Poles in military organizations. The attitude of the [Lithuanian] population towards the Germans is positive and friendly, and it expects that it will be granted independence similar to that of Slovakia.

The Belorussian population is still reserved. The Poles fear that they will be discriminated against by the Lithuanian institutions ...

According to Lithuanian data, the Catholic clergy is under strong Polish influence and has anti-German tendencies, in particular Archbishop Jelsmykowski, whereas Bishop Rainys, who is Lithuanian, occupies a foremost position among his compatriots and is apparently friendly towards the Germans.[4]

Lithuanian activity in Vilna and the efforts to impart a Lithuanian complexion to the city were conducted at several levels and in sundry directions. The composition of the city's popula-

4 Einsatzgruppen Report (No. 17) of July 9, 1941, YVA, 0-51/57-1, pp. 10-12.

tion was presented to the Germans in such a way as to make the Lithuanian community appear to be larger than the Polish, which did not correspond to reality. This action was synthesized with an attempt to show that the Poles were enemies of Germany. The Lithuanian political police conceived its main goal to be the investigation of the activity of the Polish populace. Lithuanian political police circles sent out a flow of information stating that the Poles were forming underground military organizations. Actually these had already existed in the period of independent Lithuanian rule and under Soviet government between 1939 and 1941.[5] Moreover, the Lithuanians took measures against Polish cultural institutions in order to blur the Polish character of Vilna. On July 3, 1941, Polish—as well as Jewish—theaters were closed down in Vilna. The order for their closure came from the Provisional Lithuanian Government at Kovno.[6]

The population of Vilna was mainly Catholic, and the clergy was predominantly Polish. Control over the Church was extremely important and constituted a focal point in the struggle for power between the Lithuanians and the Poles. The Lithuanians did not feel they were strong enough to carry out changes in the ecclesiastical hierarchy, so they tried to persuade the Germans to take steps against the Primate of the Catholic Church in Vilna, Archbishop Jelsmykowski. The Archbishop was Polish and hence presented as anti-German; his opponents wanted the Lithuanian Bishop Rainys appointed in his stead.

The policy concerning the Polish population in the occupied areas of the Soviet Union was laid down in Berlin, and an order to this effect was published by Reinhard Heydrich. It was incorporated in Report No. 10 on the activities of the Einsatzgruppen in July 1941, and stated that "Actions of the Einsatzgruppen" must be directed against the Bolsheviks and the Jews

---

5 Einsatzgruppen Report (No. 10), YVA, 0–51/57–1, pp. 16–17, specifies the Polish underground organizations active in Vilna.

6 *Gitlerovskaya okupatsiya*, p. 35.

and that there should be no operations at this time against the Polish intelligentsia.[7]

This order also influenced the attitude of the Germans toward the Poles in Vilna. Lithuanian attempts to incite the German military administration to adopt an anti-Polish posture resembling its anti-Jewish stance were unsuccessful.

Vilna Jewry under the German-Lithuanian Joint Administration
During the brief period of joint German-Lithuanian administration, no mass executions of Jews in Vilna nor any anti-Jewish pogroms were carried out. There were persecutions and molestations and Jews were murdered,[8] but these were not the type of pogroms and massacres that occurred in those days in the other cities of Lithuania, especially in Kovno and Shavli.

By July 7, 1941, nearly 5,000 Jews, mostly males, out of a total Jewish population of 36,000 in Kovno had been killed by the Lithuanians. In Shavli, the third largest city in Lithuania (after Vilna and Kovno), 1,000 Jews were killed in the first week of occupation, out of a total Jewish community of about 8,000.

Throughout the cities and townships of Lithuania (within its inter-war boundaries, excluding the Vilna district), the Lithuanians carried out pogroms in which thousands of Jews were

---

7 Trial of Dr. Filbert, Commanding Officer of Einsatzkommando 9, Yad Vashem Archives TR–10/388, pp. 60–61; the following passage is quoted from the proceedings: "...The Chief of the Security Police and the SD issued the following order to all Einsatzgruppen on July 1, 1941: Order No. 2: The Polish inhabitants in the occupied areas in the East, especially in the areas which were formerly Polish, appear to be... anti-Communist and anti-Jewish. Purges must primarily encompass the Bolsheviks and the Jews. As regards the Polish intelligentsia, apart from cases in which there is danger in delaying the matter, it is strictly forbidden to take measures against them. This will be spoken of later on..."

8 Shur in his diary speaks of several dozen Jews and Soviet soldiers who were murdered on June 24 in the garden of the Franciscan Church.

murdered even before the Einsatzgruppen began the systematic slaughter of the Jewish population. The Lithuanian pogroms held during the first days of the German occupation in the cities of Ponevezh, Plungian (Plunge), Kretinga, and Keidany, among others, claimed thousands of Jewish lives, primarily among the men.

Sixty Jews and 20 Poles were seized as hostages in Vilna on June 24 and 25, 1941. Order No. 1, published on June 25, 1941, and carrying the signatures of Zakevicius and Von Ostman, stated that the hostages had been apprehended in order to make certain that the population would obey the instructions contained in that order and warned that further hostages would be taken if all the instructions were not carried out. The Jewish hostages were held in the Lukiszki prison until July 22, at which time six were released and the remainder murdered. They were not killed as a reprisal for any particular hostile act against the Germans, but within the framework of the plan for the liquidation of Vilna Jewry.[9]

This incident involving Jewish and Polish hostages was exceptional. The seizure of Poles as hostages together with Jews was apparently undertaken at the instigation of the Lithuanians and was meant to brand them, in the eyes of the Germans, as potential enemies on the same level as Jews.

One of the initial anti-Jewish operations was the kidnapping of Jewish males from the streets of the city. These abductions began on June 27, 1941. Most of the kidnapped persons were taken away to work for the Germans and were returned to their homes when their tasks were completed, but some of them failed to return and according to rumor had been sent to work in distant places.

The kidnapping of Jewish males, and the uncertainty as to the fate of those who were missing after finishing their work, incited fear among the Jews. Balberyszki wrote: "We waited impatiently for the moment when a German administration

9 *Documents Accuse,* pp. 80–81; Dworzecki, *op. cit.,* p. 23.

would be organized, no matter what its character, so that the Lithuanian lawlessness could be put to an end."[10]

On June 29, 1941, the Lithuanians introduced two lines outside the food shops—one for Jews and one for non-Jews. Jews began to be ousted from their places of employment. Jewish houses were searched by Lithuanians who ostensibly were looking for arms, but who actually stole every article of value that they found. The kidnappings increased.

Kruk wrote:

> 1 July — It is now apparent to me that many of those who were seized for work had been sent to the Lukiszki jail. It is stated that this was to be the assembly point from which the people were to be sent to work. Many women congregate in front of the prison.
>
> 3 July — Incidents such as this have been occurring lately: They come at night, evict all the family from the house, take the males away and leave the rest with their bundles under the open sky. The houses are sealed and there is no one to talk to.

Einsatzkommando 7-A, which was to advance to and operate in Minsk, was detained in Vilna upon orders of the army command. While standing by in Vilna for immediate departure, the Einsatzkommando was not very active. Report No. 10 of July 2, 1941, dealt with the arrests of Communists and Jews in Vilna, but did not mention any massacres of Jews.[11]

The commander of Einsatzgruppe B, Nebe, tried to spur the Lithuanians in Vilna to wage a pogrom against the Jews. This method of inciting local elements to carry out pogroms against the Jews was a common practice among the Einsatzgruppen. In the report of Einsatzgruppe A, its commander, Stahlecker, described how an advance unit of his (which had entered Kovno

---

10 Balberyszski, *op. cit.*, p. 124.
11 Einsatzgruppen Report (No. 9) of July 1, 1941, and of July 2, 1941, YVA, 0–51/57–1.

several hours after the capture of the city by the Wehrmacht) agitated the local anti-Communist forces and their commander, Klimaitis (Klimavicius), to carry out a pogrom among the Jews.[12]

The Jews of Vilna were not exposed to the wave of assaults carried out at the instigation of the Lithuanians and encouraged by the advance detachments of the Einsatzgruppen. The Lithuanians in Vilna and vicinity "had no time" for Jewish affairs. Their basic problem in Vilna was not, in their eyes, the problem of the Jews, but rather that of the Poles, who jeopardized their position and the Lithuanian character of the city and who had been their enemies for dozens of years. A summation report by Einsatzgruppe A, dated October 15, 1941, stated: "In the view of the Lithuanian population in the Vilna district, the Jewish question . . . takes second place after the Polish problem. The strongest argument of the Lithuanian populace in the Vilna area against the Poles is that some of them are cooperating with the Jews."[13]

The Lithuanian minority in Vilna did not deem itself strong enough to tackle the Poles on the issue of giving the city a Lithuanian character and at the same time wage pogroms against the Jews. Rioting was bound to cause disorder and snatch authority—the authority of a small minority—from their hands. As the Jews did not take precedence in the Lithuanian scale of priorities in that city, they were in effect spared the carnage wrought upon the Jews in most of the other sections of Lithuania in those days. The systematic extermination

12 Filbert's trial, TR–10/388, p. 59; Einsatzgruppe A, Report of October 15, 1941, Nuremberg Document, L–180, YVA, 0–51/57–1. During this pogrom, 3,800 Jews were killed. SS *Brigadeführer* Nebe, Commanding Officer of Einsatzgruppe B (then still C) encouraged the formation of a Lithuanian auxiliary police force to launch the savage execution of Jews.
13 Einsatzgruppe A, Report of October 15, 1941, YVA, 0–51/57–1, p. 112.

of the Jews of Vilna started only when Einsatzkommando 9 arrived and began its activities.

Stabilization of German Military Government and Restriction of the Lithuanian Administration in Vilna

The German-Lithuanian joint administration in Vilna was short lived and came to an end in early July 1941. The military government disbanded some Lithuanian institutions and restricted the powers of those that continued to function. The Germans were guided in their measures in Vilna by their basic policy toward the Baltic countries: precluding their autonomy and preparing conditions for rendering them as German colonies.

The anti-Lithuanian steps effectively transformed the status of the Lithuanian Committee from a body representing a sovereign government, as the Lithuanians wished it to be, into that of a municipal authority directly subject to the local German military commander. Lithuanian military units were disbanded. Parts of the disbanded Lithuanian units were subordinated to the German military commander for guard duties over various military facilities. Part of the Lithuanian police was made subordinate to the Einsatzkommando. Lithuanian offices were prohibited from issuing orders for the public notices, and the authority to do so was vested in the German military commander of the city.

The limitation of Lithuanian power in the city was effected jointly by the army command and Einsatzkommando 9, which arrived there on July 2. The Einsatzgruppen report No. 17 dwelt upon "a series of steps taken, partly in cooperation with the military command ... of Vilna, with the purpose of circumscribing the political action of the Lithuanians and so that, in making decisions in the future, we shall not be hampered by *faits accomplis.*"[14]

On July 8, 1941, a public notice was issued on behalf of the

14 Einsatzgruppen Report (No. 17) of July 9, 1941, YVA, 0–51/57–1, p. 13.

military commander of Vilna, Zehnpfenning. With the entry of the German Army, it stated, the entire administration had passed into the hands of the German military authorities, which were also to be vested with judicial powers. Civilian life would be under the protection of the Wehrmacht. A municipal authority was to be established to administer local affairs and stipulations were made as to possession of weapons, property, curfew hours, and housing, among other matters. It was enjoined that the legal tender was to be the Reichsmark and the ruble and that the Lithuanian money previously used would not be returned to circulation. The notice made it clear to the public that full authority would be vested in the Germans and completely ignored the Lithuanian institutions that had functioned previously, with the exception of those on the municipal level. The notice in effect determined the methods of administration and life in the city and was similar in contents to Order No. 1 promulgated on June 24, 1941, by Von Ostman and Zakevicius. But whereas Order No. 1 extended recognition to the Lithuanian governing agencies, Zehnpfenning's broadsheet did not take them into account, except for the municipal ones.

On July 16, 1941, an order was promulgated by the German military governor of the Vilna region, General von Ditfurth, decreeing that all Lithuanian establishments therein must function in accordance with the instructions and under the supervision of the German Military Government. The German Military Government bade members of the Lithuanian Committee to travel to Kovno and maintain communications with the Lithuanian Provisional Government still functioning there.[15]

To further limit the activities of the Lithuanians, a number of measures were adopted to enhance non-Lithuanian national groups in Vilna. Within the framework of this action, Belorussian organization in the city was encouraged.[16] The Poles were

15 *Documents Accuse,* pp. 80–81, 84–87, 90–92, 99–100.
16 Einsatzgruppen Report (No. 17), YVA, 0–51/57–1; p. 11 states: "As a counterbalance against the most active operations of the

also given a higher status than the Lithuanians relished, especially when the order of July 16 proclaimed the equality of the Lithuanian, Belorussian and Polish languages, and the Poles were granted permission to publish a Polish newspaper in the city.

The anti-Lithuanian measures introduced in Vilna preceded similar practices elsewhere in the country. The execution of these measures in Vilna before they were introduced in other provinces in Lithuania may be due to the following reasons: The position of the Lithuanians in Vilna was weak from the outset, as they were in a minority there; Vilna fell within the sphere of responsibility of the "Central" Armies Group, and sovereign Lithuanian administration in the city was a singular phenomenon in contrast with the other regions conquered by the "Central" armies. Other parts of Lithuania were under the military rule of the "Northern" Armies Group, which had captured all the Baltic countries and had everywhere encountered the feature of self-government. In the areas under "Northern" rule, the repeal of "autonomy" was effected only upon the arrival of German civilian administration and their assumption of power.

Lithuanians, Wladyslaw Kozlowski, Secretary of the former Belorussian Party, was given aid and approval to establish a Belorussian nationalist organization."

Chapter 4

GERMAN MILITARY ADMINISTRATION (July 1941)

Division of Functions between the Military Administration and the Einsatzgruppen

Beginning on July 4, 1941, numerous restrictions and decrees were imposed upon the Jews of Vilna by the German military administration. Simultaneously, mass exterminations, implemented by Einsatzkommando 9, which was strengthened by Lithuanian units, began.

The German military administration acted pursuant to directives by the *Generalquartiermeister* ("Chief Administrative Officer") of the "Army High Command" O.K.H. (Oberkommand des Herres) General E. Wagner. The Wehrmacht in the Eastern territories was directly responsible for anti-Jewish activity and assisted the Einsatzgruppen in the extermination actions. The basis for the cooperation between the army and the Einsatzgruppen was an order by the "High Command of the Wehrmacht" — O.K.W. (Oberkommando der Wehrmacht) dated March 13, 1941, which comprised directives for Operation "Barbarossa." This Order stated that in the area of army operations ... the *Reichsführer* of the SS has been assigned special missions pursuant to the order of the *Führer* ... Within the framework of these missions, the *Reichsführer* will act independently and on his own responsibility ..."

During April and May 1941, Wagner and Heydrich discussed the implementation of the order. The SS demanded that the

Einsatzgruppen be permitted to operate as closely to the front as possible and to advance with the army vanguard units in order to overcome the Jews quickly in each place conquered by the Wehrmacht. The agreement reached at the end of May provided that the Einsatzgruppen operate in the proximity of the front. The Wagner-Heydrich agreements prepared the ground for coordination and collaboration between the Wehrmacht and the Einsatzgruppen and for the independent action of each within its own sphere of responsibility and powers.[1]

The action of the military government and the Einsatzgruppen could be discerned in the anti-Jewish actions implemented in Vilna in July 1941. The official overt actions were published in orders and proclamations by the military administration, while, parallel to this, the Einsatzgruppen were covertly engaged in the mass extermination of Jews.

Anti-Jewish Legal Action by the Military Government
With the invasion of the U.S.S.R., the Army High Command published an announcement to all inhabitants of the occupied territories asserting that all Jews must wear a white band on each arm, that they are forbidden to leave the settlements in which they dwelt, and that they are to surrender their radio sets. It was also affirmed that all Jews aged sixteen to fifty years were to be at the disposition of the local administration, which would utilize them in various works. The local population, the proclamation continued, must maintain and repair roads and bridges and the Jews must be used for such works.

At the outset of July 1941, the military governor of the Occupied Territories in the East published a proclamation to the local inhabitants stating that all Jews aged ten and over must wear white bands with a yellow star of David on their right

1 Directive by the OKW, March 13, 1941, Nuremberg Document, NOKW–2302; affidavit by SS *Gruppenführer* Schellenberg, November 26, 1945, Nuremberg Document, PS–3710; Statement by SS *Gruppenführer* Ohlendorf, April 24, 1947, Nuremberg Document, NO–2890.

arm. The notice defined a Jew as anyone whose three out of four grandfathers and grandmothers were Jewish; or two grandfathers and grandmothers were Jews, and who belonged to the Jewish faith on June 22, 1941; or was married to a Jew/Jewess at the time of the publication of the order. In addition, this proclamation outlawed the kosher slaughter of animals.[2]

On July 3, 1941, an order was published by Von Ostman, the German Military Commander of Vilna, requiring all Jews to wear the yellow badge. A day later, the Lithuanian authorities in Vilna issued their own order, basing themselves on Von Ostman:

> Notice: Pursuant to the Order of the German Military Commandant dated July 3, 1941, the following is hereby decreed:
> 1. All Jews, males and females, irrespective of age, must wear, prominently placed on the chest and on the back, a special badge of 4 inches diameter. A sample of the badge may be seen in all police stations in the City of Vilna.
> 2. All Jews are forbidden to remain in the streets from 6 P.M. until 6 A.M.
> 3. This order is to be implemented in Vilna as of July 8, 1941. Infractions will be punished with the utmost severity.
>
>   S. Zakevicius, Chairman of the Citizens Committee of the City and District of Vilna
>   A. Iskauskas, Chief of Auxiliary Police of the City and District of Vilna
> Vilna, July 4, 1941.

A few days after this order was published, the new military governor of Vilna, *Oberstleutnant* Zehnpfenning, abolished the

---

2 *Yerushalayim de-Lita — Illustrated and Documented Album,* ed., L. Rann, New York, 1974, p. 426, photocopy of the announcement (hereafter: *Yerushalayim de-Lita Album*).

requirement to wear the yellow badge and ordered all Jews over ten years of age to wear a white armband, 4 inches wide, with a yellow Star of David or a yellow circle on it with the letter "J" (*Jude*) in the center.[3]

The enforcement of the order to wear the special identity badges corresponded with the beginning of the Einsatzgruppen's extermination operations in Vilna. This outward mark of identification was meant to ease the task of the Einsatzgruppen in singling out and arresting their victims. It was an expression of cooperation and coordination of anti-Jewish action by the two German arms—the Wehrmacht and the Einsatzgruppen. This illustrates how the coordination reached by agreement at high level between General Wagner and Heydrich was implemented and the practical application of the agreement at lower levels.

From July 5, 1941, further restrictions were imposed upon the Jews. Separate food shops were set aside for them. The sale or exchange of food and other articles in the city squares and streets was forbidden. Sales were permissible for the general population, as well as the Jews, in certain marketplaces. Non-Jews were allowed to purchase there between 7 A.M. and noon, but Jewish customers were limited to the last two hours, i.e., between 10 and 12 o'clock, when most goods had already been purchased. The Lithuanian daily *Naujoji Lietuva,* which began appearing in Vilna on June 29, 1941, published on July 8, 1941, a notice by the Vilna Chamber of Commerce that food for Jews would be sold only in special shops. An order, applicable to the entire population, was published concerning the registration of all means of transport: cars, motorcycles, and bicycles. The Jews were forbidden to use public transport, and telephones were removed from their dwellings.[4]

On July 8, 1941, an order was published banning Jews from walking in the most central streets of the city. Jews who lived in those streets were to go from their homes to the nearest

---

3 *Documents Accuse,* pp. 86, 131.
4 Moreshet Archives, D. 1. 362; *Documents Accuse,* pp. 80–81.

corner and then turn into a side street. Another order forbade Jews from entering public baths, hospitals, cinemas and theaters, coffee-houses and barber-shops. Posted on these places were notices reading: "Admission Forbidden to Jews."[5]

Naujoji Lietuva of July 18, 1941, published a notice by the Vilna Municipal Council on the assignment of Clinic No. 2 in Zawalna Street for Jews, and stated that only Jewish doctors and nurses would be employed there. Jewish doctors were empowered to give medical treatment to Jews only. Another notice issued by Zehnpfenning forbade Jews from making contact with non-Jews, or even greeting them. Kosher slaughtering of animals was also banned. The same announcement also defined who was considered to be a Jew.[6]

Property confiscation was carried out by the local Lithuanian administration. The Jews of Vilna did not own much property, as the large enterprises and businesses had been nationalized during the period of Soviet rule. During the early days of July, the Lithuanians seized those smaller workshops and properties that Jews still retained.

A decree was issued requiring Jews to surrender radio sets in their possession. Lithuanians, carrying lists of owners of such sets, went from house to house and confiscated them. Jews who lived in the outskirts of the city or in hostile neighborhoods tried to exchange their dwellings for safer places. They tried to sell what little stationary property they had, for fear of confiscation, and because they needed the money for subsistence. Others endeavored to transfer property to non-Jewish friends,

5 Kruk, *op. cit.*, p. 18; Korczak, *op. cit.*, p. 10; *Documents Accuse*, p. 146, contains a document which does indeed specify the streets in which the Jews were forbidden to walk, but this order is based on the *Gebietskommisar's* instructions, and consequently was published no earlier than August 1, 1941. It is possible that a similar order was also published on July 8 by the German Military Commandant; Testimony by A. Rindzionski, Moreshet Archives, A. 381, p. 15.

6 Moreshet Archives, D.1.362 and A.381; *Naujoji Lietuva*, No. 22 of July 23, 1941.

in the hope that at some later date they might be able to re-
trieve it. But subsequently a directive was published forbidding
Jews to sell or transfer their property. And as of July 21, 1941,
the Housing Department of the Municipality of Vilna ceased
issuing permits to Jews who wanted to change apartments.[7]
These steps were aimed at preventing transfers of Jewish property to private non-Jewish residents of Vilna in anticipation
of impoundment by the German or Lithuanian authorities.

From the very early days of the German occupation of Vilna,
Jews were kidnapped from the streets and from their homes for
forced labor. The kidnapping of Jews was carried out by
soldiers of the Wehrmacht or by the Lithuanian police.[8]

Establishment of the First Judenrat in Vilna

The German military government established a Jewish representative body, the Judenrat, which was designed to be of assistance in implementing the anti-Jewish policy. The inception of
the Judenrat marked the first direct contact between the German military government of Vilna and the Jews without recourse to the mediation of the local Lithuanian authority.

On July 4, 1941, a car drove up to the synagogue on Zydowska (Zydu) Street, and two Germans alighted. They entered
the courtyard and asked for the rabbi of Vilna. The municipal
shamash (beadle), Chaim-Meir Gordon, a tall, burly Jew with
a long white beard, was brought to them. When asked if he
was the rabbi of Vilna, he told the men that the Chief Rabbi,
Y. Rubinstein, was in America and the second rabbi, Chaim
Ozer Grodzenski, had passed away. They then instructed the
shamash that henceforth he would be the rabbi. He was ordered
to set up a Jewish representative body that would be presented
to them on the following day.[9]

Gordon went to the former secretary of the community, Mr.
I. Verblinski, who called in a number of people for consulta-

7 Moreshet Archives, D. 1. 362
8 Kruk, *op. cit.*, pp. 12, 148; Dworzecki, *op. cit.*, p. 20.
9 Kruk, *op. cit.*, pp. 8–9.

tion. Among them were Rabbi S. Fried and Dr. G. Gershuni, and it was decided to convene a larger group that evening. Rabbi Fried, Dr. Gershuni, and Gordon went to the Commissioner for Internal Affairs of the Lithuanian Vilna Citizens' Committee, K. Kalendra, who was in charge of Jewish affairs, so that he could put them in touch with the representatives of the German military administration with regard to the establishment of the Judenrat. Kalendra informed them that the German administration did not wish to have any direct communication with the Jews and that everything was to be arranged through him. He then declared that the Judenrat, consisting of ten members, had to be established within twenty-four hours.

The Lithuanian administration, which was still fighting to retain its sovereign powers, was naturally interested in having control over Jewish affairs remain under its jurisdiction.

That evening, July 4, a number of Jewish public figures in Vilna assembled to discuss the formation of a Judenrat. The meeting was attended by fifty-seven persons who represented various groups and parties in the Jewish community of Vilna — Zionists, Bundists, members of the inteliigentsia and liberal professions, artisans, and merchants. The chair was taken by Dr. Gershuni, a veteran Zionist and well-known personality in Jewish public life in the city. Dr. Jacob Wygodzki, the foremost figure in the Jewish leadership of Vilna, was deliberately omitted from the invitations to the meeting, as in the past he had been chairman of the anti-Hitlerite committee in Vilna, and there was no wish to endanger his life. The meeting was opened by Dr. Gershuni, who stated:

> We must establish a Judenrat, and although we are aware of the peril confronting us, it is our obligation to do so. Were I younger, I would join the Judenrat myself. Consequently, I stress that all who are elected must not refuse; they must make themselves available for service.

With that Dr. Gershuni burst into tears and was joined by most of those present.

[59]

Despite his exhortation, there was an inadequate response when the nomination of ten candidates was undertaken. No one wanted to become a Judenrat member. Finally it was decided that anyone elected was forbidden to refuse. Ten members were chosen in the second round of voting. They represented different groups of Vilna Jews and provided a broad basis of Jewish representation.

S. Trotzki was elected chairman of the Judenrat; A. Fried, vice-chairman; and A. Zajdsznur, secretary. The physician Dr. Sadlis announced that, although elected, he refuses to accept membership. The next day at 12 noon, the Judenrat was received by Kalendra in his office. Thus the first Judenrat of Vilna was formed.[10]

The council of ten members, consisting entirely of persons formerly active in the Jewish community and in the public life of Vilna, was elected by the Jews, and may well be regarded as a continuation of the traditional leadership of Vilna Jewry. The people who convened the meeting—I. Verblinski, Rabbi S. Fried and Dr. G. Gershuni—had themselves been prominent in public and party life in Vilna, and those whom they invited were previously active workers in the community, in public and party institutions, and in the professional organizations in the city. The short time allotted them to form the body, together with the reality of street and home abductions and the absence of organized groups or Jewish institutions precluded any method of establishment other than individual approaches to a large number of people in public life, bringing them to-

---

10 *Ibid.,* pp. 9–12. The ten Judenrat members were: Rabbi Shuv, noted religious figure; E. Kruk, artisan, member of the Community Council Board of Directors; A. Zajdsznur, tradesman, member of the Community Board of Directors; Advocate P. Konn, newspaper reporter, active in Vilna YIVO; Engineer S. Trotzki, industrialist, member of the Community Council and of the City Council; Engineer A. Fried, Director of the Savings Fund in Vilna; Dr. R. Shabad-Gawronska, leader of "Toz-Oze"; Dr. E. Sadlis; J. Shabad; I. Verblinski, Secretary of the Community.

gether, and choosing the council from their midst. Most of those elected had no wish to be members of the Judenrat, and heavy moral pressure was brought to bear to obtain their consent.

Little information is extant as to the activity of the first Judenrat. Its offices were at No. 6 Straszuna Street, in the building that had previously belonged to the Jewish community. Among other matters, the council dealt with finding accommodations for Jewish families who had been evicted from their homes. They were put up in Jewish houses, in accordance with special permits issued by the Judenrat. The most difficult experience for the Jews at that time was the kidnappings. Men were taken off the streets and from their homes and did not return. Their families were told—and some believed—that they had been taken for labor. The Judenrat attempted to regulate this problem of kidnappings for labor purposes by becoming the sole supplier of Jewish manpower. A representative was appointed by the Judenrat for each city district, with the duty to provide the requisite labor force and thereby to prevent the abductions.[11]

On July 15, 1941, the German military commandant of the district published a public notice in which the articles referring to Jews declared that a Judenrat must be elected by each community. A Jewish community with less than 10,000 persons would have a Judenrat with ten members, but in places with a large population, the membership of the council would be twenty-four. Each Judenrat would elect its chairman and his deputy from among its members. The chairman of each of these councils would be obliged to inform the local military commandant of the composition of the membership by July 31. The notice further stipulated that the chairman of the Judenrat and his colleagues would take their instructions from the military government and would be personally responsible for carrying them out. They would also be liable for any hostile act

11 *Ibid.*, pp. 14, 16, 23.

directed at the German administration by Jews. It was further stated that Jews in every city would be concentrated in separate quarters, and those who fled would be returned to their former residences.[12]

Pursuant to this directive, the military commandant of Vilna, *Oberstleutnant* Zehnpfenning, instructed the Judenrat to increase its membership to twenty-four. The existing Judenrat resolved to appeal to public figures and former active party members to join. The requests to the former party leaders were personal, as there were no longer any parties to address, following their dissolution by the previous Soviet regime.

Dr. Dworzecki writes that an emissary came to him from the Judenrat and proposed that, as a former member of the Vilna Municipal Council representing Po'alei Zion-Hitahdut, he should now join the Jewish council on behalf of Zionist Labor. Dvorzecki summoned a meeting of a number of ex-party members to discuss joining the Judenrat. It was decided that Po'alei Zion-Hitahdut would not join the council on the grounds that the Judenrat, no matter how good its intentions, would become an instrument of the Germans. Dr. Dworzecki notes that other parties, including the Bund, held similar consultations; the pros and cons of such participation were discussed, and there was an expression of great hesitancy.[13]

In a diary entry for July 30, 1941, Kruk states that previously discussions had gone on for several days between a group of Bundists and Judenrat members over the same issue. The Bund decided to join the Judenrat. These deliberations by former party activists on joining the Judenrat marked the beginning of the coalescence of party groups in light of the new situation in Vilna.

Fourteen new members joined the Judenrat on July 24, 1941, and from then on it numbered twenty-four members. The fourteen new members included Dr. J. Wygodzki, the veteran leader

12 *Yerushalayim de-Lita Album,* p. 426, photocopy of the order.
13 Kruk, *op. cit.,* p. 25; Korczak, *op. cit.,* p. 12; Dworzecki, *op. cit.,* pp. 30–31.

of Vilna Jewry; Advocate S. Milkonovicki, the last chairman of the Vilna Jewish Community Council and a member of Po'alei Zion; two active central figures of the Bund, G. Jaszunski and J. Fishman; and S. Petukhovski, former Deputy Chairman of the Municipality of Shavli.[14]

Some of the new members were part of the Jewish traditional leadership of Vilna, while others were party leaders and active public officials from other cities (for example, G. Jaszunski and S. Petukhovski). The membership of the enlarged Judenrat represented various social groupings and parties. While it included two Bundists and three Zionists, there were no persons identified as Communists or Revisionists. In spite of this, its social basis was a wide one.

The scope of activity of the enlarged Jewish council was identical with that of the smaller one: housing homeless families and sending groups of Jews to work in establishments run by the Lithuanians and German military units.

The attitude of the Jewish populace toward the first Judenrat is described by A. Rindziunski, a Jew who lived in Vilna at this time:

> The Jewish population believed, in its innocence, that the Judenrat could ease the position of the Jews and could successfully intervene with the German administration to secure facilities. Consequently, Jews—males and females—came to the Judenrat offices and wept and begged for mercy to save their relatives. The members of the Judenrat, too, were no less naive than the remainder of the Jews and believed they could do something by interceding.[15]

14 Additional members of the Judenrat were Advocate L. Katznelson; Rabinowicz; S. Hoffman, tradesman, former member of the Community Council, Zionist; A. Zalkind, President of the Tradesmen's Association in Vilna; Dr. L. Holem; Advocate N. Sofer; J. Shkolnitzki; Rabbi Katz; Advocate B. Parnass, Zionist, former Chairman of the Vilna Jewish Community.

15 Rindziunski's testimony, p. 15.

C. Grossman writes in her book of the appeal that she, herself, together with Mordechai Tenenbaum-Tamaroff, addressed to Judenrat member I. Verblinski concerning the need to find work for Halutz members within the city's surrounding district so that they would not be kidnapped. Mrs. Grossman compares the first Judenrat to the former Jewish community council (Kehillah): "On Mordechai and me was imposed the task of testing the possibilities expected from the temporary Kehillah, the first Judenrat."[16] This appeal indicates that, during the tenure of the first Judenrat, from July to August 1941, the Zionist youth movements did not have a negative attitude toward it, although later opposition was to develop from them.

The Jews of Vilna perceived the first Judenrat as a continuation of the city's traditional leadership and of the Jewish community council and had confidence in it. This identification was furthered by the fact that members of the first Judenrat had been on the former Jewish community council, and even among its leaders.

Extermination Actions of Einsatzkommando 9 in Vilna
While they were still stationed in the assembly area of the Einsatzgruppen, in the vicinity of Düben in Saxony, the commanders of the Einsatzgruppen and Einsatzkommando were summoned to a conference at the beginning of June 1941, and were briefed by Heydrich concerning the tasks assigned to their formations. Heydrich informed them that Hitler had given orders to kill the Jews in the occupied parts of the U.S.S.R. and that it would be the special duty of their outfits to fulfill this command. He emphasized the need for complete secrecy in all that pertained to the execution of the mission.

Heydrich's briefing on the Einsatzgruppen tasks in the U.S.S.R. was limited exclusively to the rank of *Brigadeführer* (Major-General) and *Standarteführer* (Colonel). It was not transmitted to the lower ranks while the formations were still in Germany,

16 Grossman, *op. cit.*, p. 20.

but only when they were about to cross the frontier into the Soviet Union. In an address that Heydrich delivered to all troops prior to their departure from Düben for the U.S.S.R., he dwelt on the arduous tasks confronting them, of a kind in which they had had no experience, to be discharged under especially difficult conditions. He withheld information as to the nature of these tasks.[17]

On June 26 or 27, 1941, Einsatzkommando 9 left its base at Düben. It reached Warsaw on June 28, where it was reinforced by a platoon of *Ordnungspolizei* of the 9th Police Regiment. On June 29, Einsatzkommando 9 departed Warsaw and halted overnight near the city of Treuburg in east Prussia.

On June 30, the day before the crossing into the U.S.S.R., at the bivouac near Treuburg, the commander of Einsatzkommando 9, Dr. Filbert, informed his deputy commanders about the mission assigned to them in the Soviet Union—the extermination of the Jews. Filbert explained that the command came from Hitler, who had ordered the execution of the Jews, and finished his briefing by demanding complete obedience from the officers and men. In outlining the task, Filbert did not resort to military necessities to justify the murder of the Jews, but adduced the argument that this was in the spirit of National Socialist ideology, that ideology that called for the liquidation of inferior species of mankind. The sub-commanders of the Einsatzkommando 9 conveyed the orders to the soldiers. All orders to the Einsatzgruppen relating to the general extermination of the Jews were communicated verbally. Heydrich's briefing in the base area in the Düben zone and the order to Filbert and others were also made verbally; this in order to preserve secrecy and so that no documents would remain for future reference.[18]

---

17 Filbert's trial, YVA, TR–10/388a, p. 30.
18 *Ibid.*, pp. 31–32. *Gruppenführer* Schellenberg of the RSHA testified in his evidence at Nuremberg that the orders were transmitted verbally.

Einsatzkommando 9 crossed the old border of the Reich en route to Vilna on July 1, 1941, and arrived in the city the following day. The first two days, July 2 and 3, were devoted to familiarizing themselves with the conditions and arrangements for the extermination actions. E.K. 7-a, which had remained in Vilna until then, left upon the arrival of E.K. 9 and proceeded to Minsk.

The murder of small groups of Jews by the Lithuanians had already begun before the arrival of E.K. 9. The Lithuanians seized Jews on the streets and killed them in the forest near Ponar (Paneriai). Filbert learned of this Lithuanian action on July 2, after reaching Vilna.[19] The information was helpful to E.K. 9 because Ponar could be used for mass murder, and the Lithuanians could be helpful in the murder actions. This enabled E.K.9 to launch the extermination campaign without delay and on a large scale.

The Einsatzkommando completed its organization in Vilna, and on July 4, 1941, began its massacres. The number of victims mounted daily.

The Process of Extermination
The process of extermination carried out by E.K.9 was conducted in three simultaneous and successive stages:

> Stage I: Kidnapping Jews from the streets and from their homes and concentrating them in the Lukiszki prison.
> Stage II: Detention of the victims in prison as a transit station to Ponar.
> Stage III: Transporting the Jews from Lukiszki to Ponar and murdering them there.

The problem of manpower needed to discharge the functions of extermination on such a large scale was solved by incorporating Lithuanian police and other units in the E.K.9 actions.

19 *Ibid.*, p. 39.

Einsatzgruppen report No. 17 of July 9 referred to "units of the Lithuanian police subordinate to E.K.9." Einsatzgruppen Report No. 21 of July 13 stated:

> In Vilna ... the Lithuanian *Ordnungspolizei*, which was placed under the command of the Einsatzkommando after the disbandment of the Lithuanian political police, received instructions to take part in the Jewish extermination actions. Consequently, 150 Lithuanians are engaged in arresting and taking Jews to the concentration camp, where after one day they were given "special handling" (*Sonderbehandlung*).

The integration of the Lithuanians into E.K.9 activity made it possible to increase the number of Jews kidnapped and killed daily at Ponar. The E.K.9 was organized in such a way that each stage and type of *Aktion* had its own special force, permitting the operation to be carried out simultaneously.

Stage 1—Kidnapping of Jews and their Transport to Lukiszki
The unit used to kidnap Jews from the streets and from their homes was composed of German E.K.9 soldiers, Lithuanians under their command, and Lithuanian civilians who helped in abducting Jews. Dr. Dworzecki writes:

> The Gestapo men come in cars and stop in front of Jewish houses. They take out the males and order them to bring along a towel and soap. These people are ostensibly taken to work for several days, but they never return. Groups of Lithuanian and Polish youths wearing white armbands appear in the streets and snatch the Jews, whom they lead off to the police stations or prison. Some of them break into the houses and haul out the Jewish males. People call them *hapunes* [abductors] ... It was said that the price paid to the abductor for a kidnapped Jew was 10 rubles.[20]

20 Dworzecki, *op. cit.*, pp. 20–21; Sutzkewer, *op. cit.*, pp. 12–13;

The "abductors" were mainly Lithuanians, but German sources also indicated that there were some Poles among them. Report No. 17 of the Einsatzgruppen, dated July 9, 1941, described the situation in the Vilna district: "... The Lithuanian military units are inspected as to whether there are Poles in their ranks. They are subsequently disarmed and discharged from military service."

Developments and changes occurred in the kidnapping actions during July. The changes were in the locations from which the Jews were abducted, the hours during which this was done, and the scale of the actions. The number taken away increased daily, particularly during the period of July 8–17, when the system of shootings at Ponar became more efficient.

The Judenrat was required by the German military government and by the Lithuanian authorities to send Jews to forced labor daily. Many Jews assigned by the Judenrat for work were kidnapped on their way there or when returning. There were cases in which the kidnappers entered the courtyard of the Judenrat offices and seized the Jews assembling there even before they were sent to work. The Germans, who had demanded these laborers, would then come to the Judenrat demanding the requested labor force. They naturally gave no consideration to the fact that the men they had asked for had been taken away en route.

Shur stated that some Wehrmacht soldiers helped the Jews in a number of instances and saved them from their Lithuanian captors. Korczak and Kruk also reported similar incidents.[21]

This situation—in which, on the one hand, there was a demand for Jewish labor by German military units and factories operated by the local Lithuanian authorities and, on the other hand, the capture of Jews on their way to work and their subsequent removal to Lukiszki and Ponar to be murdered—

Rindziunski's testimony, p. 13. The Jewish museum set up in Vilna after World War II contained documents with confirmations of payments made to Lithuanian abductors for each kidnapped person.

21 Korczak, *op. cit.,* p. 11; Rindziunski's testimony, p. 21.

arose from the coexistence of two separate authoritative bodies, each functioning in accordance with its own objectives and powers. One of these was the German military government; the other Einsatzkommando 9.

The duty of the German military government was to organize the rear area to serve the needs of the frontline and to maintain the orderly operation of factories, railroads and the like, as well as to supply army units with essential services. These requirements made it necessary to utilize Jewish labor. On the other hand, to E.K.9 fell the task of wiping out the Jews of Vilna. The easiest way to accomplish this was to snatch organized groups of Jews on their way to work, and these groups became the principal target of the abductors.

This situation led to friction between E.K.9 and the German military government, which insisted that Jews working for German army units not be kidnapped. It was agreed that the Jews would be equipped with special permits testifying that the bearers were employed by the army. This pass was to shield them against the kidnappers. Following the example set by the military government, the local Lithuanian authorities also issued their own passes for Jews employed in plants and factories managed by Lithuanians. The value of a pass given by a Lithuanian establishment was inferior to a German one, as the kidnappers thought less of the former.[22]

But even the passes, including those with a German stamp, issued by a German body, did not prevent the kidnapping of groups of Jews on their way to work. Finally, in some cases Wehrmacht soldiers came to the Judenrat to protect their Jewish workers.

The street captures failed to garner the requisite number of Jews for Ponar, and, to complete the daily quota, Jews were seized in their homes. At night the captors entered the houses, took the males and brought them to Lukiszki.

---

22 Dworzecki, *op. cit.*, pp. 20–21; Sutzkewer, *op. cit.*, pp. 12–13; Rindziunski's testimony, p. 13.

The constant abductions at homes and in the streets, the insecurity and the lack of knowledge as to the fate of those taken, stimulated the Judenrat to seek ways of regulating the problem. The prevalent view among the Jews was that the men who disappeared were taken to work-sites outside the city and therefore could not come home. The massacres at Ponar were not yet known in those early days of July. The Judenrat sought an authority to which it could apply to halt these abductions and organize an orderly method of supplying people for work. Finally the Judenrat found the Lithuanian unit that engaged in these kidnappings. Kruk writes:

> When the Judenrat received a report that the matter was connected with the *Ypatingi buriai* ("The Special Ones") at 12 Vilna Street, the former secretary of the community council, Verblinski, went there. He suggested they should cease the kidnappings and the Judenrat would give them workers. The *Ypatingi* willingly agreed ... The Judenrat soon realized that it had made a mistake. How could they send people *without* any certainty as to their fate. After the agreement a demand was received for 150 males. The Judenrat decided by a vote of twenty-four to one not to send the people. But according to the "agreement," it published a notice appealing to people to register for work as the Lithuanians requested. Fifty-three people registered, but by the time of departure only twenty-one remained ... The twenty-one went off and did not return ... [23]

Nothing came of the agreement between the Judenrat and the *Ypatingi*. From the moral standpoint, the Judenrat was unable to furnish Jews for the Lithuanians if they did not know their destination. The *Ypatingi* were ready to receive the help of the Judenrat in capturing Jews, but they could find them on the streets and in their homes even without any arrangement with

23 Kruk, *op. cit.*, pp. 18–19.

the Judenrat. Verblinski apparently had not received the prior approval of the Judenrat for an agreement with the *Ypatingi,* as was evidenced by the twenty-four to one vote against it. The single vote was apparently Verblinski's.

Within a short while the street and home abductions were also insufficient. The abductors now met with difficulty, as Jews began to go into hiding. The terms *malines* and *farmalineven,* (Yiddish slang) came into used and persisted among Jews in Vilna and elsewhere until the end of the Nazi period. The *maline* was a hiding-place from the kidnappers. Even before the Jewish public became fully aware of the fate of the captives, they realized that it was better not to be caught, and the natural reaction was to hide. During the initial phase of the kidnappings, house searches were not thorough, and places such as attics with a hidden entrance, tiny roomlets with a door concealed by a heavy wardrobe, or even chimneys and cellars all provided *malines.* These hideouts are mentioned in Jewish sources dealing with the events in Vilna in July 1941. Kruk writes that on July 12, he and a number of males took cover in a *maline* and that for two days the tenants of his house were on guard near the house for sixteen hours daily in order to warn of the approach of kidnappers so as to allow the others to scramble quickly into a *maline.* Women played an important role as guards and in warning of approaching captors. Other sources also refer to the *malines* in this period.[24]

To increase the number of victims, the E.K.9 adopted new tactics. To surprise the Jews in their homes, they began coming during the day as well as at night; they also made use of larger forces. This intensification was facilitated by the employment of 150 Lithuanians. This reinforcement doubled the strength of E.K.9. The E.K. used cars for the kidnappings, so that they were able to arrive swiftly, by surprise, and before any warnings could be given. The Lithuanian reinforcements and the use

24 *Ibid.,* pp. 20–21; Dworzecki, *op. cit.,* p. 27; Sutzkewer, *op. cit.,* p. 26.

of vehicles enabled the E.K. to widen the scope of its activities and increase the number of victims.

Large forces of E.K.9 men and Lithuanians surrounded residential quarters and went from house to house, arresting every Jewish male and carrying him off to Lukiszki prison. This large-scale operation began on July 13, 1941, and included the Nowogrod (Naugarduko) and Zarecza (Uzupio) districts. The kidnappers did not take the time to verify the ages of their victims, and young boys who looked older than their years were also seized.

This rule of taking only males characterized the Einsatzgruppen's actions in other areas of Lithuania during July. The report by Einsatzkommando 3 of Einsatzgruppe A, which was operating in Kovno and other regions in the country, stated that 2,930 males, as compared with 47 women, were killed in Kovno between July 4 and 6, 1941. Jewish sources confirm the fact that the Jewish males were the main victims of the Einsatzgruppen activities in Lithuania during July 1941.[25]

The kidnapping of males only was a deliberate policy of the Einsatzgruppen in the first phase of their campaign. We find confirmation of this in the statement of the Commanding Officer of E.K.9, Filbert, who told his officers at the close of the Vilna action: "We shall, in the future, have to murder Jewish women and children, as the number of those liquidated so far has been too small."

An additional criterion in choosing victims was to liquidate the Jewish leadership and intelligentsia. Einsatzgruppen Report No. 17 of July 9, 1941, stated:

> Lithuanian police units under the command of E.K.9 received an order to prepare lists of Vilna Jews and to give priority to the intelligentsia, party activists, and the wealthy.

The same line of selection is evident in the report of Einsatz-

25 *Documents Accuse*, pp. 231–232; Kruk, *op. cit.*, pp. 13–23.

gruppe No. 13 of July 15, which tells of the action of an E.K.9 sub-unit operating in the Grodno region: "The leaders of the Jewish intelligentsia, especially teachers, lawyers and Soviet officials, were liquidated."[26] This singling out was evident elsewhere. Over 500 Jews, all members of the liberal professions, were killed in Kovno in a special action directed against them on August 18, 1941.

In spite of the instructions there was no special action in Vilna against the intelligentsia or Jewish leaders.[27] The extirpation of the Jewish leadership and intelligentsia in Vilna was carried out within the general framework of the destruction of the Jews. The murder operations against Vilna Jewry assumed a mass form, and E.K.9 could not, and possibly also did not wish to, devote special means and efforts to deal with individual and comparatively small groups, which would have limited the scope of the mass extermination.

The male kidnappings, coupled with the tendency to single out the Jewish leadership and intelligentsia for elimination, verifies the assumption that in the first phase the Germans intended to remove those elements among the Jews which could organize resistance, and this before the Jews realized the fate in store for them.

An additional factor that dictated male kidnappings in the initial stage was the need to keep the Jews in the dark with regard to the fate of those who had been taken away. The fact that, simultaneously with the seizure and disappearance of male Jews, others actually were taken as laborers and returned home at the end of the day, gave grounds for the assumption that those who did not return had been sent to work in places far from Vilna. The Germans encouraged the Jews in this belief by ordering the men to equip themselves with towels and soap, on the grounds that they would not be returning home that night.

26 Filbert's trial, TR–10/388, pp. 61, 66; and TR–10/388a, p. 41.
27 Dworzecki, *op. cit.*, pp. 24–25, writes that during the night of July 13–14, 1941, rabbis were arrested.

The illusion that the men were being taken for work could continue only as long as the seized males were of working age. Had women and children been included, it is reasonable to assume that the illusion would have been quickly shattered and the Germans would have encountered more difficulties in their murder campaign.

The kidnapping and killing of males only was more convenient for the Einsatzgruppen from a psychological viewpoint. When Filbert briefed his deputy commanders at the end of July 1941, when the E.K.9 left Vilna and was stationed at Vileyka, Belorussia, he told his staff that, from then on, Jewish women and children would also be massacred. One of the commanders remarked, "it is difficult to expect that people who are themselves family men can do this with any enthusiasm." Another commander pointed out that "a part of the E.K.9 personnel is composed of young men, and it is not desirable that they should participate in such executions."[28]

The objective of killing the males first also stemmed from the need to determine priorities in the extermination of the Jews, for it was not possible to slaughter all Vilna's Jews at once.

Stage II — Lukiszki Prison, the Transit Station to Ponar
The Lukiszki prison served as a transit station to Ponar throughout the Nazi occupation of Vilna. The Jews knew that the captives were taken there, but they had no idea of their destiny after leaving the prison. On July 1, H. Kruk wrote: "Why just the Lukiszki prison? I have now learned that many of those kidnapped on the way to work have been sent to Lukiszki jail. It is said that this must be the place of assembly from which men are sent to work. Many women congregate outside the prison." On July 5, he made this entry in his diary: "The woman assembling outside the prison tell of large groups of men being led in the direction of Legionowo [in the direction of Ponar]."

28   Filbert's trial, TR–10/388, p. 41.

The seized Jews spent indeterminate periods in the prison, from several hours to a number of weeks. The bottleneck of the killing operations was Ponar, viz., the number of Jews that the firing-squad could deal with in one day. The prison was the regulator between the number of Jews caught in the streets and at home and the murder capacity of Ponar. It always contained a ready reservoir of victims.

Not all the Jews on the way to Ponar passed through Lukiszki. Several hundred Jews captured on July 13 were kept for one night in the courtyard of the Gestapo building at 36 Mickiewicza Street and on the morrow were transported to Ponar, where they were slain.[29]

Stage III — Ponar: The Valley of Death
Ponar was a wooded area some 8 miles south of Vilna on the highway to Grodno and had been used in the past for holidays and recreation. It was served by a road and a railway from Vilna. In the Ponar area the Soviet authorities had dug deep pits for fuel tanks. The holes were of various depths, from 2 to 7 meters, and with a diameter from 15 to 50 meters. During the digging, large, high embankments had been built up around the pits from the extracted earth, with passageways through them to the pits. These pits, planned for fuel storage, became the mass graves of tens of thousands of Vilna Jews and thousands of Soviet prisoners of war and civilian opponents of Nazism.

The E.K.9 Commanding Officer appointed *Obersturmführer* Schauschutz as responsible officer at Ponar and placed him in charge of the Lithuanian contingent that implemented the murders on the spot. The Lithuanian system of killings did not comply with Schauschutz's demands, so he introduced a new method of killing. He forbade the use of machineguns and permitted the use of rifles only. Thus there were no volleys directed at groups, but rifles sighted and fired at individual

29 Kruk, *op. cit.*, p. 8; Rindziunski's testimony, p. 17.

victims only, a method that eliminated the chance of men being only wounded or even remaining unhurt. Schauschutz also improved the organization of the massacres so that a larger number of Jews was executed in less time. This new organizational method enabled the killing of 100 men per hour.

The German–Lithuanian force responsible for bringing the Jews to Ponar and putting them to death there consisted of three units: the first, comprised of E.K.9 personnel and Lithuanians, had charge of transporting the victims from Lukiszki prison to Ponar in E.K.9 trucks. The second was responsible for security at Ponar and sealing it off from within and without. It was to prevent victims from escaping—and to shoot down those who tried—and to prevent the local population and German soldiers from entering the area of execution and discovering what was happening there. This detachment included mainly Germans of E.K.9, as only they, and not the Lithuanians, could prevent inquisitive German soldiers from coming in to watch the shooting of Jews. Notwithstanding this precaution, there were men of the Wehrmacht who saw the murders being committed at Ponar. A third detachment, under the command of Schauschutz himself, was composed of riflemen who perpetrated the actual killings. Each of the three units had a German officer in charge. The Lithuanians were in the majority in each group involved in the actual killing.

The victims brought from Lukiszki prison to Ponar were marshaled into a waiting zone some hundreds of yards from the firing pits. They were made to undress and relinquish whatever valuables they possessed. They were then marched in groups of ten to twenty from the waiting area—naked and holding hands—in single file. Such was the procession to the scene of slaughter. Once one line had left, the next had to make ready. There were at times 100 or more Jews amassed in the waiting area.

The victims were arranged at the edge of the embankments above the pits and shot down by rifle-fire. After they had fallen, no effort was made to ascertain if all were dead. If any-

[76]

one moved, another bullet was fired at him. The corpses were covered with a thin layer of sand and the next batch was brought in. Those in the waiting zone could hear the firing, but were unable to see what transpired.

The organization of the murder actions at Ponar was based on a number of parallel stages: bringing the victims from the town prison to Ponar; preparing the victims in the waiting zone; and firing at the pits. By this method E.K.9 was able to increase their number to 500 daily, beginning on July 8, 1941. During the period of E.K.9 operations in Vilna from July 4 to 20, 5,000 Jews were murdered.[30]

Complicity of E.K.9 Personnel in the Massacres

During the first week of the E.K.9 operations in Vilna, the German soldiers of E.K.9, except for a few, did not take direct part in the killings at Ponar. There was no immediate need for them, as there was a sufficient number of Lithuanians ready to carry out the killings. The E.K.9 soldiers dealt mainly in administration, planning, and supervision, and worked as drivers, signal men, and liaison officers, who were not required to participate directly in the murders.

To ensure that each one of the Einsatzgruppen members was personally and directly associated with the crimes perpetrated by his unit, there was a standing order whereby each soldier, whether in an administrative or clerical capacity, or even a driver, was personally obliged to take part in at least one execution and to fire at the victims with his own weapon. To implement this order, the commander of E.K.9 took advantage of an "incident"—which in all likelihood, under the circumstances, he himself staged.

During the night of July 10, 1941, several shots were fired at E.K.9 quarters. No one was hit, nor was it known who the

30 Filbert's trial, TR–10/388, pp. 63–64; and TR–10/388a, pp. 34–36, 40; Einsatzgruppen Report (No. 21) of July 13, 1941, YVA, 0–51/ 57–1.

assailants were. The next day, July 11, the C.O., Filbert, ordered a search of the adjacent Jewish quarter, the arrest of all males as hostages, and the confiscation of valuable articles. Filbert directed that part of the hostages be taken out and executed by commanders and soldiers of E.K.9. He chose a spot at the edge of the city limits and ordered a group of Jews to dig the pits. They were brought in on trucks to a distance of about 100 yards from the firing place. A firing party of ten men, all E.K.9 personnel, was formed. Two men directed their fire at each victim. Filbert personally commanded the first squad. Another took its place for the next batch of victims. After each fusillade, Lithuanian police inspected the bodies to verify that no one had remained alive. Thus Filbert turned each individual in his unit into accomplices in crime.[31]

The action was presented by Filbert as retaliation for the shots fired at his men's quarters. He served as a personal example, first in leading one of the firing squads, and then as an ordinary member of a firing party. Other officers in the E.K.9 followed his example. From July 11 until the end of their activity in Vilna, the E.K.9 men were integrated into the firing squads.

E.K.9 operated in Vilna until July 20, 1941. On the 23rd it departed for Minsk and left behind a rearguard that was to be relieved by Einsatzgruppe A, which had assumed responsibility for all of Lithuania, including Vilna. The rearguard stayed until August 9, when E.K.3 of Einsatzgruppe A took over in Vilna.[32]

With the departure of the main body of E.K.9, the kidnappings and murders of Ponar decreased, but did not cease. The small rearguard company and the Lithuanians under E.K.9 command continued to take anti-Jewish action, but on a reduced scale.

---

31 Filbert's trial, TR–10/388, p. 64; and TR–10/388a, p. 37.
32 *Ibid.*, pp. 66–67, and TR–10/388, p. 40. Summation Report of K. Jäger, Commander of Einsatzkommando 3, of December 1, 1941, YVA, 0–18/245.

The seizure of thousands of Jewish males and their disappearance, the absence of information about their fate, the insecurity everywhere—at home, outdoors, on the way to and from work, during the day, during the night—the fear of footsteps or approaching cars all characterized the atmosphere in Vilna during that July in 1941. On August 1, 1941, the military authorities yielded the reins of power to the German civilian administration.

Chapter 5

GERMAN CIVIL ADMINISTRATION

German Administration in the East—Authority and Organization
Within the framework of preparations for the invasion of the
U.S.S.R., on April 20, 1941, Hitler appointed Alfred Rosenberg
responsible for the group that was assigned to inquire into the
potential problems that had to be met in ruling the vast Eastern
territories; they were asked to study the alternatives and draft
the necessary plans. During the months of April and May,
Rosenberg formulated the guidelines and underlying principles
of German administration in the conquered territories of the
Soviet Union.[1]

Several days after the invasion, at the beginning of July 1941,
the chief of staff of the Wehrmacht, General W. von Keitel, requested that Rosenberg take over the administration of those
parts of the Baltic states that had already been subdued by the
German Army, viz., all of Lithuania and most of Latvia. This
request came before the German civil administration for the
East had been officially established. The Army High Command
had no interest in having the army deal with the political problems that had arisen in the Baltic states with the creation of
autonomous governments in Latvia and Lithuania. Rosenberg

---

1 Rosenberg *Denkschrift*, April 2, 1941, Nuremberg Document, PS-
   1017; April 25, 1941, Nuremberg Document, PS–1020; Trial of
   Franz Mürer, YVA, TR–11/233, p. 7.

transmitted Von Keitel's proposal to Hitler. On July 8 he received a reply that "the *Führer* is not interested, for the time being, in civilian administration in the conquered territories in the East, and he reserves for himself the right to decide about the proper time for it."

Simultaneously, and without waiting for Hitler's approval, Rosenberg reached an agreement with the Wehrmacht (on July 14) by which the lower echelons of the civilian administration in any case would begin to function, and the German Army and civil administration would withhold any recognition from the armies and local governments established in the Baltic states and Belorussia.[2]

The directive to establish civilian administration in the Eastern territories was given in an "Order of the *Führer* on the Administration of the New Territories in the East," promulgated on July 17, 1941. The order prescribed that those areas captured in the East, and in which combat activities had already been terminated, should be transferred by the military government to a civilian administration to be organized for that purpose. It further prescribed that the head of the civilian administration would be the *"Reichminister* for the Occupied Territories in the East," Alfred Rosenberg, who would sit in Berlin. The "Order" also set forth the organizational structure and geographical and political divisions of the Eastern areas and provided that the principal geographical and political unit in those territories should be the *Reichskommissariat,* headed by a *Reichkommissar* directly subordinated to the *Reichsminister.* The *Reichskommissariat* would be comprised of a number of areas, each known as a *Generalbezirk* (*Generalkommissariat*) headed by a *Generalkommissar.* The *Generalbezirk* would be divided into subdistricts, each called *Kreisgebiet* (*Gebietskommissariat*) under a *Gebietskommissar.*

An additional order by the *Führer* published the same day

2 A. Dallin, *The German Rule in Russia, 1941–1945,* London, 1957, p. 189.

provided for two *Reichskommissariate*: *Reichskommissariat Ostland* embraced the areas of Lithuania, Latvia, Estonia, and part of Belorussia, and was headed by *Reichskommissar* H. Lohse, who had his headquarters in Riga, Latvia; the second *Reichskommissariat* was the *Reichskommissariat* Ukraine, under *Reichskommissar* E. Koch.

On July 17, too, the *Führer's* "Order" concerning police security in the New Territories in the East was also promulgated.[3] According to this "Order," Heinrich Himmler and his SS cohorts were made responsible for police security, rather than Alfred Rosenberg's ministry. Himmler was given vast powers in all matters that concerned police security. The "Order" stated that, within the limits of his responsibility, Himmler was to issue instructions directly to the *Reichskommissar*, except on general subjects or those of political and economic significance, which were not specified by the above-mentioned order. This actually left to Himmler the ultimate determination of his position. The "Order" established SS authority in the East, which would operate concurrently with the German civilian administration on all levels. Although the SS apparatus in the Eastern territories was officially subordinated to the civil administration, as each of the civilian regional heads had a Senior SS and police commander subordinate to him, there was no practical significance to this system. It was Himmler, and not Rosenberg, who was nominated as the head of the network in the security domain.

This order sanctioned the possibility of directives issued to the *Reichskommissar* to go through SS channels, and not through Rosenberg's Ministry for the East (*Ostministerium*). Hence, in reality, instructions from Himmler's Command H.Q. in Berlin went directly to the *Gebietskommissariat*, the lowest rung of the hierarchical ladder, to which senior SS and police

3 Nuremberg Document, PS–1997; Trial of Gewecke, *Gebietskommissar* of Shavli, YVA, TR–10/657, pp. 17–18; Dallin, *op. cit.*, p. 99.

commanders were attached. Instead of a unified German administration with a distinct hierarchy, carefully defined and well-understood powers, Hitler's orders established dual administration in the Eastern territories, and wherever a German civilian government functioned, there was also a corollary SS body.

Apart from the civil administrators and SS agencies which operated under separate directives and orders, there were additional bodies in the *Ostland* that functioned independently. By order of the *Führer* and the High Command of the Wehrmacht, as of July 25, 1941, General F. Brämer was appointed Military Governor of the *Ostland*. He was made subordinate to the O.K.W. and not to Rosenberg. On July 24, General Brämer issued a circular in which he announced his own appointment and the areas falling within his jurisdiction.[4]

Goering, who was in charge of the Four-Year Plan, was also responsible for the economic exploitation of the occupied territories in the U.S.S.R., in accordance with Hitler's "Order" of June 29, 1941.[5] Goering established an "Economic Staff in the East" (*Wirtschaftsstab Ost*), but because of Rosenberg's opposition, Goering's staff functioned only in the areas that were under military administration. In the *Ostland,* economic matters were the responsibility of the civilian administration, with the exception of production requirements for the army, which were under the supervision of the Army Quartermaster. A special Inspector of the Army Ordnance (*Rüstungsinspektor*) had been appointed for the *Ostland,* and he operated subordinate units (*Rüstungskommandos*) under his command. These ordnance units exploited the economic resources of the Eastern territories

---

4 *My Obvinyaem, Dokumenty i materialy o zlodeyaniyakh gitlerov-skikh okupantov i latyshskikh burzhuaznykh natsionalistov v Latviskoy Sovetskoy Sotsialisticheskoy Respublike 1941–1945,* Riga, 1967, pp. 36–37 (hereafter: *My Obvinyaem*). General Brämer was Supreme Commander of the Wermacht in the *Ostland* from 1941–1944.

5 Führer's Order of June 29, 1941, Nuremberg Document, PS–012.

for the German war effort, especially for the requirements of the Eastern front. Industrial establishments and workshops producing for the German Army came under their jurisdiction. The use of skilled and unskilled Jewish labor in the factories that produced goods for the army and other military establishments caused these army authorities to become involved in the Jewish affairs policy in the East.

In a series of orders, Hitler specified the various authorities for each territory: e.g., the civil administration, the SS, the Wehrmacht, and economic agencies. In many cases the areas of responsibility overlapped. Contradictions in basic policy on the future of the occupied territories, conflicts of personal interests, both at the local and policy-making levels in Berlin, created a situation which, throughout the period of German government in the East, generated continuous friction among the various authorities.[6] Each of the agencies functioning in the East apparently had some contact with Jewish matters, and the conflict of interest among them extended also to the Jewish problem.

The German civil administration began its activities on September 1, 1941, pursuant to the *Führer's* Order of August 20, although, actually, it had been active for about one month prior to the official date. The activation of the civil administration a month before its formal inception had been made possible by the agreement reached on July 14 between the Wehrmacht and Rosenberg.

The civil administration in the *Ostland* began organizing at the end of July. *Reichskommissariat Ostland* encompassed four countries—Lithuania, Latvia, Estonia, and part of Belorussia. Because of the multiple German agencies in the territory and the absence of clear definitions of areas of responsibility, the functionaries at the lower echelons enjoyed broad powers. Heinrich Lohse, who held the post of *Ostland Reichskommissar* from the end of July 1941 to the end of July 1944 (several days before the liberation of the territory by the Soviet Army), deeply

6 Dallin, *op. cit.*, p. 89; Mürer's trial, p. 8.

influenced the developments in the area under his rule. The historian Alexander Dallin wrote about Lohse's personality:

> A fanatical Nazi ... Lohse strove for a personal empire independent of Berlin. In an attempt to make the *Ostland* precisely this, he exerted strenuous and at times childish efforts to "centralize" everything in his own hands ... The result was a flood of directives, instructions and decrees which covered thousands of pages ... Lohse saw as his basic task the reconstruction of the areas entrusted to him. *Aufbau und Kultur* was his somewhat hypocritical slogan ... The people had to be "used" and therefore given, or at least promised, something in return ... if better treatment could increase production ... as many concessions as were necessary and safe had to be made.[7]

This is the man who had in his hands the destiny of the Jews of Vilna and of all the *Ostland*.

SS *Obergruppenführer* H. Prützman was appointed as Senior SS and Police Commander of the *Ostland*. He held his post until November 15, 1941, when he was replaced by SS *Obergruppenführer* F. Jeckeln. The extent of cooperation that existed between the SS and the civil administration was dependent mainly on these SS commanders.

On July 27, 1941, the *Reichskommissar* Lohse called a conference at Kovno of the *Generalkommissare* and *Gebietskommissare* who were scheduled to take over the administration in the *Ostland*. At this meeting Lohse announced the directives pertaining to the civil administration in the Eastern territories. He stressed that stimulation of the economy and of agricultural activity would be the principal aims of the civil administration, as it would be called upon to supply the goods required by the German armed forces on the Northern front and those posted to the *Ostland*.[8]

7   Dallin, *op. cit.*, pp. 85, 185–186, 187.
8   Gewecke's trial, TR—10/657, p. 40; Mürer's trial, p. 8.

The Civil Administration in Lithuania

Lithuania became a *Generalbezirk*, headed by *Generalkommissar* von Renteln, who had his headquarters at Kovno. The Lithuanian *Generalbezirk* was divided into *Gebietskommissare*—City of Kovno, Kovno District ("Kovno Land"), City of Vilna, Vilna District ("Vilna Land"), and Shavli.

The SS and police commander in the *Generalbezirk* of Lithuania was *Brigadeführer* Wysocki, who served in that capacity until mid-1943. All SS and police units, German as well as Lithuanian, were under his command. SS *Standartenführer* Jäger, C.O. of E.K.3 (of Einsatzgruppen A), who had operated in Lithuania from July 2, 1941, and had been primarily engaged in the massacre of Lithuanian Jewry, had been appointed, with the inception of the civil administration, as chief of the Security Police and SD in the *Generalkommissariat* of Lithuania and held that office until 1943. The officer in charge of Jewish affairs at SS and Police Headquarters in Lithuania was *Hauptsturmführer* H. Schmitz, who held that post from July 1941 to July 1944.

On July 28, 1941, *Generalkommissar* von Renteln announced that, on behalf of the Reich, he was taking power in the territory of the former state of Lithuania. The German civil administration began to dissolve the Lithuanian institutions that had been previously established and that bore a sovereign political character. The Lithuanian units were disarmed in the last days of July and were organized as regular police battalions. They were placed under the command of a German police officer, F. Lechthaller, on July 30, 1941.

On August 5, 1941, members of the Provisional Lithuanian Government were received by *Generalkommissar* von Renteln, who informed them that the Lithuanian Government would henceforth cease to function as such and that the ministers would continue as general advisors (*Generalräte*) to the civil administration. The Acting Prime Minister of the Lithuanian Government, Ambraze Vicius, refused to accept the appoint-

[86]

ment and resigned on August 9. General Kubiliunas agreed to accept the post.[9]

On August 15 the Germans published an order concerning the registration of labor forces, also specifying that laborers could be used for work outside their places of residence. Instructions were issued on August 20 as to the fulfillment and delivery of quotas of agricultural produce to the Germans. To the bitter disappointment of the Lithuanian farmers, the lands nationalized by the Soviets were not restored to the original owners. When the new scholastic term began, the Germans prohibited teaching toward higher degrees in the universities, with the aim of keeping the conquered nations stagnant at a lower cultural level.

These measures taken by the German civil administration disappointed the Lithuanians. Various Lithuanian organizations, including the general advisors, submitted memoranda to the German administration in which they protested the non-restoration of land, the restrictions at the universities, and the withholding of independence to Lithuania. The memoranda were of no avail, and German policy remained unchanged.[10] These disappointments notwithstanding, Lithuanian dissatisfaction with the Germans did not take the form of cessation of cooperation. During the second half of 1941, the Lithuanians served the Germans faithfully, and Lithuanians units enthusiastically participated in the murder of the Jews.

Vilna Gebietskommissariat

The *Gebietskommissar* was officially the ultimate German authority in the area under his control. The scope of his functions included:

(1) police measures;

(2) ultilization of economic factors in the district to serve the requirements of the army and the German war effort;

9 *Documents Accuse,* pp. 101, 104–105.
10 S. Neshamit, "Ben Shituf Pe'ulah le-Meri," *Dappim le-Heker ha-*

(3) ensuring the flow of essential war supplies and equipment;

(4) assistance in the operation and reactivation of inland shipping, postal services, and the railroad network;

(5) supervision of the civilian population, cooperation with the security services, and recruitment of the populace to provide necessary services;

(6) dissolution of hostile organizations still in existence.

The *Gebietskommissariat* had four departments: General, Political, Economic, Engineering.

The functions of the *Gebietskommissar* and the structure of his organization were published in "The Brown File," issued by the Ministry for the East on September 3, 1941, over one month after the civil administration actually began to operate there. "The Brown File" had a special chapter entitled "Directives on How to Deal with the Jewish Problem."[11]

The first duty of the *Gebietskommissar*, as defined in "The Brown File," as to deal with police measures (*polizeiliche Massnahmen*). *Reichsminister* Rosenberg intended thereby to emphasize that police security matters in the territories of the East fell within the orbit of the civil administration. Actually, the Senior SS and police commanders (H.S.S.P.F.), the Security Police and SD were subordinate to Himmler, in accordance with the *Führer's* order in the matter of police security in the East.

The *Gebietskommissar* of the City of Vilna was H. Hingst, who arrived there in the last days of July 1941, and took over the reins of government in the city from Military Governor Zehnpfenning. The *Gebietskommissar* of the Vilna district was H. Wulff.[12]

Sho'ah ve-ha-Mered, 2nd series, Vol. I, 1970, pp. 164–167. *Gitlerovskaya okupatsiya*, pp. 54, 74.

11 "The Brown File," YVA, 0–4/53/1–107. The "Brown File" contains detailed organizational instructions and directives of the civilian administration for the East. "The Brown File," Part II, Chapter II, 3, contains directives for the treatment of the Jews.

12 *Documents Accuse*, p. 103; Kruk, *op. cit.*, p. 29; Trial of Weiss, YVA, TR–10/381, p. 9.

The *Gebietskommissariat* had no special section dealing with Jewish affairs within its structural organization. The handling of these matters fell within the scope of responsibility of the Political Department of the *Gebietskommissariat*. A separate section for Jewish Affairs existed at the levels of the *Reichskommissariat* and the *Generalkommissariat*. The utilization of Jewish labor was the function of the *Arbeitsamt* ("Labor Office"), which dealt with all the manpower in the area, Jewish as well as non-Jewish.

F. Murer, as Hingst's *aide-de-camp* and righthand man, in addition to his defined duties as director of the Food and Agriculture Department and the Price Supervision Section, was in charge of Jewish affairs on behalf of the *Gebietskommissar*. As the official in charge of food matters, he was responsible for supplies to the ghetto and for controlling the ghetto gate, a most vital matter for the life and survival of the enclosed quarter. The official in charge of Jewish affairs for the local Lithuanian authorities in Vilna was Petras Buragas.

Major-General of Police Wysocki was the first commander of the SS and police forces in the city of Vilna and its environs, including the Lithuanian *Ordnungspolizei* and Lithuanian police companies from the early days of August 1941. SS *Obersturmbannführer* Paul Reinhard Krieg was named to succeed him as SS and police commander in Vilna and its environs in September 1941.[13]

Security Police and SD in Vilna
The Security Police and SD units in Vilna began to function on August 9, 1941, with the arrival in the city of about thirty SS men of E.K.3, who assumed responsibility for the district from E.K.9.

13 *Documents Accuse,* pp. 166, 218, 253–254, 291; *Naujoji Lietuva,* No. 43, August 24, 1941. Wysocki remained in Vilna a short time (approximately one month) and was appointed Chief of Police and SS for all of Lithuania, with his HQ in Kovno. Krieg also occupied this post in 1942.

The Security Police and SS force in Vilna was comprised of the following departments: (1) Administration (Manpower); (2) Quartermaster; (3) SD (Information and Intelligence); (4) Gestapo; (5) *Kripo* (Criminal Police). The head of the Vilna office was a SS officer with the rank of *Hauptsturmführer* or *Obersturmführer*. The various departments were headed by SS men with the rank of *Obersturmführer* or *Untersturmführer*.

The Security Police and SD unit in Vilna was commanded at first by SS officers *Obersturmführer* Schäfer and *Obersturmführer* Wolf, and later, at the beginning of September, by *Obersturmführer* Gerth, who served in that capacity until January or February 1942. From that date until October 1943, *Obersturmführer* Neugebauer was in command of the unit.

Police handling of the Jews and extermination actions were the responsibility of Department 4 (Gestapo), which consisted of the following subdivisions: "Section for Jewish Affairs"; "Section for Polish Affairs"; and "Section to Combat Partisans and Other Resistance Organizations." The officer in charge of the Jewish Affairs' Section was *Hauptsturmführer* Mayer. A special Lithuanian unit, which at various times had a force ranging from 45 to 150, was under the command of the Security Police and SD in Vilna. The officers in charge of the unit were a Lithuanian, First-lieutenant Lukoschos, and his assistant, Second-lieutenant Norvaisas. The men in this formation, who served as executioners at Ponar, were all volunteers. Department 4 had a special officer who served as liaison between it and the Lithuanian unit and was responsible for its operations. The first to hold this post was a German SS man named H. Schweinberger, who served until January 1942. Another SS man, A. Hering, served from January to June 1942 in that capacity and was succeeded by M. Weiss. The entire Lithuanian police force in Vilna was subordinate to the SS and German police command and was organized on the same lines and with the same departments and sections as the German model. The commander for the city and environs of Vilna of the Lithuanian regular police (*Ordnungspolizei*) was A. Iskauskas, a former

Lithuanian army officer. The Lithuanian security police unit in Vilna was subordinate to the Commanding Officer of the Security Police and SD; the officer in immediate charge was A. Lileikis, and the head of its Jewish Affairs Section was B. Sidlauskas, a former Second-lieutenant in the Lithuanian Army. Sidlauskas was also in charge of a special section that dealt with individual executions.[14]

The Ostland *German Administration's Policy Toward the Jews*
At Lohse's first meeting with the *Generalkommissare* and *Gebietskommissare* subordinate to them, which was held at Kovno on July 27, 1941, he delivered an oral briefing on German policy toward the Jews in the Eastern territories. The briefing included information on "the Final Solution" to the Jewish problem, which was being implemented by the Security Police on its own responsibility.

The first comprehensive published document containing directives on German policy toward the Jews in the Eastern Territories and methods of its implementation was issued by H. Lohse on August 13, 1941, at Riga, Latvia, the permanent headquarters of the *Reichskommissar* for the *Ostland* (see Appendix 1).

A covering letter signed by Lohse pointed out that these directives were not for publication, but should serve as a basis for the Notices and Orders by the Civil Administration and also for transmitting verbal instructions to the Judenrats.[15]

14 Jäger Report, p. 1; Trial of Weiss, YVA, TR–10/29, p. 8; and TR–10/381, pp. 10–12. *Gitlerovskaya okupatsiya*, p. 100; *Documents Accuse*, pp. 127, 131, 213, 216–218, 231, 289, 292, 295. A. Iskauskas was an army officer in independent Lithuania and a member of the Fascist organization known as Gelezinis Vilkas ("Iron Wolf"). A. Lileikis served in the Lithuanian security police in independent Lithuania. When Lithuania became a Soviet Republic in July 1940, Lileikis fled to Germany to return later to Lithuania during the German Army occupation.
15 "Provisional Directives," YVA, 0–18/133; *Documents Accuse*, pp. 153–159; Lohse's covering letter, YVA, 0–4/53–2, 825.

"The ultimate solution," the primary objective of German policy towards the Jews in the Eastern territories, as stated in the first passage of the document, actually meant extermination. All other anti-Jewish steps, as detailed, were only temporary until the extermination process could be accomplished. These measures were divided into two categories: those to be introduced immediately and everywhere; and those to be influenced by local conditions. The authority to introduce the latter was vested in the *Generalkommissare* who were empowered to delegate their power to *Gebietskommissare*.

Article 4 of the document outlined the anti-Jewish measures to be initiated immediately and everywhere. These included a census of the Jewish populace; the obligation to wear the yellow badge; the ban on changing dwellings, on visiting public institutions and places, and engaging in certain professions; the confiscation of Jewish property, including property held for Jews by non-Jews.

Article 5 stipulated measures relating to local conditions, particularly economic factors. These were introduced neither immediately nor simultaneously into all the *Ostland* areas. The various German authorities, functioning at different levels of the German administration in the East, more than once gave their particular interpretation to what constituted "local conditions" and the implementation of the anti-Jewish steps prescribed in this article.

Article 5 also stated that rural districts should be purged of Jews. The operational meaning of this provision was to wipe out the Jews physically in the *Ostland* townships and villages. This directive was dictated within the framework of the orders dependent upon the decision of *Generalkommissare* and/or *Gebietskommissare*, thus giving them the power to determine where and when to liquidate the Jews.[16]

16 According to this article, small ghettos such as Svencionys, Oshmyany, Sol, and Mikhailiscki were permitted to remain in eastern Lithuania and some areas of Belorussia.

Most stringent conditions were defined in these directives with regard to the means of subsistence of the Jews in the ghettos. The intent of the Germans was to subject the Jews in the ghetto to a gradual process of starvation, enfeeblement and consequently certain death. The conditions of forced labor that were imposed upon them were designed to further contribute to this process. The forced labor that the Jews had to undertake, and the payments that were made in return to the *Gebietskommissar*'s fund, turned them into means of augmenting the revenues of the local German administration.

On August 25, 1941, Lohse wrote a letter to the *Generalkommissare* in which he elaborated the contents of the provisional directives. The letter stated:

1. All telephone connections with the ghetto must be cut. Orders will be conveyed to the Judenrat over the telephone by the guard on the ghetto.
2. No postal communications to or from the ghetto will be permitted.
3. If bridges are built over the streets to connect separate parts of the ghetto, barbed-wire should be installed in such a manner as to make it impossible to jump off the bridge footwalks.
4. All cattle in Jewish possession must be confiscated.
5. The removal of timber from houses—doors, windows, floors, and rooftops—for use as fuel must be prevented.
6. The number of auxiliary police assigned to guard the ghetto must be limited to the essential minimum.
7. In all cases in which Jews are found guilty of breaches of order in any form, the strongest measures of reprisal must be taken in accordance with the directives of the *Gebietskommissare*.

The *Generalkommissar* of Lithuania, Von Renteln, transmitted the "Provisional Directives Concerning the Jews in the Territories of the *Reichskommissariat* of the *Ostland*" to the five

Gebietskommissare in Lithuania on August 26, 1941, together with Lohse's covering letter of August 25.[17]

The Provisional Lithuanian Government published a "Jewish Law"—instructions on how to deal with Jews throughout the country. The date of enactment was August 1, 1941, five days before the Provisional Government was dissolved by Von Renteln. It was signed by Lithuanian Prime Minister J. Ambrazevicius and Minister of Interior J. Slepetys. By this law, the Jews were divided into two categories: Communists and activists during the Soviet regime who were to be arrested at once and brought to trial; and all other Jews. It made wearing the yellow badge mandatory and provided for the establishment of ghettos for Jews, restrictions on their movements, limitations on the use of property, and other prohibitions. Jews who had been decorated with high Lithuanian orders or had fought for the independence of Lithuania were exempt from all restrictions set forth in the "Jewish Law." The law did not refer to the extermination of the Jews.[18] In fact, it had no practical significance at all, as the German administration did not recognize the Provisional Lithuanian Government and German policy towards the Jews was directed towards extermination.

Enactment of Anti-Jewish Policy in Lithuania
Prior to the issuance of the provisional directives on August 13, 1941, by Lohse and the transmission of these orders to *Gebietskommissar* Hingst on August 26, the civil administration in Vilna began to operate and invoke its anti-Jewish policy. The first such order enacted by Hingst was published on August 2, 1941:

Regulation No. 1
1. All Jews, irrespective of sex, residing in Vilna must wear a yellow Star of David on the left side of their

17 YVA, 0–18/202, Nuremberg Document, PS–3659.
18 *Documents Accuse*, pp. 144–146.

chests and on their backs for purposes of identification.

2. The Jewish population is forbidden to use sidewalks. Jews must use only the right hand verges of roadways and walk in single file.
3. The Jewish population is forbidden to use promenades and to enter public parks and also forbidden is the use of beaches.
4. The Jewish population is forbidden the use of all means of public transportation, such as taxis, carriages, buses, shipping, and similar conveyances. The owners and managers of public transport must display in a clearly visible place on their conveyances a sign with the inscription "For non-Jews only."
5. Transgressors are liable to severe punishment.
6. This regulation is effective immediately.

Gebietskommissar of Vilna, Hingst
2 August 1941

Until the order was published, every Jew in Vilna from age ten upward had worn a white band on his sleeves as an identifying mark. During the first few days of August, Hingst issued an order prohibiting Jews from walking in sixteen main thoroughfares in the city. They were permitted only to cross these streets, while those who lived there were allowed to go to the nearest street-corner and from there take a side-street. The daily *Naujoji Lietuva, No.* 35, for August 7, published a report to the effect that the governor of the city had imposed fines of 1,000 to 15,000 rubles on eighty-six Jews who had not worn the yellow badges or had trespassed.[19]

On August 6, Mürer summoned representatives of the Judenrat. The three members who went to the meeting were S. Petukhovski, E. Kruk, and A. Zajdsznur. Murer did not receive them in the offices of the *Gebietskommissariat,* but in a nearby

19 *Ibid.,* pp. 143–144, 146–147; Moreshet Archives, D. 1. 362.

alley; he told them that by the next day, August 7, the Jews were to hand over to him five million rubles (10 rubles = 1 Reichsmark). Murer ordered that by 9 o'clock the following morning, the members of the Judenrat appear before him with two million rubles, with the remainder to be brought during the course of the day. If the two million rubles were not delivered by the appointed time, all other Judenrat members would have to appear before him at 10 o'clock in order to receive the bodies of their colleagues who had come without the money. The deputation returned to the Judenrat and told the others of Murer's demand. H. Kruk describes the scene in his diary:

> When the deputation returned to the Judenrat and told them of the demand, a feeling of panic seized them. It was permitted to be on the streets only until 6 o'clock in the evening. Many streets were entirely closed to the Jews. How would it be possible to collect the amount by the morning? Old Wygodzki raised his voice and shouted that there was no time to despair. They must begin to collect.

The report about the fine was quickly spread among the Jews of the city. Subcommittees representing streets and suburbs were spontaneously organized and began to collect money, gold, and valuable articles. By 6 o'clock in the evening 667,000 rubles, one pound of gold, watches, and diamonds had been collected. Many Jews believed that by giving the amounts demanded they would save their lives. There were others who hoped that the tribute would help in regard to the abductees, about whom no news had been received.

The three Judenrat members who had been to see Murer on the previous day took the money and objects of value and appeared before him at 9 o'clock on the morning of August 7. Murer sent them down to a cellar, counted the money, and asked where the rest of it was. The Judenrat members explained it was still being collected. Murer ordered Zajdsznur to go back and tell the Judenrat that the other members must appear before him and bring the entire amount. Two others in the deputation were detained.

All the Judenrat members came to Murer. Dr. Wygodzki introduced himself and asked for a ten-day extension to raise the money, explaining the difficulties involved. Murer detained three Judenrat members and warned that their fate would be identical to that of the other two if the amount demanded was not forthcoming. When he had finished speaking, he took the suitcase of money and valuables and left. The Judenrat members decided to send three representatives to *Gebietskommissar* Hingst, in order to try to rescue their detained associates. Murer met the trio outside the *Gebietskommissar's* office, and this time he was more moderate in his demands. He did not insist that all the money be handed over that day, but told them that they should continue to collect it for several more days and deposit the proceeds into the bank daily. The detained members of the Judenrat were released at 1 o'clock that afternoon. The collection continued for several days, and altogether yielded 1,490,000 rubles, 33 pounds of gold, and 189 watches. No receipts were given for the valuables.[20]

The imposition of the tribute on the Jews, the character and form of its assessment, was unique to Vilna and had no parallel elsewhere in Lithuania. In Kovno, four days after the ghetto was established, German soldiers and Lithuanian policemen proceeded from house to house demanding that Jewish residents relinquish all their money, gold, valuables, and expensive clothing, especially furs. This operation lasted about two weeks, until every house in the ghetto had been canvassed by the Germans.

While the Jews were being ghettoized in Shavli, on August 15, a special Lithuanian committee combed their belongings

---

20 Kruk, *op. cit.*, pp. 30–31; Korczak, *op. cit.*, p. 13; Balberyszski, *op. cit.*, pp. 136–137. See also *Documents Accuse*, pp. 218–219 for evidence of Murer on the "Contribution," according to which Hingst and SS General Wysocki assigned him the task of collecting money.

for money and valuables. Valuables were confiscated by the committee during the examination.[21]

The contribution in Vilna was not the sequestration of Jewish property in the spirit of the "Provisional Directive" and was dissimilar to what happened in Kovno and Shavli. It seems that this was a private operation by *Gebietskommissare* Hingst and Murer, which was intended to channel a substantial part of the money and valuables into their own pockets. The manner in which it was extorted, the furtive meeting-places, and the small number of German administration personnel deployed (only Murer in effect) all contributed to the suspicion that Hingst and Mürer benefitted personally from this tribute.

Order No. 2, issued by Hingst on August 12, established rules concerning market-places. Market hours for Jews were limited to 10 A.M. to 12 noon daily, namely, the two last hours of trading, after which most of the goods available had already been sold. Jews were permitted to buy in shops from 4 to 6 P.M.[22]

On August 24, Dr. Wygodzki, the leader of Vilna Jewry for twenty years, was arrested. He was taken to prison although he was seriously ill. An attempt was made to secure his release through the local Lithuanian administration, but to no avail. Dr. Wygodzki could not survive long in the harsh prison conditions, and a few days later he passed away at the age of eighty-six. During the brief period of his life under Nazi rule, the Judenrat turned to him for counsel on every important question. When the first Judenrat was established, and when the tribute was imposed, in his stance and moral force he shined above the others. His death and his fight to defend Jewish honor under the Nazi scourge served as a symbol.

Dr. Wygodzki's death was a severe blow to the Jews of Vilna. They did not have another leader of his stature, and his person-

---

21 L. Garfunkel, *Kovnah ha-Yehudit be-Hurbanah*, Jerusalem, 1959, pp. 58, 62; E. Yerushalmi, *Pinkas Shavli*, Jerusalem, 1958, p. 36.
22 A photograph of this order is contained in Kruk, *op. cit.*, p. 33.

ality and influence had guided them during a difficult period. His passing was the beginning of the end of the Jewish leadership that had represented the Jewish public of Vilna for many years. A new leadership, centered around the Judenrat, arose in its wake, to fill the void that had been created.

No major actions against the Jews took place in Vilna during the month of August. The absence of a Security Police and SD unit in the city until August 9, removed an element that could have organized and carried out the massacres. A summation report of the activities of E.K.3 from the beginning of the war until December 1, 1941, stated that between August 12—three days after the E.K.3 unit assumed responsibility over Vilna— and September 1, the detachment of E.K.3 killed 425 Jews, 19 Jewish women, 8 Communists, and 9 Communist women, a total of 461 persons.[23]

During this period of comparative relaxation in August, the Jews of Vilna reacted to the mass abductions of July by seeking places of work that entitled employees to safe-conduct passes. It became an accepted theory that working for Germans or Lithuanians, which provided a worker with such a pass, endowed him and his family with security from detention and sudden kidnappings and from being deported to unknown destinations.

Hermann Kruk wrote on August 26: "I am going to work!... Everyone today is saying *Mazal Tov* to me ... Thousands of people have worked ... All my relatives and friends advise me to give up hiding. I have decided that tomorrow I shall go to serve the Germans by forced labor."

The following day he wrote: "At last my first day of labor has passed by. I carried bricks at a running pace, but the main thing was that I walked freely in the streets for the first time — I went with a pass ... "

The work arrangements were organized through the Judenrat, which established a special department for that purpose. Early

23 *Documents Accuse,* p. 237.

every morning thousands of Jews congregated outside the Judenrat offices and from there groups set out for the work sites.
Some Jews arranged to work for Germans and Lithuanians
privately and not through the Judenrat. Working gave the Jews
the two things they sought—the illusion of safety, and the
possibility to obtain food through contact with the non-Jewish
population at the work-places or en route to and from them.

The Jews of Vilna still labored under the same illusion concerning the thousands of males who had been carried off and
massacred and were ignorant of the bitter fate that awaited
them in the very near future.

The conclusion that the Jews reached through their short experience was that working for the Germans and thus procuring
passes ensured them comparative safety from kidnapping and
deportation to unknown destinations. Both private and collective
initiatives, therefore, were directed towards obtaining these
work-passes. It was a spontaneous reaction, paralleling the demands of the German and Lithuanian establishments for manpower to carry out their urgent needs.

Chapter 6

EXTERMINATION OPERATIONS AND THE
CREATION OF THE GHETTO
(August 31–September 12, 1941)

"The Great Provocation"

During the closing days of August 1941, the *Gebietskommissar* of Vilna, Hingst, received "Provisional Directives" from Lohse. These "Directives" inaugurated the second and principal wave of mass destruction of Vilna Jewry—the phase during which the major part of the Jewish community was murdered.

The first action in this wave of extermination was the choice of a site on which to erect the ghetto. Murer stated at his post-war trial:

> The *Generalkommissar* of Lithuania, Von Renteln, in- structed the *Gebietskommissar*, Hingst, to erect a ghetto in the city. As I was his personal adjutant, I was ordered by him to organize the ghetto. Pursuant to these instruc- tions, I chose the place for the ghetto together with the mayor of Vilna, Dabulevicius.[1]

The place chosen for the ghetto was the old Jewish quarter in the center of the city, which was inhabited by thousands of Jewish residents. The choice coincided with Lohse's stipulation in his "Provisional Directives," viz., that the Jews be concen- trated in the cities or suburbs of large cities that already had a large Jewish population. This order was meant to ensure that

1 *Documents Accuse,* p. 219.

the number of non-Jews to be shifted from the area designated as a ghetto would be minimal. On the other hand, the "Directive" facilitated the task of the executors in that fewer Jews would have to be relocated.

These two factors were taken into consideration in choosing and establishing the ghetto sites in Kovno and Shavli. The ghetto area at Kovno was even reduced when pressure was exerted by local non-Jewish inhabitants who did not wish to evacuate their dwellings.[2]

Variegated interpretations were given in Vilna as to the instructions for selecting a ghetto site. Although there was indeed an overwhelming majority of Jewish residents there before the establishment of the ghetto, the entire quarter was cleared of thousands of Jewish residents who were sent to Ponar and murdered. The Jews dubbed this action "the Great Provocation."

On Sunday afternoon, August 31, 1941, at 2 o'clock, two Lithuanians in civilian attire entered a house at the corner of Szklanna (Stiklu) and Wielka streets from where there was a clear view of the square in the vicinity of a movie house. Some German soldiers were standing near the cinema when the two Lithuanians fired a volley of shots and ran from the house, shouting that the Jews had fired. These Lithuanians, together with the German soldiers standing outside, broke into the apartments from which the shooting had come, hauled out two Jews, accused them of having fired at the German soldiers, beat them, and shot them on the spot.[3] This provocative act triggered the great purge of the entire zone designated to be the ghetto. On September 1, a notice was published by Hingst, the Vilna *Gebietskommissar:*

NOTICE: Yesterday, Sunday afternoon, shots were directed from an ambush at German soldiers in Vilna. Two of these cowardly bandits were identified—they were Jews. The attackers paid with their lives for their

2 Garfunkel, *op. cit.,* pp. 42–45; Yerushalmi, *op. cit.,* pp. 34, 37.
3 Kruk, *op. cit.,* pp. 42–43; Balberyszski, *op. cit.,* p. 159.

act—they were shot on the spot. To avoid such hostile acts in the future, new and severe deterrent measures were taken. The responsibility lies with the entire Jewish community.

All Jews, men and women, are forbidden to leave their homes from today at 3 o'clock in the afternoon until 10 o'clock in the morning. Exceptions will be made only for those Jews and Jewesses who have valid work-passes. This order is for the security of the population and to protect the lives of the inhabitants. It is the duty of every honest citizen to cooperate in preserving quiet and order.

Vilna, September 1, 1941

> *Gebietskommissar* of the City
> of Vilna, Hingst [4]

The eviction of the Jews from the old Jewish quarter and their incarceration in Lukiszki took place between August 31 and September 2. During the night of August 31/September 1, the Jewish occupants of houses in the area and also on Szklanna, Zydowska and Niemiecka streets (one side only) were removed. The following night, September 1/2, the Jews residing in Niemiecka (second side), Ozmianska, Jatkowa, Lidska, Rudnicka and Szpitalna streets were arrested and taken to Lukiszki. They were obliged to remit the keys to their apartments to the superintendants, who were non-Jews.

The Lithuanian guards at Lukiszki confiscated the Jews' money and valuables from their persons. They were kept in cells and in the open courtyard without food, water, or sanitary provisions. Several Jews were released from the prison by German soldiers who were given money and valuable articles by Jews requesting intervention on behalf of their relatives.[5]

On September 1-3 the Jews in Lukiszki were taken to Ponar— the men on foot and the women with children in motor-vehicles—and were massacred. The men were shot first, then the

---

4 Dworzecki, *op. cit.,* p. 38, photocopy of the announcement.
5 Balberyszski, *op. cit.,* pp. 161–162; Kruk, *op. cit.,* pp. 42, 48, 52, 57.

women and children. The executions were carried out in groups of ten persons, who were lined up at the edge of the pits. The shooting squads were Lithuanian *Ypatingi* commanded by a German. Six Jewish women who were only slightly wounded scrambled out of the pits during the night and made their way to Vilna during September 3–4.[6]

A German report stated that on September 2, 3,700 Jews were executed in Vilna as a reprisal for Jewish shooting of German soldiers. The report also specified that this number was composed of 864 males, 2,019 females, and 817 children. The large disparity between the number of females and males stems from the fact that many of the men were at work when their wives and children were seized.[7] Moreover, some 5,000 men had been seized in the *Aktionen* during July, which created a plurality of females in the Jewish community.

The Judenrat was liquidated on September 2, during the course of "the Great Provocation," as its offices were located in the area in which the *Aktion* was carried out. On September 1 the Judenrat received an order from *Zugwachtmeister* Schweinberger to place ten carts and horses at the disposal of the *Ypatingi* from 9 o'clock the next morning. The Jews had neither carts nor horses, as they had been confiscated previously. Nevertheless, the Judenrat members succeeded in hiring five carts and horses from non-Jews and they reported to the *Ypatingi* offices at 10 A.M. on September 2, one hour later than specified in the order.

Schweinberger and three *Ypatingi* appeared at the Judenrat offices at 11 o'clock. Schweinberger ordered that all twenty-two Jews present in the office line up, and he examined their papers. Sixteen—ten of them Judenrat members—were taken to Lukiszki and then to Ponar; among them was S. Trotzki, the

6 *Ibid.*, pp. 51–54; Dworzecki, *op. cit.*, p. 39.
7 Kruk, *op. cit.*, pp. 42, 44, 53; Korczak, *op. cit.*, p. 31, gives the figure of 5,000 Jews deported and murdered; Rindziunski's testimony, p. 27; Dworzecki, *op. cit.*, p. 39, gives the figure of 10,000 Jews murdered; Jäger Report, p. 5.

chairman. The six others were employees of the Judenrat or Jews who had come to transact business. Of the six released, four were Judenrat members — A. Fried, the vice-chairman; A. Zajdsznur; G. Jaszunski; and J. Fishman. The Judenrat offices were closed and sealed.[8]

The Judenrat had clearly not been liquidated because of its inability to allocate the requisite number of carts and horses for the *Ypatingi*. The real reason was that the German administration no longer needed their cooperation in the future operations it planned for the removal of Jews to the ghetto. The liquidation of the Judenrat in this summary fashion was one of the measures taken by the Germans to instill terror among the Jews and part of the extermination policy to expunge the Jewish leadership. It may well be that the location of the Judenrat's headquarters—in the area purged of Jews during the course of "the Great Provocation"—contributed to the decision to liquidate it. The German administration did not want to maintain premises in a *judenrein* locality, which would have invited continuing Jewish movement within it. The authorities were interested, moreover, in maintaining secrecy around their preparations to establish the ghetto in an area emptied of its inhabitants, and a Jewish institution there would have infringed upon that secrecy.

The liquidation of the Judenrat created a situation in which the Jewish community of Vilna was left leaderless, devoid of a representative body recognized by the authorities, or any institutionalized means of communication between Germans and Jews.

The Jews of Vilna were in a state of fear and uncertainty as to what awaited them during those days. No information was available as to the fate of the thousands of Jews who had been seized during "the Great Provocation." Rumors spread in the city concerning the intention to set up a ghetto and its probable location.

8 Kruk, *op. cit.*, pp. 46, 48–49. The Judenrat members sent to Ponar were S. Trotzki, J. Shabad, N. Sofer, L. Katznelson, P. Konn, A. Zalkind, B. Parnass, J. Shkolnitzki, S. Petukhovski, and Katz.

Apart from the absence of news on the situation and the waves of rumors, there were urgent problems requiring immediate solution. The offices of the *Chevra Kadisha* ("Burial Society") had been closed down, as they had occupied the same premises as the Judenrat. People who had died during those days were not interred. The uncertain position of the Jews and the burial problem demanded initiative and action. The Judenrat members who had escaped arrest met and decided to continue to act. They formed a deputation to call on the person in charge of Jewish affairs at the Vilna municipality, P. Buragas. They saw him several times on September 2 and 3, urging him to clarify the situation, inquiring about the possibility of reestablishing the Judenrat, and asking for permission to activate the *Chevra Kadisha.* Buragas replied that the position of the Jews and their future was unclear and that the authorities did not recognize any Jewish representation. He promised to get permission for the resumption of the activities of the *Chevra Kadisha,* and the next day, September 4, permission was given to reopen the Jewish cemetery and resume interments.

The answers proferred by Buragas were not sufficient for the Jews. On Thursday, September 4, they called on the Lithuanian mayor, K. Dabulevicius, to whom they posed questions on the Jewish position in the city, asking for clarification of the rumors concerning the formation of a ghetto, and urging the reinstatement of the Judenrat. The mayor replied that all that had occurred in Vilna during the previous days had been instigated by German initiative and the Lithuanians bore no guilt by complicity. He also said that a ghetto would be established and the Judenrat reconstituted, but he did not indicate when this would take place.[9]

The Jewish delegations did not seek out the German administration, but rather the Lithuanian authorities, for several reasons. During this initial phase of German civil administration, no ties had yet been established between the Jewish representation and

9 Balberyszski, *op. cit.,* p. 163; Kruk, *op. cit.,* pp. 57–58.

the Germans who had been in Vilna only about one month. On the other hand, communication did exist with the Lithuanian authorities who had been there longer. At this time the Jews still believed that the Lithuanian authorities exercised some influence over their fate. The fact that the *Ypatingi* had engaged in kidnapping operations and in seizing Jews from their homes during "the Great Provocation" and that Lithuanians were staffing the Lukiszki prison created the impression that the Lithuanians were a powerful force, capable of exerting influence. Actually, the local Lithuanian administration in Vilna had no say whatsoever in formulating policy pertaining to the fate of the Jews. It was only a factor used to assist in enforcing that policy.

The approach made by the Jewish delegation to the Lithuanian mayor concerning the reconstitution of the Judenrat underscored the fact that the Jews perceived the need for a body to represent them with the administration.

"The Great Provocation" marked the inception of the mass massacre of Vilna Jewry. In the previous *Aktionen* implemented by the Einsatzgruppen in July, only males were taken, and consideration was given to holders of work-permits; in "the Great Provocation" no detainees were freed because of work-permits. "The Great Provocation," which began a few days after Lohse's "Provisional Directives" were received in Vilna, marked the end of the selective murder of males and the beginning of general massacre.

Yet "the Great Provocation" failed to arouse Vilna Jewry to the looming menace of total extermination, and before they could comprehend its full significance, they were overwhelmed by further *Aktionen*. The labelling of the initial operation as a "retributive act" for the shooting of German soldiers was apparently intended to stamp it with the character of a one-time sortie limited to a specific event. Cunning German deception succeeded once again.

Vilna Jews to the Ghetto—September 6, 1941

During September 3–5, 1941, the German administration engaged in preparing the area cleared of Jews during "the Great Provocation" for the establishment of two ghettos. Niemiecka Street would separate them. The street itself was outside the limits of both ghettos and served as a barrier between them. Each ghetto was enclosed by a wooden fence, and the entrances of houses facing the outside were blocked off.

Ghetto No. 1, the larger of the two, was established south and west of Niemiecka Street, and encompassed Straszuna, Oszmianska, Jatkowa, Rudnicka, and Szpitalna streets. Ghetto No. 2 was north and east of Niemiecka Street, and incorporated Zydowska, Szklanna and Kliaczko streets. Each ghetto had just one gate for entry and exit. The gate of Ghetto No. 1 was located in the southern section, in Rudnicka Street; whereas in Ghetto No. 2, it was in the northern part, in Gaona Street. The gates were placed at opposite ends, thus eliminating any possible encounter between those entering and leaving each of the ghettos.

Rumors began to circulate in the city on Friday, September 5, that the immurement of the Jews in the ghetto was imminent, but no official announcement was made. Contradictory reports circulated as to its probable site. A notice was published to the effect that all non-Jewish owners of carts and horses must appear the next day at 5 A.M. in the timber market. This notice accentuated Jewish fears of imminent danger. Some of the Christians who dwelt in houses adjacent to Jewish tenants painted crosses on their doors to distinguish them from their neighbors. The night before September 6, 1941, was one of vigil for the Jews of Vilna.[10]

Y. Rudashevski wrote in his diary:

> The night between September 5–6, the sleepless night of a bright September day, a night of people staying awake,

10 *Ibid.*, p. 59; L. Epstein, "Geto Vilna," Diary (Yiddish) in: YVA, JM–2822, p. 15; Dworzecki, pp. 44–45, 47; Korczak, *op. cit.*, p. 18.

despondent, resembling shadows sitting with their bundles in anguished expectancy and helplessness. Tomorrow we will be led into the ghetto.[11]

The task of expelling the Jews from their homes was assigned to the Lithuanian municipal police, whose Commanding Officer was A. Iskauskas. Several Lithuanian units of police-guard regiments were added to his command.[12] At dawn on September 6, 1941, groups of policemen fanned out into the streets in which Jews lived, in the places designated as assembly points, and the site of the ghetto. The Jews were forbidden to leave their houses or go to work. Although no official notice was published, it was evident to all that ghettoization had begun. Jews found at work were forced to return home, and those who had hidden themselves for fear of an *Aktion* came out of hiding to join the others.[13]

Ghettoization was implemented in strict accordance with a detailed schedule prepared by the German administration in the city. Vilna was divided into three zones: the first, from which Jews were led into Ghetto No. 1; the second, into Ghetto No. 2; and the third, from which they were driven to Lukiszki prison and then to Ponar. It was arbitrarily decided that Jews residing south and west of Ghetto No. 1 would be sent there. Most of Vilna's Jews dwelt in this quarter. The area from which Jews were sent to Ghetto No. 2 lay north and east of the latter. And the Jews in the northwestern area of the city were sent to Lukiszki prison.

11 Y. Rudashevski, *The Diary of the Vilna Ghetto*, Tel Aviv, 1973, p. 31.
12 *Documents Accuse*, pp. 217–218, 228. Part of these Lithuanian units were organized as police units under the command of the German police. The report of the German Police Chief in Vilna, of October 24, 1941, refers to five Lithuanian police units functioning in Vilna, the total strength of which was 2,048 soldiers and officers.
13 Balberyszski, *op. cit.*, p. 167; Epstein's diary, p. 15; Kruk, *op. cit.*, p. 62.

A report submitted on September 9, 1941, by the officer in charge of the ghettoization, the Lithuanian Police Commander of Vilna, Iskauskas, stated:

> The Ghetto Operation in Vilna began at 6 A.M. on September 6, 1941. The *Aktion* was carried out in accordance with a prepared plan, whereby the police districts of the city were divided into quarters and sub-quarters. Guards were posted along all roads out of the city to prevent Jews from fleeing. Simultaneous *Aktionen* began in all police districts from the outer perimeters, and gradually closed the ring in the direction of the city center.
>
> The operation was executed by police and soldiers from guard units. The police evicted the Jews from the houses, and the soldiers herded them into the places chosen for their future residence. Invalids were temporarily left in their dwellings, and the City Council received notification to this effect.[14]

The expelled were permitted to take with them only those belongings that they could carry on their person. They were given no means of transport and had to make do with the most essential articles. They packed in such a way that every one could be independent, each carrying what was most essential. The people took their clothing, a little food, a pillow and blanket, and, in addition, dressed in as many layers of clothing as possible.

They were forced to leave behind most of their personal belongings, household utensils, and all their furniture. Some of these possessions were put into storage—in cellars, attics and other hiding-places—in the hours during which they awaited their expulsion. Many goods were turned over to Christian neighbors, especially janitors. Some of the Christian neighbors exploited the Jews' plight in order to amass goods, and stole or extorted larger amounts against various promises, but there

14 *Documents Accuse*, pp. 217–218.

were also those who displayed real compassion and aided in every way possible in the packing and secreting of goods and belongings.[15]

The eviction of the Jews from their homes was supervised by squads of two to three policemen. They went from house to house giving the tenants fifteen to thirty minutes to assemble in the courtyards or in front of the buildings with their chattels. They were then marched to assembly points, to which people from nearby places had already been brought. These central points were the marketplace in Nowogrod (Naugarduko) and Wilkomierska (Ukmerges) streets; and from there, in huge contingents of hundreds and even thousands, they proceeded to one of the ghettos or Lukiszki along prearranged routes.

The march to the ghetto was very difficult. It was a hot day; people wore many layers of clothing and were weighted down with bundles, and the Lithuanian policemen continuously urged them on, allowing them no respite. The young Rudashevski described the trek in these terms:

> We dragged along, a group of Jews with parcels. The street was full of Jews with parcels ... People walked along harnessed to bundles they dragged after them on the road. People fell, packages broke open. Before me a woman was bowed under a bundle from which rice trickled endlessly like a necklace on to the roadway. I walked laden down, angry. The Lithuanians egged us on, not allowing us to pause ... I did not see the streets in front of me, the passersby. I only felt a terrible fatigue; I felt a storm of indignation and pain burning within me.[16]

The way was particularly difficult for Jews who lived far from the ghetto and who had to walk miles under these conditions. Thousands of non-Jews lined the streets along which the Jews

15 Balberyszski, *op. cit.*, pp. 167, 169, 171; Kruk, *op. cit.*, p. 62; Rudashevski, *op. cit.*, p. 32.
16 *Ibid.*, p. 32.

were led to the ghetto. There were some Poles among them who showed sympathy for the Jews. Others chortled with joy and joked aloud, uttering such cries as: "You wanted the Bolsheviks—you have the ghetto," or "You wanted Palestine—now you're off to the ghetto." There were even those who snatched parcels from the Jews. But most stood by indifferently, looking on silently. Among the spectators were German soldiers photographing the Jews and also the Lithuanians who escorted them to the ghetto.[17]

There were several control points near the two ghettos at which the influx of people was checked and from which they were directed to various entrances. These points were manned by SD and Security Police personnel.

Admittance into the ghettos was permissible only through the gates and the gaps in the fences that had been left for that purpose. People filed into Ghetto No. 2 from two directions: from the north through the gate in Gaona Street, and from the southwest through a gap in Zydowska Street. Admission into Ghetto No. 1 was possible from three entrances: from the west, from Straszuna and Lidska (Lydos) streets; from the south, through the gate on Rudnicka Street; and from the north, through Mikolaja Lane. There was considerable congestion at each entrance.

The entire ghettoization and transports to Lukiszki were implemented on the Sabbath, September 6, and through the ensuing night. The dense congestion around the gap in the wall on Straszuna Street made it necessary to divert part of the crowd streaming from various directions into Lidska Street. It may well be that, during the afternoon hours, those responsible for the operations realized that the ghetto was too small to accommodate all those expelled according to plan, or that the number of Jews entering Ghetto No. 1 was larger than expected, and it was decided to divert part of the crowd (about 2,000) into

17 Kruk, *op. cit.*, pp. 66–67, 74; Dworzecki, *op. cit.*, p. 48; Balberyszski, *op. cit.*, p. 174.

Lidska Street and to send them to Lukiszki. Many of those driven in the direction of Ghetto No. 1 during the night of September 6/7 and who reached Novogrod Street (near the ghetto) were not admitted, but taken directly to Lukiszki.

The night march to Lukiszki was accompanied by terrifying scenes. One of the women among them wrote:

> The march to Lukiszki was terrible. Thousands of Jews were rushed along like sheep, and beaten with rubber truncheons in the darkness of night ... The elderly stumbled and fell, and died; children lost their mothers, and parents lost their children. Everyone was wailing, and their cries filled the dark. We were taken to prison. Hundreds of Germans and Lithuanians opened the gate for us and, in doing so, beat the children, fathers, and mothers. Many of them jeered at us and promised us death.[18]

The ghetto operation ended in the morning hours of September 7. The report by Iskauskas, the Lithuanian police commander, stated: "... The operation ended in Police Precinct 1 at 9 P.M. on September 6; Precinct No. 2 at 11 P.M. that evening; Precinct 3, at 5 A.M. on September 7; Precinct 4, at 8 P.M. on September 6; Precinct 5, at 8 P.M.; Precinct 6, at 10 P.M.; Precinct 7, at 7 P.M."[19]

During Sunday, September 7, the transfer of groups of Jewish invalids who had been left overnight in their homes continued. Carts were used to convey the old and sick. The *Aktion* was terminated on Sunday evening, and the victims were locked into the two ghettos and Lukiszki. Ghetto No. 1 contained 29–30,000 Jews; Ghetto No. 2, 9–10,000; and about 6,000 were incarcerated in Lukiszki.[20]

18 Klibanski, *op. cit.,* p. 284.
19 *Documents Accuse,* p. 218.
20 This data is based on Kruk, *op. cit.,* pp. 71, 259. Murer testified in a trial before a Soviet court (*Documents Accuse,* p. 219), that 40–42,000 Jews were placed in the two ghettos. *Gitlerovskaya okupatsiya,* p. 155, specified the number of people murdered in the *Aktion* as 8,000.

Lukiszki prison served, as in previous *Aktionen,* as the intermediate stop to Ponar. It absorbed thousands of Jews who had been evicted, and preparations and arrangements were made there for sending them to Ponar. These preparations included appropriation of money and valuables found on the persons of the victims; return to the ghetto of workers and skilled hands required by the Germans; and separation, according to sex and age, and dispatch (in groups) to Ponar.

The prison did not have sufficient space for such a large number of people, and they were kept in cells and in the courtyard in great congestion. Rooms of approximately 9–12 yards had some 800 people crowded into them. The heat was intense, and the few existing windows were partly closed over with tin sheets. Each room had two toilet cubicles and one water faucet. Food was not distributed, and people could only eat the provisions they had brought with them. There was no room to sit or lie down. The situation of the people outdoors was little better. The crowding was oppressive, and people sat or lay on the ground. SS men accompanied by Lithuanians went through the rooms and yards and ordered the Jews to hand over their possessions, threatening to shoot anyone who refused to do so. Empty buckets were positioned to receive the money.[21]

During the afternoon of September 7, the prison authorities announced that all doctors, engineers, and skilled workers were required to register. No reason was given, but according to rumors, these people were to be released and sent to the ghetto. On the other hand, there were also rumors that the registered professionals would be sent to work in the front-line areas and that only the remainder would be transported to the ghetto. The registration continued throughout the day and extended for several hours into the evening. Those who were registered had to show documents testifying to their occupations.

---

21 Testimony of S. Bronowski, YVA, 0–3/2335, p. 2; Klibanski, *op. cit.,* p. 284; Rindziunski's testimony, pp. 30–31.

The next morning, September 8, SS men passed through the cells and yards and called names from prepared lists. These persons were gathered together and told they would be removed from Lukiszki, and they were in fact escorted by Lithuanians to Ghetto No. 1. In the morning hours of September 9, a second group of skilled workers was removed from the prison, together with their families, and brought to Ghetto No. 2. Altogether some 200 Jews were released from prison during those two days. Some of them were freed due to the enterprising activity of Jews who worked in German factories and units and had good contacts with their employers; they succeeded in persuading or bribing some of the Germans to release their relatives and friends.[22]

The transfer to Ponar and the executions of those held in the prison took place on Wednesday and Thursday, September 10–11. The Vilna teacher Sima Katz, who was taken to Ponar and escaped, related:

> ...We were imprisoned there until Thursday... At 2 A.M. the courtyard of the prison was suddenly flooded with lights. We were loaded onto trucks, each of which had 50–60 people and several Lithuanians armed with rifles. We were thus driven in the direction of Ponar. We reached a wooded spot...lay down, tired...Not far away we heard volleys of rifles fire... The Lithuanians began marshalling us into groups of ten, and led the tens into the hillocks from which the firing was heard. Suddenly it became clear to us what this was all about. The women began pleading with the Lithuanians...to no avail...when their turn came, they rose up, quiet and despairing, without protests or pleas...Thus family after family proceeded on their final journey...Our turn came at about 5:30. I set my face for the walk, my daughters

22 Bronowski's testimony, pp. 2–3; Rindziunski's testimony, pp. 32-36, 38; Dworzecki, op. cit., p. 56.

with me...we were lined up and I felt how my elder daughter slipped out of my hand...[23]

The summation report of Einsatzkommando 3 of December 1, 1941, stated: "On 12 September, 993 Jewish males, 1,670 Jewish women, and 771 Jewish children, a total of 3,334, were liquidated in Vilna."[24]

The plan and execution of the ghettoization of Vilna Jews differed considerably from what happened in the other two ghettos in Lithuania—Kovno and Shavli. In these two cities the Jews who lived in the area appointed to be the ghetto remained in their places of residence, and the Jews from other parts of the respective cities were sent there. The German and Lithuanian officials in Kovno announced to the Jewish representatives on July 8, 1941, their decision to establish a Jewish ghetto. The transfer to the enclosed area took place between July 15 and August 15, and was implemented in accordance with a plan drawn up jointly by the Lithuanian municipality and a Jewish committee appointed by the Germans for that purpose. The Jews were provided with carts in which to convey their belongings and were escorted by Lithuanian squads. The transfer to the ghetto at Shavli took two weeks, from August 15 to the beginning of September, and proceeded in an organized fashion and with the help of planning committees in which Jewish observers were also included. Judenrat representatives directed the people to their new dwellings inside the ghetto.[25]

In Vilna, the Jews were dragged out of the area designated as the ghetto and put to death in Ponar during "the Great Provocation." The transfers to the ghetto took only twenty-four hours and were carried out without any prior notice and in the absence of any Jewish representatives. About 46–48,000 Jews were uprooted during the mass expulsions and without any knowledge of what was to happen; 6,000 Jews were sent to Lu-

23 Korczak, *op. cit.*, pp. 62–63.
24 Jäger Report, p. 6.
25 Garfunkel, *op. cit.*, pp. 38–50; Yerushalmi, *op. cit.*, pp. 35–37.

kiszki, and later met their deaths in Ponar. The German plan in Vilna, which comprised the ghetto immurements and the murder actions, had no place for Jewish representatives, and therefore the Judenrat was also liquidated.

The vast discrepancies among the methods of implementation in the three places in which ghettos were established in the area of the *Generalkommissariat* of Lithuania underscores the wide powers vested in the local elements of each *Gebietskommissariat*. The practical interpretation of the general directive to establish a ghetto in each place was left to the *Gebietskommissariat*, the Security Police, and SD detachments there. It was the administration in each *Gebietskommissariat* that determined the dimensions of the ghetto, the time and the conditions of the transfers, what property the Jews would be permitted to take with them, and whether liquidation actions would be conducted simultaneously to the removals.

Mixed Marriages, Mischlinges and Converts

Mixed couples, children of mixed marriages, and converts constituted a very small and marginal group among the Jews in Vilna. A group of converts was immured in the ghetto. R. Korczak, in her description of the ghettoization, writes:

> They stood against the grey mass ... making themselves distinctive, as if to demonstrate their difference, their lack of affinity with the mass, sometimes even smiling contemptuously with a feeling of superiority ... this group which stood out isolated, carrying its pride and contempt for the mass, seemed more miserable than all the other pitiful masses ... [26]

Christian spouses wedded to Jews were permitted to join their Jewish mates in the ghetto and thus share in the fate of the Jews. On September 10, 1941, four days after the Jews of Vilna were forced into the ghetto, Franz Mürer wrote to Major Stützel,

26 Korczak, *op. cit.*, p. 23.

Senior Commander of the SS and Police in Vilna, who was also in charge of the Lithuanian police:

> In accordance with the directives of the *Reichskommissar* dated August 18, 1941, clause 1-b states that surveillance should be imposed on non-Jewish spouses who do not wish to share the fate of their Jewish partners...As I have begun receiving reports referring to non-Jewish spouses, I would ask you to instruct the Lithuanian police to find these people and keep them under surveillance. Moreover I ask you to send me a list of the persons so identified.[27]

On October 29, 1941, the *Gebietskommissar* of Vilna published a notice which stated *inter alia* that the public must report all Jews and half-Jews living outside the ghetto and that severe penalties would be incurred by anyone concealing Jews and half-Jews.[28]

On November 26, 1941, Mürer wrote to Buragas, the Lithuanian who was in charge of Jewish affairs at the Vilna municipality, as follows:

> I would ask you to immediately investigate the following details through the Judenrat and Jewish police:
>
> 1. The total number of mixed marriages;
> 2. The number of persons so married living within the ghetto;
> 3. The number of mixed couples who have separated, and the number of Aryans from among them living outside the ghetto;
> 4. The number of children, specifying how many of them live inside, and how many outside, the ghetto;
> 5. Dates of birth of children and partners of mixed marriages;

27 *Documents Accuse*, p. 160.
28 *Naujoji Lietuva*, October 29, 1941 in Moreshet Archives, D.1.362.

6. If these children and the Aryan spouses belong to the Jewish religious community or not;

7. List of names of the mixed couples.

Buragas submitted the request to the Judenrat and Jewish police on November 27, 1941. Fried gave his letter to Glazman, Deputy Commander of the ghetto police, and attached a memo: "To Glazman. Submit the requested information as soon as possible. Engineer Fried, Chairman of Jewish Council, November 27, 1941."[29]

Little information was furnished by the non-Jewish public, and little cooperation was extended to the German administration in anything pertaining to Aryan partners of mixed marriages who dwelt outside the ghetto. The local population felt that those who had not embraced the Jewish faith were Christians and was not prepared to report them to the authorities. Moreover, it would seem that the spouses did not appear at police-stations to register as required by the published instructions. Mürer tried to identify such persons through their Jewish husbands/wives residing in the ghetto; hence the request to the Judenrat. Glazman did not submit any information.

Partners in mixed marriages, their children, and the converts who were forced to take up residence in the Vilna ghetto shared the fate of the Jews there. The majority was exterminated in the various *Aktionen*.[30] The others found refuge among the non-Jewish population much more easily than among the Jews, because of their family ties and religious affinities.

---

29 *Documents Accuse*, pp. 167–168.

30 *Documents Accuse*, p. 255. One incident of a German woman married to a Jew is recounted herein. She divorced her husband and was sent to Germany. Her two children, aged 9 and 13, were sent to Ponar and murdered, by decision of *Gebietskommissar* Hingst.

Chapter 7

INTERNAL ORGANIZATION OF THE GHETTO

Housing Problems
There was no authority within the ghetto to receive the incoming Jews and direct them to their new dwellings. The Lithuanian security escorts accompanied the people as far as the outer gates and then left them to their own devices. Since the liquidation of the Judenrat, there was no Jewish authority capable of establishing order inside the ghetto.

Many Jews felt a sense of relief upon entering the ghetto. The Lithuanian guards, who had harried and harassed them along the route, remained outside the walls, and the tired Jews could divest themselves of their belongings and rest. The taunts and insults of the Lithuanians and the Poles, who had watched and enjoyed the spectacle of the marchers, could no longer be heard. The fact that they found themselves inside the ghetto, and not at Lukiszki or at some unknown destination, also greatly relieved them. They hoped that once inside the ghetto, isolated from the animus of the outside world, they would be free from the constant menace of abductions and humiliations to which they had been subjected for more than two months.[1]

The primary concern of every Jew entering the ghetto was to find lodgings. Those who had come during the Sabbath morn-

---

1 Dworzecki, *op. cit.*, p. 50; Sutzkewer, *op. cit.*, p. 40; Balberyszski, *op. cit.*, p. 178.

ing of the expulsion had no difficulty. However, within a few hours all the vacant apartments were occupied, and those who arrived later in the day were compelled to crowd into rooms that were already occupied, or to seek accommodations in basements, attics, hallways, or even in open yards. People who had already managed to find apartments took in relatives or friends who arrived later. Some of the apartments had been closed since "the Great Provocation," and the people had to force them open.[2] Several families were crowded into one room. The density was 1–2 square yards per capita.[3]

Many of the newcomers experienced severe trauma upon entering the empty dwellings and finding possessions left by the previous tenants, who had been expelled only a few days before. R. Korczak writes:

> When we first came in, a shocking sight was revealed to us: This room is alive! It was still pulsating with the lives of the previous occupants... Pictures of children smiled down on us, the thousand voices of torn letters cried out, books were strewn all over the floor... unmade beds stood mute, and on the table were vestiges of a meal, the last evening's supper.[4]

Some of the people discovered a little furniture and some other articles left behind by the previous inhabitants, but many of the apartments had been looted by non-Jewish neighbors or government officials in the interval between "the Great Provocation" and the enforced removals into the ghetto. Balberyszski writes:

> Some household articles were found in the apartments

---

2 Epstein, p. 16; Kruk, *op. cit.*, pp. 68, 74; L. Engelshtern, *In Getos un velder*, Tel Aviv, 1972, p. 13; Balberyszski, *op. cit.*, p. 179.
3 Engelshtern, *op. cit.*, p. 13, writes of twenty-three people who lived in two small rooms; Dworzecki, *op. cit.*, p. 52, refers to seventeen people living in one room; Epstein's diary, p. 18; M. Rolnik, *Ani Hayevet le-Sapper*, Jerusalem, 1965, p. 33.
4 Korczak, *op. cit.*, p. 24.

which the neighbors had not time to remove during the few days. Houses had small stores of fuel-wood, coal, potatoes and other goods the Jews had laid in for the winter, but had not been able to consume ... Several apartments had furniture, household goods and clothes.[5]

These remnants were of considerable help to the newcomers, who of course had been unable to bring much furniture or utensils with them. The first arrivals in the morning had the advantage of being able to take possession of these articles. The majority of these who entered the ghetto in the morning had lived in neighborhoods adjacent to the ghetto area, and they succeeded in bringing more of their own goods. Thus, a gap between property owners of some degree and those entirely destitute was created in the ghetto from the very first day.

Some people who only yesterday had been poverty-stricken became, by ghetto standards and in comparison to others, wealthy overnight, and vice-versa. By virtue of the reality of the absence of any authority in the ghetto, some underworld types forcibly appropriated dwellings containing some property. From the very first hours, a process engendering sociological change—a process of class transformation and the creation of "new poor" and "new rich"—began.

People soon learned of the existence of the two ghettos and also that many had been locked up in Lukiszki on the first day of the ghettoization. Many families had been separated or had lost touch with one other during the transfers. People began searching for relatives; many were reunited, but others had parted forever, some having been thrust into the ghettos and others taken off to Lukiszki and Ponar. Several days after the erection of the two ghettos, family reunions between the two sectors took place; this was implemented by the Judenrat with the consent of the German administration.[6]

5 Balberyszski, *op. cit.*, p. 183.
6 Rolnik, *op. cit.*, pp. 30–31; Kruk, *op. cit.*, p. 71

Establishment of the Judenrats in the Two Ghettos

On Sunday, September 7, 1941, the day after the ghettoization began, a separate Judenrat was established in each of the two ghettos. Balberyszski writes that he was told by A. Fried that on the day they entered the ghetto, Fried met Murer inside, and, as they had been acquainted when the latter was active in the first Judenrat, Murer ordered him to establish a Judenrat of five members, of which Fried was to be the head. Fried chose the other four members; three from the former Judenrat and engineer G. Guchman. The latter did not want to join, but Fried succeeded in persuading him by stating that he would deal only with technical matters and that the Judenrat needed a man of his caliber.

The head of the new Judenrat, A. Fried, was an assimilated Jew, a bank manager, who had not previously participated in Jewish public life. G. Jaszunski, a lawyer, had arrived in Vilna from Warsaw in 1939, and was one of the leaders of the Bund. J. Fishman, a shoemaker by profession, one of the Bund leaders in Vilna, had been a member of the Jewish Community Council. S. Milkonovicki, a lawyer and Zionist, had been for many years deputy chairman (and later chairman) of the Jewish community in Vilna. G. Guchman, construction engineer, had not previously adhered to any particular party, but showed Bundist tendencies.

After his appointment as head of the Judenrat, Fried assembled some twenty persons who had been active in the former Judenrat and requested that they cooperate with the new Judenrat. The majority agreed to help in establishing an administrative body in the ghetto and to participate in its work. The Judenrat offices were to be situated at 6 Rudnicka Street.[7]

The appointment of the Judenrat evoked no particular reaction in the ghetto community. The fact that four out of the five members had been part of the first Judenrat gave the impression of the continuity of Jewish leadership in Vilna. The re-

7 Balberyszski, *op. cit.*, pp. 253–254; Kruk, *op. cit.*, pp. 69, 71.

constitution of an official Jewish representation, recognized by
the authorities, added to the illusion of stability and security
which the Jews felt upon entering the ghetto.

In Ghetto No. 2, the Judenrat was appointed by Schweinberger, SD and Security Police Officer in Vilna. Schweinberger entered Ghetto No. 2 and met I. Lejbowicz, a merchant, and
appointed him head of the Judenrat. Schweinberger also stopped
four other Jews on the street and coopted them to the Judenrat.

The Judenrat of Ghetto No. 1 was composed of public figures, party activists, and members of the intelligentsia. The
majority of the Judenrat of Ghetto No. 2 was composed of
ordinary people. The newly appointed Ghetto No. 2 Judenrat
invited a group of public figures and members of the intelligentsia to a meeting and requested that they organize the administration of the ghetto. The appointed members contended,
at this meeting, that they were unable to handle affairs as the
realities of the situation demanded, and they therefore proposed
that while they would continue officially to represent the ghetto
community vis-à-vis the authorities, the actual administration
should be in the hands of the group invited to the meeting. In
this way, in addition to the official Judenrat, an internal leadership of public figures was created in Ghetto No. 2. Among the
prominent persons on this panel were Dr. Vladimir Poczter, M.
Balberyszski, and the advocate Smilag.[8]

In a census conducted on September 13–14 at the request of
the German administration, the Ghetto No. 2 Judenrat registered
all incarcerees according to occupation and place of residence.
The census showed that there were 9,000 inhabitants in this
ghetto.[9]

Formation of a Jewish Police Force
Following these initial steps in the organization of an internal
administration in the ghetto, steps were taken to form a Jewish

8 Balberyszski, *op. cit.,* pp. 182, 196; Kruk, *op. cit.,* p. 85.
9 Minutes of a meeting of the Judenrat in Ghetto No. 2 on September 13, 1941, Moreshet Archives, D.1.398.

police force. On September 7 notices were posted on the walls of Ghetto No. 1, calling for young people to enlist in the ghetto police. Jacob Gens, a former captain in the Lithuanian Army, was chosen as its commanding officer.[10] Fried nominated him

10 Jacob Gens was born in the district of Shavli. His father was a merchant. Jacob was the eldest of four brothers. He studied in a Russian school in the township and then spent two years in a secondary school in Shavli. In 1919, he joined the Lithuanian Army, which was then being formed. He was sent to the officers' academy and graduated as a second lieutenant. Dr. N. Karni writes of this period in the officers' school (see his testimony in Yad Vashem Archives 0-33/1274), as they were together in the course:

"I knew Gens — this was in the second half of 1920 — in the school for officers of the Lithuanian Army at Kovno...he stood out...from the beginning because of his fine military performance...He had great personal charm. I do not remember him ever being in a bad mood. He adapted quickly to the conditions of the harsh regime then practiced in the school...He was an excellent student...He had leadership qualities, he had personality, he was a man of principles. I recall the following incident: Every Sunday morning the entire school would be marched to prayer in the large church in Kovno. The cadets went quite willingly, and I am sure that more than 90 percent did not go to pray. It was an event in the daily routine. The church was filled with girls on those Sundays when the cadets went there. Actually, we Jews did not care very much, but Gens claimed that we must stress our position as Jews and approach our superiors collectively on this matter. Gens submitted a memorandum through official channels and stated that, as a Jew, he did not regard himself as duty bound to attend church. As a result, an order was issued to exempt us Jews from the duty of going to church. Gens remained etched in my memory as a positive youngster. After we finished school our way parted and our meetings were accidental."

After completing the course, Gens was sent to an infantry regiment, was promoted to the rank of lieutenant, and won a decoration. In 1922 (approximately) he married a Lithuanian woman, by whom he had a daughter. Gens left the army and began to study at Kovno University. He made his living teaching in the Hebrew school at Vilkomir, in which he taught language, literature, and athletics. Later on he also taught at the Jewish school in Juburg.

as the Chief of Ghetto Police on the basis of previous acquaintance with him when Fried was a patient in the Jewish Hospital;
Gens had been the Administrative Director before the establishment of the ghetto.[11]

Gens' deputy was Joseph Muszkat, a Zionist-Revisionist and a
lawyer by profession, who had arrived in Vilna in 1939 as a refugee from Warsaw. Former Betar (Revisionist: Brit Trumpeldor)
members were appointed to other key posts in the ghetto police.
Among them Salk Dessler, a resident of Vilna, and Meir Levas,
who had come to Vilna after its annexation to Lithuania. The
fact that within the ranks of the new police force, and especially among its officers, there were many Betar members, was because priority was given during enlistment of personnel to those
who had served in the army, had received army training, and
had held commissioned ranks. There were more former service-
men in Betar than in other movements. It seems also that Gens
favored Betar over other groups.

A few days after the police force had been formed, a conflict

---

To further his studies at the university, he left teaching, moved
to Kovno in 1927, and became Accountant in the Ministry of
Justice. He completed his studies at the Kovno University in 1935,
and received a diploma in jurisprudence and economics. Gens
resigned from his government post and began work in the Shell
Oil Company. Two years later, he changed to the Lietukis company, which was the largest cooperative concern in Lithuania.

In spite of his marriage to a Lithuanian gentile, Gens had a
Jewish national consciousness and was close to the Zionist Revisionists. In 1938, he was called up as a reserve officer for special
study in a staff officers' school and received a captaincy. After
Lithuania became a Soviet Republic in July 1940, he was dismissed from his post at Lietukis and moved to Vilna, where his
brother Solomon and his mother resided. With the aid of a Lithuanian friend, who was the director of the Department of Health
in Vilna, Gens was given a position in that department. From the
outset of the German occupation, Gens was made Administrative
Director of the Jewish Hospital.

11 Balberyszski, *op. cit.*, p. 254; testimony by J. Mushkat, YVA,
0–3/3748, p. 2

arose over the character it was to assume, and especially over the composition of its senior command. The Judenrat, which had appointed Gens as the Chief of Police, nominated Hermann Kruk, a Bundist, as the first Deputy Chief. This seems to have been at the insistence of G. Jaszunski, a member of the Judenrat, who was a Bundist and close friend of H. Kruk, and wielded extensive influence over the Jewish council. The Bund wished to reduce Betar domination over the police force.

H. Kruk wrote in his diary:

> Fr. H., on the third day after becoming Deputy Commander of the militia, went to the chairman of the Judenrat and asked to be relieved of that post. What is the reason? The discussion over the formation of a militia or a police force ended in favor of the police. Jacob Gens the Chief ... his second associate Joseph Muszkat ... the two of them want to set up a ghetto police ... all the claims by Fr. Kr. as to the important function of the militia, if it adopted other methods, were to no avail. Meanwhile, these two are enrolling the Betar camp in the militia ... The chairman wanted to defer the resignation. Kr. refused and resigned. He does not want to sit together with this leadership and especially with Betar ... [12]

The attempt by the Bundists to prevent Betar domination over the police and to establish a strong position for themselves in that force ended in failure. A situation was created within the

---

12 Kruk, pp. 77–78, notes 105–106. Kruk does not identify the person he dubbed "Fr.H" at the outset of the entry, and continues to refer to him as "Friend Kr." but it may be assumed that the reference was to himself; he used the initials "Fr." to be read as *Freund*, "comrade," "H" for his first name, Hermann, and "Kr." for Kruk. The same version appears in the notes to Kruk's diary; Muszkat writes in his testimony (p. 2) that at the outset, Fried offered him the post of Chief of Police, but he refused on the grounds that he did not speak Lithuanian. He agreed to accept the position of Deputy Chief.

ghetto leadership whereby the Judenrat was under Bundist influence and the police under Betarist influence.

The police headquarters and the Judenrat were located in the same building. The ghetto was divided into three police precincts, with a police station in each. The policemen wore a white armband imprinted with a blue Star of David.

A Jewish police force was also established in Ghetto No. 2. The Judenrat there had full jurisdiction over the police. The police force in Ghetto No. 2 did not have a party character, as was the case with the Ghetto No. 1 police.[13]

Organization of Institutions and Services

The Judenrat in Ghetto No. 1 was divided into five departments: General, Food, Health, Housing and Labor. The Health Department was headed by Judenrat member S. Milkonovicki; Food Department by Judenrat member G. Jaszunski; Housing, Judenrat member G. Guchman. J. Fishman, the fifth member of the council, was appointed liaison between the two ghettos and in charge of the Labor Department, of which the permanent director was A. Braude, who was not a member of the Judenrat.

The General Department coordinated all activities relating to the procedural work of the Judenrat, served as liaison between the various departments, and handled all matters in extraneous spheres of action. Fried issued his instructions to the various units through the General Department, which had a section for registration of residents and for burials. Other sections were: Treasury, Mail, Social Welfare, and Library.

The Judenrat in Ghetto No. 2 had the following five departments: Food, Health, Housing, Labor Bureau, and Education. The departmental heads were not officially members of the Judenrat, but served as active members of it and took part in its meetings.[14]

13 Balberyszski, *op. cit.*, p. 204; Minutes of the Judenrat meeting in Ghetto No. 2 on September 27, 1941, Moreshet Archives, D. 1. 398.
14 Balberyszski, *op. cit.*, pp. 196–203, 302–305, 312; Moreshet Archives, D. 1. 398.

The difference in the organizational structure between the two Judenrats was that, in Ghetto No. 1, a General Department had been set up to centralize and coordinate the work of the other divisions, whereas in Ghetto No. 2, no such department functioned, and the Chairman of the Judenrat was the liaison between the various departments. Judenrat No. 1 had no Education Department, which it apparently did not regard as a priority at that time. Its official members headed the administrative divisions. Department heads for Judenrat No. 2 were appointed from outside its official membership, because the latter did not have the suitable personal qualifications to administer the respective departmental affairs.

The various departments and essential services in the ghettos began operating after the Judenrats had been established. Health services were inaugurated in the first few days after the Jews were enclosed. A hospital and a clinic were opened in Ghetto No. 1. A clinic also began to operate in Ghetto No. 2, but in cases where the patients needed specialists, they were sent to Ghetto No. 1, under escort by Jewish policemen. Both ghettos operated sanitation epidemiological units, the function of which was to supervise cleanliness and prevent the spread of contagious diseases, a matter of extreme importance in face of ghetto conditions. A particular difficulty was the procurement of medicine and medical equipment. Part of the equipment had been brought into the ghetto by the medical personnel, and another part was found in the empty buildings when the ghetto was reoccupied. Additional equipment was secured through contact outside the ghetto.[15] The ghetto doctors displayed devotion, initiative, and a capacity for improvisation, which made it possible to conduct the ghetto health services competently.

Labor Department. On Monday, September 8, the ghetto Jews went out to work in those plants and places in which they had been employed before the ghetto had been set up. Their

---

15 Epstein's diary, pp. 19, 94; Balberyszski, *op. cit.*, pp. 199–200. The hospital was in Zawalna Street.

occupation in German and Lithuanian institutions, coupled with relevant work-permits, enhanced their sense of security, and consequently they went to work willingly. Labor departments were created in each of the ghettos and supplied manpower in accordance with the orders of the German *Arbeitsamt*.

Food Departments procured basic commodities on the outside to distribute within the ghetto. They also ran public kitchens in which boiled water could be bought for a token payment. Small quantities of food were also supplied by the municipality. The Judenrat was greatly preoccupied with obtaining and distributing food. The minutes of Ghetto No. 2's Judenrat show that the subject of food was on the agenda for every one of its meetings.[16]

The Housing Departments in both ghettos had the function of regulating accommodations. Many families had not found housing, while many others occupied apartments which were comparatively commodious by ghetto standards. It was necessary to make an inventory of available housing, find offices for ghetto agencies that had begun to organize, and also to deal with the housing problems of people who had been moved from one ghetto to the other. The department also arbitrated disputes between tenants living in the same apartments in such matters as can arise from congestion. It also appointed house superintendents and janitors, and provided for cleaning and sanitary services. The Housing departments had to invoke the help of the police in the ghetto in arbitrating some of its problems.

Firewood. The ghetto inhabitants experienced great difficulty in finding firewood for cooking and heating during the winter. To obtain the necessary fuel, they dismantled windows, doors, and fences. To prevent this, the Judenrat found it essential to arrange for adequate wood supplies.

Education. The question of schooling for children and orphans was raised at the initial meetings of the Judenrat in

16 Rolnik, *op. cit.*, p. 34; Moreshet Archives, D.1.398.

Ghetto No. 2, where an orphanage school was set up. The first schools in Ghetto No. 1 were opened at the initiative of the teacher M. Olitzky. A census taken in Ghetto No. 1 in the second half of September 1941 registered about 3,000 youngsters of school age. The Judenrat in this ghetto established a library and reading-room, headed by H. Kruk.[17]

Missing Relatives Section. Sections to search for missing relatives, set up in both ghettos, cooperated with each other and exchanged information in regard to families whose members had been separated or lost during the expulsions.

Summary

The Jews of Vilna, confined to the ghettos, succeeded in organizing themselves within a few days, in setting up the apparatus of self-government, in arranging for accommodations for thousands of people, and in operating the most essential services. Patterns of self-government were formulated from the very first days of life in the ghetto, and these were maintained and developed throughout the entire ghetto period.

Many key posts in the new Judenrat, in the police, and in other ghetto institutions were held by Jewish refugees from Poland, or those who had arrived in Vilna from Lithuania after the city was annexed to it. This aroused resentment among the veteran Vilna Jews, but these feelings subsided in the course of time. The reasons for the distribution of key posts to non-Vilnaites vary. A large number of the Vilna Jewish leaders had been murdered by the Germans in the series of *Aktionen* that preceded the establishment of the ghetto. On the other hand, leaders and activists of various parties arrived in Vilna with the stream of refugees from Poland, or Lithuania, and in the absence of the local leadership took over the key posts in the ghetto administration. The Jews from Lithuania scored by virtue

17 Balberyszski, *op. cit.,* pp. 203, 433–436; Minutes of the Judenrat meeting in Ghetto No. 2 on September 19, 1941, Moreshet Archives, D.1.398; Kruk, *op. cit.,* p. 202. The library and reading room were at 16 Straszuna Street.

of their knowledge of the Lithuanian language, which was indispensable for the constant contact with the local Lithuanian authorities.[18]

The initial organization in the ghetto complied with the immediate requirements of its inmates, but the process of perfecting the institutions and services had, of necessity, to take place over a long period of time. Before the process could be completed, the Jews of the ghetto became the target of new massacres.

18 G. Jaszunski came from Poland; J. Gens from Lithuania; Braude, who headed the Labor Office, was from Kovno; and Trapido, who headed the food department, was also from Kovno.

Chapter 8

AKTIONEN AND LIQUIDATION OF GHETTO NO. 2
(September 15–October 21, 1941)

The Jewish inhabitants of Vilna were arbitrarily thrown into Ghetto Nos. 1 and 2 in accordance with their former places of residence in the city. This, however, was to be a temporary distribution. Several days after they moved in, they learned that Ghetto No. 1 was earmarked for craftsmen and workers holding permits, and Ghetto No. 2 for all others.

Some days after the Jews had been confined within the ghettos, the transfer of orphan children, the sick, and the elderly from Ghetto No. 1 to Ghetto No. 2 began. Simultaneously, holders of work-permits and their families moved from Ghetto No. 2 to Ghetto No. 1. The first transfer of eighty people from the Home for the Aged apparently took place on September 13.

A Lithuanian reporter who visited Ghetto No. 2 wrote on September 20, 1941, in *Naujoji Lietuva*: "Many inhabitants have been moved out of Ghetto No. 1, in which experts and artisans are congregated. Ghetto No. 2 contains members of the liberal professions and people without occupations."[1]

The expulsion of thousands of permit-less persons took place on September 15, 1941, one week after their entry into the ghetto. The German authorities informed the Judenrat and Jewish police of Ghetto No. 1 that, in order to reduce the con-

---

1 *Naujoji Lietuva*, no. 72, of September 20, in Moreshet Archives, D.1.362.

gestion therein, people without work-permits would be transferred to Ghetto No. 2. On September 15, the Ghetto Police
published a notice that all those lacking work-permits would
have to move to Ghetto No. 2 that same evening. About 2,500–
3,000 people assembled at the gate and went out in the direction
of the second ghetto, but only 600 of them reached it. The rest
were dragged away to Lukiszki and from there to Ponar and
massacred.[2]

It is likely that the Germans permitted 600 people to reach
the second ghetto in order to deceive the Jews. If no one had
arrived at Ghetto No. 2, the Jews would soon have realized
what was happening, and this would have made it difficult to
remove others without work-permits from Ghetto No. 1. But
in the conditions then prevailing—the general obscurity of the
situation, the absence of regular communication between the
two ghettos, and the lack of information on the exact number
of those leaving Ghetto No. 1 and of those reaching the other—
the Germans could assume that some time would pass before
the ghetto inmates realized that most of the people had been
taken to Lukiszki. The Germans apparently believed that in this
interim they would have sufficient time to complete the remaining *Aktionen.*

The Einsatzkommando 3 report states that, on September 17,
1,271 Jews were killed in Vilna: 337 males, 687 females and
247 children.[3] According to this same German report, it is
evident that the people taken away on September 15 were held
throughout the following day in Lukiszki and taken on the 17th
to Ponar and there slaughtered.

The removal of the elderly, sick, and orphans to Ghetto No. 2
continued after the September 15 *Aktion.* The Jews were so
unaware of the Germans' real intentions that in Ghetto No. 2
they thought that the "consignments" were made upon the initiative of the Ghetto No. 1 Judenrat, which wanted to get rid of

2 Kruk, *op. cit.,* pp. 76–77; Epstein's diary, p. 19.
3 Kruk, *op. cit.,* p. 77; Jäger Report, p. 6.

elements endangering the productivity and image of their ghetto, and had not been ordered by the German administration. A proposal was made at a meeting of the Ghetto No. 2 Judenrat, held on September 27, to the effect that the other Judenrat be requested to cease transferring people. It added that, if this practice were to continue, the No. 1 Judenrat should also send the staff members who had dealt with those people and the necessary food supplies. The transfers continued until mid-October, and they demoralized the inhabitants of Ghetto No. 2. Balberyszki writes:

> One of the most difficult things of all that we endured was to look at the consignments of "living merchandise" which that aristocratic Judenrat sent us day after day. It was almost certain that the fate of our ghetto had been sealed. It was said in the ghetto that Hitler would not feed and maintain such "merchandise."[4]

Simultaneously, there was a reverse movement of those who held work-permits. Kruk writes of 200 Jews who were brought into Ghetto No. 1 on September 16, 1941. A considerable number of inmates of No. 2 managed to escape and infiltrate No. 1 when they returned from their work in the city or by wriggling through the fences during the day or at night.[5] It is estimated that 2–3,000 persons confined to Ghetto No. 2 came into Ghetto No. 1 by legal or illegal means.

On September 18, Murer issued new directives in order to tighten control over the ghetto, segregate its inhabitants, and prevent illegal departures. Orders were given that all telephones should be removed. Instructions to the Judenrat would be transmitted by the authorities through the guardpost at the ghetto gate. All postal connections would be severed. In addition, to prevent escapes from the ghetto, the fences would be

4 Minutes of the Ghetto No. 2 Judenrat meeting on September 27, 1941, Moreshet Archives, D.1.398; Balberyszki, *op. cit.*, pp. 212–213, 226.
5 Kruk, *op. cit.*, p. 78; Rolnik, *op. cit.*, p. 36.

reinforced by barbed-wire and the windows of houses overlook-
ing the non-Jewish parts of the city would be boarded over.[6]

The Yom Kippur Aktion *of October 1*
Aktionen were carried out in both ghettos on the Day of
Atonement, October 1, 1941. The first began at noon in Ghetto
No. 2, when the synagogues were crowded with worshippers.
Squads of Germans and Lithuanians, commanded by Schweinberger, burst in and began arresting people. The swoop came
as a surprise, and the mixed squads were thus able to round up
hundreds of people from the synagogues, houses, and streets
without difficulty. They were assembled near the gate, and at
1:30 P.M. some 800 persons were led out. The ghetto residents
thought this had ended the operation, but in the afternoon Germans and Lithuanians entered the ghetto again and resumed the
mass arrests. This time the *Aktion* went more slowly and lasted
until the evening, because many Jews has gone into hiding. By
6:30 P.M. another 900 had been taken. The operation ended in
the evening hours. The people of No. 2 were taken to Lukiszki —
1,700 in all.

The Ghetto No. 2 Judenrat had received no advance notification of the action, nor was it requested by the Germans to
gather people together or take part in the round-ups in any
form.[7]

During the afternoon Schweinberger contacted the Ghetto
No. 1 Judenrat and demanded that they hand over 1,000 Jews
from their ghetto, to be assembled near the gate by 7:30 P.M.
He told them that if this were not done, Germans and Lithuanians would enter the ghetto and take the people away themselves. The Judenrat decided to acquiesce and surrender 1,000
persons without passes.

The police went through the ghetto and proclaimed that
persons without permits were to report to the ghetto gate. Those

6 *Documents Accuse*, pp. 166–167.
7 Kruk, *op. cit.*, pp. 88–89; Balberyszski, *op. cit.*, pp. 215–218.

of them without passes who had already experienced the September 15 *Aktion* abstained from doing so. By 7: 30 that evening, only forty-six persons had come forward. Schweinberger then demanded that the Judenrat order everyone in the ghetto, with or without passes, to assemble near the gate, and he would then select 1,000 of them. The Jewish policemen passed the order on to the ghetto inmates. Simultaneously, mixed squads of Germans and Lithuanians began pulling people out of their houses. Those who lived near the gate were first. Several managed to elude the grasp of the Germans and Lithuanians by on-the-spot ransom payments. The majority of those without passes again failed to appear, either hiding themselves or remaining at home. But people with passes came forward with their families, believing that their work status assured them immunity, and 2,220 of them gathered at the gate in response to the announcements by the Jewish police. They were surrounded by German and Lithuanian squads and taken to Lukiszki.[8]

The captives were held in prison during the day of October 2. German establishments and units succeeded in effecting the release of a number of their employees who were taken from Ghetto No. 1 on the night of Yom Kippur and returning them to their homes. Other releases were secured by relatives or friends against large ransom payments to the Germans. Germans of different army units came to Lukiszki and called out names from prepared lists. The number of Jews who were freed was between a few dozen to a hundred.[9]

In the summary by E.K.3 dated December 1, 1941, this is the only *Aktion*, for the time period covered, which is not mentioned.

The Yom Kippur *Aktion* shattered the Jews' illusions — until

---

8 Kruk, *op. cit.*, pp. 87–88, 260; Epstein's diary, pp. 21–22; Rudashevski, *op. cit.*, p. 38.

9 Balberyszski, *op. cit.*, pp. 221–222; Korczak, *op. cit.*, pp. 36–37; Epstein's diary, p. 21.

then the majority had believed that a work-pass ensured safety for its holders and their families.

The role played by the Judenrat and the Jewish Police undermined the confidence placed in them by many Jews. It was the first *Aktion* in which both bodies had helped round up groups of inmates in response to German orders. It also marked the inception of the "ideological" argument, introduced by the Vilna Ghetto Judenrat, that in order to forestall the unrestricted abduction of Jews from the ghetto, it was better that the Judenrat itself assemble and hand over the Jews.

The justification for surrendering Jews was expressed by A. Fried, Chairman of Ghetto No. 1 Judenrat, in these terms: "When the Germans order us to supply 2,000 persons, we are obliged to obey them in order to save the other Jews. If we do not hand them over, they [the Germans] will take anyone they please, and as many as they please, and this will make it worse for the thousands of remaining Jews."[10] As a result, the Judenrat was ready to help the Germans in removing a small number of unproductive elements among the Jews in order to save the working majority and their families. In accordance with this decision, the Jewish police tried to assemble the requisite number from among the inmates without passes. When they failed, they issued an announcement that everyone, with or without permits, assemble at the gate, believing that in this way the luckless non-holders could be selected and the remainder sent home. But this device failed when only the permit-holders turned out and were seized by the Germans. The removal of skilled persons from the ghetto weakened its productive base and thus the right of the ghetto's future existence in accordance with the Judenrat's assumptions as to its usefulness. The *Aktion* was similarly unsuccessful from the viewpoint of the German administration, which was fundamentally concerned with retaining the skilled and unskilled workers necessary to production and placing them last in line for extermination.

10 Balberyszski, *op. cit.*, p. 210.

The German institutions and units from which the Jewish employees in Ghetto No. 1 were seized protested against their removal to Lukiszki and, due to intervention by German military units, some Jews were released. This may well be the reason why the entire *Aktion* was deleted from the E.K.3 report of December 1, 1941.

Liquidation of Ghetto No. 2

Three more *Aktionen* were carried out by the Germans after Yom Kippur, and, in due course, all the remaining Jews in Ghetto No. 2 were taken to Ponar. These three operations took place between October 3 and 21.

During the night of October 3/4 the Germans seized 2,000 people from Ghetto No. 2, telling them that they were being removed to a third ghetto in which there was a shortage of laborers. The last group in this *Aktion* was taken out of the ghetto at dawn on October 4, but when the Jews realized they were being led in the familiar direction of Lukiszki, they lay on the ground and refused to budge. Sutzkewer writes:

> Moshe Frumkin, a lad of eighteen, cried out to the people who were being taken with him on the way to prison: "Don't let them take you! Escape into the streets!" Panic seized the column, women lay prone on the road, the elderly stood petrified, and the youngsters ran away. Schweinberger ordered his men to fire. Dozens of people fell dead, and the survivors were compelled to carry them. Nevertheless, many escaped, including Frumkin.[11]

It was the first instance of mass passive resistance by Vilna Jews.

The people seized in Ghetto No. 2 on the night of October 3/4 were taken to Ponar. The E.K.3 report of December 1,

---

11 Sutzkewer, *op. cit.*, p. 50; Korczak, *op. cit.*, p. 37, points out that the group that opposed going to Lukiszki was returned to the ghetto.

1941, stated that on October 4, 432 Jewish males, 1,115 Jewish females, and 436 Jewish children, totalling 1,983 persons were shot in Vilna.[12]

Following these two *Aktionen* there were still approximately 6–7,000 people left in Ghetto No. 2. Groups of workers still left the ghetto for their jobs on the outside.

In spite of the gloomy atmosphere, which had been generated by the *Aktionen* and the continuing transfer of the aged and sick of Ghetto No. 1, there was still no general awareness that the ghetto was on the verge of liquidation. This lack of perspective was reflected in the proceedings of the Judenrat. Many dwellings remained vacant in this ghetto, still containing the possessions of those caught up in the preceding *Aktionen,* and the dwellings with their contents were locked and sealed by the Judenrat. The latter, at a meeting on October 4, several hours after the *Aktion* held the previous night had ended, decided not to allow other residents to occupy the empty apartments but to remove the contents in an organized manner to the Judenrat warehouse.

The Judenrat meeting held on October 5 focused on problems of food and a proposal received from Judenrat No. 1 to prepare dwellings for 1,200 persons who were to be transferred from Ghetto No. 1. On the agenda was the demand of Police Chief Gens urging the suspension of transfers from No. 2 to Ghetto No. 1 without prior approval by the Ghetto No. 1 authorities. At the meeting it was decided that only Judenrat No. 2 had the right to approve the transfer of people to Ghetto No. 1. This decision coincided with the No. 2 Judenrat's attitude that opposed weakening Ghetto No. 2 by removing able-bodied workmen, doctors, and other skilled hands, as it rendered the place a compound of the elderly, sick, unskilled, and their families. A meeting of Judenrat No. 2 on October 6 discussed problems of food, firewood, and care of children.[13]

12 Jäger Report, p. 6.
13 Minutes of the Ghetto No. 2 Judenrat meeting on October 6, 1941, Moreshet Archives, D.1.398. This date was the last recorded in the book of minutes of the Ghetto No. 2 Judenrat meetings. Either

On October 13, a letter was sent to the Judenrat in both ghettos by the Vilna municipality requesting that rents be collected from the tenants of dwellings there, and the proceeds be remitted to the municipal authorities. Precise instructions were given as to how to record the amounts and where to send them.[14] This letter aroused a certain amount of confidence in the inmates of Ghetto No. 2 in regard to its continued existence. It is likely that the letter was intended to delude them, or that the Lithuanian municipality had no idea of the intention and time schedule for the final dissolution of Ghetto No. 2.

Another *Aktion* in Ghetto No. 2 took place on the last two days of Succot, October 15–16. The E.K.3 report of December 1, 1941, stated that 382 Jewish males, 507 Jewish females, and 257 Jewish children, a total of 1,146 persons, were killed in Vilna on October 16.[15]

Aktion of *October 21, Final Liquidation of Ghetto No. 2*
The *Aktion* of October 15–16 had left 3–4,000 people in Ghetto No. 2. An atmosphere of despair prevailed. People sought ways to leave and cross into Ghetto No. 1. Several hours before the liquidation *Aktion,* on the evening of October 20, P. Buragas, the Lithuanian in charge of Jewish affairs at the municipality and the liaison between the German administration and the Judenrat, came into Ghetto No. 2. At a meeting with the Judenrat that evening, he discussed the subject of new "yellow passes" issued by the German *Arbeitsamt,* which were to replace all existing passes. The Judenrat asked Buragas for 200. At the end of the meeting, he gave ten "yellow passes" to Chairman Leibowicz: five were earmarked for furriers—who were to proceed at once from the ghetto to the "Kailis" furs workshop operated by the German Army—and five others, not filled out, to be issued at Leibowicz discretion.

<hr />

no more meetings took place, or the minutes never reached us.
14 Balberyszki, *op. cit.,* p. 232.
15 Kruk, *op. cit.,* p. 260; Jäger Report, p. 6.

Early in the morning of Tuesday, October 21, the Germans launched the final liquidation of Ghetto No. 2. It proceeded slowly; German and Lithuanian troops went from house to house, searching thoroughly, breaking down doors, windows, walls, ceilings and floors, in a hunt for secret hiding-places. There were instances of ransom paid to the Lithuanians or the Germans in return for which people escaped to Ghetto No. 1. The operation lasted all day, until the evening, and about 2,500 persons were removed to Ponar and there massacred.[16] The Einsatzkommando 3 report of December 1 stated that 718 males, 1,036 females, and 586 children, a total of 2,367 Jews, were killed in Vilna on October 21, 1941.[17] During the ensuing days, Lithuanians and Germans came to the empty Ghetto No. 2 and continued to search for people who might be hiding. *Malines* with dozens of persons existed in Szklana, Jatkowa, Zydowska, and other streets. Some were occupied for weeks; from others the concealed fugitives managed to filter into Ghetto No. 1. Still more were uncovered by the Lithuanians and their inhabitants sent to Ponar.[18] About 2–3,000 of the 9,000 people who had been incarcerated in Ghetto No. 2 were officially transferred or escaped into Ghetto No. 1.

16 Balberyszski, *op. cit.*, pp. 231–233, 237–241, 244; Testimony of A. Auerbach, YVA, 0–3/2733, pp. 7–8; Kruk, *op. cit.*, p. 260, shows that Ghetto No. 2 was completely liquidated on October 29, but this is an error. Shur records the date of the liquidation as October 21. A report on the history of the ghetto prepared at the request of the Germans at the Rosenberg Institute states that Ghetto No. 2 was liquidated on October 21. The document appears in full in Korczak, *op. cit.*, pp. 303–309.

17 Jäger Report, p. 6, gives a total of 5,500 persons who were murdered during the *Aktionen* in Ghetto No. 2. This figure includes people transferred from Ghetto No. 1, who were murdered during the liquidation operation in Ghetto No. 2. This figure should be increased by 1,700 people living in Ghetto No. 2, who were seized during the Yom Kippur *Aktionen*, which were not mentioned in the report. This would bring the final total to 7,200.

18 Kruk, *op. cit.*, pp. 260, 360; Balberyszski, *op. cit.*, pp. 244–246, 248.

Chapter 9

AKTIONEN IN GHETTO NO. 1
(October 22–December 22, 1941)

Yellow Passes

No *Aktionen* had been waged in Ghetto No. 1 during the time of the three liquidation *Aktionen* in Ghetto No. 2, from October 3 to 21, 1941. But simultaneously with the implementation of the operations in Ghetto No. 2, the German administration had been preparing the gradual liquidation of Ghetto No. 1.

Those to be taken first for extermination were persons without work-passes. The work-passes were issued by German establishments and units employing Jewish workers. There was no limit to the number of people that could be employed there, nor to the number of passes issued. These passes were not uniform in appearance and contents, and each factory and unit granted its own. The Judenrat also issued documents to its employees. The German employers applied directly to the Judenrat for the manpower it required.

This system of receiving and utilizing Jewish manpower and distributing the passes was enforced until the centralization of powers in the German *Arbeitsamt,* which was affiliated with the *Gebietskommissariat.* It was decided in mid-October that a single German authority, the *Arbeitsamt,* would approve the employment of Jewish manpower in all establishments, prescribe the number of workers in each, and issue new, uniform passes.

[143]

Ross, a German in charge of the Employment Bureau at the *Gebietskommissariat* (*Beauftragter für die Berufsverbände*) issued a circular, marked No. 1, on October 15, to all institutions and units in Vilna. Article No. 1 referred to the method of payment to Jews according to the category of the workers—male, female and children. Article 2 provided that "all institutions and authorities employing Jews immediately report the number of those employed . . . " Article 3 stated that "requests for Jewish manpower shall be made only through the Employment Bureau in Vilna."[1] The report on the number of Jews working for the various establishments furnished the administration with an up-to-date picture of the work-places and total number of workers in each.

The *Arbeitsamt* canceled the employment of people in a number of work-places, reduced the number in others, and in some cases approved the full total. The managers of factories and army-unit commanders whose request for Jewish workers was either canceled or reduced appealed in a number of instances but the appeals were not always granted.

Once the total of Jewish workers had been determined in each place, the *Arbeitsamt* issued a new, uniform pass to each person. Because of its hue, it was called "the yellow pass" (the Yiddish equivalent was *geler shain*). The employing institutions determined which of its workers should receive a pass, and the lists of names were then submitted to the *Arbeitsamt*, which issued the passes for the Jews.

Jewish workers in these places naturally tried to be included in the favored category, and in many cases paid their German superiors for the privilege. Jews who were foremen and work group leaders ("brigadiers," as they were called) had influence over the composition of the lists, and "protection" money was an important factor. Yet, notwithstanding the cases of bribery and "protection" payments, the artisans and employees who

1 Kruk, *op. cit.*, p. 90, gives a photocopy of the circular issued by Ross.

worked in places important to the German economy were those who received the passes. A large quantity of yellow passes was given to the workers at the "Kailis" fur factory, which produced fur coats and other items of wearing apparel for the German Army.[2]

The yellow pass was issued by the *Arbeitsamt Wilna* and bore the caption: *Facharbeiter-Ausweis Nr...* ("Work-Permit of Artisan No. ..."). On the pass was written the name of the holder and members of his family, place of employment, occupation, the statements that the holder could not be transferred from his work-place without the consent of the *Arbeitsamt,* and that it was valid only when presented together with the *Personalausweis* (identity card). The identity cards were issued later by the Jewish Ghetto police and were available only to yellow-pass holders. The yellow passes issued in October 1941 were valid until March 31, 1942, and with their issue all previous passes were abrogated. The *Arbeitsamt* granted 3,000 yellow permits, of which 400 were given to the Judenrat.[3] Many workers thus remained without valid passes when the new ones appeared.

The 400 passes given to the Judenrat were intended for distribution among its own personnel and those in ghetto institutions. They bore the *Arbeitsamt* stamp, and the Judenrat had to add the name of the person to whom it was given. The most difficult problem was upon whom to bestow them. The number of employees of Judenrat bodies and Jewish police was greater than the number of passes received, and, moreover, thousands of ghetto inhabitants who had been unable to receive these permits from their own places of employment tried to wheedle them out of the Judenrat's quota.

Balberyszski notes that on October 23:

> Thousands of people congregated outside 6 Rudnicka Street. All had the old white *shainen,* none of them had

2 Balberyszski, *op. cit.,* pp. 228, 266; Epstein's diary, p. 27.
3 Dworzecki, *op. cit.,* p. 82; Korczak, *op. cit.,* p. 38; Rolnik,, *op. cit.,* p. 43.

any prospect at all of getting yellow ones ... The crowds shouted that the Judenrat members had taken all the yellow *shainen* for themselves and had no interest in saving Jews, and thought only of saving themselves and their relatives ...

Gens asked the German administration for additional yellow passes, but received a negative reply.[4]

A small number of permits remained for distribution to teachers, doctors, nurses, and other people employed in the ghetto. The Judenrat decided how and to whom they were to be given. Dworzecki writes of the tense anticipation preceding the decision as to whether a pass would be given to him or to his close friend, a physician, Dr. Kolocner:

> Both of us sat in the dark corridor of the Judenrat waiting for the judgment upon us. We talked together, but at the same time we knew that a life voucher for one of us meant a death warrant for the other ... and here, the life voucher was issued to me and my friend was condemned. I was ashamed to raise my eyes but nonetheless I took the document."[5]

Pursuant to the directives by the administration, the yellow pass granted immunity to the holder and three members of the family: the spouse of either sex and two children up to age sixteen. If the nominee had no relative in these categories, it was forbidden to register anyone else. Under this specification, Ghetto No. 1 in Vilna was to have 3,000 permit-holders and no more than 9,000 dependents, a total of 12,000 Jews. In defining the family members entitled to the immunity of the yellow pass, the German authorities intended that there be actually less than 12,000 Jews in Vilna, as many of those entitled to a pass were unmarried (male or female) and had no children. When the authorities began to distribute the permits, in mid-

4 Balberyszski, *op. cit.*, pp. 259–260.
5 Dworzecki, *op. cit.*, pp. 82–83.

October 1941, the population of Ghetto No. 1 totaled 27–28,000.[6] Hence, 15–16,000 of them were condemned to extermination.

When it became known in the ghetto that the *shainen* extended immunity to the relatives of its nominal holder, a process of "composing" fictitious families began. Every holder of a pass, male or female, added to his or her family in order that it total four individuals. A bachelor added a "wife" and "two children;" an unmarried woman did the same. A married but childless couple, or a couple with one child, filled in two. Fictitious families were first filled in to take care of actual family members. A mother was registered as her son's wife, and to this end all possible kinds of cosmetic devices were used to ensure that she appeared younger than her real age. A father was inscribed as the husband of his daughter who held a pass, or a daughter might be written in as her father's wife. Nephews and nieces or younger brothers and sisters of the pass-holders went down as their children. But if, after such rounding out of families, some passes remained uninscribed with four persons, the family members of friends and acquaintances were included. Cases occurred of pass-holders who had more than two children under sixteen or above that age, and it was necessary to find new families for them.

During the composition of fictitious families, it also became a practice to add new family members against payment. A male or female permit-holder asked for, and even received, such payments. Many people sold all their belongings in order to raise the necessary money. The registration was carried out at the Judenrat, and two witnesses were needed to testify that "John and Jane Doe" were married and the children were theirs.

---

6 About 29,000 Jews were placed in Ghetto No. 1 on September 6, 1941. In the *Aktionen* implemented on September 15 and October 1, 1941, about 4,000 persons were taken out, between 2,000 and 3,000 persons having come from Ghetto No. 2.

The family relatives of the permit-holder were listed on the reverse side of the document.[7]

Two classes of people were thus created in the ghetto—those who had permits and thus a feeling of security for a certain period, and a second class, lacking such passports to life, who knew they were doomed to immediate expulsion from the ghetto.

Creation of the "Kailis" Labor Camp Outside the Ghetto
In October 1941, the workers at the "Kailis" fur factory were removed from the ghetto and accommodated in two blocks of houses on Szeptycka Street, which had previously housed the "Electrit" factory. The workers and their families totaled 800–1,000. "Kailis" was operated by the supply branch of the German Army, and its products, including fur coats, were destined for the army. The approach of winter, and the urgent needs of the army for warm apparel, had placed the factory and its production personnel in the "highly essential" category, and they were among the first to receive yellow passes.

The initiative to operate "Kailis" on a large scale and render it an essential adjunct of the German military, by virtue of its Jewish hands, came from a Jew, Oscar Glick. He had been educated in Vienna and arrived in Vilna as a refugee. When the Germans occupied Vilna, Glick met a German soldier, a friend of his during their younger days in the Austrian capital, who arranged for him to be employed at "Kailis." Glick secured forged papers for himself as a German from Vienna and posed as a *Volksdeutsche*. During the course of the anti-Jewish *Aktionen*, the "Kailis" plant faced closure due to the disappearance of its Jewish personnel. Glick suggested to German Army Major Gauzler, who was in charge of military supplies for the entire district, that he take over the "Kailis" factory for the German Army and that it be moved to the larger premises of the former

7 Dworzecki, *op. cit.*, pp. 61, 82, 85; Balberyszski, *op. cit.*, pp. 266–268; Epstein's diary, p. 22.

"Electrit" plant. He proposed to accommodate the workers and their families in a special wing of the plant. The German officer accepted the plan, and Glick was made manager of the factory. A fire broke out at the factory in January 1942, and during the Security Police inquiries it became known that Glick was Jewish. He and his wife were arrested and shot in February 1942. The German Security Police report stated: "During the investigation into the circumstances of the fire at 'Kailis'... it was established that the manager of the plant, who posed as a *Volksdeutsche*, was a *Volljude* ('full Jew')."[8]

First "Yellow-Pass" Aktion—October 24, 1941
The distribution of the yellow passes was completed on October 23, and the previous ones were invalidated. During the evening of October 23, the ghetto police announced that all holders of the yellow passes and their families must present themselves that night at the police-stations in the ghetto in order to register and receive blue slips for their families. A feeling that this was the eve of an *Aktion* pervaded the ghetto. Long lines of people, running into the thousands, formed outside the police stations. Holders of the yellow passes received numbered blue cardboard slips. The numbers were then copied on to the backs of the passes themselves.

After midnight on October 23/24, the ghetto was cordoned off by heavy detachments of German troops and Lithuanian auxiliaries. The inmates passed a sleepless night. Compared with the "fortunate" ones—those who had the yellow permits and their families—the thousands who were not so favored were indeed in a grievous position; they knew that within a few hours they were to be the targets of an *Aktion.* Korczak writes :

> Thousands are now dashing about in the streets frantically not knowing what to do, where to hide, how to save themselves... Women drag weeping children by the hand...

8 Kruk, *op. cit.,* pp. 152, 156; *Meldungen aus den Besetzten Ostgebieten,* YVA, 0–51/33, p. 6.

> Men run from place to place, to relatives, to friends, to
> the Judenrat ... any place where there is some hope of
> being added to a *"shain."*[9]

These thousands of luckless people were not expecting a
miracle. They went into hiding-places prepared during the preceding weeks. Others tried to escape the ghetto and sought
refuge outside. The Lithuanians fired at the running fugitives.
Many were killed, but some succeeded in escaping. There were
also cases in which the sentries allowed the fleeing Jews to
escape through the fences against payment of bribes.

Towards the early morning hours of October 24, the ghetto
police announced that all yellow-pass holders working outside
the ghetto should be gathered at the gate, together with their
families, by 6 o'clock. The announcement added that family
members would accompany the workers to their places of employment outside the ghetto that day. Judenrat employees having
yellow passes, and their relatives, were told to gather in the
theater hall in the yard of the Judenrat building by 6 A.M.

As the licensed workers and their families left the ghetto, the
documents were checked and the ages verified. The check was
superintended by Weiss of the SD and Security Police and
Murer, the *Gebietskommissar's* adjutant, who was in charge of
the ghetto. Family members who, in their opinion, were of different ages or family status than those registered on the passes
were pulled out of the lines and taken to a building near the
ghetto gate. From there they were sent to Lukiszki. All the
others went to their places of employment accompanied by
their families.

Judenrat employees with passes, their families, and many Jews
who had no passes assembled in the Judenrat courtyard. At the
entrance to the theater hall there was a document check. Jewish

9 Korczak, *op. cit.,* p. 39, writes that the Jewish Police and Gestapo workers could have more than three relatives on their yellow
passes; Rudashevski, *op. cit.,* pp. 22–23, 25; I. Kowalski, *A Secret
Press in Nazi Europe,* New York, 1969, p. 62.

police also permitted members of their own families who had no blue cards to enter the hall. In spite of the strict control at the entrance to the hall, people without yellow passes managed to infiltrate. About thirty people succeeded in hiding under the stage in the hall until the completion of the *Aktion*.

German and Lithuanian squads entered the ghetto and began searching for people without passes. The streets of the ghetto were empty, and no one left his house willingly. People clustered in *malines*, in basements, attics, or any place that offered a safe refuge. Parties of Lithuanians went from house to house, searching. Many *malines* were revealed and their occupants removed. One of these contained 300 people. In some of the *malines* people resisted or refused to leave, and they were shot dead on the spot.[10]

Other *malines* went undiscovered, but the people crowding into them experienced many hours of fear. One of these experiences was recounted by the boy Rudashevski, who survived the *Aktion*:

> ...A noise is heard...shots...I feel that the storm is approaching...We are like beasts surrounded by hunters...Locks are smashed, knocking, doors creak, hatchets, hacking...breaking in, tearing up...Suddenly a child breaks into tears...A despairing sigh goes up. We are lost. Sugar is desperately thrust into the child's mouth, but it doesn't help. He is covered with pillows. The child's mother weeps. People cry out in wild fright: "Choke the child." The child's wailing rises. The Lithuanians hit harder on the walls, but gradually everything dies down of itself and we understand that they have gone away.[11]

The captives were assembled on Rudnicka Street near the ghetto gate and then led outside. People were told they were

10 Dworzecki, *op. cit.*, pp. 61, 84–86; Epstein's diary, pp. 22–23; Rolnik, *op. cit.*, pp. 44–45.
11 Rudashevski, *op. cit.*, pp. 38–39.

being taken to places where permanent work awaited them. The *Aktion* continued into the afternoon hours. At almost 5 P.M., the yellow-pass holders in the Judenrat courtyard were allowed to go home.

The workmen who had gone out in the morning with their families now began to return to the ghetto. People who survived the raid came out of hiding during the night of the 23/24. The sight that met their eyes was one of devastation: doors and walls broken and smashed, belongings scattered on the floors of apartments and in the yards, and the bundles of the people taken captive strewn in the streets.

None of those taken in this action were released from Lukiszki, and all were taken to Ponar to be shot.[12] The report of Einsatzkommando 3 stated that 1,766 women and 812 children were killed on October 25, making a total of 2,578, while two days later 946 males, 184 females, and 73 children met their deaths, totaling 1,203. This report therefore revealed that 3,781 persons perished in the *Aktion*.[13]

The Aktion *of October 29, 1941*
Several days after the October 24 *Aktion*, the ghetto police, acting on the instructions of the German administration, announced that Ghetto No. 2 would continue to function, and that all those who had no yellow passes from Ghetto No. 1 were to report there, adding that their "legal" existence would thus be ensured. Hundreds of people without passes who had hidden out in the *malines* during the *Aktion* believed in these assurances and went to Ghetto No. 2. Among them were people who had already run away from that ghetto and taken refuge in Ghetto No. 1. After a few days they were rounded up and marched to prison, from where they traveled the death route to Ponar.[14]

12 Epstein's diary, pp. 23–24; Rudashevski, *op. cit.,* pp. 39–40; Rolnik, *op. cit.,* p. 46; Kruk, *op. cit.,* p. 260.
13 Jäger Report, p. 5.
14 Balberyszski, *op. cit.,* pp. 248, 278–279; Epstein's diary, p. 31; S. Kaczerginski, *Hurbn Vilne,* New York, 1947, p. 64.

The second liquidation of Ghetto No. 2 took place on October 29, when the people were removed to Lukiszki. It is reasonable to assume that this was the basis for the information in Kruk and other Jewish sources that Ghetto No. 2 was liquidated on the 29th of that month, and not the 21st. The report of E.K.3 stated that 382 men, 789 women, and 362 children, a total of 1,533 Jews, were slain on October 30.[15] These were the people taken from Ghetto No. 2 the previous day.

Second "Yellow-Pass" Aktion—November 3–5, 1941
It had become evident to the German administration that a one-day *Aktion*, as that of October 24, was insufficient for thorough searches in the ghetto to locate all the "illegals." Even after the German authorities had succeeded, deceptively, to induce people to voluntarily leave Ghetto No. 1 for Ghetto No. 2, and put them to death on October 30, there were still many survivors without valid permits.

Reports of Jews who had fled the ghetto during the October 24 *Aktion* and had gone into hiding reached the Germans. On October 29 the *Gebietskommissar* issued a directive, signed by Murer, relating to Jews hidden on the Aryan side. The populace was ordered to report Jews and half-Jews living outside the ghetto and was informed that if a Jew was found hiding in a house outside the ghetto after October 30, the homeowner would face severe penalties.[16]

On Monday, November 3, the German administration put up a notice in the ghetto that all holders of yellow passes and their families who held blue cards were to move to Ghetto No. 2 for three days. They were to gather at the ghetto gate and organize into family groups in accordance with their places of employment. They were permitted to take food and other items with them.[17]

15 Jäger Report, p. 5.
16 *Naujoji Lietuva*, October 29, 1941, in Moreshet Archives, D.1.362.
17 Balberyszski, *op. cit.*, p. 284; Epstein's diary, p. 31; Korczak, *op. cit.*, p. 43.

The personnel of Judenrat institutions gathered in the courtyard of their premises, where a check of passes was held at the
entrance to a small garden in the center. Jacob Gens and the
Jewish police carried out the check under the eyes of the German officials.

Dworzecki writes of a family with three children—two
passed the check, but the third, a boy aged twelve, did not.
Several minutes after this incident, a family with only one
child moved along to be checked. Gens began yelling at the
father, reproaching him for not looking after his children, for
here was the child he had "mislaid." He then pushed forward
the boy of twelve to become part of this family. All this transpired under the scrutiny of the German officials, who evidently
had no idea of what was going on.

Another verification of pass-holders and families took place
at the ghetto gate. It was a strict one, and the Germans removed those whom they felt to be incompatible with the particulars on the permits in regard to age and family status: these
were sent on the familiar route to Lukiszki and Ponar. Balberyszski records that Gens and his police took part in this
check and did all they could to save people.[18] Then the people
from No. 1 who had been checked went over to Ghetto No. 2.

Employees of German factories and units went to work as on
any day and returned to Ghetto No. 2 in the evening. The
appearance of Ghetto No. 2 resembled "filthy alleys filled with
furniture randomly strewn about; demolished houses completed
the nightmare. Many houses had contained *malines* and these
were piled with corpses which were beginning to decay..." In
some other *malines* there were many dozens of people who had
concealed themselves at the time of the liquidation. These fugitives, upon hearing Yiddish, left their hiding places and joined
those who had been brought over from Ghetto No. 1.[19]

18 Dworzecki, *op. cit.*, pp. 88–91; Rudashevski, *op. cit.*, p. 45; Balberyszski, *op. cit.*, pp. 284–285.
19 Dworzecki, *op. cit.*, pp. 93–96; Rudashevski, *op. cit.*, pp. 45–46.

In Ghetto No. 1, house-to-house searches continued all through Monday, Tuesday, and Wednesday, November 3–5. Parties of Lithuanians thoroughly combed the entire ghetto, looking for Jews in hiding. Those without passes, who had remained behind, camouflaged their hideouts and improved upon them. Some, however, were uncovered. At times it was a child's crying which led to discovery. Korczak writes that in a certain *maline,* a young mother choked her infant who had burst out crying when the footsteps of approaching Lithuanians were heard. Balberyszski tells of an old woman in his hideout who had an attack of nerves and began to talk out loud and make noise, until some people cried: "Suffocate the witch, otherwise we'll all go to Ponar." The stuffy atmosphere in these places, crammed with dozens of people, made it necessary to open air vents for several minutes, and it was often at such times that the *malines* were spotted and the occupants taken to Lukiszki.[20]

Some of the people captured or discovered in their hideouts in the course of the *Aktion* were immediately shot, apparently for failing to obey orders. Groups of Lithuanians returned to the same houses several times, not content with one-time searches.

On Wednesday, November 5, 1941, the pass-holders in Ghetto 2 were informed that the *Aktion* was over and they could return to their residences in Ghetto No. 1. The Germans held no inspection during the return, neither at the exit from Ghetto No. 2 nor at the entry to No. 1. Those returning to No. 1 were accompanied by people from Ghetto No. 2 who had hidden there during the liquidation process.

In Ghetto No. 1 many *malines* were found gaping and smashed, their occupants having been taken to prison and Ponar. Those who managed to evade detection emerged tired and broken, frightened and tense after their three-day ordeal.[21]

20 Korczak, *op. cit.,* p. 46; Rolnik, *op. cit.,* p. 48; Balberyszski, *op. cit.,* pp. 283–285.
21 Epstein's diary, p. 32; Korczak, *op. cit.,* pp. 40–41.

The summation report of E.K.3 on December 1, 1941, stated that 340 males, 789 women, and 362 children, a total of 1,341, were killed in Vilna on November 6. The same report specified that on November 19, 76 males, 77 females, and 18 children, a total of 171, were killed there. It seems that those murdered on November 19 either had been taken during the November 3–5 raids or had been caught hiding outside the ghetto after fleeing the November 3–5 *Aktion*. The Vilna press during that time carried reports of Jews caught hiding with non-Jews.

After the *Aktion* during the first week of November, 12,000 Jews, "legitimized" by yellow passes, remained in Vilna. Thousands of "illegals" had been in the ghetto during the *Aktion*. The majority of these, who had no papers, managed to elude their would-be captors and survive because of the *malines*, although the operation took longer and was more thorough than expected.

Dworzecki writes that a group of rabbis turned to Gens after the "Yellow-Pass" *Aktionen* and told them that he had no right to select Jews and hand them over to the Germans, to which Gens replied that by surrendering the few, he was rescuing the others from extinction. The rabbis responded that Maimonides had ruled, "Better all be killed than one soul of Israel be surrendered."[22]

The Germans adopted a new tactic in the "Yellow-Pass" *Aktionen*, based on the lessons they had learned in the Yom Kippur operation, when their attempt to remove non-legitimized residents from the ghetto failed. At that time they had seized and killed 2,200 artisans and other workmen armed with passes, which aroused protests from the German employers. So the initiators of the liquidation program devised a new method based on the following stages:

(1) Segregation of the two groups of ghetto dwellers, those who had yellow passes, and whose extermination was therefore deferred, and those who had no passes.

22 Dworzecki, pp. 282–283.

(2) Removal of the pass-holders and their families from the ghetto, as it was clear that non-holders would disobey orders and it would be difficult to delude or coerce them.

(3) Combing of the area by Lithuanian units who had complete freedom of action, as it was evident that any person they came upon was necessarily there illegitimately.

The full significance of the use of two separate ghettos became clear after the second "Yellow-Pass" *Aktion*. The creation of these two sectors, without any physical connection or visual link-up, was part of the total extermination program and its methodical implementation. City transportation requirements played no part in a decision that Niemiecka Street was out of the ghetto bounds, as the problem could have been solved by diverting traffic into other streets, or by linking the two ghettos by an overhead footway and permitting traffic to pass freely underneath. The creation of two separate ghettos in this case simply allowed the Germans greater flexibility in their methods of extermination and tactics of deceit and distraction. During the extermination operations, from September to November, two ghettos were also set up in Kovno and Shavli and were utilized by the Germans in the same way.[23]

Ghetto No. 2 was used as an assembly place or to beguile the Jews during the German death-swoops from September to November. On December 1, 1941, the entire area of Ghetto No. 2 was transferred by Murer to the Municipality of Vilna in order to prepare it for habitation by non-Jews.[24]

The "Selective" and "Pink-Pass" Aktionen *of November 6– December 21, 1941*

No further *Aktionen* took place during November. Following the forcible removal of many thousands in the two "Yellow-Pass" operations, there was an increase of dwelling-places in the ghetto. They were reorganized according to the location of the fac-

23 Kruk, *op. cit.*, p. 260; Jäger Report, p. 6; *Naujoji Lietuva*, November 20, 1941, in Moreshet Archives, D.1.362.
24 Garfunkel, *op. cit.*, pp. 70–76; Yerushalmi, *op. cit.*, pp. 44, 50.

tories and units in which the workmen were employed. The employees of these German establishments were grouped in houses of neighborhoods known as *Blocks*.

The initiative and demand to institute this arrangement came from the German establishments themselves. The first *Blocks* were for artisans and service personnel employed by the Security Police and SD in Vilna. These people were known in the ghetto as "the Gestapo workmen," and they were regarded as an elite and were protected during *Aktionen*. Their superiors requested that the Judenrat allocate two *Blocks* in the ghetto to them, and the Judenrat complied. Germans managing various factories and units requested the Judenrat to provide their workmen with special housing in the ghetto, probably in the wake of the latter's urgings. The workmen believed that this segregation in separate *Blocks* would endow them with greater security in any future *Aktion*. Also contributing to this hopefulness was the removal of the workmen of the "Kailis" fur factory from the ghetto during October and their accommodation in special *Blocks*. These people remained untouched during the "Yellow-Pass" operations.

The Judenrat fulfilled the requests, and separate *Blocks* were established in the ghetto for the Jewish workmen of the *Beutelager* ("captured arms' warehouses"), *Sanitat-Depot* (military hospital store), and others. These *Blocks*, set up on a particularist basis, according to places of employment, evoked resentment among other ghetto residents, who regarded this as the creation of an elitist class for purposes of protection and personal safety to the detriment of the rest of the ghetto population, especially the thousands who still remained without legal permits. The heads of the labor groups in the ghetto, the "brigadiers," argued, on the other hand, that this centralization of dwellings according to places of employment ensured greater control of their personnel and mobility in getting to work.[25]

25 *Masines zudynes Lietuvoje (1941–1945)*, Vol. I, Vilna, 1965, p. 161 (hereafter: *Masines*).

Murder of Vilna Jews in Voronovo

Many Vilna Jews fled to Belorussia when the mass *Aktion* started. No mass executions of Jews took place in the regions of Belorussia close to Vilna during the second half of 1941. By the beginning of November 1941, over 300 Jews had arrived from Vilna to the township of Voronovo, some 45 miles south of Vilna. A notice was published in the township, at the beginning of November, that all Jewish refugees were obliged to register with the local municipality within ten days.

Over 250 Vilna Jews were detained by the Belorussian police in mid-November. Some days later, Lithuanians, brought in specially for the purpose, shot them outside the railroad station. Jewish residents of Voronovo were brought to the firing-area and forced to bury the victims. Jewish sources affirm that 265 persons were thus murdered. The E.K.3 report of December 1, 1941, stated that 171 Jews were killed in Vilna on November 19, but the allusion was apparently to the Vilna Jews of Voronovo.[26]

Aktion *against the "Underworld"*

During the night of December 3, 1941, a group of Germans and Lithuanians entered the ghetto and, on the basis of a prepared list, removed sixty-seven persons with criminal pasts (who were dubbed in the ghetto *di untervelt* ["the underworld"]). On the following night, another ninety persons with criminal pasts were dragged out of the ghetto in the same fashion. Jewish policemen accompanied the Lithuanian squads. Several of the arrested men managed to escape on the way to Ponar and make their way back into the ghetto after overcoming their Lithuanian escorts. Differing opinions were held in the ghetto with regard to the removal of these "underworld characters." Some held that it had been done at the request of the Judenrat, which deemed these men to be a risk to the ghetto; others claimed

26 Kaczerginski, *op. cit.*, pp. 67–68; Kowalski, *op. cit.*, pp. 63–64; Engelshtern, *op. cit.*, pp. 25, 27; Jäger Report, p. 6.

that the Germans had insisted on having more Jews for extermination, and it was Gens who decided to hand over these
undesirables.[27]

The fact that these people had been seized from their homes
according to a list prepared in advance strengthens the assumption that the Judenrat did have a hand in this action.

Aktion *against Gestapo Employees*

Jewish employees of the Gestapo and their families dwelt in two
Blocks in Straszuna Street. On their yellow passes they were
allowed to include not only a wife and two children under sixteen, but also parents, brothers, and sisters.

A few minutes before midnight on December 15, a small
group of Germans and Lithuanians entered the ghetto, went to
the *Blocks* where the Gestapo employees lived, and requested
that they and their families leave the ghetto. These people believed that another *Aktion* was imminent, and that "their" Germans had come to save them, as had been the case in previous
"yellow-pass" operations. Several families who lived in the same
Blocks, but were not Gestapo employees, joined the others of
their own free will. The evacuation was accomplished quietly
and in an orderly fashion, with only a small police escort, as
the people involved believed they were being taken to a safe
place. They were, however, removed to Lukiszki.

Upon arrival at the prison, the Gestapo employees were told
that most of them had been dismissed from their work, and
only a small number had been retained and were now to be
released. The released persons were permitted to take their
wives and children—only those under sixteen—as was the
rule with all yellow-pass holders. Some 300 persons were executed in this *Aktion,* and 200 returned to the ghetto. The entire
undertaking came as a severe shock to the ghetto, as the workers concerned were considered to be the safest group. What this

27 Kruk, *op. cit.,* p. 260; Rann, *op. cit.,* pp. 140–141; Rolnik, *op. cit.,*
    p. 57.

operation proved was that possession of a yellow pass did not imply complete immunity.[28]

The Security Police and SD post command in Vilna evidently decided that they did not need all the Jewish employees and their families. It may also be that they wanted to set an example for other German establishments that employed Jewish workers, to demonstrate that it was possible to dispense with Jewish workers. The *Aktion* might also have been an outcome of the discussion among the various German authorities over the issue of suspending the extermination of Jewish skilled labor.

The German administration had once more succeeded in decoying hundreds of Jews to their deaths.

The Pink Passes

After the second "Yellow-Pass" *Aktion*, thousands of Jews not in possession of these certificates—"illegal" from the standpoint of the German authorities—remained in the ghetto. The German estimate was that 15,000 people, of whom about 3,000 were illegal, lived in the ghetto.[29] The number of the non-legitimized residents was, however, much higher.

Rumors of an imminent new *Aktion* circulated in the ghetto in mid-December and caused great alarm. The rumors had arisen over the issuance of new passes, this time pink. These were at first allocated to relatives of yellow-pass holders, i.e., those who previously had held blue cards. The new passes were called *Familienmitglied-Ausweise*. The pink permits were issued by the ghetto police and were valid only inside the ghetto. Their distribution began in the early days of December 1941.

The ghetto police announced that artisans who lacked the yellow passes had to register together with their families at the Judenrat for pink passes, and they would thus be legalized. The new passes were also issued to former public figures, rabbis,

28 *Ibid.*, p. 52; Kruk, *op. cit.*, p. 262; Korczak, *op. cit.*, p. 66; Balberyszski, *op. cit.*, p. 293.
29 Jäger Report, p. 7, states that there were 15,000 Jews in the Vilna Ghetto.

and members of the liberal professions. The distribution was based on previously composed lists of names and vocations. The response was not great at first, as some of the people without passes did not register out of fear that the pink passes were another German trap to ferret out the "illegals" in the ghetto. Nevertheless, within several days all those who could receive pink passes did register. Some, however, gave false names and addresses as a safeguard.

On December 19, information was received that the distribution of pink passes was due to end the following morning. The Judenrat apparently had prior knowledge of the deadline. Chairman Fried sent a circular to all heads of departments and units on December 17 to the effect that within three days (viz., before December 20) a list of all Judenrat employees holding pink passes must be in the hands of the General Department. The distribution of the permits in the Judenrat offices went on through the night of December 19/20. Still there remained thousands of people in the ghetto without any passes at all.

On the morning of December 20, parties of Germans and Lithuanians entered the ghetto, searching for people with neither yellow nor pink passes. The house-to-house verification lasted three days, until December 22. The workmen in the ghetto were ordered to report to their places of employment as usual. Many of those holding yellow permits were afraid to leave without their families; they anticipated an *Aktion*. The Jewish police promised that no harm would come to families with passes and, at the same time, warned that anyone not going to work would have his permit revoked. The combined promise and threat had its effect, and the workmen left. People without passes at all and those with pink ones who did not believe the Germans went into hiding in *malines*. About 400 of those without passes were caught in their hiding-places, removed from the ghetto, loaded on trucks, and driven off to Ponar. This *Aktion* became known in the ghetto as the "Pink-Pass *Aktion*." [30]

30 Balberyszski, *op. cit.*, pp. 294–296; Rolnik, *op. cit.*, pp. 52–54;

During the course of the operation on December 22, the Lithuanians discovered a *maline* at 13 Spitalna Street and ordered those inside to come out. They refused, and when the Lithuanians entered, they were assaulted by several of the men in hiding. They were led by Haus and Goldstein, who were both shot during the struggle in the hideout. Illegal notices were posted in the ghetto calling on the public to attend the funerals. This act of resistance had wide repercussions inside the ghetto.[31]

The "Pink-Pass" *Aktion* was the last in the series of mass exterminations of Vilna Jewry, which had begun with the occupation of the city by the German armed forces and ended during the last days of 1941. A long period of relative tranquillity followed this operation.

Epstein's diary, pp. 32–33; Kruk, *op. cit.*, pp. 93, 133, 257, 260; Einsatzgruppen Report (No. 154) of January 12, 1942, YVA, 0–51/ 59–2, records the number of Jews murdered in Vilna on December 22, 1941, as 385.
31 Kruk, *op. cit.*, pp. 93, 122–123; Dworzecki, *op. cit.*, p. 109; Epstein's diary, p. 33.

Chapter 10

SUSPENSION OF THE MASSACRES

The objective of the German anti-Jewish policy in the Eastern Territories was the extermination of the Jewish population there. The first section of Heinrich Lohse's "Provisional Directives" of August 18, 1941, mentions the verbal instructions he issued, as *Reichskommissar* of the *Ostland,* in connection with the "Final Solution to the Jewish Problem." All other anti-Jewish measures adopted, among them the creation of ghettos, forced labor, restrictions and humiliations of various kinds, were of a provisional nature, until the completion of the extermination process.

The enactment of the "Final Solution to the Jewish Problem" had been assigned to the Security Police and SD. This policy was fully implemented during the early months of civil government. All the Jews living in smaller towns and villages were wiped out without any distinction as to age, sex, occupation, or fitness for work; in other regions, with large Jewish populations, the extermination was conducted in stages.

The mass murders in Vilna ended after the second "Yellow-Pass" *Aktion* on November 3–5, 1941. Three more smaller *Aktionen* took place there in December, but they marked the culmination of the massacres until their resumption in mid-1943. In Kovno, the last mass *Aktion* took place on October 28–29; in Shavli in the early days of September; and in Swieciany on October 7–8.

The cessation of the murder campaign against the Jewish

[164]

population of Lithuania, in December 1941, and the continued existence of the ghettos were the outcome of a struggle within the German administration as to whether all Lithuanian Jewry should be wiped out, or that segment which was employed in German industrial plants and army installations be left alone. Three German authorities operating in the *Ostland* participated in the controversy: the civil administration, the SS, and the Wehrmacht. This conflict was waged at the lower level of the *Gebietskommissariat,* as well as on the level of the *Generalkommissariat* and *Reichskommissariat,* and extended even to the highest echelons in Berlin; it waged on through September and October. The controversy originated in the Wehrmacht's need for supplies and maintenance work and the situation that had been created in Lithuania and other regions of the Eastern Territories as a result of mass killings and the consequent reduction in Jewish skilled workers.

The first intercession by members of the civilian government in the murder campaign by Einsatzkommando 3 in Lithuania apparently took place in Shavli. The mobile detachment of E. K.3, commanded by *Obersturmführer* Hamann, arrived in that city in the beginning of September in order to exterminate all the Jews there. Gewecke, the *Gebietskommissar* of Shavli, forbade and deterred the E.K.3 unit from implementing the operation on the grounds that these Jews were engaged in important economic undertakings and their elimination would bring those activities to a complete halt. Hamann, through his superior officer Jäger, lodged complaints with the *Generalkommissar* of Lithuania against these acts by Gewecke, and Von Renteln asked Gewecke for a report on the incident. This account, furnished on September 10, stated:

> ...When all the deportation *Aktionen* have been completed, 4,000 Jews, including members of their families, who are needed as skilled workers, will remain in the Schaulen (Shavli) region...It is impossible to carry on work without Jews. This is especially the case in the

[165]

leather-tanning industry. Every single artisan in this industry is Jewish ... On the basis of the conversation I
had with you, and in light of this report, you may be
convinced that we have acted in the Jewish question in
the Schaulen region with the necessary intensiveness and
with National-Socialist stubbornness.

Gewecke, evidently ceasing to rely on Von Renteln to back
him up in the tussle with the Security Police, then communicated
directly with *Reichskommissar* Lohse in writing, to whom he
complained of Jäger's *Aktionen* and requested Lohse's intervention.[1]

The official who headed the German *Arbeitsamt* in the *Generalkommissariat* for Lithuania, Peschel, urged Von Renteln not
to murder the Jews who were still alive, as they were a source
of manpower. This apparently took place in September or the
beginning of October. Concurrently, Peschel contacted Wehrmacht headquarters in Kovno on the matter. Kramer, *Gebietskommissar* of Kovno, was in favor of preserving the Jewish
artisans. A conference was called there at the beginning of
October and was attended by *Generalkommissar* Von Renteln;
the Chief of Security Police and the SD, Jäger; *Gebietskommissar* Kramer; Peschel; P. Kubiliunas, the *Generalrat* (Chief Ad-
visor) in Lithuania, himself a Lithuanian; and a number of
others of lower rank. It was decided to urge the *Reichskommissariat* in Riga to stop the liquidation of Jewish artisans and
their families. Peschel personally traveled to Riga to intervene there and to obtain immunity for the Jews still residing
in the ghettos of Lithuania.[2]

Applications to Lohse to suspend the murder of Jews also
came from other areas in the *Ostland*. The *Gebietskommissar*

1 YVA, 0–18/139; 0–18/142; 0–18/144.
2 Evidence by G. Hermann given before the Historical Commission
at Landsberg, September 2, 1946, YVA, M–1/E–6, pp. 3–4. Murer,
p. 5, states that Lohse and Gewecke acted for the retention of
Jewish skilled workmen.

of Libau (Liepaja) in Latvia, wrote, on October 11, to the *Generalkommissar* of Latvia, Drechsler: "The liquidation of the Jews which was resumed last week is arousing resentment... especially the shooting of women and children, which stirred up general opposition... Even the officers ask me whether it was necessary to liquidate the children..."[3]

This report appeared to have been passed on by Drechsler to Lohse, who thereupon forbade further murders in Libau. The Security Police and SD headquarters opposed the ban and protested to the *Reichsminister* for the Eastern Territories in Berlin. On October 31 the *Reichsministerium* sent a memorandum, signed by Dr. Leibbrand, head of the Political Department, stating that the Chief Office for Reich Security had received a complaint that the *Reichskommissar* for the *Ostland* had forbidden further *Aktionen* against Jews in Libau. Leibbrand demanded a report on the affair. The request was received in Riga on November 5, and to it Lohse replied:

> I have forbidden the wild executions of Jews in Liepaja because the manner in which they were carried out was not justifiable.
>
> I should like to be informed whether your inquiry of October 31 is to be regarded as a directive to liquidate all Jews in the East? Shall this take place without regard as to age and sex and economic interests (of the Wehrmacht, for instance, in the case of specialists in the armament industry)?
>
> Of course, the cleansing of the East of Jews is a necessary task; its implementation, however, must be coordinated with the necessities of war production.
>
> So far I have been unable to find such a directive either in the regulations regarding the Jewish question in the "Brown File," or in other decrees.[4]

3 *My Obvinyaem,* pp. 182–183.
4 YVA, 0–18/156.

The reply from Berlin dated December 18, 1941, reads as follows:

> Clarification of the Jewish question should be achieved through verbal discussions. Economic considerations should basically not be considered in the settlement of the problem. Moreover, it is requested that questions arising be settled directly with the Senior SS and Police leader.[5]

Two criteria were laid down in this reply to Lohse: first, that economic interests should not be the determining factor in the postponement of the extermination of Jewish workmen; secondly, that the authority to decide on total annihilation or the continued existence of a sector of the Jewish community had to be in agreement with the local SS command.

Before this reply arrived from Berlin, however, a decision had been taken in the *Ostland* in favor of leaving a segment of the Jewish population alive. The intervention of the Wehrmacht Quartermaster-General's branch against the execution of its Jewish employees prevailed.

Trampedach, head of the Political Department in the *Reichskommissariat* in Riga (Dept. IIa), who had charge of Jewish affairs, noted in his records:

> On November 7, 1941, Mey, an officer in the Quartermaster-General's Command in the *Ostland,* appeared before me and swore that Jewish artisans employed in workshops and other armament factories of the Wehrmacht were being liquidated in Vilna, and that it was impossible to replace them by local workers. In these factories vehicles of combat units are repaired.

On that same day, November 7, 1941, Trampedach telegraphed the *Gebietskommissar* of Vilna—with copies to the General Officer commanding the Wehrmacht in the *Ostland,* to the senior SS and police commanders, and to the *Generalkom-*

5 YVA, 0–4/53–1, 180; Nuremberg Document, PS–3666.

missar of Lithuania—to the following effect: "I hereby request you to prevent by all possible means, depriving the Wehrmacht of Jewish manpower which is irreplaceable for tasks of war economy."[6]

It would appear that the Wehrmacht's entry into this contentious issue was prompted by the Yom Kippur *Aktion*, during which almost 2,200 Jews were put to death, most of them skilled workmen and their dependents who had been employed in army units and repair shops.

Trampedach's message arrived in Vilna two days after the second "Yellow-Pass" *Aktion* on November 3–5. It was the last of the large-scale operations there. Those implemented in December, after receipt of Trampedach's insistent message, were of a selective and limited character.

Pursuant to these requests by the Wehrmacht and others, Trampedach prepared a general memorandum prohibiting the killing of Jews working for Wehrmacht plants and other facilities essential to the war effort. A draft of the instructions was circulated on November 12 for comment by various members of the *Reichskommissariat*. After comment and discussion at this level, the following "Order" was promulgated:

> The Chief Quartermaster (*Chefintendant*) of the Wehrmacht Command for the *Ostland* complains that, in the course of the process of liquidation, Jewish skilled workers in armament factories and workshops, who cannot be replaced at present, are being taken away from the Wehrmacht.
>
> I unequivocally demand that the liquidation of Jews employed as skilled workers in the armament factories and workshops of the Wehrmacht be stopped, as there is no possibility of replacing them by other local workers at the present time. It should be determined with the *Gebietskommissare* (Department for Social Administration) which Jewish workers cannot be replaced by others.

6 YVA, 0–18/157.

Arrangements should be made to train local workers as replacements as quickly as possible.

This Order also refers to Jewish skilled workers in factories which do not serve the Wehrmacht directly, but perform important tasks for the war economy.

(Illegible signature)[7]

It was this order that put an end to the massacres that had begun with the German invasion of Lithuania. The net result was that three large ghettos remained in Vilna, Kovno, and Shavli, and a small one at Swieciany, in eastern Lithuania. The last sentence in the order left it to the *Gebietskommissar* to permit not only Jews in Wehrmacht employ to remain alive in the ghettos, but all Jewish workmen. The *Gebietskommissar* asserted this prerogative to sanction the survival of Jews who worked in factories other than those under Wehrmacht control. The Security Police and SD, which were assigned the task of wiping out Jews, were forced to submit to the "Order."

In his summation of December 1, 1941, of E.K.3 operations in Lithuania, *Standartenführer* Jäger, Commanding Officer of E.K.3 and head of the Security Police and SD in Lithuania stated:

> I can state today that the goal of the solution of the Jewish problem in Lithuania has been reached by Einsatzkommando 3. There are no longer any Jews in Lithuania except the working Jews and their families which total
>
> in Schaulen some 4,500
> in Kauen some 15,000
> in Vilna some 15,000
>
> I intended to kill off these working Jews and their families, too, but met with the strongest protest from the civil administration (*Reichskommissar*) and from the Wehrmacht, and I received an order prohibiting murdering these Jews and their families.

7 YVA, 0–18/203; Nuremberg Document, PS–3664.

I consider the bulk of the *Aktionen* against the Jews to be finished as far as E.K.3 is concerned. The working Jews and Jewesses left alive for the time being are badly needed, and I presume that even when winter is over this Jewish labor force will still be badly needed ... [8]

The summary by Einsatzgruppe A, operating in the *Ostland,* which was published apparently in December, stated that:

The goal of the systematic cleansing operation in the *Ostland* was a complete purge of the Jews, in accordance with the basic "Order." This objective was achieved in the main ... the remnants surviving in the Baltic lands are needed to fulfill urgent work requirements ... [9]

The suspension of the massacres towards the end of December 1941 was the outcome of the conflict of interest among the different German authorities. It continued during a period in which the demand for manpower in the German war effort was on the increase. The Wehrmacht was the main factor in the decision to halt the *Aktionen* and leave the remnant of the Jews of Vilna alive. The *Reichskommissar* for the *Ostland,* Lohse, made the decision to stop the extermination of Jews upon receiving urgent requests from the Wehrmacht and various branches of the civil administration. The letter from the ministry in Berlin, which reached him on December 18, 1941, did not change the substance of the order promulgated at the beginning of December, which suspended the slaughter of skilled Jewish workers. The Jews of Lithuania, including those in Vilna, were granted a bit more time.

8 The Sweciany ghetto is not mentioned in this report, probably because it was very small, or was left untouched by the German officials on the spot without Jäger's knowledge.

9 Nuremberg Document, PS–2273.

Chapter 11

JEWISH REACTION TO THE MASS *AKTIONEN*
(July–December 1941)

Knowledge of the Mass Murders at Ponar

The annihilation of European Jewry began with the German invasion of the U.S.S.R. Lithuania was subdued during the first few days of the war, and Lithuanian Jewry was the first to be subjected to massacre. The process of mass extermination was rendered immediately possible by the fact that Einsatzkommandos 2, 3 and 9, which operated in Lithuania and combined a force of several hundred soldiers, were joined by tens of thousands of Lithuanians, ready to implement the massacres. The latter had launched the mass murder of Jews even before the E.K. formations began to operate in the early days of July 1941.[1]

Since they were the first to be annihilated, the Jews of Lithuania could have no previous knowledge of German intentions. The Jews of Vilna became aware of the murders at Ponar only

1 Jäger writes in his report, p. 7, that: "The goal to clear Lithuania of Jews was rendered feasible because of the formation of a mobile unit under the command of SS *Obersturmführer* Hamann, who adopted my goal without reservation and succeeded in ensuring the cooperation of the Lithuanian 'partisans' and of the civil institutions concerned in this matter." Hamann's detachment numbered eight to ten Germans of EK3 personnel. A Lithuanian battalion commanded by Major Jmpulevicius murdered thousands of Jews in Belorussia (in Slutzk, Borisov, and Minsk) in the fall of 1941.

during the actual course of the annihilation. But information trickled out slowly, and several months passed until the combination of rumor and fact turned to belief and awareness.

Ponar was located in the midst of a non-Jewish populace. The inhabitants witnessed the convoys of Jews being transported daily, throughout July, into the closed area, and saw that none returned. Ponar inhabitants testified that at the beginning of July 1941, they saw groups of hundreds and then thousands going by. They saw them being taken to the closed area of Ponar and then heard the sound of shooting from that same direction.[2]

V. Sakovich, a journalist who lived at Ponar, kept a diary. His entry for July 12 reads:

> Today, everyone is talking of the executions carried out yesterday. It seems that people are being shot. Several hundreds were said to have been shot yesterday, today another 300 or thereabouts were taken there ... a short time later shots were heard, indicating that they too were shot.

The entry for July 27: "... Shootings take place day after day, it is said that about 5,000 have already been shot this month ... "

For August 19: "The same picture day after day. With the first light, large groups of people laden down with valises are led by." Similar commentary, with different details, appears in the entries for September 2, 21, and October 30.[3]

Hermann Kruk notes in his diary that "rumors reached the Judenrat on July 10 that there are shootings at Ponar. But the Judenrat refused to heed the warning because it was idle gossip." Later on, Kruk recorded that "on July 15 people appeared at the Judenrat who repeated in the strictest confidence what was happening at Ponar ... this time too the Juden-

2 YVA, 0–53/31, p. 3.
3 *Gitlerovskaya okupatsiya*, pp. 173–174.

rat did not believe it ... " Kruk also touched on the transport of people in the direction of Ponar on July 30–31.

Rindziunski recorded:

> On July 17 a man living in the vicinity of Ponar came and reported that such shooting and the voices of people being molested are to be heard there daily. But even after that, the Jews refused to believe. It was hard to believe that innocent people were being taken and shot for no reason. Rumors began to circulate that maybe only a few were being shot, those who were guilty of political offences, from the viewpoint of the Hitlerite authorities.[4]

The Jews still believed, in July and August, that the thousands of men abducted had been taken for labor. H. Kruk writes of a demonstration by 400 women in the Judenrat courtyard during August. The women's husbands had been gone for three weeks—presumably working in an unknown place; they demanded their return and that other males be sent by the Judenrat in their stead. On August 30–31, Kruk adds, a non-Jewish railroad worker who arrived in Vilna from the Minsk area brought with him a list of eighty-seven Jews from Vilna who were then working in the Minsk region. A Polish railway worker brought a note to a woman in Vilna from her husband who had been kidnapped and was in the Minsk area, and with whom he said there were thousands of Vilna Jews. Whether or not the appearance of the workman with a list was a fact, and whether or not he had been put up to it by the Germans in order to mislead the Jews, the Jews believed the story.

R. Korzcak writes:

> The Germans have been in Vilna two months and have already been able to send thousands of young able-bodied males away, and people indeed believe the Germans are sending them to *Arbeitslager,* as workers are needed in

4 Rindziunski's testimony, p. 18; see also Kruk, *op. cit.,* pp. 23–24, 27.

the East. This belief is substantiated by reports on transports of men for work from the Greater Reich and the General Government... No one knew in Vilna of the mass murders in Kovno which is so close... they did not know what happened to the Jews in the towns near Vilna... towns which were the scene of the first massacres... so far nothing is known about them. ...[5]

The fragmentary reports on Ponar that reached the Jews in July and August 1941, did not come from people who were present at the scene of the murders, but told about people being driven to a closed area at Ponar and the sounds of shooting from that direction. The first direct reports were given by people apprehended during "the Great Provocation."

On September 3–4, six wounded women escaped to Vilna from the pits at Ponar. They were secretly taken to the Jewish hospital in Zawalna Street, where they received medical attention. The stories they told were identical: they had been taken to Lukiszki and then to Ponar during "the Great Provocation." Upon arrival at Ponar, they were kept in the waiting area for hours, and from there they were led to the pits in groups of ten, blindfolded. The wounded women who came back were all in the last groups, which were taken to the pits toward evening. They had to stand at the edge of the pits before a firing squad and were mowed down with machine-guns. The women fell wounded into the pit. The Lithuanians who fired at them left the area at nightfall, and each, separately, climbed out and escaped. They arrived at nearby farms and were brought by the peasants to Vilna.[6]

The first to hear their stories about Ponar were the doctors at the Jewish hospital. The hospital personnel who listened to their tale kept it secret; they were afraid that if the German authorities learned of the survivors, they would be taken back

5 Korczak, op. cit., pp. 17–18; see also Kruk, op. cit., pp. 31, 41; Lazar, op. cit., pp. 52–53.
6 Kruk, op. cit., pp. 51–54; Kaczerginski, op. cit., pp. 14–15; Dwor-

in order to scotch further circulation of the reports. Kruk, who heard the story, wrote on September 4: "It is impossible to describe the shocking event in writing ... the hand trembles ... were all these taken away really murdered, shot at Ponar?" In a small pocket-diary kept in Vilna, containing only comments, one finds: "September 4 — first greeting from Ponar ... conflicting rumors."[7]

The first Judenrat, which served during July–August and was liquidated on September 2, during "the Great Provocation," had no verifiable news of what was transpiring at Ponar. Although there were intermittent scraps of information to the effect that Jews were being murdered there, no initiative was taken to check them, and they were not connected to the disappearance of the kidnapped persons. When the female survivors returned and told their tale, there was no longer a Judenrat. It had been liquidated some days earlier. Thus, the first direct evidence on Ponar found the Jews of Vilna devoid of leadership and with no institution or body to which they could turn. Only a few people heard the grim story. Two days after the women returned, the ghettoization of Vilna Jewry began, along with the *Aktion*. The story of Ponar was swallowed up by the fresh tragedy.

The Jews taken off to Lukiszki during the forcible transfers to the ghetto were murdered at Ponar on September 12. Several women managed to return to Ghetto No. 1 from this massacre. They were brought before the heads of the Judenrat, to whom they recounted their experiences. They were ordered not to speak about Ponar in the ghetto. Testimony by some of these fugitives was recorded by the Judenrat. The women who survived the massacre of September 12, gave evidence similar in detail to the stories of the women who eluded their killers during "the Great Provocation."[8]

zecki, *op. cit.*, pp. 39–41. The names of three of the survivors were P. Aharonowicz, I. Schloss, and Y. Trojak (a girl of 11).
7 Moreshet Archives, D.2.102; Kaczerginski, *op. cit.*, p. 15.
8 Korczak, *op. cit.*, pp. 62–64; Lazar, *op. cit.*, pp. 54–56.

On September 15, 3,550 people were sent from Ghetto No. 1 to No. 2, but only 600 arrived there; the others were transported to Lukiszki and Ponar. The inhabitants of the ghetto still labored under illusions as to their fate. The entry in Kruk's diary for September 15, after the *Aktion*: "...Where are the other people? What is happening to them now?..." Ghetto residents surmised that there was a Ghetto No. 3 of Vilna Jews at Ponar, in addition to the first two in Vilna. The German administration used the term *Lager* Ponar ("Ponar camp") in its correspondence, and in its web of deceitful propaganda it took pains to ensure that the allegation about a third ghetto in Vilna reached the ears of the Jews. Abba Kovner writes: "Although the first living witnesses arrived at the ghetto from Ponar, the Jews refused to believe that all those dragged there had been murdered. 'Documents' were brought to the Jewish police that proved the existence of a third ghetto, and mothers consoled each other that their children were alive 'somewhere.' "[9]

Several people also succeeded in escaping from Ponar during one of the operations conducted in October, and one of them, Pnina Arkian, returned to the ghetto. She relates:

> When I returned to the ghetto, the Jewish police saw me, and let me enter. Then one asked me: "Where have you been?" and I said, "Ponar..." After reaching home, I didn't tell my mother what I had witnessed...Hardly ten minutes had passed when the Jewish police came... They took me to Gens...He asked me, "Where have you been?" I told him all that had happened to me, how we were taken and how I succeeded in escaping. He asked me, "Do you want your parents and family to live? Then, don't say a word of what you saw. I'll help you to get work, but just keep quiet. You saw and heard nothing." I promised him...and kept my promise.[10]

9 A. Kovner, "Nissayon Rishon le-Haggid," *Yalkut Moreshet*, No. 16, April 1973, p. 10. Balberyszski, *op. cit.*, p. 207.
10 Testimony of P. Arkin, YVA, 0–3/2048, pp. 4–6.

The few who succeeded in escaping from Ponar in September and October were all females. The males were shot first, in the morning hours and at midday, and although there were some who did not die immediately, they could not hold out until evening. The women were shot in the afternoon and toward dusk. Almost all those who escaped were in the last groups, lined up just before nightfall, and their miraculous survival went unnoticed by the killers. The Germans and Lithuanians left the area as darkness closed in, which enabled the women to escape.

Despite the fact that these women returned to the ghetto in September and October, the Jews of Vilna had no inkling of events at Ponar throughout the period from July to November 1941, during which time tens of thousands of Jews were put to death. Rumors were not believed.

Abba Kovner describes the situation in Vilna at the end of 1941:

> As the Jews of Vilna had no paradigm of such a dreadful slaughter, and as they had heard of the existence of the Warsaw Ghetto with its half million Jews who remained there for three years, and of the Bialystok Ghetto with 40,000 Jews in it, they believed that while they would face a life studded with vicissitude, the slaughter of millions was outside the realm of possibility.[11]

The Judenrats' Information and Activities
The Judenrat in Ghetto No. 1 learned from survivors of Ponar what had been transpiring there during the second half of September 1941. The majority of these survivors were brought before Gens and apparently also before the Judenrat leaders and related their experiences to them. Gens warned against spreading their stories in the ghetto. The wounded were taken to the hospital, where they were kept in secrecy and forbidden

11 Kovner, "Nissayon Rishon," *op. cit.*, p. 10.

even the visits of relatives so that their stories would not circulate.[12]

Information on the events at Ponar reached the Judenrat gradually, but it would appear that by the second half of September, and no later than the beginning of October, the upper echelons of the Judenrat and Jewish police in Ghetto No. 1 were aware of the truth.[13]

The information reaching the Ghetto No. 2 Judenrat was much more limited. The fate of the thousands who had been removed from Vilna and whose whereabouts were unknown was brought up during several discussions in this Judenrat. Among the various conjectures ventured, there were surmises that they were no longer alive. The Judenrat decided to ascertain from non-Jews what they knew on the subject. As a result of inquiries, it was learned that the Jews seized in various *Aktionen* were taken to the railway-depot at Ponar, from where they were marched to a closed and well-guarded area not far away. No details were known as to their fate in that closed area, for it was guarded so that no one could approach. Residents of Ponar stated that after the people were taken into the closed zone, the sound of shooting with automatic weapons was always audible. Such was the information that reached the Ghetto No. 2 Judenrat at the end of September or beginning of October.

Notwithstanding these reports, the Judenrat leaders remained unaware that the people of Ghetto No. 2 were doomed to extinction. Problems of food, housing, education of the children, and budgetary matters were what took up the Judenrat meetings throughout September, until October 5.

At the end of September 1941, Ghetto No. 2 Judenrat decided to request a meeting with Ghetto No. 1 Judenrat.[14] The conference took place in the offices of the Judenrat No. 1. Five

12 Korczak, *op. cit.*, p. 60; Lazar, *op. cit.*, p. 54.
13 Mushkat's testimony, pp. 5–7.
14 Balberyszski, *op. cit.*, p. 208; Minutes of the Ghetto No. 2 Judenrat meeting, Moreshet Archives, D.1.398.

members of Judenrat No. 2, headed by their chairman, Lejbowicz, attended, and No. 1 was represented by Fried and three other members. From the outset Lejbowicz raised the question of the fate of people seized in various *Aktionen* and apparently proposed that a joint approach be made to the German administration. He proposed cooperation between the two Judenrats. A. Fried replied as follows:

> We have no contact with the Germans. All business is conducted through Buragas' mediation. When the Germans come and demand 2,000 people, we are compelled to agree, since in this way we save the other Jews. If we didn't turn them over, they would themselves take anyone they pleased, as many as they pleased—which would be much worse for the thousands of others. There is no point in interceding with the Germans ... We once tried to intercede with Murer and Schweinberger in connection with the congestion in the ghetto. The answer we received was: "This crowding is not a problem." They took out 2,000 people and now there's no longer any congestion. Insofar as contacts between the two ghettos: we have no objection, but we cannot conduct joint action as this may be prejudicial to us. Our ghetto is designed for working and creative elements, whereas your ghetto is for the elderly, the weak, people unfit for work.[15]

The meeting did not yield the results anticipated by Judenrat No. 2, and its representatives left downcast. They had at last clearly learned the distinction between the two ghettos. Balberyszski, who attended the meeting, writes: "Evidently the Judenrat from Rudnicka Street [Ghetto No. 1] had certain information that its ghetto would continue to function whereas ours would be eliminated."[16] In spite of this, the Judenrat in Ghetto

15 Balberyszski, *op. cit.*, pp. 208–210; Moreshet Archives, D.1.398; Kruk, *op. cit.*, p. 155.
16 Balberyszski, *op. cit.*, pp. 211–212, writes that the conclusion

No. 2 had no clear warning, nor was it aware of the fact that its ghetto was due for imminent dissolution.

After Judenrat No. 1's refusal to cooperate with Judenrat No. 2 and appear together before the German administration, a working relationship was established between the Jewish police forces in both sectors. On October 5, Shafir, commander of the Ghetto No. 2 police, announced at a meeting of his Judenrat that "the Chief of Police in Ghetto No. 1 has sent a demand that crossings from Ghetto No. 2 to Ghetto No. 1 must be terminated."[17]

Judenrat No. 1 feared that a joint appearance might impair the distinctive character of Ghetto No. 1 as a "working ghetto" in the eyes of the authorities.

The Ghetto No. 1 Judenrat leaders evidently concluded that, due to the policy of the German administration and its methods of implementation, there was no way to prevent the annihilation of a part of Vilna Jewry. The Judenrat hoped that it would be possible to maintain the existence of one ghetto, and thereby save those Jews who worked in factories and industrial establishments, and to increase this number by incorporating more Jews into the labor cycle. The retention of the ghetto in Vilna, with its working elements, would also enable the survival of those employed in ghetto institutions and services. The Judenrat assessed that within the German administration itself, there were supporters of the idea to retain a "worker" ghetto. Muszkat, who was the deputy to Gens during the first period in the ghetto, states: "The Judenrat chairman, Fried, believed that the Germans needed Jewish labor, and therefore did not intend to exterminate them entirely. Consequently, everything should be done to sustain the ghetto. Thus the head of the ghetto implemented the Gestapo's instructions."[18]

This policy could be implemented as long as secrecy was

reached at a meeting of the two *Judenräte* was that Ghetto No. 2 must be self-sufficient.

17 Moreshet Archives, D. 1. 398.
18 Mushkat's testimony, pp. 8–9.

preserved as to the fate of the people seized from the ghetto and as to the happenings at Ponar. The Judenrat was apprehensive lest the spread of information on the events there create difficulties in removing non-working elements from Ghetto No. 1 and assembling there the workers from Ghetto No. 2. The failure of this plan would, of course, have endangered the existence of the ghetto and the lives of those Jews in Vilna whom the Judenrat believed could be saved.

Through this policy of silence, the Judenrat succeeded in concealing news of the Ponar massacres, and most of the Jewish public knew nothing at all about them until the completion of the "Yellow-Pass" *Aktionen* on November 5, and even thereafter.

In a manifesto read at a rally of Pioneer Youth in the Ghetto on January 1, 1942, its authors appealed to inhabitants to "discard your illusions as to the fate of those thousands who have been taken away from Vilna, and understand that Ponar is not a camp, but a place where all were shot."[19] The manifesto indicated that, at the beginning of January 1942, when the greater majority of the Jews of Vilna had already been murdered, there were people in the ghetto who continued to delude themselves as to the fate of these victims. Only in December 1941/January 1942, viz., after the series of massacres, did the reports begin to sink in.

In all the *Aktionen* implemented in Ghetto No. 1, the "Orders" of the German authorities were given through the Judenrat and Jewish police to the Jews. In the *Aktionen* of September 15 and October 1, the Judenrat and Jewish police did not have full knowledge that the people taken out from the ghetto were sent to Ponar. Yet during the two "Yellow-Pass" *Aktionen,* the Judenrat knew that the German instructions it passed on and implemented were intended to save the Jews removed from the ghetto and leave to precarious fate the "illegals" who remained.

The four *Aktionen* directed against Ghetto No. 2 were con-

19 See Chapter 15.

ducted differently than those in Ghetto No. 1. German and Lithuanian squads swooped down on the ghetto in a surprise
sortie, proceeded from house to house, seizing the occupants.
The Judenrat and Jewish police were not required to transmit
"Orders" to the Jews, nor implement them in any way and had
no previous knowledge of the *Aktionen*. In Ghetto No. 2 the
annihilation of all the Jews was effected without any selection,
so the German administration had no need for the assistance
of the Jewish bodies therein. They needed such cooperation
when they wished to exterminate only part of the populace, but
when their policy called for total annihilation, they bypassed
the Judenrat. Ghetto No. 2 was completely liquidated without
the help of its Judenrat or Jewish police.

In Ghetto No. 1, the Germans intended to gradually exterminate certain categories of Jews, while temporarily leaving
others alive. The Judenrat based its policy on the assumption
that the Germans could wipe out all the Jews, but because of
their need for manpower, they intended to retain some Jewish
workers and their dependents. This tragic reality established the
basis for cooperation between the German administration and
the Judenrat. The Germans wanted the Judenrat to continue
separating the working and non-working segments, in order to
implement the tactic of partial extermination; whereas the Judenrat was in need of the goodwill of the authorities in order
to save at least a part of the Jewish community. But the Germans dispensed with Judenrat cooperation in those instances
in which it passed from partial to wholesale extermination in
the ghetto.

The gradual liquidation process created three groups in the
ghetto population: (1) Jews who were employed in German
establishments and believed their work insured them and their
families. This group also included those employed in the Judenrat and Jewish police; (2) Jews who, from the standpoint of age
and physical fitness, hoped to find a way of being incorporated
into the first category; and (3) all those whose age, state of

health, and inability to work deprived them of any prospect of remaining alive.

The Judenrat policy was supported by the first group and served its immediate interests. This group included most inmates of Ghetto No. 1, and all holders of yellow passes. The strenuous efforts by the ghetto inmates, especially those in the second category, to be admitted into the work cycle and obtain yellow permits, testified to the fact that they saw no way of surviving other than within the framework of German dictates. In the Kovno ghetto, the Germans, through the Judenrat, distributed "white passes," which had the same validity as the "yellow passes" in the Vilna ghetto. When the proposal arose in the Kovno Judenrat to remit the permits to the Germans—"if we're doomed to die, then let's all die together"—the artisans entitled to receive the "white passes" congregated outside the Judenrat offices and argued against that stand, declaring: "What right have you to deprive us and our families of the possibility of remaining alive?" They demanded that they be given the passes assigned to them.[20]

The struggle for passes in Vilna and in Kovno illustrates that in the face of the situation in the ghettos of Lithuania during September-October 1941, large sectors in the ghetto identified with the Judenrat's course of action—which sought to assure the survival of as many Jews as possible within the confines of German policy—and that they even encouraged the Judenrat to act in this way.

Parties and Youth Movements

The Judenrat constituted the official and recognized leadership of the Vilna Jewish community. The Jews, on the whole, accepted that fact and obeyed the Judenrat's instructions. But an alternative potential leadership was to be found among the activists of former Vilna parties and youth movements. True, they had been dissolved during the Soviet regime and many

20 Garfunkel, *op. cit.*, pp. 64–65.

of its members were killed during the Nazi *Aktionen,* yet some had survived. The question is what were they doing during the months of mass extermination. Could they have warned of the ongoing annihilation process and propose suitable reactions and possible avenues of rescue?

These political circles maintained contact and had consulted among themselves in the early months of German rule.[21] The activists of the He-Halutz movements continued to remain in contact with one another within the framework of a "He-Halutz Coordination" during the period preceding the creation of the ghetto. Within this orbit were He-Halutz, represented by Mordechai Tenenbaum-Tamaroff; Ha-Shomer ha-Za'ir by Edek Boraks; and Ha-No'ar ha-Ziyyoni by Nissan Reznik.[22] The "He-Halutz Coordination" continued to be active inside the ghetto. At its first meeting, which was apparently held in the second half of September, and was attended by representatives of the various movements, it was decided to undertake a program of organization, material aid and concerted effort for the security of the members. The group set up a small workshop in a room at 2 Straszuna Street to prepare forged identity-cards and work-permits for all the members and for underground activity. Members, especially females, of the "He-Halutz Coordination" infiltrated outside the ghetto bearing "Aryan" papers.[23]

Concurrent with their activity within the "He-Halutz Coordina-

---

21 Dworzecki, *op. cit.,* pp. 30–31, 172. Dworzecki writes that a group of the Po'alei-Zion party met in July 1941; Grossman, *op. cit.,* p. 20. Grossman writes that she and M. Tenenbaum-Tamaroff met with a member of the first Judenrat as representatives of the He-Halutz.

22 Korczak, *op. cit.,* p. 16; N. Reznik, "Ha-Tenu'ah be-Getto Vilna u-be-Ya'arot Lita," *Massua,* Vol. I, Tel Aviv, 1973, p. 52.

23 Korczak, *op. cit.,* pp. 28, 31–33; Grossman, *op. cit.,* p. 38; Reznik, "Ha-Tenu'ah," *op. cit.,* p. 53. There was a public soup kitchen that had been set up by the Judenrat, managed by a member of the Zionist Youth Organization, S. Antin. His office, on the kitchen premises, served as a workshop for the fabrication of forged documents.

tion," the youth movements continued to function in their separate ideological frameworks. A group of He-Halutz ha-Za'ir-Dror members led by Mordechai Tenenbaum-Tamaroff carried on its activities within the ghetto. Zippora Birman writes:

> ... The movement met to decide on what to do. It was decided to organize the youth ... but there was no time at our disposal ... The first *Aktion* came suddenly ... When things quieted down we met again ... We tried to ensure that everyone had food and lodgings ... No sooner had we come through one *Aktion*, then the fury of a second one befell us ...

Mordechai Tenenbaum-Tamaroff, disguised as a Karaite (regarded by the Nazis as Aryans), succeeded in finding work as the "watchman" of a house in one of the Vilna suburbs close to the city. The house served as a refuge for members of He-Halutz ha-Za'ir-Dror during the "Yellow-Pass" *Aktionen*.[24]

Tenenbaum-Tamaroff writes about his activity during this period:

> The first *Aktion* began in Vilna (the term emanates from Vilna) ... From that day it was one *Aktion* after another. We still had no inkling that this would be the fate of all Polish Jewry. We sought the cause for it in the conduct of local authorities, in the attitude of the Lithuanians, and the like ... We did our work on the quiet days; on the pogrom days we preserved our members ... And again: building the movement, lectures, the struggle for power in the Judenrat ... There was also an attempt to leave Hitler's domain in German vehicles to Libau [Liepaja] in Latvia and then, in the winter, over the ice to Sweden. The numerous *Aktionen* made it impossible to implement this aim.[25]

24 Klibanski, *op. cit.*, pp. 284–285; Korczak, *op. cit.*, p. 43.
25 M. Tenenbaum-Tamaroff, *Dappim min ha-Delekah*, Tel Aviv, 1948, pp. 123–124.

The plan to escape from Vilna to Sweden across the Baltic Sea was a daring one and offered some real prospects. It was to have been implemented with the aid of Anton Schmidt, a German *Feldwebel* (Sergeant) in the Wehrmacht. The people involved were to have left Vilna in Schmidt's truck for the port of Libau, and then on fishing vessels proceed to the Swedish island of Gotland, in the Baltic Sea. Polish underground members had used the same escape route. A Jew named Hermann Adler, who established the contact between Tenenbaum-Tamaroff and Schmidt, handled the arrangements. According to the plan, the first group was to consist of twenty-four persons. The plan failed chiefly because the Germans discovered the escape route, and succeeded in frustrating the flight of several Polish groups. The idea of escaping to Sweden was shelved.[26]

Chaike Grossman has also written about plans to find refuge in Sweden through a Pole who dealt in smuggling people abroad against payment. But this, too, came to no avail when the Polish smuggler vanished.[27]

26 P. Friedman, "Tsi is in der nazitsayt geven an ander Daychland?," *YIVO Bleter.* Vol. XXXIX, New York, 1955, pp. 154–164. This part: "Dokument fun der yidisher untererdisher organisatsie vegn Anton Schmidt" was found in the Ringelblum underground archives in Warsaw, giving an account of the activities of Schmidt in Vilna, apparently written by L. Kozibrodska, who was a courier. The document tells of the plan to flee to Sweden. A. Schmidt was born in Austria on January 16, 1900. He was arrested in the second half of January 1942, for helping the Jews of Vilna, was tried by German court martial, and executed by a firing squad on April 11, 1942. Yad Vashem conferred upon him the title of "Righteous Gentile" posthumously. Hermann Adler arrived in Vilna as a refugee from Czechoslovakia, where he had been a member of Po'alei Zion ZS. His wife was Viennese and knew Schmidt when both were still in Vienna. Schmidt helped Adler and his wife during the *Aktionen.*
27 Grossman, *op. cit.,* p. 39. It is probable that the plan to flee to Sweden, of which Tenenbaum writes, and the plan to which Grossman refers were one and the same, in spite of the difference in the accounts of the details. Reznik, "Ha-tenu'ah," *op. cit.,* p. 54,

Korczak writes of sixty members of Ha-Shomer ha-Za'ir who remained in Vilna after the capture of the city by the Germans and of "the first meeting held in a private apartment... The issues discussed were mutual help and contact between members. The further existence of the movement was also discussed... Finally work-permits." Ha-Shomer ha-Za'ir succeeded in finding refuge in a convent of Dominican nuns, located 5 miles from Vilna, for seventeen of its members, including Abba Kovner. The hiding-place was found with the assistance of a Polish woman, Jadwiga Dudziec, of the Polish Scout movement, who had been on friendly terms with Ha-Shomer ha-Za'ir from pre-war days.

On September 30, 1941, the eve of Yom Kippur, Ha-Shomer ha-Za'ir held a meeting of activists in the ghetto. Those activists who were outside the ghetto came in for the meeting, which took place in a small room at 15 Straszuna Street and was attended by twenty members.

Further meetings of Ha-Shomer ha-Za'ir activists were held in the convent where Kovner's group took refuge. Ha-Shomer ha-Za'ir members met with members of the Polish underground, which had persevered in Vilna since the Soviet era, and from an ideological and organizational standpoint was linked to the Polish Government-in-Exile in London. The contact with the Polish underground had been established with the help of Jadwiga Dudzec. At these meetings, problems of Polish underground aid to the Jewish underground in providing forged documents, shelter, and procurement of weapons were discussed. These encounters had no positive results and were eventually stopped.[28]

The Po'alei Zion-Hitahdut party resumed its clandestine

also dwells on a plan to escape to Sweden by way of the Baltic Sea.

28 Korczak, *op. cit.*, pp. 16, 29–31; Grossman, *op. cit.*, pp. 21, 34–40; J. Dudzec, a Polish woman born in 1919, helped many Jews during the Holocaust. She was killed by an aerial bombardment of Vilna in July 1944.

activity in the ghetto. On September 10 a Vaad Eretz Israel Haovedet ("Working Eretz Israel Committee") was established in the ghetto with representatives from Po'alei Zion Z.S.-Hitahdut, He-Halutz ha-Za'ir-Dror, and Ha-Shomer ha-Za'ir.[29]

Nissan Reznik has written about the Ha-No'ar ha-Ziyyoni activities in the ghetto during the initial phase. There were some gatherings of Akiva movement members held in the ghetto.[30]

The group of Betar activists maintained contact among themselves inside the ghetto. Joseph Glazman, one of the Betar leaders in Lithuania, returned to the Vilna ghetto at the end of October or beginning of November 1941, from the labor camp at Rzesza. He took over the leadership of the Betar group in the ghetto, focusing its action during that period on mutual help for its members.[31]

The Zionist parties and youth movements nominated a Co-ordinating Committee in the ghetto. It was called "Umbrella." Its function was primarily to coordinate Zionist activity in the ghetto, teach Hebrew and conduct cultural programs in that language, and receive information from messengers who arrived from other ghettos. The Zionist "Umbrella" launched its activities in the ghetto at the end of October 1941.[32]

A group of Bundists, including G. Jaszunski and H. Kruk, was active in the Vilna ghetto.[33]

There was also a nucleus of activists in the Vilna ghetto who had formerly been members of the Communist Party. Its leaders were Itzhak Witenberg, B. Szeresznyevski, Ch. Borowska, and S. Madeysker. The members of this group maintained contact among themselves during the early months of the German occupation and after the establishment of the ghetto. Their principal activity was to extend mutual assistance in order to save those

29 Dworzecki, *op. cit.*, pp. 172, 175.
30 Reznik, "Ha-Tenu'ah," *op. cit.*, p. 53; H. Zeidel, *Adam be-Mivhan*, Tel Aviv, 1971, p. 50.
31 Lazar, *op. cit.*, pp. 49–52; Kowalski, *op. cit.*, p. 65.
32 Dworzecki, *op. cit.*, pp. 153, 183–184.
33 *Ibid.*, p. 184; Kruk, *op. cit.*, pp. 70–71, 93, 169–170

in the group who were in double jeopardy—as Jews and as Communist activists. This Communist nucleus sought contact with other Communist underground cells outside the ghetto, but no such cells existed in Vilna during the second half of 1941.[34]

During the period of the mass extermination of Vilna Jews, from July to November 1941, the party activists failed to play any significant role that might have enabled them to direct and lead the Jews in face of the recurring massacres. The activists of the Po'alei Zion–Z.S. party and the Bund discussed joining the Judenrat and other problems relating to the situation, but they did not seek new solutions to the problems. The veteran Jewish parties did not act as an independent factor during this period, when the Jewish public stood in need of guidance and leadership. Some of the veteran leaders and activists met their deaths in the waves of kidnapping and initial mass *Aktionen*; others found their way into the Judenrat and affiliated agencies and were eventually incorporated into them.

In comparison with the absence of any tangible activity on the part of the veterans, the conduct of the Zionist and pioneer youth movements was noteworthy. These dynamic young men remained in contact with one another, within the framework of the respective movements, as they had done during their days of clandestine activities under the Soviet regime. Members of these youth movements implemented a variety of plans in an organized fashion, directed mainly at extending material aid and attempting to rescue their comrades taken during the abductions and various ghetto *Aktionen*. These rescue efforts were carried out by procuring passes over the quota assigned by the Germans, forging "Aryan" identity-cards, and finding hideouts outside the ghetto. During this period, the struggle assumed a de-

---

34 Dworzecki, *op. cit.*, p. 185; I. Witenberg, born in Vilna in 1909, had been active in the trade unions and was chairman of the Leather Workers' Union. C. Borowska, Vilna-born and a trainee in Ha-Shomer ha-Za'ir, went over to the Communist Party in 1932. S. Madeysker, born in Vilna in 1914, served eight years in jail for Communist activity.

fensive character in order to preserve the members of the movement. The concept of armed resistance had still not evolved at this time.

The young activists of the youth movements had still not realized that the total annihilation of all Jews had begun, and they had no idea of Ponar's true purpose. They lacked the ability and organizational means, the training and public authority, to coalesce and direct the Jews of Vilna, even when at the end of September the first reports of what was transpiring at Ponar filtered through. Both as a community and as individuals, the Jews of the city were left without guidance and counsel; each stood alone in his struggle for existence and search for means of rescue.

The Lone Jew in the Fight for Life

The following outlets were available to the individual Jew in his struggle to remain alive:

— Obtain a pass or join the holder (male or female) of a pass by fictitious marriage;
— Hide out in a *maline* in the ghetto;
— Find a hiding-place among Christians outside the ghetto;
— Flee to Belorussia, where Jews lived in comparative quiet at that time.

Passes and Fictitious Marriages. The acquisition of work-permits was legitimate and had been prescribed by the German administration. In order to take full advantage of this legal road to survival, fictitious marriages and the addition of children's names to the passes were used to fill the numerical quota.

There are no statistics extant as to how many persons were saved by this device, but apparently many hundreds, and possibly even thousands, succeeded in "legalizing" themselves. Both the Judenrat and the Jewish police were aware of these fictitious compilations, since they issued the passes to both genuine and fictitious dependents. The Judenrat knew the people in the ghetto well and was aware which were true and which were fictitious entries.

The Malines. The origin of the concept of the *maline* as a place of concealment is to be found in July 1941, the period of kidnappings, when male Jews hid from Lithuanian abductors. The *malines* became the means of rescue, for many Jews, from the horrors of Ponar. The *maline* in the ghetto was the chief instrument in rescuing thousands who had not secured passes and were unable to "attach" themselves as "dependents." Some *malines* were large enough for only one person—chimneys, ovens, double-partitioned cupboards or closets; others were large enough to hold tens of hundreds of people—basements, garrets, rooms, and even apartments with camouflaged doors. The high stone buildings and the housing congestion in the ghetto offered many likely places for concealment in well-devised *malines* and enabled the practice to be developed on a large scale. Thousands of people invested their initiative, imagination, and hard labor for weeks and months to prepare *malines*, for they required ventilation, water, and food.[35]

The use of *malines* as havens for thousands of human beings was made feasible by the existence of a ghetto in Vilna and of a legal population within that ghetto. Thousands who sought rescue in these coverts could hide for several days during the house-to-house searches and then emerge and continue to live openly until the next *Aktion*. During the "Yellow-Pass" *Aktionen* on October 24 and November 3–5, 1941, thousands of people hid in *malines* in Ghetto No. 1. Thus they were spared to come out a few days later and be swallowed up once again by the legalized community.

These hiding-places were unviable in an area denuded of inhabitants. Incessant combing by the police and the greed of the local Gentile populace for Jewish property prevented hiding in the areas from which Jews had already been evicted.

---

35 Korczak, *op. cit.*, pp. 44–46; Balberyszski, *op. cit.*, pp. 282, 284, 244–246; Sutzkewer, *op. cit.*, pp. 144–146.

The *malines* were the ingenious device of Vilna Jews, who were the first to use them, and enabled 7–8,000 persons to survive. (Regarding the number of "illegals" in the ghetto see chapter 13.)

Refuge in Non-Jewish Neighborhoods. The non-Jewish population of Vilna was largely Polish, with Lithuanian and Belorussian minorities. These inhabitants were divided into three categories in respect to their attitude towards the Jews and their liquidation: one group aided the Jews; a second collaborated with the Germans; and a third stood indifferently aside. The overwhelming majority of the Vilna population, especially the Poles, stood on the sidelines. The second largest group was composed of those who sided with the Germans and took an active anti-Jewish stance. These were mainly Lithuanian residents of Vilna and the vicinity, who joined the German administration and extermination units. The third and smallest group numbered no more than a few dozen to several hundred people, mainly Poles and some Lithuanians.

The attitude of the Christians in Vilna towards the Jews was not static. Rindziunski states in his testimony:

> ... If, in the early days, most of the Polish neighbors, who were under the fresh impact of parting from their neighbors, displayed human sentiments and regret, within a few months it was possible to discern a change ... The economic factor, the desire to grab Jewish property decisively influenced the feelings of many Poles. Some of them thought that it would be better for "their" Jews to be wiped out so that they could retain all the property. Of course, generalizations cannot be made and this cannot be described as a general phenomenon.[36]

A Jew could seek safety in a non-Jewish environment in two ways—by hiding, or by passing as an "Aryan." The substantial difference between rescue by hiding and rescue by means

36 Rindziunski's testimony, pp. 45–46.

of "Aryan" papers was that, to conceal himself, the Jew had to physically disappear, whereas the other way he was obliged to integrate into his surroundings and make certain he would not be discovered.

Finding a hideaway was conditioned by the readiness of the non-Jewish side to grant such refuge. Generally, this privilege was based on previous acquaintance or friendship, however persons harboring Jews also did so out of various motives—against large monetary payments, for humanitarian or religious reasons. There were also cases in which Jews found sanctuary in monasteries or churches.

The practical significance of being sheltered by a non-Jew was that the Jew had to remain secreted either in the house or near the house of his protector for months, and sometimes even years, without anyone, save those directly involved, knowing about it.

Security through exchanging Jewish for "Aryan" identity meant procuring the necessary papers, finding a place to live, obtaining work, and assimilating into non-Jewish society. Vilna Jews who sought this means of escape became "Poles" or "Belorussians," but not "Lithuanians," as they were not fluent in the language. An "Aryan," or at least a non-Jewish, appearance was a *conditio a priori* for successful assimilation.

From time to time, Vilna newspapers published reports on the execution of Jews caught in hiding-places or carrying false "Aryan" papers and the harsh penalties, including execution, imposed on those who harbored them. The German administration disseminated propaganda among the non-Jewish public against helping Jews. Vilna newspapers, published in Polish and Lithuanian, ran articles explaining why Jews should not be helped, although the Catholic religion dictates dispensing relief to those in distress. This anti-Jewish incitement was accompanied by notices of severe punishment for abettors.[37] Yet,

37 Rindziunski's testimony, p. 32; *Naujoji Lietuva,* October 29 and November 20, 1941, in Moreshet Archives, D.1.362; *Documents Accuse,* pp. 135–136, 244; Kowalski, *op. cit.,* p. 69, gives a photocopy of

despite the propaganda and heavy punishment threatened, there were Christians who hid Jews, including small children and infants.

Forged identity documents were obtainable from offices of the local Lithuanian government, which were responsible for their issue, through intermediaries, against bribes. An additional source was the Jewish underground, which developed a veritable "industry" in these papers. Jews paid non-Jewish suppliers from 10–15,000 rubles for preparing the document, and up to 500 rubles for a photograph to be placed on it, as Jews were forbidden to own cameras. These payments were divided between the intermediaries and the "principals," but there were also cases of Jews obtaining counterfeit documents without payment or at cost.[38]

There was considerable difficulty in finding dwellings. Permits to lease apartments or rooms to new tenants had to be obtained from the Municipal Housing Department, and it was hazardous for a Jew with false identity papers to apply. Ch. Grossman writes that, before she made an application for a housing permit, she located a house destroyed in the bombardments and of which, in her opinion, it was impossible to determine the previous occupants. She then explained to the city official that her house had been wrecked in a bombardment, and she had had nowhere to live for many weeks, but now that she had found a place she needed a permit. She was successful.[39]

Still another problem was finding work. According to German regulations promulgated in August and September 1941, all persons of working age were obliged to register at employment exchanges. A place of work was necessary in order to avoid being sent to work in Germany, for subsistence, and in order

Murer's order concerning Jews outside the ghetto; Sutzkewer, *op. cit.,* p. 57.

38 Testimony of S. Trotzki, Moreshet Archives, D.2.55, pp. 5–6.

39 Grossman, *op. cit.,* pp. 20–22; *Documents Accuse,* p. 140, contains a circular issued by the Lithuanian administration on the obligation to report people coming to rent apartments.

to avoid undue attention and questions as to sources of liveli-hood. People generally found jobs in unskilled occupations, in domestic service, restaurants, and the like. Assimilation into a Christian society called for playing by the rules of the new milieu, including church attendance and intimate knowledge of prayers and ecclesiastical rites of various kinds. For many it was their first visit to church.[40]

Evasion through change of identity was a personal venture. Each in his own fashion, and by virtue of personal connections, obtained "Aryan" papers and set out to fight for his life. As this was an individual and not an organized enterprise, it is impossible to gauge the number of Jews who tried and suc-ceeded, or who failed and lost their lives in the process. The number who were successful must have been minimal owing to rigorous police control, the difficulty in obtaining documents, dwelling and employment. It is estimated that they totaled several hundred. Part of them returned to the ghetto after December 1941.

A possibility of haven in a non-Jewish surrounding was dic-tated by two basic conditions—the attitude of local inhabitants, and the punishment awaiting those who extended help. Both were disadvantageous to the Jews. A big segment of the local public was animated by anti-Semitism, profited by illicit gains from abandoned Jewish property, and favored or was apathetic toward the extermination of the Jewish community. Those who might have been ready to assist the Jews were intimidated by the likelihood of punishment. Very few overcame their fears and extended help.

Flight to Belorussia. During the months of July–November 1941, when mass *Aktionen* against the Jews were carried out in Vilna, as in the rest of Lithuania, the situation in Belorussia was different, and in the towns and townships adjacent to Vilna, such as Voronovo and Lida, the Jews still dwelt in comparative

40 *Gitlerovskaya okupatsiya,* pp. 74–79; Grossman, *op. cit.,* pp. 30–32; Trotzki's testimony, pp. 5–6.

[196]

tranquility. No mass *Aktionen* were undertaken and the Jews were not enclosed in ghettos. Many Vilna Jews therefore felt that Belorussia offered safety to them and their families.

A document dated the beginning of 1942, written by a member of the Jewish underground, states: "The feeling was rife among the Jewish population of Vilna at the end of 1941 that the whole of Lithuanian Jewry had been condemned to extermination—it was safer for Jews in areas of Belorussia."[41]

Following the concentration of the Jews in the Vilna ghetto early in September and the inception of the liquidation *Aktionen*, groups of refugees succeeded in fleeing to Belorussia.

The refugees went on foot, in carts rented from local farmers, and on trucks, including those of the German Army. Jews and non-Jews acted as intermediaries for those who handled the traffic—for money—and there were also cases of fraud and provocation: people who paid the amount demanded were led straight to the German or Lithuanian police, instead of to Belorussia.[42]

An extraordinary instance of the rescue of Jews by transporting them to Belorussia was organized by Anton Schmidt, the German sergeant-major. He was in charge of a small military unit called the Versprengten Sammelstelle, which served as a transfer point and collection depot for German soldiers who had been separated from their units. This unit was located in three buildings near the Vilna railroad station. In their basements were workshops for repairing beds and mattresses, and tailoring-shops in which Jews worked. Dozens of Jews were employed by Schmidt's outfit. During the "Yellow-Pass" *Aktionen*, Schmidt hid many of his Jewish workmen in the basements below his unit's quarters. He sent Jews to Belorussia in his military trucks. At the outset there were five or six Jewish passengers for each trip, but in the course of time the number grew to 20–30 in each truck. They would come to

41 Friedman, *op. cit.*, pp. 157–158.
42 Trotzki's testimony, pp. 5–6; Balberyszski, *op. cit.*, p. 271.

his unit from the ghetto, stay there several days, and then travel by night to Belorussia. There were also cases in which Schmidt actually took people out of the ghetto.[43]

There is no data as to how many Jews fled from Vilna to Belorussia during July–December 1941. In Voronovo there were some 300 Jews originally from Vilna, and in Lida there were approximately 1,000.[44]

Resistance to the Expulsions. Instances of resistance by individuals and groups took place during the period of the expulsions and shooting at Ponar. These outbursts were spontaneous. Cases of Jewish women stoning the Lithuanian kidnappers occurred during the July abductions, when they tried to free the captives. Rioting by local inhabitants against the Jews, which the Germans had instigated, took place on Novogrodska Street in July, and the Jews defended themselves. Resistance also surged up during the transfers to the ghetto. Kaczerginski writes that, on the day of the expulsion, a Jew, Feivel Banski, age twenty-one, fired and hit a German officer and two local policemen and was killed by their bullets when he attempted to escape.[45]

In the October 4 *Aktion in* Ghetto No. 2, a large group of people refused to proceed in the direction of the Lukiszki prison, and many began to escape. It was the first instance of mass resistance. Some of the people were shot on the spot; others succeeded in escaping; and the rest were taken by force to the prison.

Many Jews were shot in the ghetto during the "Yellow-Pass" *Aktionen* when they refused to emerge from the *malines* or forcibly resisted expulsion. The permit-holders who returned to the ghetto found many bodies.

A group of people was discovered in a hideout during the "Pink-Pass Operation." The group, headed by Haus and Gold-

43 Bronowski's testimony, p. 4; Friedman, *op. cit.,* pp. 156–158; Engelshtern, *op. cit.,* pp. 19, 21–23; on Schmidt, see supra, note 26.
44 Engelshtern, *op. cit.,* pp. 25, 31; Kowalski, *op. cit.,* p. 63.
45 Kaczerginski, *op. cit.,* p. 25.

stein, attacked the Germans and Lithuanians who came in, and were shot in the course of the struggle.

These manifestations of resistance encompassed both individuals and groups who acted spontaneously, but their scope was limited. In his diary, Shur analyzes the causes of this behavior:

> How could so many people go to their deaths without resisting... People died unresistingly because the Germans adopted the principle of "Divide and rule." Not all of them were taken at the same time... In this way the Germans did not incite everyone against them... Besides this, the people who were seized did not believe they were being led to their deaths, that guiltless people would be killed. They thought there would be interrogations and those found to be Communists would be punished, but ordinary people would never be killed. They went to Ponar with these thoughts in mind.[46]

46 Shur's diary, [7].

Chapter 12

THE FATE OF JEWISH PROPERTY

Decrees and Seizures of Property
During the early days of German administration in Vilna, the local Lithuanian authorities impounded the workshops and businesses which were still owned by Jews and which had not been confiscated by the Soviets. An order forbidding Jews to sell or transfer their property was published in the second half of July 1941. In addition, the Lithuanian municipality ceased issuing permits to Jews for the exchange of dwellings. On August 6, 1941, a "contribution" amounting to five million rubles was levied on the Jewish community, and a part of the cash and valuables remaining in their possession was seized, seriously impinging on their economic position.

Pursuant to Lohse's "Provisional Directives" of August 18, 1941, all property and cash in Jewish possession, except for household utensils and a little cash, was to be confiscated by the German administration. Lohse explicitly stated that all powers, for that purpose, were vested in the civil administration—the *Generalkommissariat* and the *Gebietskommissariat*—and not in the SS and police.

On September 1, 1941, concurrent with the Great Provocation, *Gebietskommissar* Hingst published an order concerning registration of Jewish property:

Order No. 4

Obligation to Register Jewish Property

1. All property of the Jewish population must be registered by September 8, 1941.
2. Any Jewish owner of property, or the person holding it, is liable for such registration, as well as anyone who, legally or practically (*de jure* or *de facto*), holds or is capable of holding such property—even if he is not the owner of that property or had acquired or holds it.
3. The duty to register resides with, according to the above, not only the legal owner of Jewish property, but with any person managing Jewish property, who has taken it over for safeguarding or obtained it in any other manner.
4. Registration of the property must be effected on a form which may be procurred at the district police-station, and should be returned there upon completion.
5. Any person knowingly concealing Jewish property, smuggling it, or failing to provide information about it will incur the most severe penalties.
6. Commanders of police-stations are personally responsible to me for the seizure of Jewish property in its entirety at the suitable time.

Hingst, September 1, 1941[1]

The contents of this order duplicated the provisions of Lohse's directives on the subject of Jewish property. The timing of the publication of the order was related to "the Great Provocation" and the plan to confine all Jews in a ghetto. The administration knew that, in the course of these *Aktionen*, the bulk of Jewish property would be left unprotected, and the non-Jewish populace would be tempted to pillage it, or that the Jews themselves might transfer it to their non-Jewish neighbors and friends.

---

1 Kruk, *op. cit.*, p. 47, photocopy.

The order, as was made patently clear in clauses 2 and 3, was meant to apply equally to Jews and non-Jews. Enactment of the order at the height of "the Great Provocation," when the Jewish quarter was emptied of its Jewish inhabitants and their property remained unguarded, was intended as a warning to the non-Jewish population.

Concomittant with "Order No. 4," non-Jewish janitors began to make lists of movable property in Jewish homes, and they were made responsible by the German authorities for these items. Nonetheless, the despoilment of Jewish property began with the evacuation of the Jewish quarter, especially during the night. The janitors and, later, the Christian neighbors profited the most. There were also many cases of looting apartments still tenanted by Jews. Criminal elements and/or anti-Semites exploited the difficult position of the Jews and robbed them, fortified by the knowledge that they would not dare resist or summon the police.[2]

The date of September 8, 1941, fixed as the deadline for completing the registration of Jewish property, took into account that ghettoization of the Jews was to be implemented on September 6.

On September 3 an additional order was enacted with regard to Jewish property; this obliged Jews to immediately relinquish cash, gold, foreign currency, and valuables in their possession to the police. The Jews were permitted to retain 300 rubles.

Long lines of Jews, especially women, formed outside the police-stations. Dworzecki describes the scene:

> Jews rush to the police-stations carrying goblets, candlesticks, wedding rings. They ask for their names to be registered as having brought these valuable items, and hasten home to bury every other item of value in their possession in cellars and attics . . . [3]

2 Balberyszski, *op. cit.,* p. 163; Rindziunski's testimony, p. 28.
3 Dworzecki, *op. cit.,* p. 44; Rindziunski's testimony, pp. 27–28; Kruk, *op. cit.,* pp. 56, 59.

The order issued on the third of the month was meant to enlarge upon "Order No. 4," which had stipulated the registration of Jewish property, but did not require its seizure forthwith. No specific reference was made in "Order No. 4" to cash and valuables, and it could have been construed as directed against stationary and movable Jewish property. In that phase, the administration found registration to be sufficient and left the actual seizure to be undertaken at another time.

But with regard to money and other articles of value, this was not the case. The administration was aware that cash and valuables not relinquished by the Jews themselves would never reach official headquarters. They may have learned this lesson during "the Great Provocation." Most of the cash and valuables that the Jews took along with them to Lukiszki and Ponar were apparently taken by the Lithuanian murder squads and/or the Germans. The September 3 "Order" was intended to ensure that the Jews relinquish their valuable belongings before they went into the ghetto and were taken to Ponar.

Several days after "Order No. 4" appeared, another directive was issued to the Lithuanian authorities and police engaged in acts of extermination. The Lithuanian district and municipal officials were ordered to emphasize to their subordinates that the Jews' property must be held for the benefit of the German Reich, and anyone misappropriating it would suffer the ultimate penalty. Cash, foreign currency, valuables, etc., had to be precisely registered and kept in safekeeping in Lithuanian municipal offices.[4]

On September 6, 1941, the day of ghettoization, the Jews left most of their movable property and took with them only such articles as they could carry. The Lithuanian police who implemented the ghetto operation received orders to close and seal Jewish apartments with the movable property intact. The report on the *Aktion* submitted by the Lithuanian police chief stated: "Jewish property remained in the houses. Doors were locked

4 *Documents Accuse*, pp. 161–162.

and sealed." Yet, in spite of these precautions, the superintendents and Christian neighbors succeeded in breaking in and removing many items.[5]

The Vilna municipality was assigned authority over Jewish
apartments and property. On September 10, Mayor Dabulevicius submitted a report to *Gebietskommissar* Hingst on confiscated Jewish property, listing it at 429 houses, 5,886 hec-
tares of land, and 71 workshops. Hingst was dissatisfied, and
on September 22 asked the mayor for a more detailed report.
Three days later, a report was submitted with the required details, but it did not offer any particulars as to furniture, clothing, and utensils which the Jews had left behind. Dabulevicius
promised Hingst to provide these as soon as possible.[6]

On October 13, 1941, Lohse issued a further order concerning
Jewish property to complete the instructions on this subject
that had been outlined in the "Provisional Directives." The
new order instructed that "all property belonging to the Jewish
population in the areas subordinate to the *Reichskommissar*
of the *Ostland* shall be confiscated and assigned by the *Gebietskommissare* for management, i.e., the seizure of all Jewish property. In the new order, too, Lohse declared that "seizures shall
not affect parts of household equipment serving the basic necessities of existence, money, bank deposits, and valuable securities
not exceeding 100 *Reichsmarks*."[7]

No particular significance was attached to the new order insofar as the Jews of Vilna were concerned, as their property
had been wrested from them during their enclosure in the
ghetto, and they were in the process of being extirpated. Rather,
the order gave the "official" stamp of approval for the civil
administration in Vilna to assume ownership of all Jewish property from the local non-Jews who had misappropriated it.

5 *Ibid.*, p. 218; Balberyszski, *op. cit.*, pp. 170–171; Korczak, *op. cit.*,
p. 19.
6 *Documents Accuse*, pp. 225–226.
7 Official newspaper of the *Reichskommissar* of the *Ostland*, No. 6,
pp. 26–27, of October 24, 1941; *My Obvinyaem*, pp. 72–77.

Hingst published another "Order on Jewish Property" on October 23, 1941, again emphasizing the obligation to report Jewish property, including furniture and clothing, in the hands of the civilian population and the punishment to be meted out to those concealing such possessions.[8]

Furs destined for the troops on the Eastern front were collected in Vilna during the last days of December 1941. The Jews of the ghetto were ordered to relinquish all furs in their possession under threat of death. The Jews were also required to report on furs left with Gentiles outside the ghetto. On December 30 searches for furs were conducted within the ghetto confines by Germans and Lithuanians.[9]

The Conflict over Property

Despite Hingst's orders and threats of the death penalty for anyone found in possession of Jewish property, most did not file these reports. The desire to enrich oneself and benefit from the Jewish property was stronger than the fear of punishment. Even local Lithuanian government workers and the Lithuanian police retained large amounts of Jewish goods—orders notwithstanding. Lithuanian nationalist circles deemed themselves legal heirs to the property of the Lithuanian Jews, and stated this in their underground publications. The German administration lacked any accurate inventory and means to investigate whether property had been previously owned by Jews, especially when dealing with movables, cash, or articles of value. The Vilna newspapers from time to time printed notices on the obligation to surrender Jewish property and remonstrated that anyone found in possession of such property would be regarded as having stolen it from the Third Reich.[10]

8 *Naujoji Lietuva*, October 25, 1941, in Moreshet Archives, D.1.362.
9 Kruk, *op. cit.*, pp. 102–105, 107.
10 A memorandum by the Lithuanian nationalist underground stated that the "Lithuanians believe that Jewish property should be surrendered...to the Lithuanian people." Yerushalmi, *op. cit.*, p. 224; Kruk, *op. cit.*, p. 426.

Those segments of the non-Jewish population who benefited
from sizable portions of Jewish property, and enriched themselves
through the disaster that had befallen the Jews, had an interest
in seeing that the original Jewish owners did not remain alive
to return and claim their property. Only a few of those who
took possession of these items used them to profer help in
various ways to the Jewish proprietors and their families who
were still alive.

Hand in hand with the seizure of Jewish property, a conflict
raged between German civil administration officials and the SS
as to which of them was to gain ownership of the items, especially cash, valuables, and movable goods. The conflict waged
not only between those two branches of the German local
administration, but also between individuals on opposite sides
who wanted to derive personal benefit and amass wealth for
themselves.

Among the documents found in *Reichskommissariat Ostland*
was a report from Riga dated September 23, 1941, referring to
Jewish property confiscated by SS personnel in Vilna and stating
that *"Gebietskommissar* Hingst had established that *Brigadeführer* Wysocki, Senior Commander of the SS and Police in the
Generalkommissariat of Lithuania, had taken at least five consignments of furniture out of Vilna..." A document dated
September 24, 1941, stated that, on August 15, 1941, SS personnel had confiscated over 2,500,000 rubles, which were in
closed Jewish accounts, from the Lithuanian State Bank, and
on September 2, 1941, had withdrawn from the same bank
securities and other valuables belonging to Jews, worth over
1,240,000 rubles.[11]

Gewecke, *Gebietskommissar* of Shavli, wrote letters to Lohse
in which he complained that Security Police and SD personnel
had appropriated valuables belonging to Jews. In his communication of September 11 he wrote: "When *Standartenführer*
Jäger sends his men into my area to confiscate Jewish property

11 YVA, 0–18/148–9.

of which I, as *Gebietskommissar*, am held responsible for the seizure and delivery, then there is no guarantee that the Jewish property will be turned over in its entirety, as good order obliges." Writing to Lohse on September 8 and 16, Gewecke set forth in detail instances in which Jäger's men had seized valuables belonging to Jews, contrary to the directives issued by the *Reichskommissar* and *Gebietskommissar*, according to which the exclusive authority to deal with the subject of Jewish property was vested in the officials of the civil administration.[12]

Lohse wrote to Prützman, Commanding Officer of the SS and Police in the *Ostland*, on September 25, 1941, on the subject of "Police Measures and the Handling of Jewish Property." Lohse emphasized in his letter that "the handling of Jewish property is the exclusive concern of the *Reichskommissar*, as established in the 'Provisional Directives of How to Deal with Jews in the Area of the *Reichskommissariat Ostland*.'" Lohse further stressed that the valuables seized by SS personnel must be returned to the *Gebietskommissariat*. He sent a copy of the letter to the *Generalkommissare* of Lithuania, Latvia, and Belorussia, demanding that they take the necessary steps to carry out his directives. Lohse's personal appeal to Prützman was to no avail.[13]

On November 15, 1941, a meeting took place between Himmler and Rosenberg during which Lohse's charges against SS personnel on the seizure of Jewish property were aired. Himmler described "Lohse's petty attitude" towards "the confiscation of essential items to the SS and the Police."[14] The Jewish property and valuables impounded by the SS remained in their hands. Hingst ceded a large amount of gold articles and foreign currency that had belonged to Vilna Jews—consisting of more than 700 gold rings, hundreds of other gold articles, and over 250 gold coins, in addition to dollars and other mon-

12 *Ibid.*, pp. 141, 144.
13 *Ibid.*, pp. 150–151, 154.
14 R. Hilberg, *The Destruction of the European Jews*, Chicago, 1967, p. 239.

ey—to the Finance Department of the *Generalkommissariat* at Kovno at the end of 1942. Yet the state coffers were not the sole beneficiary of all Jewish property. Hingst retained some of it for his own personal use and distributed still more among German administrative officials serving in Vilna.[15]

All Jewish landed property and the majority of the movable goods were sequestrated from Jewish ownership. Those ghetto incarcerees who survived the *Aktionen* succeeded to save part of their money, gold, and other valuables for themselves. A small amount of the movables that they had left with Christian neighbors was returned to them while they were in the ghetto, and served as an additional source of livelihood, to be used in exchange for food.

Jewish property, which had been built up and accumulated over a period of generations, was wrested from its owners in the course of several months. The landed property was officially transferred to Reich ownership, but movable goods, cash, and valuable objects only partly reached the Reich coffers. The greater part remained with the local non-Jewish population, including Lithuanian government officials and policemen. A sizable segment went into the private pockets of the Germans in the civil administration and SS personnel who served in Vilna and vicinity, following the bitter struggle between them over who would inherit the booty from their murdered victims.

15 *Documents Accuse,* pp. 219, 266–267.

Chapter 13

THE TOLL OF THE EXTERMINATION OPERATIONS
(July–December 1941)

The estimate of the number of Jews murdered in Vilna, from
the time of the German occupation until the end of December
1941, is based on both Jewish and German sources. The latter
include the reports of the Einsatzgruppen and the trials of the
Nazi war criminals that operated in Vilna.[1] The principal Jewish sources are the diaries of Kruk and Shur, which specify the
number of victims, and a document about the Vilna ghetto
prepared by Dr. Heller—at the request of German scientists
of the Alfred Rosenberg Institute, which operated in Vilna—
that gives figures identical to Shur's.

It is highly probable that Shur drew his data from that document. An investigation was undertaken in the Vilna ghetto by
a group of Jews whose goal was to compute the number of
victims. Kruk ends a passage in his diary that deals with the
total of murdered with these words:

> This tragic total is published after it was checked a num-
> ber of times and was confirmed by consultation with all
> those who could add something in this respect. With
> trembling hand, and full responsibility towards history,

1 Filbert's trial, TR–10/388; Jäger Report, *passim;* Einsatzgruppen
Report (no. 154) of January 12, 1942, YVA, 0–51/57–1, p. 28.

NUMBER OF JEWISH VICTIMS IN THE *AKTIONEN*, JUNE 24—DECEMBER 23, 1941

The Aktion	Date on which Aktion was carried out	Date of Extermination	No. of Victims		
			German Source	Kruk	Shur/Heller
Lithuanian units	June 24–July 2, 1941		(No data, ca. 500 according to estimation)		
E.K. 9 operations (kidnappings)	July 2–August 8		5,000		
E.K. 3 operations	August 9–30		444		
Great Provocation	August 31	September 2	3,700		
Total from Occupation of City to Creation of the Ghetto	June 24–September 5		9,644	21,000	38,000
Transfer to the Ghetto	September 6	September 12	3,334	6,000	6,000
Ghetto No. 1 *Aktion*	September 15	September 17	1,267	2,950	2,000
Yom Kippur *Aktionen*	October 1				
Ghetto No. 1				2,200	2,300
Ghetto No. 2				1,700	
Ghetto No. 2 *Aktion*	October 3–4	October 4	1,983	2,000	2,000
Ghetto No. 2 *Aktion*	October 16	October 16	1,146	3,000	3,000

Aktion	Date	Date			
Liquidation Ghetto No. 2 Aktion	October 21	October 21	2,367	2,500	1,500
Aktionen against Elderly People and the Sick	October 21	October 21		140	120
First Yellow-Pass Aktion	October 24	October 25	2,578	5,000	5,000
		October 27	1,303		
		October 30	1,533		
Transfer to Ghetto 2	October 27–29				
Second Yellow-Pass Aktion	November 3–5	November 6	1,341	1,200	1,200
"Underworld" Aktionen	December 3–4			157	78
Gestapo Employees Aktion	December 15			300	300
Pink-Passes Aktion	December 20–22	December 22	385	400	400
Total: September–December 1941			17,237	27,547	23,898
Total: June 24–End of December 1941			26,881	48,547	61,898

have these figures been computed as reported herein. Vilna Ghetto, May 1942.[2]

The estimate of fatalities in the various *Aktionen* beginning with "the Great Provocation" on August 31–September 1, 1941, and culminating with the suspension of mass exterminations at the end of December 1941, was formulated within the ghetto itself. No great disparity exists between Kruk and Shur over this assessment. On the other hand, it was difficult to estimate the number of Jews caught and murdered during the phase of abductions perpetrated mainly in July 1941 by Einsatzkommando 9. Kidnappings took place daily. Jewish dwellings were scattered all over the city, and the victims were apprehended either as individuals or in small groups, with no possibility of authenticating estimates of their number. Jewish sources about this period are very general.

The table on pages 210–211 shows the schedule and number of victims in the various *Aktionen* according to German and Jewish sources.

Kruk's estimate of fatalities is based on three basic assumptions: first, that the number of Jews in Vilna on the day of German occupation was 60,000; second, that about 39,000 were placed in the ghetto—the conclusion drawn from this is that 21,000 were murdered in the *Aktionen* preceding the enforced confinement; third, that the number of Jews living in the ghetto on January 1, 1942, was 12,600, based on the number of food cards distributed in that period. The conclusion is that out of those forcibly transferred to the ghetto up to January 1, 1942, a total of 27,547 persons were put to death.

Dr. Heller and Shur base the estimate of victims on numerical evaluations similar to that of Kruk, but they differ as to the original number of Jews in Vilna. Dr. Heller and Shur estimate the number as 76,000 on the day the Germans occupied the city, and venture that 38,000 Jews were forced to take up resi-

2 Kruk, *op. cit.*, pp. 258, 261; Dr. Heller's report is reproduced in full in Korczak, *op. cit.*, pp. 303–309.

dence in the ghettos. Therefore, 38,000 people were killed before ghettoization.

Kruk, Heller, and Shur, however, err in their basic assumption; namely, that all those Jews who did not enter the ghetto were murdered in the pre-ghetto phase. They ignore the fact that in the intervening period, between the capture of Vilna and confinement in the ghetto, many hundreds of Jews fled to Belorussia and others eluded the abductors by showing "Aryan" identity papers and by hiding with Christian friends.

Kruk, Heller, and Shur also err in their estimate of the number of Jews in the ghetto at the beginning of 1942, after the succession of large-scale *Aktionen*. All three rely on the 12,600 food cards distributed in the ghetto in December 1941, but they ignore the fact that food cards were issued only to holders of passes and their dependents, and, during that period, thousands of people had no passes and were "illegals." Dr. Heller's report was written for the Germans in April–May 1942. The German administration in Vilna believed, according to the number of food cards issued, that, in March 1942, the ghetto had 15,000 Jews. Dr. Heller specified this number of Jews and ignored the thousands of Jews living illegally. The report must be viewed in light of its tendentious character. Shur apparently drew upon Dr. Heller's findings.

The objective of the Einsatzgruppen and the Security Police and SD affiliated with the civil administration was the murder of Jews. It is reasonable to assume that, in the reports to the upper echelons of command, they had no interest in minimizing the number of Jews they murdered. The system of the killings at Ponar enabled the Germans to maintain an accurate check on the number of deaths. As the victims were marched to the pits in groups of ten—men separate from women and children—it was possible to calculate the exact number of persons executed.[3] In principle, the Einsatzgruppen report on the number of Jews killed must then be accepted as reliable.

3 See the Indictment of Weiss, YVA, 0–4/7–1; on Weiss' responsibility for the murders at Ponar see the testimonies given on August

[213]

To test the reliability of Jäger's report, we compared the number of victims given for areas outside of Vilna with Jewish sources dealing with the same subject, in comparison with the number of Jews residing in these places before the Holocaust. These centers were Kovno, Ponevezh, Utian (Utena), and Keidan. There is considerable similarity between the number of Jewish inhabitants and the number of those killed according to Jäger's report. The book, *Gitlerovskaya okupatsiya v Litvie,* published in the Soviet Union, quotes passages from Jäger's report, as well as his detailed statistics, without questioning their accuracy.[4]

Jäger's report on the number of victims in Vilna underscores an additional fact. From August 12, when the E.K.3 murder operations began in Vilna, until November 25, 1941, the last date in Jäger's report, the total number was given as 5,901 males and 10,682 females, almost 5,000 more women than men. The numbers of males and females in the surviving Jewish community in Vilna were basically equal, because every yellow (and subsequently pink) pass bestowed immunity upon one male, one female and two children. It may also be assumed that there was no substantial disparity between the number of Jewish males and females in the city before the war. The figure of approximately 5,000 male victims less than females, as specified in Jäger's report, may be explained by the murder of 5,000 Jews, almost exclusively males, during the period of Einsatzkommando 9 operations in Vilna (July 1941). The families from which the husbands were kidnapped during the July abductions were the first to be seized in the various ghetto *Aktionen,* as in the absence of the *pater familias,* who were generally the worker entitled to the pass, they were singled out. This tragic statistic adds credibility to the figures given in Jäger's reports and the E.K.9 report.

10, 1949, by M. Snowski, C. Schlossberg, and F. Wellner, YVA, 0-4/7-1.

4 Garfunkel, *op. cit.,* pp. 15, 83; *Yahadut Lita,* Vol. III, Tel Aviv, 1967, pp. 285, 336, 347; *Gitlerovskaya okupatsiya,* p. 109.

After the second "Yellow-Pass" *Aktion* and the "Pink-Pass" *Aktion* of December 20–22, thousands of people continued to live in the ghetto without permits. No precise figures are available, and only a rough estimate can be ventured. The yellow passes granted legal recognition to 12,000 persons, while in November 1941, the Judenrat issued 12,000 food cards. Those issued in December totaled 13,000; in January 1942 — 13,600; in February—14,746; in March—15,880; and in April 1942—18,500 food cards.[5] These totals reflect the process by which "illegals" were legitimized in the ghetto by joining the labor force. In addition, in April 1942, the ghetto contained people who by reason of age, health, and inability or lack of desire to work preferred to continue "illegally" rather than receive food-ration cards.

The additional 6,500 food-card recipients recorded between November 1941 and April 1942 had been "illegals" in December 1941. No substantial number of Jewish refugees entered the Vilna ghetto between December 1941 and March 1942, as the murder of Jews in the townships of Lithuania ceased prior to November 1941, and the mass executions of Jews in Belorussia did not begin until the spring of 1942. Therefore, there were some 20,000 Jews in the Vilna ghetto at the end of 1941, among them approximately 8,000 of illegal status.

The table on pages 216–217 gives a composite picture of the dates of the various operations in Vilna and the number of victims during the six months between June 24 and December 23, 1941.

In conclusion, the total number of victims, from the German occupation until the end of 1941, based on a total population of 57,000 at the time of the occupation, was 33,500. About 3,500 fled to Belorussia[6] or went into hiding outside the ghetto, and 20,000 remained within the ghetto.

5 Kruk, *op. cit.*, p. 257; Balberyszski, *op. cit.*, pp. 294, 315; Epstein's diary, p. 111.
6 Most of those who fled to Belorussia met their death in the extermination *Aktionen* which were perpetrated there during 1942.

Date	Murder Operation	No. of Victims
June 24–July 4	Murder by Lithuanian units. No statistics; it may be assumed that the daily figure was about 50, in keeping with first report of E.K. 9 before they "improved" the methods of murder.	500
July 4–July 20	Murder campaign of E.K.9.	5,000
July 20–August 8	A small mopping-up unit of E.K. 9 operated in Vilna. Number of victims dropped in this phase, but abductions and murders continued. No data available for the period; impossible to estimate other than a general average of 50 victims daily, the same figure as prior to the arrival of E.K.9.	1,000
August 9–November 30	Mass *Aktionen* of civil adminstration and E.K. 3, according to figures given in Jäger's report.	21,381
	The Yom Kippur *Aktion* on October 1 was carried out in both ghettos and is reported by all Jewish sources. This *Aktion* is also mentioned in Weiss' trial, but Jäger's report does not refer to it; reasons unknown.	3,900
December 3–22	*Aktion* against "underworld" elements and Gestapo employees and their families; not mentioned in German reports, but figure appears in Jewish sources. "Pink-pass" *Aktion* recorded both in the Einsatzgruppen reports and in Jewish sources.	850

July–December   Hundreds of individual Jews and small groups were murdered during this period while trying to escape, to hide, or to pass on Aryan papers, or because of vengeance perpetrated by local inhabitants. These do not figure in the reports on mass killings; numbers can only be surmised.   500–1,000

Total No. of Jews Murdered: 33,000–33,500

Part Three
PREPARATION FOR COMBAT

Chapter 14

THE CRYSTALLIZATION OF THE CONCEPT
OF ARMED RESISTANCE

Communication Between the Ghettos
The German administration wanted to conceal its plans for extermination from its Jewish victims in order to catch them unaware and preclude flight or resistance. Therefore they enclosed the Jews in the ghettos, forbade them the use of any means of transportation, and forbade them to leave under penalty of death. In this way they hoped to block the spread of information on the murder campaign from one ghetto to another. To thwart the German aim, it was necessary to send messengers with news of the *Aktionen* to the Jewish communities in the ghettos of Belorussia and the General Government; there the mass extermination had not as yet begun and there was no knowledge or awareness of impending doom. Vilna, Bialystok, and Warsaw were in three separate zones of German administration. Bialystok and Grodno constituted a separate *Generalbezirk;* Warsaw was part of the General Government. Even for non-Jews to pass from one zone to another, it was necessary to be in possession of a special police pass. Transportation was possible only by train, which was under constant surveillance, especially at the junctions near the Grodno and Malkinia stations, between Bialystok and Warsaw.

The ghetto "messengers" were assigned the difficult task of maintaining a living link between the Jews in the ghettos. While traveling between the ghettos, as they had to pose as non-Jews, they had to be of non-Jewish appearance, to speak fluent Polish with a non-Jewish accent, to be armed with non-Jewish identity documents and to have transit passes. Most of the ghetto messengers were girls, since it was easier to conceal their identity, and they distinguished themselves by their courage and resourcefulness.

The He-Halutz youth movements were the first to create a link between the Vilna ghetto and the ghettos in Belorussia and Warsaw. These messengers breached the wall of isolation within which the Germans had placed the Jews. They brought news of the Vilna massacres in Vilna and Lithuania to the ghettos of Grodno, Bialystok, and Warsaw, where the Jews lived in comparative quiet. The Zionist youth movement's emissaries in Vilna carried with them the idea of armed resistance, which they had begun to consider toward the end of 1941. The messengers who came to Vilna brought news of life and activity in the ghetto communities in Grodno, Bialystok, and Warsaw. These reports had a considerable influence on internal developments and reactions among the youth movements in Vilna and on the course of action decided upon in ghettos elsewhere.[1]

The first contact between the Vilna and Warsaw ghettos was established when a courier, Henryk Grabowski,[2] arrived from Warsaw to the Polish underground in Vilna at the end of September 1941. Simultaneously, he had undertaken to be the liaison between the Ha-Shomer ha-Za'ir and He-Halutz ha-Za'ir-

1 Y. Zuckerman writes on the inference drawn in Warsaw: "A tremendous shock-wave went through the movement from that day in the fall of 1941, when the Polish scout returned from his mission in Vilna and brought with him the gloomy tidings on the extermination of the Jews...We felt that the pinions of Death were being spread over all of us. No educational work had any savor in those days unless an armed Jewish defense force arose alongside, and by virtue of it. Tenenbaum, *op. cit.*, pp. 7–8.
2 H. Grabowski, member of the Polish scout movement, was active in the Polish underground and in maintaining contact with the Jewish underground. Zuckerman, supra, note 1, alludes to him as the "Polish scout."

Dror movements in the two cities and to investigate the situation in Vilna.[3]

Henryk Grabowski established contact in Vilna with Chaike Grossman, Edek Boraks, and Abba Kovner. Grabowski brought with him letters from Kaplan and Zuckerman to He-Halutz friends in Vilna. He reported on the situation in Warsaw and on the extensive activity of the youth movements there. Grabowski reported that, when he passed through Troki, he saw Jews in that township being led to extermination. He remained in Vilna for several days and returned to Warsaw in mid-October.[4] He brought with him news of the German massacre of the Jews of Lithuania and of the tens of thousands that were already dead.[5]

The underground organ of Ha-Shomer ha-Za'ir, *Neged ha-Zerem* ("Against the Tide"), which was circulated in the Warsaw ghetto, published an article on "the gory days of Vilna" in its issue at the end of October 1941. It was apparently the first printed intimation of what was transpiring in Vilna. The article mentioned, among other facts:

> Within three months the Jewish population of Vilna, which totaled 70,000 in Soviet days, declined to 35,000.... Scant news arrives from the depths of Lithuania, but it is certain that there have been massacres of the Jews in those areas too. In some of the townships in the Vilna district, the Jews have been wiped out down to the last one...[6]

Apparently this article was prepared by Arieh Wilner, a native of Warsaw and active in Ha-Shomer ha-Za'ir there, who decided

---

3 W. Bartoszewski, *Ten jest z ojczyzny mojej*, Cracow, 1966, p. 497.

4 *Ibid.*, p. 497; Grossman, *op. cit.*, pp. 40–42.

5 N. Blumental and J. Kermish, *Ha-Meri ve-ha-Mered be-Getto Varshah*, Jerusalem, 1965, p. 108; (hereafter: *Ha-Meri ve-ha-Mered*); I. Gutman, *Mered ha-Nezurim*, Tel Aviv, 1963, p. 178.

6 "Krwawe dni Wilna," *Neged ha-Zerem*, No. 7–8 (18–19), p. 39; YVA, JM/1178/1.

to return from Vilna to Warsaw. He arrived in Warsaw in mid-October 1941, several days after Grabowski's return.[7]

Several messengers of He-Halutz ha-Za'ir left Vilna at the end of October on the initiative of Mordechai Tenenbaum-Tamaroff. Tamara (Tama) Schneiderman left for Warsaw, while Bella Hazan was dispatched to Grodno, where she arrived on October 31, a day before the ghettoization in that city. Hazan lived as a Christian outside the ghetto and had succeeded in finding work as a translator for the Gestapo. She maintained communications with the ghetto and with a He-Halutz ha-Za'ir group that was organized in the ghetto. Hazan returned to Vilna for several days at the beginning of December, with news about the Grodno ghetto. She reported that there had not yet been any mass extermination *Aktionen* there against the Jews. In Vilna, she obtained authoritative information on the shootings at Ponar. She returned to Grodno, succeeded in entering the ghetto and met there with Dr. David Brawer, chairman of the Judenrat, to whom she transmitted information on the massacres in Vilna and Ponar. According to Hazan's evidence, Dr. Brawer received these reports with disbelief.

Hazan's apartment outside the ghetto served as a meeting place for emissaries of the He-Halutz movements during their journey between Warsaw and Vilna. Bella Hazan remained active in Grodno until May 1942, when she proceeded to the Bialystok ghetto.[8]

No further messengers arrived in Vilna from Warsaw after mid-October 1941. The Zionist youth movements in Vilna decided to send a delegation to Warsaw in order to renew the

---

7 Bartoszewski, *op. cit.*, p. 497. Grabowski recounts that he was present when the decision was made that Arieh Wilner return to Warsaw, and apparently Wilner reached there towards the middle of October. See also, Gutman, *op. cit.*, p. 179.

8 *Sefer ha-Partizanim ha-Yehudim*, Vol. I, Tel Aviv, 1958, p. 54 (hereafter: *Sefer ha-Partizanim*); Klibanski, *op. cit.*, p. 284; Korczak, *op. cit.*, pp. 70–71; Testimony of B. Hazan, YVA, 0–33/298, pp. 1–2. Additional testimony by Hazan, YVA, pp. 19, 21–23.

contacts. A party of four members—Edek Boraks of Ha-Shomer ha-Za'ir, Shlomo Antin of Ha-No'ar ha-Ziyyoni, and Israel Kempner and Yehuda Piczewski of Betar—left for Warsaw during the second half of December. Their journey had been made possible through the help of *Feldwebel* Anton Schmidt, with whom Tenenbaum-Tamaroff, on behalf of the "He-Halutz Coordination" and Esther Jaffe, active in Betar, had maintained contact. Tenenbaum-Tamaroff and Esther Jaffe reached prior agreement that the number of people whom Schmidt would be able to transport to Warsaw be equally divided between members of the "He-Halutz Coordination" and Betar.[9]

The task assigned to the delegation was to transmit news of the extermination operations in Vilna and Lithuania to the Warsaw Jews and youth movements. They left Vilna in an army truck at Schmidt's disposal and safely reached Warsaw, where they met with active members of their movements and public figures, and briefed them in detail on the situation in Vilna. Most of the public figures with whom they met refused to believe the reports, and those who did believe argued: "It won't happen in Warsaw, because the Germans would be afraid of Europe." Boraks and Antin proceeded to Vilna separately in February or March 1942. The Betar members did not return to Vilna.[10]

Tamara Schneiderman and Lonia Kozibrodska, both members of He-Halutz ha-Za'ir, came to the Vilna ghetto several days after Christmas 1941, which they had spent with Bella Hazan in Grodno. Tossia Altman, a messenger for Ha-Shomer ha-Za'ir, arrived in Vilna from Warsaw at about the same time. The three messengers reached Vilna after the four-man dele-

9 Korczak, *op. cit.*, p. 50; Grossman, *op. cit.*, p. 45; Lazar, *op. cit.*, pp. 393–396; Friedman, *op. cit.*, p. 161.
10 Grossman, *op. cit.*, pp. 45, 52: she quotes the statement by T. Altman on the meeting of the delegation with the public representatives in Warsaw; *Ha-Meri ve-ha-Mered*, pp. 108–109; M. Neustadt (ed.), *Hurban u-Mered shel Yehudei Varshah*, Tel Aviv, 1946, pp. 233, 240; Lazar, *op. cit.*, pp. 393, 396.

gation had left for Warsaw. The girls told of life in the War-saw ghetto, the hunger and hardships, and the extensive activities of the youth movements. They arrived at a time when the youth movements in Vilna faced crucial decisions as to their future course of action; the girls' arrival hastened the adoption of these decisions, Kozibrodska and Altman remained in Vilna for several days, and left separately in the first days of January 1942 for Bialystok and Warsaw.[11]

Armed Resistance Considered

The comparative quiet that had descended on the Jews of Vilna in the period between the second "Yellow-Pass" *Aktion* (November 3–5) and January 21, 1942—a lull that was disturbed by the small-scale swoops and by the "Pink-Pass" *Aktion*—made it possible for the Zionist youth movements to undertake a reassessment of the situation and adopt decisions as to future courses of actions. In the interim, reliable reports on Ponar and the fate of the people taken there, accounts of what was happening elsewhere in Lithuania, and particulars as to the situation in Belorussia and the General Government were accumulating. Although many members had been killed in the *Aktionen*, the youth movements succeeded in legally and illegally preserving a nucleus of activists. When the *Aktionen* were halted, they were confronted by the problem of how to proceed.

Abba Kovner expressed the mood of introspection and groping at a meeting of Ha-Shomer ha-Za'ir activists held in the ghetto at the end of December 1941:

> It is incumbent upon us to determine our further course of action. We stand before the end of an epoch, an epoch of efforts, the purpose of which was to save our members. We have been able to save the majority, but the problem we are confronted with is a different one. The question to be asked is whether the path we have so far

11 Grossman, *op. cit.*, pp. 49–52, 55–56; Klibanski, *op. cit.*, p. 285; Korczak, *op. cit.*, pp. 45, 49, 51–52, 60.

trodden is the right one; is it to be the future path of the movement?[12]

One of the pivotal questions was whether the policy of extermination, as applied to the Jews of Vilna and Lithuania, was a result of local decision and conditions, or whether it was the inception of a process that would extend into the recesses of Belorussia and other places in occupied areas. Differences of opinion existed among the activists of the youth movements. Tenenbaum-Tamaroff wrote: "We still did not know whether this would be the fate of all Polish Jewry. We sought the reason for the extermination among the local authorities, in the attitude of the Lithuanians."[13]

Another view was expressed by Kovner: "It is still hard for me to explain why the blood of Vilna has been spilled, and by contrast Bialystok is quiet... One thing is clear to me: Vilna is not Vilna alone, Ponar is not a unique episode... It is a complete system."[14] These variegated evaluations had practical significance. If the exterminations in Lithuania were the result of Lithuanian and local German initiative, then perhaps the proper recourse was to leave that country and move to the more "placid" areas in Belorussia or the General Government. If, on the other hand, the massacre were the result of a general German policy, it would also be implemented in territories outside Lithuania; consequently, departure from Vilna would offer no long-term solution, and other avenues of action had to be sought.

Korczak describes a debate among members of the "He-Halutz Coordination" over the question of leaving Vilna for the more "tranquil" ghettos of Bialystok and Warsaw. Tenenbaum-Tamaroff urged:

> We are living without knowing what will happen tomorrow, what we can expect. If we stay here and struggle

12 Korczak, *op. cit.*, p. 52.
13 Tenenbaum, *op. cit.*, pp. 123, 125.
14 Korczak, *op. cit.*, p. 53.

for existence from day to day, we shall face the eradica-
tion of the movement. Our aim and duty is to preserve it
for future work. Multitudes of Jews live in the large
ghettos in Bialystok and Warsaw; there is an active He-Halutz movement there. It is our obligation to transfer our
members there, to get them away from here, a place
where extermination awaits them. We must begin evacuating at once.

Boraks presented a different viewpoint:

Naturally it is our duty to preserve the movement, its
activists, but as a movement we are necessarily linked to
the Jewish masses in the ghetto, and we have no right to
desert them. There is no certainty that the fate of Vilna
will not overtake Bialystok too, and maybe also Warsaw...where shall we go when an *Aktion* is implemented
in Bialystok?[15]

The discussions within the He-Halutz Coordinating Committee
were influenced by the fact that hundreds of Jews in the Vilna
Ghetto had fled to the ghettos in Belorussia. Tenenbaum-Tamaroff's ties with *Feldwebel* Anton Schmidt, and the opportunities to enlist his help in fleeing to Bialystok or Warsaw,
added a dimension of reality to the exchange of views.[16]

Simultaneously, the idea of armed resistance began to take

15 *Ibid.,* p. 47. This dispute apparently took place in the first half of
   December 1941, before Boraks and Antin left on their mission to
   Warsaw. Abba Kovner, in his testimony given to the Institute of
   Contemporary Jewry, (12)83, pp. 4–5, 45–46, indicates a version
   similar to Korczak's. See also Collective Interview, YVA, 0–3/
   3882, pp. 2–3 (hereafter: Collective Interview — FPO). Those
   who contributed to this interview were Kovner, Korczak, and V.
   Kempner.
16 Friedman, *op. cit.,* pp. 161–162; Grossman, *op. cit.,* p. 47, writes
   of a meeting with Anton Schmidt, which was attended by Tenenbaum-Tamaroff, Esther Jaffe and herself, where she learned that
   Mordechai and Esther had previously met with A. Schmidt; Collective Interview—FPO p. 3.

form. It had arisen during discussions within many of the youth movements. At a meeting of several dozen Betar members held during Hanukkah, at the end of December 1941, Joseph Glazman called for "No surrender to fate and no acquiescence to annihilation!" Glazman dwelt on the necessity to establish one united force, which, in the face of danger, would embrace the youth of all factions.[17]

At a gathering of Ha-Shomer ha-Za'ir members, held at the Convent of the Dominican Nuns in December, there was talk of creating a combat organization that would encompass "all the organized anti-Fascist forces in the ghetto." It was therefore decided that Kovner and other comrades living outside the ghetto should return. Kovner did so on Christmas Eve.

At a meeting of activists in the ghetto, Kovner affirmed that uprising and armed defense were the only honorable resort for the Jews. But not all subscribed to his views. Several raised the problem of "the collective responsibility involving every Jew in the ghetto."[18] If resistance were employed, retaliation would not necessarily come to the fighters, but all the Jews would become possible targets.

N. Reznik writes that members of Ha-No'ar ha-Ziyyoni spoke of the need to embark on preparation for armed resistance.[19] The desire to organize for armed struggle also developed among a group of active Communists within the ghetto.[20]

Tenenbaum-Tamaroff of He-Halutz ha-Za'ir-Dror wrote:

> The force that has overcome Europe and destroyed entire states within days could cope with us, a handful of youngsters. It was an act of desperation...We aspired

17 Lazar, *op. cit.*, pp. 59–60; "Der Witenberg tog in vilner Geto," *YIVO Bleter*, Vol. XXX, No. 2, 1947, p. 189 (hereafter: "Der Witenberg tog").
18 Grossman, *op. cit.*, p. 37; Korczak, *op. cit.*, pp. 49, 53, 55–56; Kovner's testimony, p. 11, ICJ, (12)83.
19 Reznik, "Ha-Tenu'ah," *op. cit.*, p. 53.
20 Kowalski, *op. cit.*, p. 73; Sutzkewer, *op. cit.*, p. 129.

to only one thing: to sell our lives for the highest possible price... We began our preparations for defence in
Vilna...

In Tenenbaum-Tamaroff's opinion, the idea of resistance was
linked to his plans to leave Vilna. In one of the discussions, he
said:

Altogether, 18,000 Jews have remained in Vilna, exhausted, broken, and drained of strength. Let us go some
place where we'll have the strength to fight. We'll muster
our limited forces, we must not dissipate them. I can see
no possibility at all of recovering here.[21]

The female emissaries who came from Warsaw to the Vilna
ghetto in the last days of December 1941, Kozibrodska and T.
Schneiderman brought with them a proposal from the He-Halutz
ha-Za'ir-Dror in Warsaw that the Vilna members of the
movement proceed to the Bialystok ghetto. Tossia Altman proposed that the Ha-Shomer ha-Za'ir members in Vilna move to
Warsaw.[22]

These appeals from Warsaw placed the members of He-Halutz
ha-Za'ir-Dror and Ha-Shomer ha-Za'ir face to face with the
need to decide whether to stay in Vilna or move on to other
ghettos. Toward the end of December 1941, a group of He-
Halutz-Dror members decided to leave Vilna for the Bialystok
ghetto. Members of Ha-Shomer ha-Za'ir, however, were divided
in their approaches. Some favored leaving for Warsaw, "where
there are opportunities for rescue and continuation of the
work," whereas in the Vilna ghetto "we are weak and defenceless... There are no prospects of our struggling on in these
conditions." Kovner's views prevailed in the debate, and the

21 Tenenbaum, *op. cit.*, p. 126; Reznik's testimony, YVA, 0–33/419,
   p. 7.
22 Tenenbaum, *op. cit.*, p. 127; Korczak, *op. cit.*, pp. 49, 51–52; Collective Interview–FPO, p. 4.

majority of the activists voted to stay in Vilna and organize armed resistance.[23]

The "He-Halutz Coordination" decided to convene a conference of members of all He-Halutz youth movements on New Year's Eve. In anticipation of this assembly, Kovner was assigned the task of preparing a call to revolt which would express the concept of armed resistance. The choice of New Year's Eve for the conference was by no means accidental. The German and Lithuanian police would be celebrating and consequently less vigilant. Other social gatherings were to be held in the ghetto that evening, and the conference of youth movement adherents could be presented as a social event to welcome in the New Year.[24]

About 150 members of the He-Halutz youth movements gathered on New Year's Eve in the public soup-kitchen at 2 Straszuna Street. The manifesto, "Let us not be led like sheep to the slaughter," composed by Kovner, was read aloud for the first time. It was declaimed in Yiddish and Hebrew:

> Jewish youth!
> Do not place your trust in those who deceive you. Of 80,000 Jews in "Yerushalayim de Lita," only 20,000 are left. Our parents, brothers, and sisters were torn from us before our eyes. Where are the hundreds of men who were seized for labor?
> Where are the naked women and the children seized from us on the night of fear? Where were the Jews sent on the Day of Atonement?

23 Korczak, *op. cit.*, p. 54; Grossman, *op. cit.*, p. 48; Kovner's testimony, ICJ, (12)83, p. 13.

24 Reznik, "Ha-Tenu'ah" *op. cit.*, p. 54; Kruk, *op. cit.*, pp. 108–109, writes that Gens held a reception for the officers of the Jewish police in the ghetto on New Year's Eve. Kruk also writes of a meeting of Bund leaders that night; N. Reznik, p. 18, notes a connection with the choice of this evening for the meeting "... Maybe on that night the Germans or the Lithuanians would make merry and celebrate, and then it will be quiet for us ... "

And where are our brethren of the second ghetto?
No one returned of those marched through the gates of
the ghetto. All the roads of the Gestapo lead to Ponar.
And Ponar means death. Those who waver, put aside all
illusion. Your children, your wives, and husbands are no
more. Ponar is no concentration camp. All were shot
dead there. Hitler conspires to kill all the Jews of Europe,
and the Jews of Lithuania have been picked at the first
line. Let us not be led as sheep to the slaughter!
True, we are weak and defenceless. But the only answer
to the murderer is: To rise up with arms!
Brethren! Better fall as free fighters than to live at the
mercy of murderers. Rise up! Rise up until your last
breath.
January 1, 1942.[25]

This was the first underground meeting in the Vilna ghetto
to be attended by so large a membership of He-Halutz ha-Za'ir-
Dror, Ha-Shomer ha-Za'ir, and Ha-No'ar ha-Ziyyoni. The gathering represented important progress in bringing the thinking of
the pioneer youth movements closer to the creation of a combat
force within the ghetto.

Tenenbaum-Tamaroff had been absent from the New Year's
Eve meeting. That evening he had been, with Kozibrodska and
other comrades, among the guests at a festive party given by
Anton Schmidt at his home.[26] He was at the time engrossed in

25 Kovner's testimony, ICJ, (12) 83 p. 11; This version of the mani-
    festo was taken from Kovner's article: "Nissayon Rishon," op. cit.,
    p. 11. The archives of Beit Lohamei ha-Getta'ot contain the Yid-
    dish manuscript of the manifesto, with the caption "We must not
    go like sheep to the slaughter" (author's translation — YA), bear-
    ing the date January 1, 1942. The manifesto extends three and a
    half pages and its contents include the version of the manifesto
    drafted by Kovner, but contains additional items, such as an appeal
    to Jewish policemen to help their brethren and to Jewish women
    not to have relations with German soldiers. There is no indication
    as to who composed the manifesto.
26 Collective Interview—FPO, p. 2; Friedman, op. cit., pp. 162–163;

preparations to move a group of He-Halutz ha-Za'ir-Dror activists to Bialystok with Schmidt's help. Tenenbaum-Tamaroff and his He-Halutz ha-Za'ir-Dror group left Vilna in the first half of January.[27] Schmidt took the party to Bialystok by car. Tenenbaum-Tamaroff did not accompany the others but traveled separately, using a false passport. He met with B. Hazan in Grodno and visited the ghetto there.[28] Some of the He-Halutz youth members in Vilna stamped the departures for Bialystok as "desertion of their posts," but at the same time a small number of Ha-Shomer ha-Za'ir members also left for Bialystok. Their motivation was the same as Tenenbaum-Tamaroff's.[29]

The discussions on the move from Vilna to "quieter" ghettos devolved around the conditions for organizing armed resistance and the prospects of rescue. The evaluations of these issues influenced He-Halutz ha-Za'ir-Dror to support departure, but there were also additional factors that favored leaving the ghetto.

Tenenbaum-Tamaroff and most of his colleagues who left Vilna arrived in that city in 1939 as refugees from Warsaw and other places and envisaged it only as a stop on the way to Eretz Israel. Reports emanating from Bialystok and the General Government zones on the activities of the movement there inspired the urge to return. The appeal made by leaders in

Testimony of H. Adler, in Anton Schmidt File in the department of Righteous among the Nations in Yad Vashem, states that he and his wife, Tamara Schneiderman, and Lonia Kozibrodska were also at the reception. Dworzecki writes, in *Yediot Yad Vashem*, No. 19/20, Jerusalem, May 1959, p. 6, that Tenenbaum-Tamaroff was at Anton Schmidt's on New Year's Eve.

27 Anton Schmidt was arrested by the German Military Police in mid-January, 1942, see Friedman, *op. cit.*, pp. 162–163. Consequently, Tenenbaum-Tamaroff and his colleagues left Vilna between the beginning and the middle of January 1942.

28 Klibanski, *op. cit.*, p. 285; Tenenbaum, *op. cit.*, pp. 124, 142; Chazan's testimony, p. 24.

29 Grossman, *op. cit.*, pp. 48–49; Reznik's testimony, YVA, 0-33/419, p. 10; Kovner's testimony, ICJ, (12) 83, p. 7.

Warsaw to send the Vilna nucleus to Bialystok and Warsaw determined the issue. This desire to return to the scenes of pre-war residence and action extended to many of the activists in various factions. Members of Ha-Shomer ha-Za'ir, Ha-No'ar ha-Ziyyoni, and Betar also left Vilna for Bialystok, Warsaw, and other places. These people, along with the movement's couriers, brought information from Vilna on the massacres and the concept of armed resistance and, subsequently, became the leaders of the armed undergrounds in Bialystok and other ghettos in the General Government.[30]

Creation of the F.P.O.

A group of active youth movement and party members in the Vilna ghetto met on January 21, 1942, and decided to establish the Fareinikte Partisaner Organizatzie—F.P.O. ("United Partisans Organization"). This gathering at the home of Glazman (Betar) was attended by Kovner (Ha-Shomer ha-Za'ir), Witenberg and Borowska (Communists), Reznik (Ha-No'ar ha-Ziyyoni) and Major Frucht.[31] This important meeting had been preceded by careful preparation over several months, during which the idea of armed combat was gradually formulated. Meetings and inter-movement discussions, reviewing the plans for setting up a unified underground organization in the ghetto to wage armed resistance against the Germans, were held at

30 Arieh Wilner was one of the commanders of the fighting organization in Warsaw, and fell during the revolt. Tenenbaum-Tamaroff, Grossman, and Boraks were among the leaders of the Bialystok underground. Tenenbaum-Tamaroff and Boraks fell in action during the uprising. S. Antin was among the organizers of the underground in the General Government. He was caught while on an underground mission and tortured to death in the Pawiak jail in Warsaw.

31 Major A. Frucht served in the Polish Army and in the ghetto police was the Commanding Officer of a precinct station in the ghetto. He was invited to the founding meeting of the organization as a former army officer. Lazar, *op. cit.*, p. 393, writes that Frucht was a member of Betar and represented that movement on the Zionist Coordinating Committee in the ghetto.

the beginning of January. Kovner met with representatives of the Communists, Betar and Ha-No'ar ha-Ziyyoni. About his contacts with the Communists, Kovner writes:

> We found a common language on two points: to establish a united organization, and eliminate all reservations as regards the composition of this organization. I was afraid that they would not want the Revisionists and Ha-No'ar ha-Ziyyoni included. There were no reservations in this matter.[32]

The readiness of the Communists in the Vilna ghetto to band together with the Zionists was a unique phenomenon. The decision had been preceded by internal deliberations within the Communist ranks in the ghetto, and the eventual decision was by no means unanimous.[33]

The combination of personal factors and local conditions persuaded the Communists to accept federation with the Zionists. The Jewish Communist underground inside the Vilna ghetto had come into being before a similar non-Jewish group was organized outside its walls. The absence of an organized Communist group outside the ghetto, as the very existence of a Zionist underground within it—which was prepared to undertake armed struggle against the Germans—and the shock sustained in the wake of the mass exterminations were the determining factors in formulating the Communist position in the ghetto.

Kovner also maintained contact with Betar leader Glazman, who was Deputy Commander of the Vilna ghetto police.[34] In

---

32 Kovner's testimony, ICJ, (12) 83, pp. 8–9, 13–14, 43–46; Reznik, "Ha-Tenu'ah," *op. cit.*, p. 54.

33 Kovner's testimony, ICJ (12) 83, p. 8, 37–40. B. Szeresznyevski, who was the secretary of the Communist organization in the ghetto, apparently opposed federation into an all-Jewish framework. Opposing him were I. Witenberg, C. Borowska, and S. Madeysker, who favored such an inclusion. Testimony of J. Harmatz, ICJ, 124/12, pp. 11–12, 14.

34 Kovner's testimony, ICJ, (12) 83, pp. 9, 39. Abba Kovner tells of

their talks, during the first half of January 1942, they came to an agreement for establishing a united combat force.

Kovner's parleys with representatives of the various movements paved the way for the general meeting of the four movements—Ha-Shomer ha-Za'ir, Communists, Betar, and Ha-No'ar ha-Ziyyoni—on January 21, 1942, at which it was decided:

(1) To establish an armed fighting organization in the Vilna ghetto. It would comprise all the movements represented at the meeting, with the aim of uniting all organized forces in the ghetto;

(2) The principal objective of the organization should be the preparation of mass armed resistance, in case of an attempt to liquidate the ghetto;

(3) Defense was a national act, the struggle of a people for its honor;

(4) The organization intends to perform acts of sabotage behind the enemy's front lines;

(5) The combat organization in the ghetto will actively join the ranks of the fighting partisans and succor the Red Army in the common battle;

(6) The organization will inculcate the idea of defense in the other ghettos, and will establish contact with fighting forces outside the ghetto;

(7) The action of the organization shall be directed by a Staff Command, headed by a Chief Commander. The Command will include three members: I. Witenberg, J. Glazman and A. Kovner. Witenberg is hereby appointed Chief Commander;

(8) The organization shall be called F.P.O.[35]

his overtures to Glazman: "The truth is that we went to him with great hesitation, because at that time his position in the ghetto was such as to make it doubtful to understand how a man wanting to build up a combatant organization could talk to him. Quite simply, he was the deputy of the Head of the Ghetto ... "; Reznik, "Ha-Tenu'ah," *op. cit.*, p. 53; Reznik's testimony, 0–33/1238, p. 8.
35 Korczak, *op. cit.*, p. 67.

These decisions were the ideological basis of the F.P.O., designed to comply with the stands of the various constituents of the F.P.O., synthesizing Jewish-national and Communist aims. Articles (1), (2), and (3) stressed the Jewish national aspects of the common platform; Article (5), which affiliates the united organization with the Soviet forces fighting the Nazi invader, was probably inserted under the influence of the Communists.

The forests could have served as a possible alternative to fighting the Germans inside the ghetto, but during the F.P.O.'s formative period, partisans were not active in the wooded areas near Vilna or western Belorussia, and, consequently, leaving the ghetto for the forests was not planned.

The appointment of Witenberg, a Communist, to command the organization, of which most of the members were Zionists, had been conditioned by several factors. Above all, the leaders assessed that contact with the Communist underground would be easier to maintain were the commander of the F.P.O. himself a Communist. Witenberg's personality, aptitudes, and experience in the Communist underground in Poland also served to recommend him to command the organization.[36]

Two political groups in the Vilna ghetto were not invited to join the F.P.O.—the Bund and a section of He-Halutz ha-Za'ir-Dror members headed by Yechiel Scheinbaum (after the Tenenbaum-Tamaroff group left). The F.P.O. Command had negotiated with these two in order to secure their participation, but the talks with Scheinbaum during the spring of 1942 yielded no positive results.[37] Those with the Bund were eventually successful.

A Bund conference held in the ghetto on February 12 adopted organizational and ideological decisions, and as a result the Bund in the ghetto became a more cohesive body, directed

36 Kovner's testimony, ICJ, (12) 83, pp. 8, 13–14, 46–47; Reznik's testimony, 0–33/419, pp. 16, 19–20, 22; Sutzkewer, *op. cit.*, p. 160; "Der Wittenberg Tog," p. 200.
37 For an account of the contact between Scheinbaum and the FPO Command, see Chapter 16.

by a Central Committee. When the F.P.O. Command initiated the negotiations with the Bund, two issues confronted it— first, a decision on the idea of armed struggle, and second, whether or not they had the right to cooperate with the Zionists and Communists. Those opposed were mainly the veterans, most of whom were members of the Judenrat and the cultural or social-aid institutions in the ghetto. The younger Bundists, who were formerly in the Zukunft ("Future") youth movement, supported joining the united organization, and did in fact adhere to it in the spring of 1942.[38]

When the Bund group joined the F.P.O., their representative Abraham Chwojnik was elected to the Command. His inclusion had been one of the conditions of their joining. It was followed by the appointment of N. Reznik, representing Ha-No'ar ha-Ziyyoni, to the Command. With this expansion of the Command structure, each component group had a member on the staff Command.

The F.P.O. included mainly the youth groups from Betar, Ha-No'ar ha-Ziyyoni, Ha-Shomer ha-Za'ir, the Bund, and the Communists. None of the older activists in the various parties joined, as they disagreed with F.P.O. ideology and activity.[39]

---

38 Kruk, *op. cit.*, pp. 168–169, 298–299, 563–564. The members of the Bund were organized into underground cells. The cell leaders constituted a quasi-council, to which the Central Committee reported and with whom they consulted. The Bund members of the Judenrat were also members of the Central Committee. Organizational changes took place in July 1942, and the Bund members were then divided into two groups—"activists" and "non-activists." The Bundists on the Judenrat were no longer automatically part of the Central Committee, but were rather elected to it.

39 Reznik's testimony, 0–33/419, p. 22, says: "There were adults... among the people in the party... their conduct did not inspire us with confidence. The truth is that we approached them, and they responded with fears." The only exceptions were some of the adult members of Hitachdut–ZS who joined the FPO.

Chapter 15

THE F.P.O.

Organizational Structure and Combat Regulations
Pursuant to the decision adopted on January 21, 1942, regarding the creation and objectives of the F.P.O., the first practical steps were taken to establish the organization. The first task was to enlist members and develop underground cells. The candidates were required to be members of youth movements and fit for armed underground action. Individuals who had no affiliation with the movements were enlisted only in exceptional cases. Potential F.P.O. members took oaths of loyalty.[1]

During the initial phase, the basic unit of the organization consisted of three members from one specific movement, who were dubbed a "trio." The representative of each movement in the F.P.O. Command selected those who were to be accepted into the F.P.O. and divided them into the "trios." These operated as separate units for four or five months and were subsequently replaced by units of five members each, called "quintets," which were composed of members of different movements who lived in close proximity to one another. The quintets became the main operational units of the F.P.O.

Three quintets composed a platoon, under a platoon commander, and four to six platoons were organized as a "battal-

---

1 Kovner's testimony, ICJ, (12) 83, pp. 12, 50; Testimony of Z. Treger, YVA, 0–3/3670, p. 13.

ion" of 100–120 fighters. The F.P.O. comprised two battalions and several staff units, directly subordinate to the F.P.O. Command. The staff units consisted of a signal detachment, arms instructors, and an intelligence unit.

The intelligence unit was formed in March 1942 under J. Glazman's command. Its function was to infiltrate German and Lithuanian institutions in order to elicit information. The unit also posted its men among the Judenrat and Jewish police personnel. Girls belonging to the F.P.O. excelled in their intelligence duties.

The signal personnel attached to headquarters formed the link among all operational levels, transmitting summonses to meetings of various groups and to arms-drill exercises, and circulating the news-bulletin, which headquarters published daily, among the F.P.O. commanders. The F.P.O. also maintained a group at the "Kailis" camp, numbering twenty men, directly subordinate to the F.P.O. Command.[2]

The essential change in the F.P.O. structure was the change from "trios" based on members from one movement to intermovement "quintets." The F.P.O. thus became a unified organization, rather than a confederation of various movements. This change showed that identification with the F.P.O. had proved to be stronger than the particularistic interests of each individual movement. The F.P.O. was the only underground organization in the ghettos that began on a particularist basis and succeeded in achieving a sufficient degree of cooperation and mutual trust to enable a change in framework.[3]

The particularist character of the movement, however, was preserved in the F.P.O. Command, which consisted of the five representatives of the movements that had established it, and the political division of the senior command posts; the F.P.O.

2 Reznik's testimony, 0–33/1238, p. 23; Harmatz's testimony, pp. 11–12; Kowalski, *op. cit.*, p. 148.
3 The individual political movements fighting in the Warsaw, Bialystok, and other ghettos continued to maintain their separate identities.

Chief was I. Witenberg (Communist), and the two battalion commanders were A. Kovner of Ha-Shomer ha-Za'ir and J. Glazman of Betar. The command, composed of representatives of all the movements, and the mutual confidence among them, made possible the reorganization and merger in the lower echelons. The creation of the F.P.O. did not eliminate the clandestine activities of the youth movements. Some of their adherents joined the F.P.O., while others remained unaware of its existence. Activity within the movements was mainly ideological, cultural, and social. In addition, each movement served as a reservoir of manpower for the F.P.O. and made its growth and development feasible.[4] The F.P.O. continually expanded, reorganized, and developed throughout its existence in the ghetto, from the end of January 1941 until September 1943.

F.P.O. Combat Regulations
The F.P.O. structure, methods of mobilization and combat conditions were published in a document entitled "Combat Regulations of the F.P.O.," in March 1943.[5]
Clause 1 of the "Regulation" dealt with the difficult conditions in which ghetto combat would be waged. Clause 2 described the structure of the F.P.O. Clause 3 prescribed the mobilization of the members for battle and preconsidered two situations—mobilization upon the initiative of the F.P.O. command and emergency mobilization. The password "Liza is calling" (after Liza Magun, a F.P.O. member who was caught by the Security Police and executed at Ponar) became the secret call-up order. During the mobilization of the F.P.O., it was the duty of each member to reach the prearranged assembly point. Emergency mobilization was to be implemented when the staff command had been forced out of action for any reason what-

4 Reznik's testimony, 0–33/419, p. 23 and his article: "Ha-Tenu'ah," *op. cit.*, p. 56.
5 Korczak, *op. cit.*, pp. 165–169; 284–285; B. Ajzensztajn, *Ruch podziemny w ghettach i obozach, Materialy i Dokumenty,* Warsaw, 1946, pp. 123–133.

soever and the ghetto was threatened by immediate danger. In such cases all fighters were required to report to assembly places, without having been personally called up. Non-reporting for duty and disappearing into hiding (into the *malines*) was branded as treason.

Clause 4 gave directives to the commanders as well as the rank and file on comportment in battle and the action to be taken if they were cut off from their units or from the F.P.O. Command. They were required to find means of communication with the Command and to continue fighting at all costs, even without contact with headquarters. This clause emphasized the need to use ammunition sparingly and to display resourcefulness during action. The battle-posts of the commanders and the system for replacing those killed or missing in action were set forth.

Clause 5 dealt with the formation of an alternative command should the F.P.O. headquarters be out of action for any reason, but primarily in case of arrest. All members of the F.P.O. central headquarters signed the "Regulation" with their underground *noms de guerre*—"Leon," the Chief Commander I. Witenberg; "Abraham," J. Glazman; "Uri," A. Kovner; "Moshe," A. Chwojnik; and "Chaim," N. Reznik.

The "Battle Regulation" was distributed to all F.P.O. members; at the sub-unit levels it was discussed, and questions were raised in order to clarify obscure points. There were those who expressed doubts as to whether the fighting was to take place in the ghetto or in the forests. The F.P.O. command published a supplement to the "Combat Regulation" on April 4, 1943, entitled "Explanations of the Regulation," several weeks after having issued the original document (see Appendix B).

The "Explanations to the Regulation" provided the answer to the two central problems in the concept of combat—time and place. The F.P.O. would rise in revolt and fight within the ghetto, if, in its estimation, a general liquidation of the ghetto and not a limited *Aktion* was being launched; and the initial site of combat would be the ghetto, not the forests.

At its peak, in April–August 1943, the F.P.O. totaled about 300 members, organized in two battalions and staff units. Some 300 more young men, mainly members of the movements and youth groups from other ghettos who had come to Vilna, formed the "periphery" of the F.P.O. They did not belong to F.P.O. underground cells, but were marginally affiliated with the organization and were available to the F.P.O. for operations in the ghetto.[6]

Spreading the Idea of Resistance

One of the F.P.O.'s basic objectives was to transmit the idea of resistance to other ghettos. The F.P.O. sent messengers to inform the political movements in other ghettos of the ideas on combat and of the united underground organization established in the Vilna ghetto.

Chaike Grossman left Vilna at the end of January or beginning of February 1942, on a mission for the F.P.O., for Bialystok and Warsaw. She carried a letter from Witenberg to the Communist leaders in Bialystok authorizing her, on behalf of the Communists in the Vilna ghetto, to request the Communists in the Bialystok ghetto to agree to a common front with the other movements in the ghetto. During her sojourn in Warsaw at the end of February or beginning of March 1942, it was her mission to disclose to the members of the pioneer youth movements and the political forces closely allied with them the news of the F.P.O.'s creation and its objectives. Moreover, she was to obtain funds for arms purchases by the F.P.O. Grossman writes that the concept of armed defense was not accepted at that time in Warsaw, but that she did succeed in soliciting funds for the F.P.O. from the director of the "Joint" there, Itzhak Gitterman.[7] Grossman returned to Vilna in March 1942,

6 Kovner's testimony, ICJ, (12) 83, pp. 16, 54–55.
7 Grossman, op. cit., pp. 60–62, 71, 80–83, 88, 93–94; Korczak, op. cit., p. 71.

with the money. Several days later Boraks and Antin also returned from their mission in Warsaw.[8]

The emissaries reported to the F.P.O. on the situation in Warsaw and Bialystok. According to the reports, the Jews in these ghettos believed that the extermination would not touch them directly; therefore, the concept of combining political forces in the ghetto and the creation of a combat organization on the lines of the one in Vilna had not gained acceptance.[9] Boraks and Grossman left Vilna for Bialystok in April 1942, and remained there to organize an armed underground.[10]

As a result of the reports it had received, the F.P.O. Command decided to send another delegation to Bialystok and Warsaw, this time composed of three persons—the sisters Sara and Ruzhka Zilber and Shlomo Antin. The emissaries were instructed to transmit written evidence to these ghettos, furnished by people who had succeeded in escaping from Ponar, in order to arouse the ghetto inhabitants to action and give credence to the reports of impending extermination. The delegation was also told to circulate a proclamation that had been drafted by the F.P.O. Command. The first part of the proclamation told of the exterminations perpetrated in Vilna, Kovno, Vilejka, and Minsk, and called upon the Jews to discard the illusion that economic considerations would influence the Germans to refrain from mass murder. The annihilation of the Jewish people was the Nazi policy, the statement declared, to

---

8 *Sefer ha-Shomer ha-Za'ir*, pp. 529, 531; Grossman, *op. cit.*, pp. 99–100, 102. Boraks and Antin came to Vilna separately. F. Plotnitzka arrived together with Antin on a mission for He-Halutz and left for Bialystok a few days later.

9 *Ibid.*, p. 76, meeting with Barasz, chairman of the Judenrat in Bialystok; meeting with the leaders of the parties in the Warsaw and Bialystok ghettos, pp. 88, 91; meeting with the Communists from Bialystok and Warsaw, pp. 82–83, 96; Y. Zuckerman, "The Jewish Fighting Organization — Z.O.B.," *The Catastrophe of European Jewry*, Jerusalem, 1976, p. 519.

10 Grossman, *op. cit.*, pp. 99–103, 105. The members of Ha-Shomer ha-Za'ir in Vilna opposed Boraks' departure.

take priority over all economic considerations. The statement concluded with a call to take up arms and fight. The delegation left Vilna in April 1942. They were in Bialystok a few days, but on the way to Warsaw, all three were detained at the Malkinia railroad station, imprisoned at Pawiak in Warsaw, and several months later executed there.[11]

In April 1942, Glazman sent a young girl to inquire into the situation in the Kovno ghetto. The girl returned to Vilna and reported to the F.P.O. on her mission.[12]

Following the arrest and imprisonment of the Zilber sisters and Antin at Malkinia, communications between Vilna and Warsaw were severed for several months, to be renewed at the end of June 1942 by Irene Adamowicz, a Polish woman from Warsaw. She brought with her letters and funds for the F.P.O., entrusted to her by Joseph Kaplan (a youth movement leader in the Warsaw Ghetto) and also the first reports of the exterminations in the General Government.[13]

Adamowicz remained in Vilna for several weeks, until the second half of July. She entered the ghetto several times, met with F.P.O. leaders, told them what was happening in Warsaw and the General Government, and was kept abreast of developments in Vilna by them. The F.P.O. Command asked Adamowicz to go to the Kovno and Shavli ghettos with letters and reports on the situation in the Vilna ghetto, and communicate the idea of armed combat to the Zionist youth movements in these ghettos.[14]

She succeeded in entering the Kovno ghetto, and there met

11 Korczak, *op. cit.*, pp. 76–77, 288. *Sefer ha-Partizanim*, p. 25.
12 Z. Brown and D. Levin, *Toldoteha shel Mahteret*, Jerusalem, 1962, p. 80. This was probably a mission for the Betar movement in Vilna to the Betar movement in Kovno, undertaken by the young girl Krapivnik.
13 Testimony of I. Adamowicz, YVA, 0-33/415, p. 1.
14 *Ibid.*, p. 2, states that Glazman remitted her letters for distribution in Kovno. Glazman had been in contact with the people in Kovno and Shavli from the time he was Betar commissioner in Lithuania.

with members of the Coordinating Committee of the Zionist parties and two Judenrat members, Dr. Elkes and Garfunkel. To these people she reported on the situation in Vilna, Warsaw, and other ghettos, and on the beginning of extermination operations in the General Government. She also met with representatives of He-Halutz and Ha-Shomer ha-Za'ir in Kovno and told them about the F.P.O. During her two days in the Kovno ghetto, she was also given a survey of the situation there for transmission to Vilna and Warsaw.[15]

The mission undertaken by Adamowicz had great influence on the underground organization in the Kovno ghetto. Her reports from Vilna prompted the decision of the "Coordinating Committee" and the Zionist parties to shift underground action from the sphere of culture and education to that of resistance.[16] Adamowicz left Kovno for Shavli again to report to the ghetto there on the situation of the Jews in the places she had visited, and on what was transpiring in the General Government. Upon returning from Shavli, she entered the Kovno ghetto again and reported on conditions in Shavli, revisited the Vilna ghetto, where she gave accounts of the situation in the two other ghettos, and then resumed her journey to Warsaw.[17]

Adamowicz was the last messenger between Vilna and Warsaw. Her visit took place during the period when the great deportations were beginning in Warsaw, but as she had left a few days earlier she knew nothing about them. The link between Vilna and Bialystok lasted only a few more months. C. Grossman, then in Bialystok, was summoned to Vilna in September or October 1942. She remained there only a short time and returned to Bialystok in October 1942.[18] It was the last direct contact between the Jewish underground organizations in the two cities. But the F.P.O. had inculcated the ideas of

15 Brown-Levin, op. cit., pp. 82–84; Garfunkel, op. cit., pp. 115–116.
16 Brown–Levin, op. cit., pp. 82–83.
17 Yerushalmi, op. cit., pp. 94–96; Garfunkel, op. cit., pp. 116–117; Adamowicz's testimony, p. 2.
18 Grossman, op. cit., pp. 142, 147–150.

resistance and unification of political forces in the other ghettos. It was the first underground group composed of active Jewish political groups to have adopted the idea of armed resistance, and it was to serve as an example for the other ghettos.

The connections between the ghettos were severed at the end of the summer of 1942. The massive expulsion from the Warsaw ghetto, from July to September 1942, and the liquidation of the majority of Warsaw Jewry also endommaged the clandestine communications among the ghettos. The Warsaw ghetto ceased to be the active Jewish center from which the links radiated.

The situation in the fall of 1942 also diminished the importance of ties between the ghettos. The murder of Jews in the General Government, which began in the spring and summer of 1942, proved that the Vilna emissaries' message—that the policy of liquidation was not a local but rather a general problem—was the tragic truth. But the idea of armed resistance, which had emanated from Vilna, had not fallen on deaf ears. Inter-ghetto communications had been initiated when the vital need arose to pass on information on the liquidation actions and the concept of resistance. The couriers to and from Vilna had accomplished this goal. Beginning with the second half of 1942, the underground organizations in the ghettos devoted their principal efforts to internal arrangements, arms procurement, and establishing contacts with local non-Jewish underground groups.

Contact with the Non-Jewish Underground and Partisans
The F.P.O. sought ways to contact non-Jewish clandestine groups active in Vilna and the partisans in the forests in order to obtain arms from these groups, but also to integrate itself into the general struggle against Nazi Germany.

The Polish national underground, affiliated with the Polish Government-in-Exile in London, was the only existing clandestine organization in Vilna when the F.P.O. was created. This underground, at first known as the Zwiazek Walki Zbrojnej

("Union for Armed Struggle") and later as A.K., Armia Krajowa ("Home Army"), began to operate in Vilna as early as
1939, after the fall of Poland, and continued its activities
throughout the Soviet period and the years of German occupation. The principal activity of the A.K. during the German
occupation in those years was the organization and mobilization
of forces for the struggle over the future of the Vilna region,
which, in its view, would be waged between the new state of
Poland, to be created after the victory over Nazi Germany,
and the U.S.S.R.[19]

The F.P.O. succeeded in contacting the Polish underground,
and negotiated with them for aid in procuring arms for the
Jewish group. The Polish underground leaders questioned the
F.P.O. on its orientation: was it Communist; what side would
it take when the Soviets returned and a struggle between the
Poles and the Soviets ensued over authority in Vilna? The
Poles were informed that the F.P.O. was not a Communist
group, but an organization fighting the Nazis, in which Communists were included but were not the majority. The F.P.O.'s
objective was to fight the Germans until the liberation; the
fate of Vilna after the liberation was not its immediate concern,
it would be decided at some later time.

Following weeks of contacts, a negative response was tendered to the F.P.O.'s requests for aid. As an outcome of this

19 A Polish underground military organization called Zwiazek Walki
    Zbrojnej (ZWZ) was established in Vilna in December 1939. Colonel
    N. Sulik, who had been sent for that purpose from Warsaw, was
    placed at the head of the organization. The group was in direct
    contact with the Polish leadership in Paris, in addition to its con-
    tacts with underground quarters in Warsaw. The function of the Polish
    underground in Vilna, during the period of Lithuanian independence
    (until July 1940) was to assist Poles in escaping to Western Europe
    in order to join the Polish forces there and to stockpile arms. The
    Polish underground continued to exist throughout the period of
    Soviet government in Lithuania (July 1940 to June 1941) and under
    the German occupation. It changed its name to Armia Krajowa

In the streets of the Jewish Quarter in Vilna before the war

The conquering German Army being received by the Lithuanians (June 30, 1941)

Officers and soldiers of the Lithuanian Corps of the Soviet Army joining the ranks of the German Army (June 30, 1941)

BEKANNTMACHUNG

ОБ'ЯВЛЕНИЕ НАСЕЛЕНИЮ

Der deutsche Soldat kommt nicht als Eroberer, sondern als Befreier von einem verbrecherischen Regierungssystem, das schaffende Bauern und Arbeiter ausbeutete und versklavte. Nach Tagen harten Kampfes, die Chaos und Zerstörung brachten, zieht mit den deutschen Soldaten Ordnung und Sicherheit ein.

Der Aufbau kann beginnen!

Bis zu einer endgültigen Regelung wird folgendes angeordnet:

Sämtliche **kommunistischen und jüdischen Organe sind mit sofortiger Wirkung ihres Amtes enthoben. Die Gemeinden wählen aus ihren Reihen einen zuverlässigen Mann,** der nicht Kommunist oder Jude sein darf, **als Führer der Gemeinde.** Den Anordnungen des Führers der Gemeinde ist unbedingt Folge zu leisten. Diese Regelung gilt, solange nicht durch eine deutsche Dienststelle ein kommissarischer Bürgermeister bestimmt wird.

Der Führer der Gemeinde hat sich, solange keine Ortskommandantur eingerichtet ist, im Falle der Belegung des Ortes mit deutschen Truppen sofort bei der Truppe zu melden.

ALLE JUDEN beider Geschlechter **haben sich durch weisse Armbinden mit dem Davidstern auf beiden Armen zu kennzeichnen.**

Alle Juden beider Geschlechter haben sich umgehend beim Führer der Gemeinde des letzten Wohnortes zu melden. **Die Freizügigkeit für Juden ist mit sofortiger Wirkung aufgehoben.** Juden, die sich ohne schriftliche Genehmigung des Führers der Gemeinde bezw. einer deutschen Dienststelle aus den Ortschaften entfernen, setzen sich härtester Bestrafung aus.

Alle Juden beider Geschlechter von 16 bis 50 Jahren **stehen dem Führer der Gemeinde zu Arbeitsleistungen zur Verfügung.**

Alle Juden haben die in ihrem Besitz befindlichen Rundfunkgeräte beim Führer der Gemeinde abzuliefern.

Feindselige Handlungen gegen die Deutsche Wehrmacht oder Zerstörung von Einrichtungen der Deutschen Wehrmacht werden mit dem Tode bestraft!

Wer Nachrichtenanlagen (z. B. ortsfeste oder feldmässige Fernsprech- und Telegrafenleitungen, Vermittlungseinrichtungen, ...) **beschädigt, wird mit dem Tode** ...

Das normale Wirtschaftsleben muss sofort in Gang kommen, sonst hungert die Bevölkerung im Winter!

Jeder bleibt an seinem Platz und verrichtet weiter seine gewohnte Arbeit.

Wer plündert wird erschossen.

Alle Maschinen und Geräte sind zu erhalten.

Alle Lebens- und Futtermittel sind zu erhalten.

Die Felder sind weiter zu bestellen, die Ernte ist einzubringen, sonst muss die Bevölkerung im Winter hungern!

Alle Warenbestände, auch die der Koperative und der Roten Armee, die die Bevölkerung an sich genommen oder vergraben hat, sind unverzüglich an eine von dem Führer der Gemeinde zu bestimmende Sammelstelle abzuführen. Nichtablieferung wird als Plünderung bestraft. **Hamstern ist bei strengster Bestrafung verboten.** Alle Schaffenden sollen Brot erhalten. **Sämtliche im Gemeindebereich verlaufenden Strassen sind instandzuhalten.** Es ist für dauernde Pflege und gute Beschaffenheit zu sorgen. Die Brücken sind zu reparieren.

a) Schlaglöcher sind mit Schotter auszufüllen.
b) Auf Schotterstrassen ist der zur Seite geschleuderte Sand auf die Schotterdecke zu werfen.
c) Notwendiges Material wie Schotter und Sand ist durch die Gemeinde heranzufahren und an den Strassenrändern so abzulegen, dass die Fahrbahn nicht verengt wird.

Zur Durchführung dieser Arbeiten sind insbesondere Juden heranzuziehen.

Neben dem Rubel gilt die Mark als Zahlungsmittel. Dabei gilt **eine Mark soviel wie 10 Rubel. Es gelten weiter die alten Preise.** Preissteigerungen sind unbegründet und schädigen das Wirtschaftsleben. Daher wird der, der die Preise steigert, wegen Wucher bestraft.

Die Spuren des Kampfes sind zu beseitigen

Wenn bisher ein deutscher Soldat durch die Bevölkerung beerdigt wurde und wenn ein unbeerdigter deutscher Soldat gefunden wird, ist umgehend der nächsten deutschen Dienststelle Meldung zu erstatten.

Rotarmisten sind zu beerdigen.

Alles von der Roten Armee zurückgelassene Gerät, wie Kraftwagen, Traktoren, Wagen, Geschütze, Waffen usw. und alle Ausrüstungsgegenstände sind an Sammelstellen zu schaffen. Ort der Sammelstelle bestimmt der Führer der Gemeinde.

In zerstörten Ortsteilen sind die Trümmer und Schutt von den Strassen zu entfernen. Abgerissene Fernsprechleitungen aufzurollen und an die Sammelstelle zu schaffen.

Tierkadaver sind zu begraben. Jedoch nicht in der Nähe von Brunnen und fliessendem Wasser.

Солдаты вооруженных сил Германии не являются завоевателями-захватчиками, а освободителями русского народа от преступного и кровожадного правительства, которое 23 года эксплоатировало и порабощало трудящихся — крестьян и рабочих!

Прошли дни жестоких боев, принесших разрушение и хаос. С приходом германских войск наступает время безопасности и порядка.

ВСЕ ЖИДЫ обоих полов **обязаны носить белую повязку на обоих рукавах.**

The German head commander's first announcement: "The German soldiers have come to free the population from Communist bondage. The Jews must wear arm bands with a Star of David; they must not leave their quarters; they must carry out their required work and yield their radios" 4·7·1941

Mass graves in Ponar

Jacob Gens

The Judenrat building, Rudnicka Street No. 6

FLIEGERHORSTKOMMANDANTUR WILNA-SÜD
ZERLEGEBETRIEB

Nr. *246*

BESCHEINIGUNG

Der Jude *Berkon Hbram 189*

wohnhaft in Wilna *Zgany-łoju 6/4. 27.*

ist in dem obg. Betriebe z. Zeit ständig beschäftigt und darf

keinesfalls für andere Arbeiten verwendet werden.

Dieser Schein verliert seine Gültigkeit am *30. /9. 41*

sofern er nicht verlängert wird.

Wilna, den *22. /8.* 1941.

Techn. Inspektor (?) a. Kr.

The white shaynen, *the work permit for
the Jewish forced laborer in the service of
the Wehrmacht*

*Bread-ration card issued to each ghetto resident after he paid all
required taxes*

Brot 25 Woche	Brot 26 Woche	Brot 27 Woche	Brot 28 Woche	Der Ghettovorsteher und Chef der Judenpolizei		Fleisch 28 Woche	Fleisch 27 Woche	Fleisch 26 Woche	Fleisch 25 Woche
Mehl 25 Woche	Mehl 26 Woche	Mehl 27 Woche	Mehl 28 Woche	**BROTKARTE**		Butter 28 Woche	Butter 27 Woche	Butter 26 Woche	Butter 25 Woche
Zucker 25 Woche	Zucker 26 Woche	Zucker 27 Woche	Zucker 28 Woche	1 Pers.		X 28 Woche	X 27 Woche	X 26 Woche	X 25 Woche
Salz 25 Woche	Salz 26 Woche	Salz 27 Woche	Salz 28 Woche	für die Zeit vom 2.7.1943 bis 30.7		Y 28 Woche	Y 27 Woche	Y 26 Woche	Y 25 Woche
Graupen 25 Woche	Graupen 26 Woche	Graupen 27 Woche	Graupen 28 Woche	(Zuname und Vorname) (Adresse)		Gemüse 28 Woche	Gemüse 27 Woche	Gemüse 26 Woche	Gemüse 25 Woche
Kartoffel 25 Woche	Kartoffel 26 Woche	Kartoffel 27 Woche	Kartoffel 28 Woche	(Unterschrift des Kartenausgebers)		R 28 Woche	T 27 Woche	U 26 Woche	W 25 Woche

Druck „Awotra" Wilna, 1741-5055

Szawelska Street No. 5, a ghetto Torah Center and children's kitchen

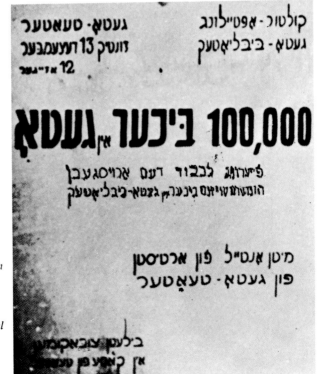

A celebration in honor of the loan of the 100,000th book from the Central Ghetto Library

A scene from the production of The Eternal Jew, *in the Vilna Ghetto,* **June 1943**

A check by the Gestapo near the ghetto gate on Rudnicka Street. Only those with special passes received an exit permit

Plan of the Vilna Ghetto

WILEŃSKA
DOMINIKAŃSKA
GAONA
SZWARCOWYZ.
TROCKA
FRANCISZKAŃSKA
ŻYDOWSKA
SZKLANNA
KIEJDAŃSKA
LIDZKI
MIKOŁAJA
NIEMIECKA
JATKOWA
WIELKA
STRASZUNA
OSZMIAŃSKA
DZISNIEŃSKI Z.
ŻMUDZKA
SZPITALNA
JATKOWA
RUDNICKA
OSTROBRAMSKA
ZAWALNA
BOSACZKOWA
HETMAŃSKA
KONSKA
KRUPNICZY Z.
STEFAŃSKA W.
KWASZELNA

Ghetto No. 1, September 6, 1941 — September 24, 1943
Ghetto No. 2, September 6, 1941 — October 24, 1941
Area that was added to the Ghetto No. 1, on September 1942
The Ghetto Gate +++
The Judenrat Building ✦

Abba Kovner

Yitzhak Witenberg

Sonia Madeysker

Mordechai Tenenbaum-Tamaroff

Joseph Glazman   *Yechiel Scheinbaum*

The remains of the house at Straszuna Street No 12, where F.P.O. fighters Yechiel Scheinbaum and friends fell

In a maline *during an* aktion *in the ghetto (drawing by M. Bahelfer)*

MAP OF VILNA AREA

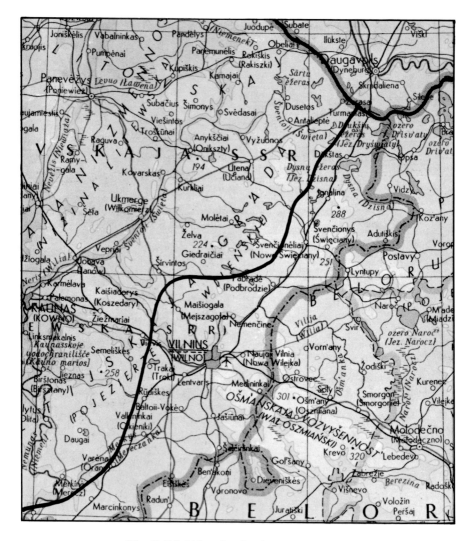

━━━━ *The Polish-Lithuanian border prior to September 1, 1939*

▬▬▬ *The border of Soviet-Lithuania: 15 June 1940—22 June 1941*

Jewish partisans in the forests

Jewish partisans from Vilna who fought in the Rudniki forests return to Vilna after the city's liberation (July 14, 1944)

The ruins of "German Street" in the Jewish Quarter

The destroyed YIVO building in Vivutska Street No. 18

The demolished Gaon Synagogue

decision, the links with the Polish underground were severed.[20]
The A.K. in the Vilna area persisted in its anti-Jewish stance.
Reports sent by this organization to the Polish Government-in-
Exile depicted the Jews in Vilna and other ghettos of former
eastern Poland as Communist or pro-Communist elements. The
Jewish partisans active in the forests were portrayed as gangs
of robbers, who behaved brutally towards non-Jews.[21] This
picture of the Jews in the ghettos was rooted in political
evaluations and inherent anti-Semitism. The result was that
many Jews of Vilna and its environs who found refuge in the
forests or with farmers, as well as Jewish partisans, were murdered by bands of Polish partisans.[22]

A Communist underground group, the first in Vilna outside
the ghetto, was organized at the outset of 1942. It was composed of Polish Communists, headed by Jan Przewalski and
bore the name of Zwiazek Walki Czynnej (ZWC) ("Union for
Active Struggle"). It numbered some sixty to eighty members.
For the first few months of its existence, this clandestine group
had no connection with Moscow, nor with partisans in the
forests.[23]

Contact was made between the F.P.O. and the ZWC in the

(A.K.). See the article by M. Juchniewicz "Udzial Polaków w litewskim ruchu oporu w latach 1941–1944," *Wojskowy Przeglad
Historyczny*, No. I (45), 1968, pp. 52–53; J. Garlinski, "Polskie
Panstwo Podziemne (1939–1945)," *Zeszyty Historyczne*, Paris, 1974;
S. Zabiello, "Ksztaltowanie sie koncepeji 'Burzy'," *Wojskowy Przeglad Historyczny*, Warsaw, 1968.
20 Kovner's testimony, YVA, 0-33/353, pp. 6–7; Grossman, *op. cit.*,
pp. 38–39.
21 Report of April 30, 1943, YVA, M–2/198, pp. 128–129; Report
of the situation in Poland, March 25, 1943, YVA, 0-25/198, p. 4.
22 For murder of Jews in the forests at the hands of the Polish
partisans, see the following sources and testimonies: N. Bazilian,
YVA, 0-3/2335, pp. 29, 32, 35; Kovner, "Nissayon Rishon," *op.
cit.*, p. 4; Haubenshtok's testimony, YVA, 0-3/1286; Dworzecki,
op. cit., p. 376; Lazar, *op. cit.*, pp. 267–294.
23 Juchniewicz, *op. cit.*, pp. 56–57, 64; J. Przewalska's testimony, YVA.
0-3/3027, pp. 3–5; *Gitlerovskaya okupatsiya*, pp. 200, 210.

spring of 1942 through Makar Karablikov, a Belorussian who was in contact with Jewish Communists in the ghetto. The first meeting, held outside the ghetto, was attended by Sonia Madeysker on behalf of the F.P.O. Other meetings took place in the ghetto as well as outside. Jan Przewalski went in and out of the ghetto disguised as a Jew. The F.P.O. and the ZWC maintained common ties and cooperated without creating a joint organizational framework. The ZWC was a small organization with sparse means, incapable of extending any substantial help to the F.P.O., which was the larger and more affluent of the two, and indeed was called upon by the former for arms.[24] The Jewish Communists in the ghetto maintained organizational ties with J. Przewalski and his comrades through the "Urban Communist Committee," established in the first months of 1942 in the Vilna ghetto.[25] The tie with the ZWC was important to the F.P.O. from the standpoint of morale, as proof that a friendly element did exist in Vilna and, despite the general alienation and hatred towards the Jews, was ready to cooperate and help as much as possible.

News of Soviet partisans operating in areas not far from Vilna began to reach the ghetto in the second half of 1942.[26] A Lithuanian Communist group was sent in from the U.S.S.R. to operate in the enemy rear. The group, numbering six persons was parachuted in and reached the Rudniki forests south of Vilna in the summer of 1942. The name of the party, led by A. Kunigenas, was "Alksnis" (Lithuanian: "alder tree"). They were in radio contact with headquarters in the U.S.S.R. The men of this group were pre-war natives of the Vilna area.

24 Juchniewicz, *op. cit.*, p. 58, and Przewalska, in her testimony, p. 7, write of the weapons that the ZWZ had acquired from the FPO.

25 The Secretary of the first Underground Urban Communist Committee in Vilna, which was established within the ghetto, was B. Szeresznyevski; J. Przewalski was a committee member. See Juchniewicz, *op. cit.*, p. 60, n. 106.

26 Kruk, *op. cit.*, pp. 330, 336, writes that, during August 1942, reports reached the ghetto concerning partisan activity in the district.

They established contact with their friends and relatives and stayed with them.[27] Contact between this group and the F.P.O. was effected by a ghetto inhabitant who worked in the Biala-Vaka (Baltoji Voke) camp and was in contact with these partisans. He succeeded in arranging a meeting between Witenberg and the "Alksnis" group somewhere in the vicinity of Biala-Vaka.

During their exchanges, Witenberg asked that they inform Moscow of the F.P.O.'s existence and that it be recognized by Moscow as a Jewish combat organization within the Vilna ghetto, ready to revolt at the time of the liquidation of the ghetto. The attitude of the Alksnis was that a fighting organization has no right to stand by until the day of the uprising and that it was imperative that the F.P.O. act at once. Witenberg was evidently placed in a grave personal dilemma when this group of Soviet fighters insisted that his organization, which he commanded, take immediate action. The demand was binding on him as a Communist and as in keeping with the Soviet line, which dictated that active combat against the Nazi enemy superseded all else. On the other hand, Witenberg commanded a Jewish organization that had been created to revolt *within* the ghetto as a means of Jewish defense against annihilation during the liquidation phase. The significance of that tenet was to defer combat until the day the ghetto was to be liquidated.

Kovner speaks of these meetings and of Witenberg's attitude in the following terms:

> He [Witenberg] reported to us ... He tried to persuade us that, without diverging from the principal objective, which was the ghetto uprising, there was a justified demand that we not sit in the ghetto and wait for the ap-

27 The Kunigenas group was one of the operational units sent to Lithuania by the Central Committee of the Lithuanian Communist Party during March–November 1942. The group had six members: W. Sinkiewicz ("Margis"), W. Zapolski ("Zalski"), A. Kott, B. Tuminskas, G. Moyseyenko; see also Juchniewicz, *op. cit.*, p. 55.

pointed day... There is no other force and we must
give a hand to the ongoing fight. They did not tell him
the truth—that there were only five of them. We
staunchly insisted that our principal and exclusive aim
was the ghetto.[28]

As to the outcome of the negotiations, the two sides reached
the following agreement:

(1) A F.P.O. group would go with the parachutists to organize a partisan base in the Vilna region;

(2) A group of F.P.O. instructors were to be sent to the partisan base for combat training;

(3) The F.P.O. was to organize the collecting of information
at all important military and economic points in Vilna and continue to commit acts of sabotage;

(4) The parachutists promised aid to the F.P.O. and upon the
outbreak of the uprising in the ghetto would provide firearms
and explosives;

(5) The F.P.O. Command would supply two of the parachutists with forged papers to enable them to operate in the
city.

The Alksnis group informed the F.P.O. people, on behalf of
the Partisan command in Moscow, that they recognized the
F.P.O. and its aims as "a Partisan organization functioning
within the ghetto, and as a link in the Soviet partisan movement." Pursuant to this agreement with Alksnis, the F.P.O.
launched an extensive effort to collect information in Vilna.
Its members were sent to work in the railroad-station to observe
and record rail traffic and the freight carried. Reports were
prepared on military units and installations in Vilna—their
location, their purpose, the manpower and equipment they deployed—and on the movement of military forces through
Vilna. These reports were transmitted to the Alksnis group and

28 Kovner's testimony, ICJ (12) 83, pp. 28–30; *Gitlerovskaya okupatsiya*, p. 200. Z. Rozonowicz was the man who established the
contact between the FPO and the "Alksnis" group.

radioed to Moscow. Contact was established, through the F.P.O., between Alksnis and the Polish Communist group led by Przewalski. This activity lasted a month or two, until the Alksnis group was liquidated by the Germans after the local inhabitants betrayed them at the end of the summer of 1942. The F.P.O. was once more left without any link to the Soviet Partisan movement, and the hope of obtaining firearms and aid from this source was thus dissipated.[29]

The F.P.O. decided to attempt to regain contact with the Soviet Union by sending couriers through the Germano-Soviet front lines. The mission was entrusted to two female members of F.P.O., Sonia Madeysker and Cesia Rosenberg. Their task was to reach the Soviet Union and convey to the authorities there, and the whole world, news of the extermination of the Jews throughout Europe and of the massacres at Ponar, and to urge that help and rescue be extended to the surviving population. According to the plan, the couriers were to approach the front in the Velikiye-Luki region, using false papers, and try to cross the lines with the aid of partisans operating in that area. The F.P.O. had learned, through its contacts with Alksnis, of a gap in the German front lines through which thousands of people and supplies had been passed in both directions by the Soviet Partisans operating there. This aperture was dubbed "the Suraz Gap" after a nearby village.

Madeysker and Rosenberg left Vilna at the end of September or October 1942, and, via Vileyka-Polotsk, reached Velikiye-Luki, in the vicinity of the front, where both were taken into custody. Neither girl was identified as a Jewess, and as their papers showed they were from Vilna, they were returned there under guard. Both succeeded in escaping from their captors in the Vilna railroad station and made their way back into the ghetto. Thus, the attempt by the F.P.O. to renew the link with the U.S.S.R. and to appeal for help was fruitless.[30]

29 Korczak, op. cit., pp. 132–133, Kovner's testimony, ICJ (12)83, pp. 28–30; Gitlerovskaya okupatsiya, p. 200; Juchniewicz, op. cit., p. 55.
30 Korczak, op. cit., pp. 133, 136; Kovner's testimony, ICJ (12) 83,

These failures—the liquidation of the Alksnis parachutists and the abortive mission to Moscow by the two girls—severed the connections between the F.P.O. and the organized Soviet *partizanka* until the spring of 1943.

Arming and Preparing for Combat

The F.P.O. had been constituted as an "armed combat organization," and its principal activity throughout its existence was the procurement of firearms and smuggling them into the ghetto. This activity was fraught with numerous hazards not only for the people concerned, but also for the ghetto community as a whole. Abba Kovner writes about the moral vicissitudes:

> ... Had we the right to endanger the lives of the thousands of remaining Jews in the event of the discovery of arms in our possession? With full realization of the responsibility we bore, our reply was: Yes. We are entitled, we are bound, to do so.[31]

Sources of firearms were limited. The non-Jewish population was in possession of firearms that had fallen into its hands on the collapse of the Polish Army in September 1939, and during the retreat of the Red Army in June 1941. Another source of arms was the German armories and the Lithuanian police personnel. F.P.O. members who were employed outside the ghetto, in German army installations and other places where they came into contact with the civilian populace, engaged in purchasing arms and smuggling them into the ghetto.

p. 34; *Gitlerovskaya okupatsiya*, p. 200. In its counter-offensive during the winter of 1941/42, the Red Army broke through the German frontline and reached an area northeast of Vitebsk. As a result of this attack, an area 30 miles wide was created between the German armies in the north and those in the center. The partisans were in control of this area, and during the spring and summer of 1942, there was considerable two-way movement through this open passage.

31 Kovner, "Nissayon Rishon," *op. cit.,* p. 13.

The Germans had established large arsenals for captured armaments and ammunition as well as weapons-repair workshops in Borbiszki (Burbiskes), a Vilna suburb. About eighty ghetto Jews worked in these places, among them a group of F.P.O. members commanded by Baruch Goldstein. This group stole several dozen weapons, including revolvers, rifles, submachineguns, grenades, and ammunition from Borbiszki and smuggled them into the ghetto. The first revolver obtained from Borbiszki was brought in by Goldstein in the latter part of January 1941, several days after the founding of the F.P.O. The appropriation of arms from Borbiszki cost the F.P.O. a victim. Z. Tiktin, a lad of sixteen, broke into a railroad car and stole fuses for grenades and ammunition. The Lithuanian sentry detected him and fired, severely wounding him. He was taken to prison by the Gestapo and interrogated as to the purpose of the theft. Tiktin answered, "I stole because you murdered my parents." He died behind bars, without revealing anything to his inquisitors, at the end of April 1943. Arms for the F.P.O. were also stolen from other Wehrmacht units where Jews were employed.[32]

Contacts between Jews and non-Jews existed at various worksites outside the ghetto, and arms in the possession of the civilian population were brought in this manner. One of the work-places was in the former Y.I.V.O. building. The Y.I.V.O. building, with all its Jewish cultural treasures, and those brought in from other institutions in the city, was controlled by the Einsatzstab Rosenberg. Some forty people were employed there, mainly members of the liberal professions, whose task was to classify the material, prepare academic surveys on various subjects, and pack the papers for shipment.[33] Among the

32 Korczak, *op. cit.*, pp. 108–109; Sutzkewer, *op. cit.*, pp. 133–137; Kruk, *op. cit.*, pp. 529–530.

33 The "Rosenberg Staff" was a special unit created by A. Rosenberg for the purpose of locating and sending to Germany cultural assets, books, archival material. The YIVO building in Vilna had been appropriated by the Germans to assemble the books, manuscripts,

employees was a group of F.P.O. members. They succeeded in purchasing arms from non-Jews and smuggling them into the ghetto. The books brought into Y.I.V.O. from other libraries included Soviet manuals on military training and the use of firearms, explosives, and mines. These pamphlets were taken into the ghetto, where they served in the F.P.O.'s training and instruction programs.[34]

Jews working in establishments outside the ghetto were under strict surveillance, and contact with non-Jews was fraught with risks, especially insofar as arms purchases. An additional hazard was the possibility that the seller was a German agent. But due to the extreme caution that F.P.O. members exercised, there were no such occurrences. A large part of the F.P.O. arsenal was thus procured from the civilian population, while arms were also bought from German and Lithuanian soldiers and police.[35]

Large funds were necessary for the arms purchasing. The F.P.O. held a fund-raising drive among its members, who contributed cash, gold rings, watches, and clothing. A group of F.P.O. men stole equipment from German stores, which they sold and donated the proceeds for the purchase of firearms. An important financial source for arms procurement was the forged food cards that were prepared by the F.P.O. A special group of the F.P.O. under staff member Chwojnik was organized to obtain food rations from the Judenrat stocks in ex-

paintings, and sculptures from libraries and museums, as well as from Jewish private homes. Valuable items were sent to Germany, and all the rest were consigned as raw material to be pulped at paper-mills. Most of the Jewish employees were scholars, writers, and newspaperman, including Prof. N. Prilutzki, H. Kruk, Z. Kalmanovitch among others. The Jewish personnel stole and smuggled out valuable Jewish material and documents into the ghetto at great personal risk. Most of this material was lost during the liquidation of the ghetto.

34 S. Kaczerginski, *Partizaner geyen!* Munich, 1948, pp. 72–74.
35 Kovner, "Nissayon Rishon," *op. cit.*, p. 7; Lazar, *op. cit.*, p. 67; Reznik's testimony, 0–33/1238, p. 15.

change for counterfeit cards. Because of the necessity for secrecy, the F.P.O. did not solicit funds from ghetto residents.[36] In some cases Gens donated money to the F.P.O. out of Judenrat funds.[37]

The Polish nationalist underground in Vilna refused to give arms. The Communist underground in Vilna was short of arms and could not serve as a source of supply for the ghetto. Kovner states that the first two pistols which the Communist underground in the city received were donated by the F.P.O., which also presented it with other kinds of weapons. The F.P.O. remitted funds to the Communist underground for the purchase of arms.[38]

Throughout the existence of the F.P.O. in the Vilna ghetto, from the end of January 1942 to the end of September 1943, arms procurement efforts were made in all directions, and the organization succeeded to arm the majority of its members, who totaled about 300. Most of these weapons were revolvers, but there were also a few rifles, submachineguns, and grenades.[39]

The smuggling of firearms into the ghetto was one of the most difficult and hazardous undertakings. The ghetto was guarded, and the Germans and Lithuanians at the gate searched all those returning from work. Despite these searches, the F.P.O. members were successful in smuggling arms by concealing them inside clothing, in toolboxes with double bottoms, in coffins, and in garbage trucks. Jewish policemen who were

36 Korczak, *op. cit.*, p. 103, 117; Kovner, "Nissayon Rishon," *op. cit.*, p. 7; Kowalski, *op. cit.*, pp. 124–127, 159–160.

37 Lazar, *op. cit.*, pp. 87–88; Reznik's testimony, 0-33/1238, p. 14.

38 Kovner, "Nissayon Rishon," *op. cit.*, pp. 6–7; Korczak, *op. cit.*, pp. 108, 153; Juchniewicz, *op. cit.*, p. 58, writes: "Ammunition, fuses for grenades, and bombs were manufactured in the ghetto and smuggled through the sewer tunnels to secret caches outside the ghetto."

39 Reznik's testimony, 0-33/419, p. 16, tells of 200–300 weapons in the hands of the FPO. This figure corresponds with the number of FPO members as given by Kovner's testimony, ICJ (12)83, pp. 54–55.

members of the F.P.O. and stood guard at the ghetto gate helped in the smuggling.

Smuggling was also done through camouflaged fissures in the ghetto walls, or through attics and basements. A daring attempt was made in the summer of 1942. Two F.P.O. members, disguised as city sewermen, put up municipal red signs and halted traffic in the street opposite the ghetto gate, opened the sewer manhole, and pretended to begin repairs. Two pipes containing rifles were thrust into the sewers. That same evening, a party of F.P.O. men crawled through the underground drains and brought the weapons safely inside. Notwithstanding the difficulties and risks involved, none of these smuggling operations on F.P.O. initiative ever failed.

Concealment and Maintenance of Arms in the Ghetto

Once inside the ghetto, the arms had to be safely hid. The firearms had to be concealed not only from the eyes of the Jewish police, but also from the ghetto inhabitants, for possession or concealment of weapons was punished by death.

In order to be able to arm swiftly in time of danger and to ensure against the likelihood of discovery, it was necessary to disperse the armories among several places to which the F.P.O. could have easy access. The hiding-places were in a basement at 3 Carmelite Street, a public kitchen at 31 Niemiecka Street, the library at 6 Straszuna Street, and the Command headquarters at 8 Oszmiana Street. For reasons of security and storage requirements, the F.P.O. was compelled to move its cache from place to place.

A special F.P.O. group was responsible for storage, maintenance, repairs, and manufacture of spare parts. Bombs were made in the ghetto from electric light bulbs, and other such appliances served as Molotov cocktails, fuses and hand-grenades. Repair of arms and manufacture of parts were undertaken at mechanical workshops at 6 Rudnicka Street, in which several F.P.O. men were employed. "Cold" weapons, such as knives, steel "gloves" and axes, were also made there. Arms that reached the ghetto in poor condition, or with parts missing, were often repaired and rendered usable.

With the creation of the F.P.O. and the arrival of the first arms, a course for arms instructors was held to train a team of instructors who would in turn teach the other members. Glazman, who had served in the Lithuanian Army, headed the course. All the persons chosen as instructors had military experience.

The majority of F.P.O. members were drawn from youth movements and had no previous military experience. Lectures on arms and combat tactics were given secretly and at night in schoolrooms, youth clubs, and ghetto workshops.[40]

Information and Propaganda Activity

The F.P.O. operated a radio set in order to keep informed on events in the outside world and at the various fronts. News reports were recorded and then printed in a bulletin which was distributed to the F.P.O. commanders every evening. Through them the news reached the members and the ghetto at large.[41]

The F.P.O. distributed a proclamation in Polish addressed to the "Citizens of All the Occupied Areas," and bearing the signature of the "Organization Fighting the German Invader." It listed the defeats of the German Army on the Eastern front in the winter of 1941–1942, and called on the populations of the conquered areas to offer armed resistance to the Germans. The manifesto was distributed in Vilna in February or March 1942. Jews were not mentioned, and nothing in it could be linked to a Jewish source. The contents made it seem that the authors were pro-Soviet Poles.[42]

An underground printing press was set up outside the ghetto

---

40 Korczak, *op. cit.*, pp. 68, 98, 101–102; Lazar, *op. cit.*, pp. 65, 67; "Der Witenberg tog," *op. cit.*, p. 206; Kowalski, *op. cit.*, p. 160.
41 Korczak, *op. cit.*, pp. 119–120. Jews had been forbidden to possess radios and to listen to them from the first days of German rule.
42 Korczak, *op. cit.*, pp. 153–154, gives the contents of the manifesto in full.

in Przewalski's home by the F.P.O. and the Polish ZWC at the initiative of Yitzhak Kowalski, a F.P.O. member. The decision was taken in May 1942. Kowalski, who worked in the German-Lithuanian *Ausra* (Aushra) printing-works, smuggled out, over the months, all the equipment needed for a printing press, with the aid of Sonia Madeysker and Przewalski. Kowalski trained Przewalski and his wife in printing techniques, and they printed the news bulletins at night. The first issue appeared on May 1, 1943. in Polish. It was entitled the *Sztandar Wolnosci* ("Flag of Freedom"), published by the Polish ZWC, which at that time had changed its title to Z.P.P. ("Union of Polish Patriots"). Shortly after the appearance of the Polish-language bulletin, another began publication, in Lithuanian, under the mast-head of *Tevynes Frontas* ("Homeland Front"), put out by the Lithuanian Communist "Union for the Liberation of Lithuania." Proclamations in Polish, Lithuanian, and German (intended for German soldiers) appeared simultaneously and called for battle against the Germans, sabotage, and refusal to accept conscription for labor in Germany.[43]

These clandestine organs and their circulars fulfilled a most important function in the activity of the Communist undergrounds and, in effect, were their principal concern. The F.P.O. played a decisive role in setting up the underground printing-works outside the ghetto. Once the first one had been installed outside the ghetto walls, another one was mounted inside as a reserve. Again Kowalski provided the equipment.

Sabotage Actions

The F.P.O. had been established with the object of "carrying out acts of sabotage and damage in the enemy rear." In June 1942, the command decided to mine the German railroad line going to the front. The mine was prepared in the ghetto. After

43 Kowalski, *op. cit.*, pp. 104–110, 121, manifesto in Polish; Przewalski's testimony, pp. 8–9; Kaczerginski, *"Partizaner," op. cit.*, pp. 111–114; *Gitlerovskaya okupatsiya*, pp. 210–213.

a preliminary reconnaissance of the railroad line from Vilna to Vileyka, Vitka Kempner and two other F.P.O. members left the ghetto, and on the night of July 8, 1942, placed the mine on the railroad, 6 miles southeast of Vilna. The trio returned to the ghetto at dawn. The next morning an ammunition train hit the mine, and the engine and several wagons were damaged. Farmers in the vicinity were arrested in a German reprisal *Aktion*, but the Jews were not touched. The Germans had no idea that it was a Jewish operation. It was the first German train to be mined in the Vilna area.[44]

F.P.O. members who worked in various German factories sabotaged equipment and armaments. Leibke Distel, who was employed in an arms-repair workshop, spoiled dozens of bolts for artillery. Yashke Raff and Feldman, mechanics in vehicle workshops of the H.K.P., where they repaired and refurbished vehicles, damaged the motors. Goldstein, Gordon, and Tiktin sabotaged German arms at the Borbiszki armory. The engineer Ratner, another employee at Borbiszki, helped the F.P.O. men to prepare chemical delaying time fuses, which were inserted in the fuel-tanks of several Panzers sent in the direction of the front. Goldberg, who worked at the Porobanek airfield, removed screws from the aircrafts parked on the field.[45]

These acts of sabotage, which caused considerable damage to the enemy, were perpetrated in such a manner that nothing was noticeable at the time, and the results were felt only during actual shooting, or when the vehicles had traveled many miles. No suspicion ever fell on the saboteurs.

Aid to Soviet Prisoners of War and Families of Soviet Officers
Many families of Red Army officers were unable to leave Vilna before the Germans arrived, and they were quartered in large buildings at 37 Subocz Street. About 600 persons lived there,

44 *Sefer ha-Partizanim*, pp. 23–24; Kaczerginski, *"Partizaner," op. cit.*, pp. 152–156.
45 Korczak, *op. cit.*, pp. 104–107; Kowalski, *op. cit.*, pp. 157–159.

and their economic situation was difficult. A Soviet P.O.W. camp, No. 344, with more than 7,000 inmates, was established in Vilna, and the inmates found themselves in extremely difficult circumstances. Hunger and typhus felled many, and the daily mortality rate averaged 50. The prisoners worked in the same places as the Jews.

The F.P.O. Command ordered its members to help Soviet prisoners of war and the Soviet Army officers' families by donating food, cigarettes, and clothing, and informing them about the situation on the front. F.P.O. members at the H.K.P. work-site helped a group of Soviet prisoners escape into the forests. The F.P.O. furnished them with forged documents, cash, clothing, and details on routes to the forests. Prisoners of war who managed to escape with F.P.O. help reached the forests and joined the Partisans.[46]

---

46 *Gitlerovskaya okupatsiya,* pp. 133, 145; Korczak, *op. cit.,* pp. 121–123; Sutzkewer, *op. cit.,* pp. 144–145.

Chapter 16

"THE YECHIEL STRUGGLE GROUP"

The "Yechiel Group"
Those members of He-Halutz ha-Za'ir-Dror who remained in
Vilna after the departure of Tenenbaum-Tamaroff and his associates merged into a group totaling 15–20 men headed by
Yechiel Scheinbaum.[1] Tenenbaum-Tamaroff's departure brought
about the severance of the ties between the He-Halutz ha-Za'ir-
Dror members left in Vilna and other youth movements with
which they had cooperated in He-Halutz. Scheinbaum was not
invited to the meeting on January 21, 1942, at which the decision was made to establish the F.P.O. The "Yechiel Group"
crystallized as an independent and isolated formation concurrent
with the organization and coalescence of the F.P.O.

During the spring months of 1942, contact was established
between Scheinbaum and the F.P.O. Staff Command with regard
to his group joining that organization. The F.P.O. proposed
that Scheinbaum's followers join the F.P.O. individually and
not as an organized body. These proposals meant the dissolution of the "Yechiel Group." Scheinbaum insisted that all
members be enrolled in the F.P.O. as a group and not individually and that he personally represent them on the Command.
The F.P.O. refused.

---

1 Collective Interview, conducted by Dr. D. Levin, with a group of
   members of "Yechiel Struggle Group," ICJ, (12)88, pp. 25, 28, 63.

The "Yechiel Group" attempted to establish contacts with other underground groups following the collapse of the negotiations with the F.P.O. One of those with whom it initiated talks was the Kampfgruppe ("Struggle Group").[2]

The "Struggle Group"
The "Struggle Group" began to organize as a clandestine body in March-April 1942. Borka Friedman was the initiator, and he was aided by Shlomo Brand and Dr. Leo Bernstein. Friedman was a friend of Glazman and a member of the F.P.O., but seceded from it and formed a separate underground faction. The impetus to this move was the personal rivalry between Friedman and Glazman for the Betar leadership in the Vilna ghetto. Another reason was that Friedman did not acquiesce in the narrow organizational structure of the F.P.O., which was based mainly on youth movements.[3]

People without prior affiliations to a specific movement were accepted by the "Struggle Group." Dr. L. Bernstein confirms:

> ... Our primary function was to recruit new members, not according to party affiliation ... but by one and only one criterion—the readiness of the person to fight ... We did not want party adherence to be the exclusive sacred principle.[4]

Nathan Ring, a ghetto police officer, and a group of those close to him joined the "Struggle Group."[5] Esther Jaffe, a F.P.O. member, seceded or was expelled from the F.P.O., and

2 Collective Interview, Yechiel Group, pp. 23–28.
3 *Ibid.*, pp. 31, 34, 40, 42, 67; Kovner's testimony, ICJ (12)83, p. 49. B. Friedman, born in Vilna, Betar member, was a ghetto policeman. He went into the forests in the spring and later fell in action.
4 *Ibid.*, p. 50.
5 *Ibid.*, pp. 46–47. Nathan Ring headed a ghetto police district. He went out into the forests in 1943, joined the partisans, and was executed by them. For the account of his execution, see *Sefer ha-Partizanim*, pp. 113–114, and Lazar, pp. 281–284.

joined the "Struggle" toward the end of 1942.[6] Many of the activists had military experience. In spite of its "unrestricted" character, the group had a nucleus of Betar members, which formed its leadership. The "Struggle Group" totaled several dozen people.

Merger of "Yechiel" and "Struggle" Groups

The merger of the "Yechiel" and "Struggle" groups resulted from the contact between Scheinbaum and Friedman in November–December 1942. The union was a combination of two factions that complemented each other: "Yechiel" brought the ideological content of the Zionists and Halutzim, while the "Struggle" injected the militarist element. Scheinbaum became the leader of the joint body. Dr. L. Bernstein says of the merger:

> The fusion was most natural for two reasons: (1) Because Yechiel Scheinbaum regarded us as a dynamic military force ... (2) Because we regarded Yechiel Scheinbaum as a moral authority who could give this unified movement that stamp which perhaps did not yet exist ... For me, the first encounter with Yechiel was a discovery. I felt that the underground and resistance movement had found its man. It was no wonder at all that Yechiel became the uncontested central figure in the movement after we had known him a few weeks.[7]

Several factors led to the amalgamation of the two groups : the idea of combat, which was common to both of them; the aspiration to a broad base for the combatant organization; the desire not to be isolated in the struggle; and the overt and

6   *Ibid.*, pp. 68–70. Esther Jaffe, a personal friend of Glazman, was active in Betar and was among the first to join the FPO. She quarreled with him at the end of 1942, was expelled from the FPO, and joined the "Struggle Group." Various and extreme views have been expressed concerning her personality and activity.

7   *Ibid.*, p. 74.

covert rivalry with the F.P.O. The groups that amalgamated into the framework of the joint organization preserved their previous entities. The command consisted of Scheinbaum as commander; Nathan Ring and Shlomo Brand, Armaments Section; Borka Friedman, Finances; and Leo Bernstein, Information.

Additional groups joined "Yechiel's Struggle Group" in January–April 1943. A Grodno group, consisting of youngsters who had arrived in the Vilna ghetto at the end of 1942, after the liquidation of their ghetto, joined "Yechiel's Struggle Group" at the outset of 1943. It was also supplemented by youths from the townships of Belorussia and eastern Lithuania, numbering several dozen, who came to Vilna after the liquidation of their ghettos. The Akiva group, which was formed in the Biala-Vaka labor camp, returned to Vilna after the camp was disbanded in the spring of 1943, and swelled the "Yechiel's Struggle" ranks. These groups brought some arms with them. Each of these adherents continued to maintain its former framework.[8]

"Yechiel's Struggle Group" was not subdivided into fixed units, nor had it a defined command hierarchy, but was rather a federation of several groups. The nucleus of the organization comprised twenty to twenty-five active persons drawn from the leaderships of the various component groups. It reached the peak of its numerical strength in the spring and summer of 1943, with 150–200 members, some of whom had only a tenuous connection with the organization.[9]

"Yechiel's Struggle Group" adopted "the ideology of the forest." Its purpose was to organize its members, and as many

8 Collective Interview, Yechiel Group, pp. 28, 61, 74–75; Zeidel, *op. cit.*, p. 53. The Akiva group comprised some twenty members under the leadership of Moshe Kalchheim and H. Zeidel.

9 Dworzecki, *op. cit.*, p. 205. It should be noted that there are no accurate membership figures for the groups which joined the organization in 1943. It may also be assumed that a substantial number formed the periphery of the organization, built up as a confederation of groups which were of indeterminate sizes.

other Jews as possible, in order to leave the ghetto and launch guerrilla warfare in the forests, a recourse which it conceived as a method of both rescue and struggle. The organization regarded combat within the ghetto as a possibility, and a national necessity should the liquidation of the ghetto begin before the organization could leave for the forests. Rejection of combat inside the ghetto as a preplanned objective was founded on the premise that it offered no realistic prospects. Dr. Bernstein states:

> It soon became apparent that a defense strategy in the conditions of the Vilna ghetto was absurd... Any resistance, any possibility of retreat, requires space, and after all we had almost none at all... We had no hinterland anywhere.[10]

Scheinbaum founded the "ideology of the forest" based on an evaluation that a preorganized sortie of many youngsters into the forests had better chances for the rescue of a much larger number of persons than did remaining in the ghetto to fight during the liquidation. This "forest ideology" was offered in contradistinction and as an alternative to the ghetto revolt thesis of the F.P.O.

The emergence of the "forest ideology" as the aim of "Yechiel's Struggle Group" evolved during the period in which Soviet partisan activity in the regions of western Belorussia was on the upsurge. The presence of Soviet partisans in areas not too distant from Vilna and the real possibilities of leaving for the forests and joining the partisans influenced the adoption of forest warfare tenets by "Yechiel's Struggle Group."

Procurement of Firearms

The problems facing "Yechiel's Struggle Group" in procuring firearms—sources of supply, bringing the weapons into the ghetto and concealing them, and maintaining them in service-

---

10 Collective Interview, Yechiel Group, pp. 41, 51, 54–55.

able condition—resembled those of the F.P.O. The "Yechiel"
and "Struggle" groups had each engaged in this activity since
their founding. The "Struggle Group" had ties with Gens and
received money from him to purchase arms. According to
Brand, the first funds for this purpose and the first pistol the
group obtained came from Gens. Yet Kowalski contends that
Ring showed Gens his plan to establish a combatant group and
asked for his assistance, and "Gens refused to help with the
plan, as he believed it would become known to Dessler." [11] Arms
purchases continued at a faster pace after the unification of the
two groups. Policemen who were members of "Yechiel's Struggle Group" were of assistance at the ghetto gate through which
the arms were smuggled. The damaged weapons were repaired
in a ghetto workshop. Arms were stored in *malines*. "Yechiel's
Struggle Group" also had its own radio receiver.[12]

Relations Between the F.P.O. and "Yechiel's Struggle Group"
The F.P.O. command staff knew of the organization and existence of "Yechiel's Group" and of the "Struggle Group," but,
until their merger they did not ascribe much importance to
either. "Yechiel's Group" was assessed as an offshoot of He-
Halutz ha-Za'ir-Dror, and the "Struggle Group" as an ensemble
of Betar and police personnel who were Glazman's opponents.
When the F.P.O. learned of the initial contacts to establish a
joint organization and of the eventual merger, it was no longer
able to ignore the existence of another armed underground in
the ghetto.

Kovner makes the following point:

> ...We learned of this group. We tried to get in touch
> with the Dror people in it, to try to find out what they

---

11 Dworzecki, pp. 206, 208–209, for acquisition of arms by the "Strug-
    gle Group." Kowalski, *op. cit.*, p. 150.
12 Collective Interview, Yechiel Group, p. 43. The firearms drill was
    held in an attic apartment at 8 Szpitalna Street. Arms were stored

were up to, how they came to join this group. This contact failed ... We suspected that the second organization was entirely open to Gens and operated under his inspiration, and that, Heaven forbid, a collision between two Jewish forces inside the ghetto was likely to ensue from this.[13]

I. Kowalski, who belonged to the F.P.O. Intelligence Department headed by Glazman, penetrated "Yechiel's Struggle Group." He writes:

> Glazman told me that my assignment was of special importance for the future of the F.P.O.... He said that a group of people was planning to establish a second combatant organization and if they succeeded, they would begin to acquire arms ... Such a thing, carried on without the supervision of the F.P.O., could bring catastrophe both to it and the whole ghetto. The F.P.O. cannot allow people not under its supervision to engage in such activities, as failure is liable to bring destruction to our great and sacred enterprise. I was assigned to join the group and obtain information on its activities ... [14]

Kowalski asked Esther Jaffe to put him in touch with the leaders of "Yechiel's Struggle Group" so that he could join its ranks. He was invited to a meeting of its Staff Command. Kowalski explained that he had left the F.P.O. and wanted to join "Yechiel's Struggle Group" because the former no longer fulfilled his expectations. He was admitted into the organization and added to its Staff Command. He attended several meet-

---

in the offices of the ghetto schools in a basement at 2 Straszuna Street. The radio receiver was in a *maline* at 21 Niemiecka Street.
13 Kovner's testimony, ICJ (12) 83, pp. 50–51; Reznik's testimony, 0–33/1238, p. 24, refers to the subject of creating a second organization and says: "More than once they, the FPO Staff, discussed the establishment of a new organization along its own line."
14 Kowalski, *op. cit.*, p. 148.

ings and learned about the acquisition of arms and that Ring maintained contact with Gens. Kowalski transmitted this information to Glazman.

Shlomo Brand relates: "... Kowalski went to Glazman and told him everything. A day later Glazman came to my home ... and asked me not to establish a second organization ..."[15]

The F.P.O. sought to frustrate the creation of a second organization in the ghetto for they would have to procure arms from the same sources as the F.P.O. and thereby complicate matters. They feared the disclosure of the arms procurement efforts might produce German retaliatory measures and accentuate supervision in the ghetto, which would also weigh heavily on the F.P.O. The latter's Command believed that the second organization was established with Gens' blessing, and they feared he would exploit it to their disadvantage. The ideological dissension between the two—ghetto revolt vs. forest warfare—did not figure as a factor in the F.P.O.'s negative attitude toward the other organization. But, despite its efforts, the F.P.O. failed to prevent the creation of "Yechiel's Struggle Group."

15 *Ibid.*, pp. 149–151; Collective Interview, Yechiel Group, pp. 43–44.

Part Four

THE "PERIOD OF STABILITY," JANUARY 1942 — MARCH 1943

Chapter 17

STABILIZATION OF THE GHETTO AND CONSOLIDATION OF ITS INSTITUTIONS

Transitional Phase

The fifteen months between the beginning of 1942 and the spring of 1943 were dubbed "the period of stability." No mass-extermination *Aktionen* were implemented, although liquidation of certain "nonproductive" elements continued. Physically fit people worked in plants and installations in and outside the ghetto. The situation in the ghetto during the period of stability required that special attention be paid to social issues and needs that had been non-existent or negligible factors during the period of the *Aktionen*.

The internal ghetto organization was broadened. The Judenrat in Ghetto No. 1 originally had five departments: General, Food, Health, Housing, and Labor Bureau. These were meant to deal with the urgent and immediate problems with which the Jew in the ghetto was confronted. With the end of the massacres and the beginning of the period of stability, new problems arose. The Judenrat had to extend its scope and therefore created new departments: Social Welfare, Education, Culture, and Finances. The new structure of the Judenrat is illustrated by the diagram on page 274.

The Staff Command of the ghetto police consisted of J. Gens, Chief, and J. Glazman (one of the F.P.O. leaders), Deputy Chief. The Command was comprised of officers, laymen, and clerks. The ghetto was divided into three police precincts, each of which had a police-station with fifteen to twenty constables. There were 200 policemen in the ghetto in the first half of 1942.

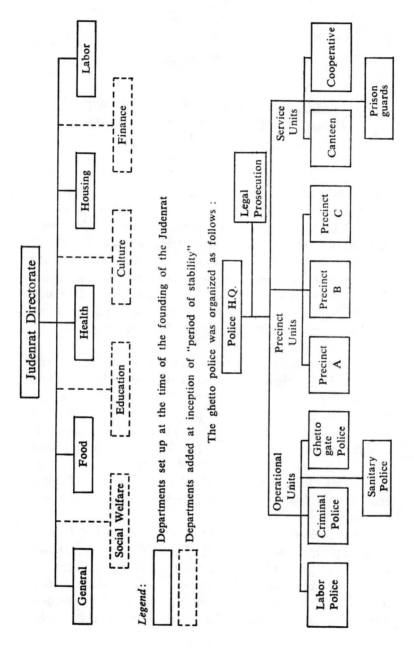

Judenrat Directorate

General | Food | Health | Housing | Labor

Social Welfare | Education | Culture | Finance

Legend:

Departments set up at the time of the founding of the Judenrat

Departments added at inception of "period of stability"

The ghetto police was organized as follows :

Police H.Q.

Legal Prosecution

Operational Units | Precinct Units | Service Units

Labor Police | Criminal Police | Ghetto gate Police

Sanitary Police

Precinct A | Precinct B | Precinct C

Canteen | Cooperative

Prison guards

The prison was located in Lida Street. A special squad of twelve policemen had charge of the jail.[1] The number of persons imprisoned during the first half of 1942 was as follows: January—135; February—211; March—341; April—849; May—693; June—1,427.

The majority of those convicted were sentenced by the police to 24–48 hours detention for misdemeanors connected with entry through the ghetto gate; the others were tried by the ghetto court.[2]

During the first months after the *Aktionen,* from January to March 1942, the inhabitants of the ghetto lived with the fear that the coming of spring would presage the liquidation of the ghetto. The yellow work-permits distributed in October 1941 were valid only until March 31, 1942. Rumors of impending annihilation circulated in the ghetto. Gens fought them, and those caught spreading these rumors were arrested and punished. Gens published a warning to this effect:

> Notice No. 3
> By the Chief of Ghetto Police, January 5, 1942.
> For circulating inaccurate reports and provoking a mood of panic among inhabitants, I punished two residents of the ghetto on January 3, 1942.
> I hereby announce that all who are convicted of the same offense will be punished with the utmost severity of the law.
>
> Chief of Police.[3]

The warning and penalties did not prevent the continued dissemination of rumors and the fear of extermination. Kruk's diary entries for the period read as follows:

> February 2: The passes expire on March 31 ... what thereafter?

1 Epstein's diary, pp. 50, 55; Balberyszski, *op. cit.,* pp. 339, 378, 421–422, 427, 431; Kruk, *op. cit.,* pp. 158, 162, 193, 579.
2 Moreshet Archives, D.1.354.
3 Kruk, *op. cit.,* p. 126.

February 9: Once again rumors about the liquidation of the ghetto. People are very afraid. Will the liquidation take place on the 15th of the month?

February 22: March will soon be here. Thousands of pass-holders are trembling when they remember that their validity will soon lapse.

March 21: Our right to the passes will terminate on the 31st . . . If they are renewed, we shall live, if not—life will end.

March 23: March 23 is connected with the end of the passes. We know today that they will be prolonged for one month. The hunt will begin again in April . . . .

The apprehensions of the ghetto Jews of course had some foundation. The decision to halt the annihilation process was temporary, and in an order to that effect sent out by the *Reichskommissariat* for the *Ostland* on December 9, 1941, it was stated that "arrangements should be made to train local people to replace Jewish skilled personnel as quickly as possible."[4] On January 29, 1942, Himmler issued instructions to the *Reichskommissariate Ostland* and Ukraine, in which he dwelt on the duty to proceed immediately with the annihilation of the Jews in the Eastern territories.[5]

Pursuant to this promulgation, a decision was taken at German government levels in the *Ostland* to resume the extermination in Belorussia—where there were large concentrations of Jews who had remained almost untouched by the mass-extermination *Aktionen*—and not to liquidate, in that phase, the ghettos in places where *Aktionen* had already been conducted and *Arbeitsjuden* ("Working Jews") had been spared.

It is noteworthy that Jäger, chief of the Security Police and SD in Lithuania, who was in direct charge of anti-Jewish

4   YVA, 0–18/203.
5   YVA, 0–4/53–1, Document 295.

Aktionen had already stated in the report of December 1, 1941, that "Working Jews" who had remained in the ghettos in Lithuania would be needed even after the winter of 1941–42.[6] This decision to retain the "working ghettos" in the Eastern territories must also be seen against the background of the needs of the German war effort, and the expression of these needs in Lithuania.

The failure of Germany's *Blitzkrieg* against the U.S.S.R. and the consequent prolongation of the war confronted the German economy with severe manpower problems. *Reichsmarshall* H. Goering, the head of the Four-Year Plan and in charge of economic exploitation in the Eastern Territories, issued an order on November 7, 1941, concerning "the utilization of manpower in the Occupied Territories in the East, and the dispatch of workers from these areas for employment in industries in Germany." The recruitment of manpower in the East was fraught with difficulties, and the shortage of labor in the German economy became worse. Sauckel, who had been placed in over-all charge of recruitment and exploitation of labor manpower in the Third Reich and the Occupied Territories, wrote to the two *Reichskommissariate* for the Eastern Territories on March 31, 1942, and demanded that they take all the necessary and most severe measures to ensure the enlistment of manpower for labor purposes.[7]

Conscription for work in Germany was intensified in Lithuania, especially in Vilna, because of its Polish population. The local Lithuanian administration, which dealt directly with labor recruitment, preferred to send Poles in order to get rid of them and to keep Lithuanians at home. A total of 4,200 people were sent to Germany from Vilna and its environs during the first half of April 1942.[8] These transports aroused resentment and

6 Jäger Report, p. 8.
7 *Prestupnye tseli-prestupnye sredstva, Dokumenty ob okupatsionnoy politike fashistskoy Germanii na Teritorii SSSR* (1941–1944), Moscow, 1968, pp. 208, 214, 219 (hereafter: *Prestupnye sredstva*).
8 *Gitlerovskaya okupatsiya*, p. 74; *Meldungen aus den besetzten Ost-*

increased underground activity. About 280 Poles were arrested in Vilna on March 27 and 28, 1942.[9]

Orders on the "Obligation to Work in Military Industry in the Reich" and an "Order on the Obligation to Work in Transportation" were issued in Lithuania on May 2 and 4, 1942. Inhabitants of Lithuania were also obliged by "Orders" to cut peat, chop trees, provide seasonal help in agriculture, and maintain transport routes. The opposition of the local populace to the German authorities was further exacerbated by these measures. The reports of the German security police recorded that "the activity of the partisans has increased in Lithuania, and the populace does not operate against them because of the 'Order' to send people to work in Germany..."[10]

Thousands of people who still lived in Vilna and other ghettos in Lithuania served as an important reservoir of manpower. Instead of having to grapple with the non-Jewish population to take more people for work, the German administration preferred to maintain the ghetto and exploit Jewish labor forces, thereby reducing the demands for recruitment among the non-Jewish population. The number of Jewish workmen did not completely fulfill the needs of the administration, but at least it alleviated the situation. In addition, there were categories of Jewish workers who could not be replaced in a short period of time, and the local German administration took no practical steps to train non-Jewish skilled workers in their place, which was what they had been instructed to do by the upper echelons. The use of

gebieten, No. 10, July 3, 1942, YVA, 0–51/33–1, states "... The order for the conscription of labor for military industry in the Reich, of May 1, 1942, called for 30,000 persons, of whom 22,000 came, all of them Poles."

9 Report of the German Security Police, Ereignismeldung No. 191, of April 10, 1942, YVA, 0–51/57–1, Nuremberg Document, NO–3256.

10 Gitlerovskaya okupatsiya, pp. 74–76; Report of the Security Police of July 3, 1942, YVA, 0–51/33–1; Kruk, op. cit., pp. 255, 261–263, 271, recounts the resistance of the Poles and the Lithuanians in the Vilna sector against being sent to work in Germany.

Jewish labor was much less expensive, and considerable sums flowed into the coffers of the *Gebietskommissar* from payments made by the employers. This factor had considerable influence on the local authorities' decision to maintain the ghetto.

Following the decision not to liquidate the Vilna ghetto, the German local administration instituted several measures for more efficient utilization of the available manpower, the intensification of control over the ghetto, and imposition of further restrictions on its inmates.

On April 7, 1942, Murer published the "Guidelines and Instructions for the Deployment of Jewish Labor Forces." This document was intended for employers of Jewish labor. It established the policy and method of utilization of Jewish manpower and covered the following points:

— "The Ghetto is under the exclusive control of the *Gebietskommissariat,* and the deployment of Jewish labor forces shall be implemented through the Social Department of the *Gebietskommissariat.*

— "Pursuant to the Order of September 20, 1941, by the Wehrmacht Commander in the *Ostland,* it is forbidden for the army to cooperate with the Jews, to employ them or to issue work-permits to Jews working for it . . .

— "Jews shall proceed to work in groups of at least ten persons, headed by Jewish group-leaders. Individuals are forbidden to move about outside the ghetto except for those with special permits.

— "The hours of departure for work outside the ghetto are from 6 A.M. and for return from 3 P.M. until dark, but never later than 8 P.M.

— "Employers shall ensure that Jews working for them do not engage in bartering nor bring with them foodstuffs or firewood upon returning to the ghetto.

— "Wages for Jewish workers shall be as follows: Males over 16–0.15 marks per hour; females over 16–0.12 marks per hour; youths under 16–0.10 marks per hour.

— All employers, except the army and municipality, are required to pay into the *Gebietskommissariat* treasury an amount equivalent to the wage paid by him for all Jewish laborers. The employer is entitled to deduct 0.30 marks for every plate of soup provided.

— "The Jew is the enemy of Germany and responsible for the war. He is a forced laborer and is forbidden to be in contact with his employers except on matters referring to work. Anyone maintaining contact with Jews shall be treated as if he were a Jew.

— "The possibility of being allocated Jewish workmen shall be denied to institutions and employers who fail to act in accordance with these instructions."[11]

This document revoked the previous one pertaining to Jewish labor which had been published by Ross, who was in charge of Labor Forces in Vilna, on October 15, 1941. The wages which Mürer specified for Jewish labor were higher than the scale proposed by Ross, and this was due to inflation and price increases. Murer's wages were approximately one-third of the pay for non-Jewish workmen.[12]

Wagner, who was in charge of the Social Department in the *Gebietskommissariat* in Vilna, issued a proclamation on April 15, 1942, concerning the invalidation of the yellow work-passes and subsequent substitution by new ones. The notice read:

11 YVA, 0-6/96.
12 Actual payment to Jewish workers for one hour's work, in German marks, according to order of Ross and Mürer:

Sex	Age	*Ross*	*Mürer*
Males	16–60	0.15	0.10
Females	16–60	0.12	0.075
Juveniles	up to 16	0.10	0.05

Gitlerovskaya okupatsiya, p. 77, noted that the average monthly pay of non-Jewish workers was as follows: skilled hand—100 marks; unskilled hand—63 marks; women were paid between 52 and 62 marks. The pay of a skilled Jewish workman for a working day of ten hours ranged from between 1 and 1.5 marks, which totaled a monthly wage of 25–38 marks.

Announcement by the *Sozialamt* [Social Department],
April 15, 1942

ANNOUNCEMENT TO BEARERS OF YELLOW PASSES

It is hereby proclaimed that the validity of the yellow
passes will expire on April 30, 1942, and by this day will
be exchanged for new certificates.

The new certificates will be issued for an unlimited time
period and will bear the signature of Government Inspector Wagner.

The replacement of the yellow certificates by new ones
will be implemented by liaison officer A. Braude. Bearers
of new certificates shall be obliged to:

1. Carry the certificate with them at all times;
2. Accept work offered to them at once;
3. Not change their place of employment without permission;
4. Obey at all times the instructions of the *Sozialamt*
   and Labor Department of the ghetto, which function on behalf of the officer of the *Gebietskommissariat*;
5. Notify the Labor Department of the ghetto at once
   should the person in possession of an *Ausweise* leave
   his place of work;
6. Notify the Labor Department of the ghetto immediately of every change of address.

Any person in possession of a new certificate who is
employed must, upon its receipt, sign the new document
at his place of employment and immediately afterward
present it to the Labor Department in the ghetto so that
it may be duly registered in the card-index.

Non-fulfillment of the above instructions will be penal-
ized.

[281]

It is hereby stated that in the event of loss or disappearance of a document, in any manner, no duplicate will be issued.

Stamp
Arbeitsamt, Vilna

Gebietskommissariat Vilna
Social Department
(signed) Wagner

The day after the publication of Wagner's order, Fried, the chairman of the Judenrat, issued one of his own. He repeated the contents of Wagner's document and addended particulars as to the distribution of the new certificates. Fried's notice stated that the new certificates would be distributed to holders of yellow passes, irrespective of whether or not the latter were employed during that period.[13]

The distribution of the new work permits (*Ausweise*) was accomplished by the Judenrat Labor Office between April 16 and 30, 1942. The new passes were numbered and bore the stamp of the German *Sozialamt* and cancelled the yellow and pink passes. The German administration was evidently concerned that the majority of those eligible for work receive these work-permits. The purpose of the *Sozialamt* in issuing the new documents was to conduct a census of ghetto manpower with a view to its utilization, and consequently no limit was imposed on the number of new work permits distributed by the ghetto Labor Office.

The *Gebietskommissariat* published a declaration in the second half of April 1942 to the effect that the bread ration allotted to Jews was increased. This indicated the growing importance of the Jewish labor force. The same order was also issued in other ghettos in Lithuania.[14]

After the *Aktionen* in the Vilna ghetto, an ideology gradually

13 Moreshet Archives D.1.343; Kowalski, *op. cit.,* p. 112.
14 Kruk, *op. cit.,* p. 245; Yerushalmi, *op. cit.,* p. 80.

evolved around the thesis that the hopes and prospects of the Jews to be permitted to live were conditional on their work and productivity. Consequently, the prospects for the ghetto in its entirety—and those of each individual—to remain alive were related to the ability to prove economic advantage to the German administration. It was an ideology of "Work to Live"; it postulated that the number of workers in the ghetto must be increased and the volume of output enlarged in order to make the ghetto more valuable from an economic standpoint, thus enhancing its prospects for continued existence.

The continuing existence of the ghetto was combined with the hope prevalent among the ghetto Jews that Nazi Germany might suddenly collapse, and if that were to happen, the Germans would have no time to liquidate the ghetto community. These hopes were encouraged by reports of defeats and retreat of the German armies on the Eastern front, by the expectation that a second front would soon be opened in Western Europe, and the possibility of a military coup in Germany itself. Soviet bombing of Vilna and the surroundings in March 1942 aroused new hopes.[15]

The ideology of "Work to Live" did not immediately take root in the ghetto. It became viable for the ghetto community only when no liquidation *Aktionen* were implemented in the spring of 1942, new work permits were issued, and demands for Jewish labor increased. The Judenrat was the main bearer of this concept, which became its official ideology and motive for activities. Gens encouraged this idea and stressed that it was rooted in the realities of life.

This approach necessitated the complete marshalling of manpower resources in the ghetto for labor purposes, in order to render it productive, to prove to the German administration

15 Epstein's diary, p. 38, entry in March 1942: "... The Russian successes and their advance westward fortify us and lend us hope... and perhaps a revolution will break out in Germany or in its army? After all, it is possible..." See also: Kruk, *op. cit.*, pp. 49, 53–54, 197, 199, 208, 216–219, 241, 245.

that the greater majority of the ghetto inhabitants worked and that there were no "superfluous elements." To achieve this, an authoritative ghetto institution was essential to compel people to work and to direct workers from place to place. During the period in which this ideology was being formulated, in the first half of 1942, an intense struggle raged in the ghetto as to who would be the person and/or institution to implement this policy. It was a fight for the rule of the ghetto.

The Struggle for Supremacy in the Ghetto
Political elements that had sprouted from the new reality of ghetto life—the Judenrat, the Jewish police and Jewish foremen ("brigadiers")—together with remnants of the political forces that had functioned in the past in "the Jewish street"— were involved in a struggle. The contest had an ideological background, but personal ambitions and lust for power were also important factors. The struggle was waged principally between Fried and the Judenrat, on the one hand, and Gens and his police, on the other.

Fried vs. Gens. The chairman of the Judenrat, A. Fried, headed the Jewish administration in the ghetto, as prescribed by the Germans. The Jewish Police should have been the executive arm of the Judenrat and its policy within the ghetto, subordinate to the Judenrat. But ghetto realities provided otherwise. A process steadily evolved in the ghetto, until mid-1942, during which the police and its chief took over areas of activity that should have been in the hands of the Judenrat and Fried. This power play by Gens and the Jewish police at the expense of Fried and the Judenrat was linked to the personality of the two principals.

Fried was an assimilated Jew and had no previous involvement in Jewish life in Vilna. Kruk writes about him:

> A Jew who lived all his life in Vilna whom no one in Jewish Vilna knew at all ... His pedigree was manager of the Public Loan Fund. It was this man who through ill chance was appointed by the Germans as a member

of the Judenrat, and matters developed in such a way that he became Deputy Chairman of the first Judenrat and *Obermann* of the Judenrat in the ghetto. Did anyone want him as Chairman? No one at all.[16]

Fried's nomination to the chairmanship was accidental. The ghetto inhabitants had no esteem nor confidence in him, and he earned many opprobrious epithets.

Fried did not enjoy any great respect among the Germans either. He applied to Murer to be permitted to walk without the yellow star and to use the sidewalks outside the ghetto, but was refused. This application aroused contempt within the ghetto. He was a man of organizational ability and can be given credit for organizing the ghetto administrative organs in the first few months of their existence. He lacked outstanding personal attributes and the leadership qualities required for the post of Judenrat chairman.

Gens stood out in sharp contrast to Fried. A fellow-student in a Lithuanian officers' academy writes of him:

> Gens was of a typical middle-class Jewish family . . . He soon came to the fore among the others at the outset of the officers' course by reason of his smart military appearance . . . He had personal charm . . . Gens was an excellent student . . . He had leadership ability, he had personality and he had principles . . . The entire school was led to church services every Sunday morning . . . Gens argued that we must emphasize our Jewishness . . . He submitted a memorandum in which he explained that, as a Jew, he did not think himself bound to attend church services. As a result, an order was issued exempting Jews from the obligation of going to church . . .[17]

16 Kruk, *op. cit.*, pp. 117–118, 155, 277. On pages 203–204, Kruk specifies the opprobrious names that ghetto residents gave Fried and quotes a poem composed in the ghetto in condemnation of Fried. Testimony of E. Haubenshtok, YVA, 0–3/1286, p. 13.
17 Evidence of N. Karni, YVA, 0–33/1274.

Gens, whose wife was non-Jewish and who mingled with the Lithuanians, did not try to escape the fate of the other Jews and went into the ghetto with them, thus greatly enhancing his prestige. His natural qualities of leadership, his Jewish national feelings, and his ambitions for leadership thrust him into prominence in ghetto life. As chief of the Ghetto Police, he had a wide area of responsibility and action within the framework of Jewish administration, but these defined spheres apparently failed to suffice. Gens usurped power-positions in ghetto institutions and became the supreme and recognized authority among ghetto Jewry. Fried admitted in a private conversation at the end of January 1942 that "Gens is the ruler of the ghetto, and he has good connections with the German administration and the Security Police."[18]

Gens and the police began to interfere in the work of the various departments of the Judenrat, and this further undermined Fried's standing. The latter dealt with this subject in a letter to Gens on April 6, 1942:

> ... Without entering into the principal aspect of the problem, I must express my astonishment at a directive which is liable to put askew all the order which has been introduced into the ghetto with such great effort, especially since it affects the heating problem. This directive is liable to destroy all existing discipline ... To prevent this in the future, I will ask you to issue appropriate instructions to the police personnel subordinate to you that, in all cases pertaining to the economy of the ghetto, they turn only to the Judenrat ... I also desire to inform you that on the Sabbath, April 4, a policeman closed all the offices [of the Judenrat] without consulting me about it ...

This letter clearly indicates police interference in areas of Judenrat jurisdiction and underlines Fried's inferior position.

On April 15, 1942, an incident occurred between Fishman,

18 Kruk, *op. cit.*, p. 143.

a Judenrat member, and the Jewish police at the ghetto gate, as a result of which Gens threatened to seek Fishman's dismissal from the Judenrat. Although he did not carry out the threat, the altercation enforced the waxing strength of the police chief within the ghetto.[19]

German Preference for Gens. The German administration gave its official stamp of approval to Gens' preferred position, and that of the Jewish police, in a document which Murer published on April 29, 1942, defining the functions of the Jewish police :

DIRECTIVES FOR THE FUNCTIONING OF THE JEWISH POLICE

Pursuant to the principle that the Jewish population must manage its own affairs, all orders of the *Gebietskommissar* of the City of Vilna will be implemented with the help of the Jewish police. Lithuanian guards will function as a supervisory body. The directives to the Jewish police are:

1. The Jewish police is subordinated to the Chief of the Jewish Police, Jacob Gens.
2. The Jewish police, under the direction of the Chief of Police, will control order and security in the ghetto.
3. Its principal function will be to carry out, without reservation, the orders and instructions of the *Gebietskommissar* of the City of Vilna. The Chief of Jewish Police whom I appointed and the policemen under his command will be responsible to me.
4. The following instructions shall be carried out with maximum precision:
   (a) Only Jews working outside the ghetto are permitted to leave the ghetto;
   (b) Without the *Gebietskommissar's* special permit the columns of workmen can leave the ghetto between

---

19 Balberyszski, *op. cit.,* pp. 424–425, gives the contents of the letter; Kruk, *op. cit.,* pp. 234–235.

GHETTO IN FLAMES

6 and 9 A.M. only. The return from the place of employment must take place between 3 and 8 P.M.;

(c) Orders for work to be undertaken in ghetto workshops, submitted by establishments or individuals, must have my approval. Invoices for work done in the ghetto shall be forwarded to me prior to being sent to customers;

(d) The employment of Jews for labor is approved only for groups of ten Jews and over, except in extraordinary cases ... Jewish police patrols will supervise and ensure compliance with this instruction;

(e) Jewish workmen will be subordinate to the orders of the "brigadier" [column leader], who will be responsible for their conduct to and from their work-places. The "brigadier" will make certain that the men under his orders do not purchase food ... ;

(f) Guards at the ghetto gate will ensure that no food or other commodities are brought into the ghetto without the approval of the *Gebietskommissar;*

(g) The right to supply food is reserved for companies approved for that purpose. The Jewish police shall confiscate food or other commodities even when Jews have been encouraged by Lithuanian or German establishments, including the Wehrmacht, to bring them into the ghetto. Reports must be made to me on the quantity of food and commodities confiscated, and also the names of the establishments which supplied them;

(h) Two policemen shall guard the ghetto gate at all times. In addition, in the hours during which the Jews return to the ghetto, it must be ensured that a sufficient number of police officers shall be at the gate to make appropriate inspection possible;

(i) The guard log must precisely record which Jewish policemen were on duty at the gate of the ghetto at all times;

[288]

(5) The death penalty will be inflicted in all cases in which Jews, "brigadiers," and Jewish police are guilty of violating the orders published by the *Gebietskommissar* of the City of Vilna.

Vilna, April 29, 1942

Gebietskommissar of the City of Vilna,
(Signed) Mürer.[20]

This document had great importance and significance for life in the ghetto. Gens and the Jewish police were nominated as the ruling element, directly linked to the *Gebietskommissar* and not requiring the intermediary of the Judenrat, in that "all orders of the *Gebietskommissar* of the City of Vilna be implemented with the help of the Jewish police." The document noted that Gens was the Chief of Police and personally empowered to execute instructions, as was not the case with the Jewish police in general. The definition implied that the Judenrat had no authority over Gens, nor the right to replace him, although Gens and the police were in theory subordinate to the Judenrat. The Judenrat was not mentioned at all in the document, and contact between the ghetto and the German administration had in effect been transferred to Gens and the police.

Gens personally was named responsible "to implement the orders of the *Gebietskommissar* without reservation." This responsibility was on two levels—the first, control over complete compliance with orders; the second, personal responsibility in the event of non-implementation.

The primary concerns of the Jews in Vilna during this period were work and food. The principal German aim was the exploitation of Jewish labor and keeping the ghetto at near starvation level. In his April 29 document, Murer transferred the handling and responsibility for fulfillment of German instructions in these matters to Gens and the police, and thus Gens became the decisive factor in the ghetto.

20 *Documents Accuse*, pp. 172–174; Kruk, *op. cit.*, p. 247.

The German administration, in resolving to continue the existence of the Vilna ghetto and control and exploit its Jewish manpower, had concluded that Gens was more suitable than Fried to implement its policy. During the period of the *Aktionen*, July–December 1941, Gens stood out in German eyes as a man of ability, ready to discharge instructions. The German authorities permitted Fried and the Judenrat to retain their official functions temporarily, but greatly restricted their executive powers.

Gens' Political Club. Gens made great efforts to strengthen his connections and influence with the political groups and among the liberal professions. He opened a "Club" in his home for lectures and colloquia, at which he held evening meetings attended by all shades of the political spectrum in the ghetto— ranging from the Zionist-Revisionists on the right to the Bundists and Communists on the left. The first gathering at the "Club" was held on May 15, 1942, and was regaled by a lecture on "A Nation and a People." It was followed by a discussion that lasted until 3 A.M. A second meeting of the "Club" took place on May 28, 1942, with a lecture and debate on "Jews and Judaism." Further meetings of the "Club" were held in Gens' home. Kruk, who was among the invited guests, participated in these sessions and wrote:

> Gens is setting up a social group around himself consisting of various strata of the public. He wants to enlist the moral support of all active factors in the ghetto. If this were done without any special intentions, it may be that the initiative should be welcomed, but this is directed at gaining influence... [21]

The "Club" became a meeting-place for the intelligentsia and party leaders of all circles. Gens added a new dimension to his image among the ghetto inhabitants, especially the liberal professions—the image not only of a police commander who

21 Kruk, *op. cit.*, pp. 262, 274, 293.

exercised his police powers, but an enlightened intellectual whose home was open to all political circles in the ghetto.

The Legal System

With the approval of the German administration, a legal system was instituted in the ghetto by the Judenrat at the beginning of February 1942. It emerged as a result of the requirements of daily life. The components were a court, judges, prosecutors, and defenders. The legal system was an integral and subordinate part of the Judenrat and the police. Until its constitution, the sole instrument of justice was Gens and the Jewish police. Even after its creation, the ghetto police retained judicial powers over such misdemeanors as leaving the ghetto without permission, misconduct at the ghetto gate, escapes from ghetto jail, and injury to policemen. The legal system dealt with offenses such as criminal acts, disputes between tenants, and noncompliance with Judenrat instructions. The prosecution, which was part of the juridical system, was subordinate to the police. An association of ghetto jurists was also established.[22]

The sentences of the court were diversified, ranging from acquittals, cash fines, imprisonment and even the death penalty. During the first half of 1942, the court dealt with 115 criminal cases, in which 172 persons were involved. During the same period, 183 persons were arraigned before a single judge or police magistrates. In one case, three persons accused of robbery in the ghetto were sentenced to prison terms. The German Security Police took them out of the ghetto jail and murdered them at Ponar. A ghetto police officer, Oberhart, was suspected of having informed the Germans, and he was dismissed from the police force several days later. The Judenrat, in its full composition of five members, was the appellate authority for court judgments, and was also required to ratify death sentences. A special Court of Appeal was established at the beginning of August 1942.[23]

22 *Ibid.*, pp. 162, 165, 343–344, 358, 367–368.
23 Balberyszski, *op. cit.*, p. 431; Kruk, *op. cit.*, pp. 165–168, 328, 357.

Murder cases also happened in the ghetto. J. Gerstein was murdered by criminals on June 3, 1942; he had been engaged in trading and black-market practices in the ghetto and had done business with his assassins. After killing him, they took his money and buried him in a cellar. The victim's wife reported his disappearance to the police, and as the result of a thorough inquiry, the murderers were arrested. They confessed and admitted having committed yet another murder—a murder about which the police were unaware. At its session on June 4, 1942, the ghetto court, with a bench of five judges, condemned the murderers to hang. The Judenrat unanimously ratified the sentence that same day.

On that day, too, another criminal, named Avidan, was sentenced to death for the attempted murder of a Jewish policeman at the end of October 1941. Avidan fled to Lida after the attempt on the constable's life; there he murdered a priest in the course of a robbery and hid out in the ghetto. The Germans learned that the cleric had been killed by a ghetto Jew, and the Judenrat was compelled to surrender him. Avidan informed the German authorities at Lida that the Judenrat had aided Jewish fugitives from Vilna and had furnished them with forged papers saying they were Lida ghetto residents.

The Germans ordered all the Jewish inhabitants to assemble in the square, and Avidan passed down the rows pointing out the refugees from Vilna. Sixty refugees from Vilna and elsewhere, and all six members of the Lida ghetto Judenrat, including the chief of police, were seized by the Germans and put to death. This occurred in March 1942. Avidan was evidently released by the Germans as a reward for his tale-bearing and returned to Vilna. A number of Vilna refugees, who fled from Lida and returned to their former ghetto, reported what Avidan had done, and he was arrested by the Jewish police upon his return to the ghetto, in the second part of March 1942. He was held in detention in the ghetto jail until June 4, 1942. The Judenrat and ghetto police availed themselves of the pretext of the trial of J. Gerstein's murderers to liquidate Avidan, who was likely to carry information to the German administration on illegal activities in the ghetto and bring disaster upon it. The charge of attempted murder of the policeman was apparently only a pretext. The Judenrat also ratified the death sentence on Avidan.

The sentences were carried out by the Jewish police in the presence of the Judenrat members on June 4, 1942. Gens addressed the audience prior to the hanging:

> Policemen and Judenrat members! Sixteen thousand out of 75,000 Jews of Vilna have survived. These 16,000 must be good, honest and diligent people. Anyone failing to uphold these precepts must expect the same end as these men sentenced today. We shall punish and eliminate them with our own hands. Today we apply the death sentence to six murderers—Jews who killed Jews. The sentence will be carried out by the Jewish Police, which guards the ghetto and will continue to guard it. The police is executing the sentence by virtue of its function. We now begin!

The ghetto inhabitants approved the sentence and were relieved when the hangings took place without incident. There was some fear that the condemned might inform the German authorities of illegal activities in the ghetto in an effort to save their necks.

The arrest and trial of the five murderers and Avidan, the approval of the sentences by the Judenrat, and the executions were completed in one day—June 4, 1942. The Judenrat and police had acted swiftly, so as to preclude the possibility of contact between the convicted men and the German administration. Gens assumed responsibility for the executions without prior consultation with the Germans.

Fried and Gens published a written notice on the hangings in which ghetto residents were cautioned that "all crimes in the ghetto will be punished with the utmost severity, and the death

penalty will be imposed for heinous crimes." The announcement was posted on June 5, one day after the hangings.[24]

No further murders for robbery were perpetrated in the
ghetto.

Financing the Activity of the Judenrat and Its Institutions
The Judenrat required funds to run the ghetto institutions and
provide services for the population. Expenditures included
wages for Judenrat employees and the Jewish police, educational and cultural programs, social welfare, technical maintenance of buildings and services, street-cleaning, and sanitation.
The Financial Department of the Judenrat, established in November 1941, administered the fiscal affairs.

Sources of Judenrat income were varied. The Food Department sold foodstuffs at higher prices than what they had paid
for them. Workers outside the ghetto paid a 20 percent income
tax. Ghetto inhabitants paid the Judenrat rentals, medical-aid
fees, and burial charges. The Judenrat taxed workshops, bakeries, store-keepers, restaurants, various categories of intermediaries, and members of the liberal professions in the ghetto.
Additional revenues were derived from fines imposed by the
police. Judenrat income and expenditure alike steadily increased.

According to the compilations of the Institute of Statistics–
Department of Accounts, in the Vilna ghetto, the total income
(in Reichsmarks) for the first half of 1942 was 658.6, and the
total expenditures were 543.9[25] (see Appendix C).

An additional source of Judenrat income was a per capita
tax, which was paid by the Jews of the ghetto beginning in the
second half of 1942. This tax was also levied upon the non-Jewish population of Vilna and served to finance the work of the
municipality. The Judenrat collected this tax for the city management by order of the mayor of Vilna, but, in effect, it was

24 Balberyszski, *op. cit.*, pp. 297–298; Kruk, *op. cit.*, pp. 209–210,
    224–225, 276–280.
25 Korczak, *op. cit.*, p. 383; Balberyszski, *op. cit.*, pp. 415–416.

used to finance the Judenrat budget. The per capita tax was graduated according to sex and age and ranged from 80 to 150 rubles per annum. It was to be levied annually. In 1942, 8,716 persons paid this tax.[26]

The Judenrat also needed money in order to provide gifts and bribes for German and Lithuanian personnel, as well as to purchase food on the black market, and it kept an unofficial account for these purposes. The confiscation of moneys, gold, property, and taxes imposed on food smugglers and speculators provided additional income. No records were kept of this account so as to preclude audit by the German administration.[27]

The Judenrat taxation of the ghetto inhabitants made it possible to provide essential services to the community.

---

26 Kruk, *op. cit.,* p. 275; Korczak, *op. cit.,* p. 259; The announcement by the Judenrat proclaimed: "In accordance with the order of the Mayor of Vilna, of August 27, 1942, a *per capita* tax had been imposed upon the Jewish population . . ." Males aged 18–20 and 50–60 were obliged to pay 10 marks; males aged 20–50, 15 marks. Women aged 18–20 and 40–60 were obliged to pay 8 marks, and aged 20–40 to pay 10 marks. People who were not fit for work paid a tax of 40–60 percent less than the regular levy. A tax reduced by 15 percent was levied upon the parents of each child up to sixteen.
27 Balberyszski, *op. cit.,* p. 419; Dworzecki, *op. cit.,* pp. 136–137.

Chapter 18

LIFE IN THE GHETTO

Labor Administration and Workers' Organization
The ideology of "Work to Live," coupled with the demand
for Jewish labor by the German administration, created the
need for efficient manpower management. The potential reservoir of working hands—males and females of fifteen and
over—totaled 14–15,000 persons, or 70–75 percent of the
ghetto population. Of these, 3,000 persons worked outside the
ghetto in some 190 military and civilian plants at the end of
1941 and beginning of 1942; approximately 1,000 persons were
employed in the Judenrat and its agencies within the ghetto.[1]
The greater majority of these were males of eighteen and over.

1 The number of yellow permits issued was between 3,000 and 3,600, of
  which approximately 400 went to employees of the Judenrat and
  the remainder to workers outside the ghetto, in various plants and
  installations. Kruk, *op. cit.*, p. 152, writes, on January 31, about
  188 work-sites where Jews were employed outside the ghetto. Balberyszski, p. 305, speaks of 1,001 persons who were employed in
  ghetto establishments during the first half of January 1942:

Members of the Judenrat	6	Hospital	147
General Department	25	Housing Department	97
Food Department	73	Technical Department	231
Child Care	22	Distribution of Firewood	6
Library	14	Workshops	6
Labor Office	16	Burial Society	8
Health Services	157	Ghetto Police	193

About 10,000 persons—of whom the majority were females and youths—were manpower potential that existed outside the work-cycle. The Judenrat, which preached greater productivity of the ghetto, based its plans and demands for labor on this yet-untapped potential. The increase in the number of Jewish workers continued throughout the entire period of the ghetto's existence.

The Labor Department of the Judenrat was the central instrument for the control and activation of Jewish manpower. This department took its orders from the German *Arbeitsamt*, and was obliged to supply the requisite labor. There were certain places in which the working conditions and the employers' attitudes were particularly poor, and it was difficult to find people willing to work there. The Labor Department at times had to compel people to do so, sometimes under duress. A special police unit, known as the "Labor Police," functioned in the ghetto in order to enforce the obligation to work, and cooperated with the Labor Department to this end. The latter was the authority for the issuance of work permits, which had replaced the yellow passes on April 15, 1942.

The Labor Department, which ruled this central area of ghetto life, became the focus of political power. Judenrat councilor J. Fishman was in charge, but actually A. Braude became its director and the person who reigned supreme over all labor matters. Braude, who was close to Gens, was in direct communication with the *Arbeitsamt* and enjoyed an important status in the ghetto.

The Labor Department became an independent body vis-à-vis the Directorate of the Judenrat. Braude wrote to the Judenrat on April 30, 1942, demanding that all able-bodied persons of suitable age be removed from their employment in the Judenrat offices and sent outside the ghetto to undertake more physical work. He proposed that the Judenrat employ women or men of much lower health standards in its offices.[2] This

2 YVA, JM/1195, Document no. 233.

demand corresponded with the propensity to increase the number of workers deployed outside the ghetto.

"Brigadiers." The organization of ghetto labor was based on place of employment. Groups of persons employed in a particular place constituted a separate labor force attached to the ghetto Labor Department that had designated it and to the German or Lithuanian employer. The link with the employer was a daily one and encompassed a number of spheres—work-permits, labor conditions, human relations, and assistance in the form of food. One person chosen from among the Jewish workers was placed in charge of the entire group at each place of employment. His title was "brigadier" (foreman).

The "brigadiers" were not appointed in advance, but there was always one in each group who stood out from the rest and automatically became the spokesman. He was obliged to know the employer's language, which was German or Lithuanian. The "brigadiers" succeeded in establishing good relations with the employers, arranged for work-permits and sometimes were able to obtain the release of laborers and/or their families from Lukiszki, generally by bribing the Germans. Some "brigadiers" were active on behalf of the entire group in dealing with employers, in procuring additional food at the work-places, better working conditions and more humane treatment, but there were others who exploited their position for their own benefit. These men misappropriated part of the bribes intended for the employers, and accepted bribes from Jews who wanted to get into places of employment that offered "good" work-permits and opportunities to obtain additional food. In addition to the "brigadiers," some of the larger locations were also supervised by column-leaders (*Kollenenführer*), who were responsible for escorting workmen, in various shifts, to and from the ghetto. These column-leaders, too, benefitted from higher standing and better conditions than the ordinary worker.

Some of the "brigadiers" achieved positions of power in the ghetto due to the ties they were able to establish with the Germans and as a result of their solid economic status. At times these power-ploys enabled them to extract favors for themselves and for their workmen in regard to housing and other needs within the ghetto. The "brigadiers" became a class onto themselves.

Several who rose to power wanted to be independent of the Judenrat and the Labor Department in all that pertained to the management of their coteries, that is, in accepting new workers and exploiting their status in order to wield influence in various spheres of ghetto life. Conflicts developed between the "brigadiers" on the one hand, and the Judenrat and Jewish police on the other. One of these clashes, which was to influence the status of this class, sprang up between "Brigadier" Weisskopf and Gens.

Weisskopf, a tailor by vocation, was the brigadier of a tailor shop (*Schneiderstube*) that had a staff of over 200 working for the German Army. Weisskopf enjoyed close ties with the German soldiers and, with their aid, brought large quantities of food and firewood into the ghetto; he also succeeded, through bribery, in freeing detainees from Lukiszki. He grew rich and used his wealth and ties with the Germans to fortify his position in the ghetto. He gave financial support to cultural programs and distributed alms, thus earning the half-serious, half-facetious title among his fellow-Jews of "King of the Ghetto."

Weisskopf's relationship with Gens was at first quite close, but as his own position strengthened, they clashed. The altercation became public at the beginning of May 1942. An agreement had been reached between Weisskopf and a quartermaster's unit of the German Army for the repair of a large quantity of army clothing. Weisskopf wanted to expand his workshop and enlist additional tailors for that purpose. Gens demanded that all these arrangements be made through the Labor Department and that a separate workshop be set up to handle the repairs. His aim was to add a new work-unit to the ghetto, expanding its creative capacity by hundreds of additional workers, and simultaneously curb Weisskopf's aggrandizement. The latter asked the army personnel with whom he was in contact to support him against Gens. The police chief reacted vigorously and ordered a search of the foreman's home, where forbidden food—flour, wines and liqueurs—was found. Weisskopf was arrested, detained for four days, and dismissed from his post as "brigadier."[3]

Gens viewed the "brigadier" class with anxiety. Their ties with the Germans at their places of work and their affluence had made them far too independent, challenged his authority and that of the Judenrat, and, in his estimation, endangered the realization of the ideology of productivity. Gens waited for a suitable moment to settle accounts with Weisskopf. The opportunity arose after Murer's order of April 29, 1942, broadening his powers in the labor sphere. Weisskopf's appeals to German Army headquarters in Vilna were to no avail as Gens had the support of the *Gebietskommissar,* who, for reasons of his own (stemming from his desire to be the exclusive ruler of the ghetto), was against work arrangements between the Jews and German or Lithuanian employers, without the mediation of the *Gebietskommissariat.* It had been expressly posited in the German *Sozialamt* and Murer's order of April 29, 1942, that the *Gebietskommissariat* must be the only intermediary.

Weisskopf's elimination as an influential factor in the ghetto checked the danger of the "brigadiers" becoming an autonomous force capable of resisting Gens' authority. Throughout the existence of the ghetto, no other Jewish foreman rose to defy Gens: they had learned their lesson from Weisskopf, whose downfall was a significant milestone in the growth of Gens' power.

Labor Arbitration Committee. This body, designed to mediate between Jewish workmen and their "brigadiers," or between a workman and his fellow-worker, was established in March 1942, upon the initiative of the ghetto police, which did not wish to deal with such problems. Glazman, then deputy chief of ghetto police, asked that a body be established to arbitrate labor dis-

3 Kruk, *op. cit.,* pp. 170–171, 184, 275; Epstein's diary, pp. 53, 98.

putes. The Judenrat decided to create a permanent instrument of arbitration consisting of two workers, two "brigadiers," and a chairman.[4]

Committee of Judenrat Employees. A Judenrat employees' committee was established by a group of Bundist leaders and Communists. The committee petitioned Fried for salary increases. The Judenrat granted the request, and the salary at each level was raised by 100 rubles. There were six pay levels: "Grade A" was the highest, at 687 rubles; "Grade F" was the lowest, at 280 rubles.

The Committee held only two meetings. The first dealt with the subject of a Public Committee for Social Welfare. The second meeting, held in June 1942, raised the issue of extra food parcels distributed to a small group of senior Judenrat employees once a week. After discussing the matter, the committee resolved to urge the Judenrat management to expand distribution of the extra rations to include all ranks, and not just a small senior group. On June 27, Gens invited the "Employees' Committee" to his office. He told them that the food distribution had been undertaken upon his initiative and was intended for echelons that bore the principal responsibility for ghetto administration and the committee had no right to interfere. He warned them that they would be sent to work outside Vilna if they continued to do so. In reaction, the Bund Central Committee met on July 4 and decided, by a majority vote, to personally boycott Gens and suspend Bund participation in the management of public institutions. Criticism was also leveled at the stand taken by the Communists, who had not supported these Bund measures. The Bund representatives thereupon withdrew from the "Public Committee for Social Welfare." At a gathering of the Bund "quintet" leaders, held several days after the central committee meeting, these decisions were criticized, and it was resolved to resume management of public institutions as soon as possible. They reasoned that these institutions

4 Balberyszski, *op. cit.,* pp. 345–347.

should not be deprived of Bund representation.[5] It was the last attempt by the Bund to openly resist Gens. Gens' reaction put an end to the Committee of Judenrat Employees' activity.

The Fight Against Hunger and Deprivation
Ghetto inmates were obsessed by the daily problem of obtaining food and staving off hunger. Food entered the ghetto through legal channels, in the form of fixed rations allotted by the German administration, and via illegal means, i.e., smuggling. This contraband traffic was conducted by laborers returning from work, by professional smugglers, and by the Judenrat Food Department, which obtained food and brought it into the ghetto illegally.

F. Murer was responsible for the food supply to the ghetto on behalf of the *Gebietskommissariat*. The ration allocated by the German administration to the Jews was less than one-half of the per capita ration for the non-Jewish population. A Jew received 1 1/3 pounds of bread weekly, and meager quantities of grits, flour, sugar, and meat. The German authorities delivered these commodities to the Judenrat Food Department in accordance with the number of people who possessed food cards. The number of people for whom the German administration provided food, and which the Judenrat distributed on the basis of the food cards, was as follows: [6]

Nov.	1941 — 12,000	Feb. 1942 — 14,746	May 1942 — 18,500
Dec.	1941 — 13,000	March 1942 — 15,850	June 1942 — 18,600
Jan.	1942 — 13,600	April 1942 — 18,500	July 1942 — 19,560

The number of food cards specified for November corresponded to the 3,000 persons possessing yellow passes. During

5 *Ibid.*, pp. 330, 347–350; Kruk, *op. cit.*, pp. 119, 135, 291–293, 295, 298. It should be noted that, despite this reaction by Gens, the number of people who received extra food rations increased gradually and, in effect, encompassed the overwhelming majority of employees of the Judenrat and its various affiliated bodies.
6 *Ibid.*, p. 255; Balberyszski, *op. cit.*, pp. 315, 318.

December and January, 1,600 pink passes were distributed and food cards issued commensurately. The rise in the number of food cards in the February–April quarter was consistent with those thousands of persons who had survived in the *malines* and gradually acquired the status of "legal" residents in the ghetto. The large increase in food cards in April was the result of the abolition of the yellow passes and the legalization of manpower by Wagner's order of April 15. Over the period November 1941–April 1942, there were thousands of "illegal" people in the ghetto for whom no food at all was supplied by the German administration, and the Judenrat was compelled to spread the rations (in any case small) to provide for these thousands as well.

The quantities of food supplied by the Germans to the ghetto rose slightly in mid-year and during the second half of 1942. Bread allocated to workers engaged in hard physical labor outside the ghetto was doubled from 1 1/3 to 2 2/3 pounds per week, equivalent to the bread ration given to a non-Jewish laborer. The increased bread ration was given to 5,600 workmen. A number of "brigadiers" were permitted by the German administration to bring food into the ghetto, over and above the rations distributed through the Judenrat Food Department.[7] These small supplements were a result of the new German policy which was aimed at more intensive exploitation of Jewish manpower.

The food allocated by the German authorities to the ghetto, including the supplementary rations in mid-1942, was insufficient for subsistence. The inhabitants were able to survive only through smuggling operations and by obtaining food from additional sources outside official channels. Thousands of Jewish laborers returned daily from their work with smuggled food.

7 Kruk, *op. cit.*, p. 245; Balberyszski, *op. cit.*, pp. 317–319; Ghetto inhabitants received a monthly average of 9–10 lbs. of bread, 1 lb. of meat, 2/3 lb. of sugar, one egg. The Judenrat bought comparatively large quantities of potatoes and brought them into the ghetto with the German administration's approval.

There were times when food could be brought through the gate without difficulty, but at other times those caught were severely punished. Some were executed. Gens tried to regulate the food brought by the workers through the gate. He summoned the "brigadiers" on January 27, 1942, and told them that returning laborers were permitted to bring "a limited quantity of foodstuffs" through the gate. This arrangement lasted only a few days.

Murer carried out an inspection at the gate on February 5, and found that the Jews were bringing food back with them. He forbade the continuation of this practice and announced that unless it was halted he would place all the gate policemen under arrest. The Jewish police officer in charge of the ghetto gate was taken off that post and transferred to another assignment. He was replaced by Levas, whose bad reputation was widespread in the ghetto.[8] Murer was dissatisfied with the control at the gate, and in a memorandum to employers, printed April 7, 1942, he emphasized that they were obliged to make certain that Jews working for them did not obtain food.

Murer's directives for the operation of the Jewish police, dated April 29, 1942, had made clear that Jews were forbidden to purchase food outside the ghetto and bring it inside. The death penalty was threatened for anyone caught smuggling food, column-leaders of groups caught in possession of food, and gate policemen permitting it to pass through. This order made the Jewish gate policeman a guarantor with his life in cases of detected food smuggling.

Murer often appeared suddenly at the gate and conducted searches. His presence led to immediate intensification of control by the policemen. Thousands of workers experienced nightmares every time Mürer unexpectedly descended upon the gate. M. Rolnik writes in her diary:

> When I returned today from work, it was still quiet at the gate. Suddenly an uproar broke out. F. Murer was

8 Kruk, *op. cit.*, pp. 149, 158.

at the gate. He stood at the entrance and examined how the gate guards checked the incomers. Sometimes he checked them himself. He found a pfennig on one woman. He ordered her to be taken into the guardhouse, stripped, and given twenty-five blows with a nightstick. Five policemen laid on the blows, but this was not enough for F. Murer, and he himself took over the cudgel...[9]

The behavior of the Jewish police at the gate—the searches and the beatings—made them and their commander, Levas, the most hated group among the Jews of the ghetto. These blows and searches were inflicted directly by the policemen themselves, and became the rule when Murer or another German was on the spot. Many Jews saw the Jewish gatemen as the oppressors who prevented them from bringing in food. The gate police more than once exceeded the necessary norm and abused their position to impound food for their own consumption and enrichment. Fried intervened in one instance and wrote to Gens that "all too often incidents occur at the gate not because of objective reasons, but because of the incautious and unjustified provocations of the gate-police commander."[10]

Gens regarded strict control by the Jewish police at the ghetto gate, including manhandling those caught with food, a necessity whenever Murer or some other German official was there. He argued that if the Jewish police were not capable of proving to the German administration that they were able to guard the gate efficiently and prevent food smuggling, the Germans would post their own guards and the surreptitious entry of food would cease altogether. In the police chief's opinion, the confidence that the German administration placed in the gate-police force enabled large quantities of food to be brought into the ghetto, for even what was confiscated at the gate remained in the ghetto. The food was sometimes restored to the person from

9 Rolnik, *op. cit.,* p. 67; Kruk, *op. cit.,* pp. 222, 237, 239, 245.
10 Balberyszski, *op. cit.,* pp. 430–431. The letter was sent on April 21, 1942. Epstein's diary p. 58.

whom it had been taken and at other times was given to the public kitchens which distributed meals to the poor and needy. There had also been several cases in which the gate police had issued prior warnings to groups of workers returning from the outside that Murer was there on the look-out. This had enabled people to refrain from bringing in food, or to rid themselves of it before reaching the gate.

There were times when control over procurement of food was tightened, and people caught purchasing or bringing it furtively into the ghetto were arrested and executed. Seventy-three Jews, including twenty-three women and two children, were shot at Ponar in March 1942. There is no information as to their supposed offense, but it is clear that some of them were put to death for attempting to smuggle food into the ghetto. The murder of Jews for buying and smuggling food continued throughout the existence of the ghetto. Dessler succeeded, at the beginning of June 1942, in releasing from Lukiszki a total of thirty-seven Jews who had been detained because of food purchases and failure to wear the yellow patch on their clothing. Six Jewish women were killed while trying to obtain food in October 1942; another ten women were murdered on November 18, 1942, for a similar attempt. Lyuba Levitska, a well-known singer in the ghetto, and another woman were detained by Germans at the ghetto gate in January 1943, on the charge of being in possession of 2 pounds of grits (groats) and a little butter. Both were shot and killed at Ponar. Gens published a notice in the ghetto on May 4, 1943, in which he stated that the Security Police had executed two persons caught in the act of buying food, and he warned that, in accordance with a Security Police announcement, every Jew caught outside the ghetto purchasing food without permission would be executed.[11]

11 *Ereignismeldung* No. 191, p. 16, YVA, 0–51/57–1; Kruk, *op. cit.*,
    pp. 208, 280–281, 370, 412, 443, 450; Z. Kalmanovitch, "A tog-
    buch fun vilner geto," *YIVO Bleter*, Vol. XXXV, New York,
    1951, p. 43; Rolnik, *op. cit.*, pp. 66–67.

Apart from food smuggling by workmen, there were also people engaged in food trafficking on a much larger scale for their own profit. These contrabandists had "connections" with the gate police, both Jewish and Lithuanian, who, against due payment, helped them to bring whole cartloads of commodities through the gate. Secret routes were sometimes used by the smugglers, including attics, cellars, and walls of houses adjoining the "Aryan" area and leading into the ghetto. One particular band of smugglers was the Jewish chimney-sweeps, who as a result became the *nouveaux riches* of the ghetto. There was a dearth of non-Jewish chimney-sweeps in Vilna, and Jews engaged in this occupation enjoyed the privilege of going to the city on their own during working hours. Their unimpeded contact with the non-Jewish populace enabled them to obtain food and conceal it in their boxes of soot-covered appliances. A second group of smugglers was the Jewish workmen in the army foodstuff warehouses. Mainly former porters, they were dubbed in the ghetto *die Shtarke* ("the strong ones"). They stole products from the German stores, including cigarettes, matches, wood for heating, and liquor of various kinds, and brought them into the ghetto. They were organized into groups and built caches in the ghettos to hide their illegally imported merchandise.[12]

A brisk trade in food and other articles developed in the ghetto in the wake of the smuggling operations. At first trading was practiced in the streets, doorways, and courtyards. In March 1942 small shops were opened in which bread, meat, butter, sugar, salt, cigarettes, matches, clothing, and firewood could be obtained. Bakeries, restaurants, kiosks, and a saccharine factory were also opened, and some people made fortunes. To open a business, it was necessary to receive a license from the police. The smugglers, middlemen, and tradesmen in the ghetto accepted a variety of articles in exchange for food and

12 Balberyszski, *op. cit.*, p. 314; Dworzecki, *op. cit.*, p. 131; Rolnik, *op. cit.*, pp. 68, 73, 81.

other items, and used these as payment in kind outside the ghetto.

On one of his inspections in June 1942, Murer discovered a quantity of liquor destined for restaurants in the ghetto. He threatened to execute 100 people in reprisal. As a result, the police closed down the luxury restaurants for which these goods were intended.

The ghetto police also fought profiteering; bakers who charged more than 35 rubles for 1 pound of bread were arrested. Ghetto prices were affected by those on the outside and by control conditions at the gate. When control was tightened a shortage of commodities ensued, and the risks of food smuggling increased, thus forcing up prices. With the relaxation of control, the prices dropped, but the ghetto price-levels always remained higher than those on the outside.[13]

It was necessary to have cash or valuables, or goods of equivalent worth to defray the cost of food and other necessities purchased outside the ghetto from non-Jews and for goods bartered inside the ghetto itself. The cash and the few belongings that the Jews had succeeded in bringing into the ghetto were soon depleted. The Jewish inhabitants made desperate efforts to recover property they left behind with non-Jewish neighbors or acquaintances before being confined in the ghetto. Part of these possessions were restored, but in some cases, Jews who came to seek their goods were arrested and taken to Ponar when the custodians of their property informed against them.

Gens reached an agreement with the German administration that Jews who had left movable property with non-Jews could recover a portion of it with their help. Gens issued an announcement on May 5, 1942, to the effect that the Jews were to provide the German administration with particulars of the property and with whom it had been deposited. The administra-

13 Kruk, *op. cit.*, pp. 154, 212–213, 248–249, 261, 283–285, 420; Epstein's diary, p. 65.

tion arranged for half to be returned to the original owners and retained the other half. Jews who had been unable to recover their possessions through other means took advantage of the arrangement, although actually they received less than one-half of the property, and the German officials kept the rest. In October 1942, Gens was authorized by the *Gebietskommissar* to detail Jewish police to repossess property that Jews had left with Christians and bring it back to the ghetto. But the paltry belongings were insufficient for food purchases over any length of time, and it was necessary to find funds from other sources. These "other sources" were the products of the Jewish workshops. Jewish artisans were forced to steal and sell part of their output, using the proceeds to pay for food. Notwithstanding, however, the nutritional level of the ghetto population continued to deteriorate, especially among those sectors that worked inside the ghetto.[14] It was necessary for the Judenrat to institute drastic measures to fight off starvation.

The Judenrat, through its Food Department, in its function as receiver and supplier of the food allocated by the authorities, found it to be insufficient and initiated other measures to obtain additional supplies and smuggle them in. The rationed food was received through a Lithuanian supply company. The Judenrat succeeded in bribing several of the company managers into providing larger quantities than those sanctioned. H. Trapido, manager of the Judenrat Food Department, was arrested on January 26, 1942, when he brought "gifts" to the company manager in order to extract more food for the ghetto. He was held in the Lukiszki jail, but released on February 19, 1942. Trapido assumed full personal responsibility for the at-

---

14 Dworzecki, *op. cit.,* pp. 130–131; Balberyszski, *op. cit.,* p. 449; Epstein's diary, p. 47; YVA, JM/1195, Document No. 224; Kruk, *op. cit.,* pp. 239, 248, 252, writes that in May 1942, the price per pound of bread in the ghetto (not on ration) was 40 rubles, one pound of potatoes, 17 rubles, and the wages of the Judenrat employees ranged between 350 and 850 rubles per month.

tempted bribery and did not implicate the Judenrat. Trapido's release was also the result of bribery.

The Judenrat brought the "illegal" food into the ghetto on carts hired for the purpose, in garbage-vans, firewood wagons, or hearses entering and leaving the ghetto.[15] The food legally allocated, as well as that obtained from illicit sources, was distributed by the Food Department to ghetto residents with food cards, who received fixed rations; employees of Judenrat bodies who worked inside the ghetto and had no way of obtaining other provisions; public kitchens which sold inexpensive meals or distributed free meals to the poor residents.

In January 1942, over 1,000 persons were employed in establishments and workshops inside the ghetto. This number rose, as time went by, in proportion to the proliferation of ghetto workshops. Work inside the ghetto was easier than in most places of employment outside, as those employed in the workshops and services in the ghetto were not at the mercy of cruel employers. On the other hand, they were unable to obtain the extra provisions available to those working outside. Large places of employment inside the ghetto founded cooperatives that were responsible for providing extra food for their workers. The Judenrat extended loans to the cooperatives for this purpose. The cooperatives, inaugurated at the outset of January 1942, included the Jewish police force, with a membership of about 200, the Judenrat clerical and services staff, with about 500 members, and the hospital employees, who totaled about 180. Each of these cooperatives was directed by an elected management.

Bundists were among the foremost leaders of the cooperative created by the Judenrat staff. Gens opposed Bund hegemony over this cooperative and decided to dissolve it and those of the hospital employees and merge its members with the police cooperative. He informed the Judenrat of his decision on the

---

15 Balberyszski, *op. cit.*, p. 314; Kruk, *op. cit.*, pp. 149, 182.

grounds that the managers of the cooperative were conducting political activities hostile to the Judenrat.[16]

All persons employed by Judenrat institutions (one per family) belonged to the police cooperative. Basic provisions were sold at low prices at the police canteen.

The quantity of food distributed through the Food Department of the Judenrat to all inhabitants of the Vilna ghetto depended on the food cards allotted by the German administration. During the first half of 1942, it remained relatively stable, in contrast with the extreme fluctuations in the quantities distributed by the cooperative (see Appendix C), for the cooperative purchases were affected by the market graph and the possibilities of acquisition. Food allocated by the cooperative constituted a significant supplement to the fixed food rations allocated against food cards.

The Judenrat decided to allot extra food parcels for several dozen of its senior officials, in addition to the extra provisions from the cooperative. Upon Gens' initiative, a plan was adopted to this effect in June 1942. The food was purchased outside the ghetto or was obtained through confiscations at the gate. Their recipients paid a small token for them.

Gens controlled all food distribution to Judenrat employees through the police cooperative and the special food allowances for senior Judenrat officials. Thus, he occupied a powerful position in one of the crucial spheres of ghetto life.

There were people in the ghetto who, for reasons of age or ill health, did not work, or were employed at jobs and places that did not entitle them to extra food allowances. The Food Department of the Judenrat set up four public kitchens, one of them Kosher, for these needy persons, and another for poor children. Also the police canteen in the ghetto sometimes served meals to the very poor. These public kitchens provided luncheons, and some of them distributed the evening meal for a low price or gratis. The free meals were served against

16 *Ibid.*, pp. 118, 142–144; Balberyszski, *op. cit.*, pp. 348–349.

vouchers issued by the Welfare Department of the Judenrat.

In the first half of 1942 the number of meals served in the public kitchens rose, reflecting the growth of the indigent population in the ghetto and its rate of economic decline[17] (see Appendix C).

Thousands of people without yellow passes received no food allocations from the end of 1941 to the spring of 1942. The number of needy people continued to increase because those who had succeeded in living from the proceeds of their possessions had long since exhausted this source of income and were now left with no means of subsistence.

The Social Aid Department of the Judenrat and the Public Committee for Social Welfare were in charge of granting free meals at the public canteens and directing financial support, free medical treatment, and part or full exemption from paying rent for housing. Expenditures of the Judenrat Social Aid Department for the first half of 1942 totaled 1,431,000 rubles, which represented about 22 percent of the aggregate income of the Judenrat during this period.[18]

The Welfare Committee, which had been set up in the ghetto in October 1941 by a group of Bund leaders, received a subsidy from the Judenrat and succeeded in organizing free meals for the poor with the help of a food allocation from the Judenrat. The latter rescinded the financial grant to the committee and its distribution of free meals at the end of December 1941, apparently to prevent the Bund from gaining exclusive control over a public body handling aid to the needy and to compel it to broaden its base of public representation. A joint request was also tendered by Po'alei Zion-Z.S., the Communists, and Agudat Israel to establish a broadly based public-welfare committee, with the participation of all ghetto circles. The Bund was compelled to comply.

Delegates of the various parties met on January 16, 1942,

17 *Ibid.*, pp. 326–327; Kruk, *op. cit.*, pp. 214–215.
18 Kruk, *op. cit.*, p. 135; Dworzecki, *op. cit.*, p. 148.

and resolved to form an all-party Public Committee, composed of eleven members: Bund — 3; Communists — 3; Zionists — 3; Social Revolutionaries (S.D.) — 1; and Agudat Israel — 1. It was also decided to form a presidium from among the members on the Public Committee.

At a meeting of the committee on January 21, 1942, S. Milkonovicki, a Zionist and head of the Judenrat Health Department, was voted to head the Public Social Welfare Committee. By way of protest, the Bund withdrew its members from the presidium of the new body. The Communists in the ghetto preferred to cooperate with the Zionists rather than with the Bund and acted to destroy the authority which the Bund had gained in the public-aid committees.[19]

The Bund wanted the Public Committee to be a public body active in various spheres of ghetto life, and not to limit itself to social welfare. The committee decided, at a meeting held May 10, 1942, to send a deputation to the Judenrat and the chief of police in order to present a written protest against the behavior of the police at the gate. The Public Committee for Social Welfare continued to be active until November 17, 1942, when, by Gens' order, personnel changes were effected, and three representatives of the "brigadiers" who were Gens' followers were enlisted.[20]

The income necessary for the welfare activities of the Public Committee was derived from a number of sources, among them the Judenrat and other institutions in the ghetto. Judenrat employees were taxed a percentage of their monthly salaries for this purpose: workmen in labor units employed outside the

19 Kruk, *op. cit.*, pp. 198, 119, 137–138, 140–141; several days after the formation of the Public Committee for Social Aid, in which Zionists and Communists joined together against the Bund, the FPO was also created in the ghetto, composed of Zionists and Communists without Bund participation.
20 Dworzecki, *op. cit.*, p. 187, minutes of the meeting of the committee on the question of the conduct of the gate-police; Kruk, *op. cit.*, pp. 406–407; Kalmanovitch, *op. cit.*, p. 47.

ghetto paid an average of 20 rubles monthly as welfare donations, and 40 percent of the proceeds of the sale of tickets to
concerts and performances held in the ghetto went to the committee. Another source of income was the occasional proceeds
from the sales of provisions seized at the ghetto gate, or the
provisions themselves, which were given to the Committee.
Donations were also received, and taxes were levied on certain
classes, such as shopkeepers and restaurant owners. Among the
recipients of the Public Committee's monthly cash and food
grants were a number of people whose past public positions
or their personal dignity deterred them from applying to the
Judenrat Social Aid Department for assistance. These benefi-
ciaries were primarily members of the liberal professions—
writers, journalists, teachers, and actors, among others. Aid was
also furnished for the Children's Home, the Children's Kitchen,
and the Home for the Aged in the ghetto. The expenditures
totaled several million rubles, as some 3,000 people were on
the welfare rolls in mid-1942.[21]

The ghetto administration started a loan fund in September
1942. Loans were extended for two weeks only, and borrowers
were obliged to furnish collateral. The directors of the fund and
the board of management were appointed by Gens.[22]

Gens appointed a "Winter Help" (*Winterhilfe*) Committee at
the end of October 1942, for the purpose of organizing clothing
collections for the needy for the winter. The committee enlisted women and children who collected clothing and donations
from inhabitants on a voluntary basis. Within several days,
some 10,000 items of wearing apparel and 80,000 rubles were
gathered. The clothing, mostly torn, was mended in ghetto

21 Dworzecki, *op. cit.*, pp. 147, 186–187; Epstein's diary, pp. 109–
110; Kruk, *op. cit.*, p. 219.
22 *Ibid.*, p. 347; Korczak, *op. cit.*, p. 270, excerpt from *Geto Yedies;*
the meaning of the term "ghetto administration" is the internal
administration established in the ghetto after the dissolution of
the Judenrat and the appointment of Gens to be "Ghetto Representative."

workshops and distributed to the needy. The action of the committee greatly aided the poor to pass the hard winter.[23]

Social-aid agencies were activated for all necessary spheres of ghetto life. Due to the efforts of Judenrat bodies, the police, and public circles in the field of social assistance, there were no cases of death due to hunger or as a direct result of exposure to the cold in the ghetto.

The Health Services

The ghetto was located in the old narrow streets of Vilna, in the sector near the medieval Jewish ghetto. The congested conditions were indescribable. The sewers, the water supply, toilets and showers were not meant for so many people. The drains clogged and were severely damaged and became a source of pollution. Pipes burst in many houses, leading to a water shortage; garbage piled up in the courtyards. These sanitary defects, along with the shortages of food, clothing, and firewood, the damp and moldiness in the rooms, the bugs and lice, created ideal conditions for disease and epidemics. But the ghetto health services grappled manfully and successfully with these hazards.

The Judenrat Health Department was headed by Councilor S. Milkonovicki. There were five physicians in the directorate, who, together with the administrative director, established and operated the health services and maintained close control over them. The health services encompassed the hospital, clinic, and a sanitary-epidemiological unit.

The hospital had been installed on the premises of the former Jewish hospital, which was located in the ghetto. It had departments for internal medicine, surgery, gynecology, children, contagious diseases, X-ray, and a laboratory. The staff consisted of over 150 persons—doctors, nurses, and technical personnel. Over 3,000 patients were treated during 1942.

The existence of the contagious diseases department had to be concealed from the German administration, since the Ger-

23 Kruk, *op. cit.*, pp. 383, 390.

[315]

mans might take the patients from this ward to Ponar for extermination. The spread of contagious diseases endangered the
very existence of the ghetto. German officials inspected the hospital frequently and checked the situation there. The contagious diseases department functioned under the guise of a Laboratory Tests Department.

Another department that operated clandestinely was Gynecology. A decree was issued by the Germans on February 5, 1942,
forbidding Jews to procreate. A verbal order to this effect was
given to the Judenrat and the director of the ghetto hospital
by the Security Police. The order made no mention of what
would be done with infants that were born, and the idea was
apparently to encourage abortions among pregnant women and
to deter further pregnancies. The order brought confusion and
fear among expectant mothers and their families, but the births
did not cease. A secret delivery room functioned in the Gyne-
cological Department at the hospital. The newborn infants were
hidden in a *maline* inside the hospital, and mothers nursed their
babies there. When the children grew up, they were registered
in the Judenrat offices as born prior to the date of the ban.

The German administration learned of the ongoing births in
the second half of 1942, and the Judenrat was ordered to act
in accordance with the order to halt such births. A birth-con-
trol campaign explaining this was launched, and the Judenrat
opened special advisory bureaus for this purpose. The birth
rate in the ghetto declined as the number of abortions performed at the hospital increased, but births continued during
the entire period of ghetto existence.[24]

The clinic in the ghetto was composed of general practi-
tioners, specialists, dentists, and a laboratory. Hundreds of
persons visited the clinic daily, particularly in the evenings after
returning from work. Clinic staff doctors also made house calls.
A special panel of three doctors was empowered to grant ex-

---

24 Kruk, *op. cit.*, pp. 157, 402, 432, 439; Epstein's diary, p. 106;
Gitlerovskaya okupatsiya, p. 155; Dworzecki, *op. cit.*, pp. 299–300.

emptions from work because of illness. Medical aid was available at the clinic twenty-four hours a day. Visits were free at first, but later patients were obliged to pay a token fee.

The Sanitation-Epidemiological Unit was responsible for combatting contagious diseases and epidemics in the ghetto. Its principal field of action was preserving personal cleanliness and hygienic conditions in the streets and homes. The ghetto was divided into several sanitary sectors, with a doctor, assisted by a team of nurses, in each. Women were appointed for each dwelling place to be in charge of cleanliness, and they were instructed in these matters by the district doctor. Extensive informative programs, lectures, and discussions on hygienic requirements and the combatting of contagious diseases were held. Strict supervision was maintained over restaurants, public kitchens, and bakeries.

During periods when there was danger of the spread of disease, large public assemblies were forbidden. The unit operated a special station for vaccinations in cases of scabies. Two public bath-houses were built, and each inhabitant was obliged to frequent them at least once a month and receive a special card confirming attendance. Monthly food cards were not issued without the stamped confirmation of the bath-house management.

This unit also dealt with garbage collection from the ghetto, using carts hired for that purpose from the outside. An isolation chamber was operated for people who had returned to the ghetto from labor camps outside Vilna. The unit also maintained a laundry and barber-shop for laborers and schoolchildren, as well as five teahouses where it was possible to buy boiled water to take home for a token payment.

Personnel of the Sanitation-Epidemiological Unit had police powers to make out summonses in matters within its sphere of jurisdiction, and they were assisted by the Sanitary Police in the discharge of their duties.

The ghetto health services were also responsible for the labor

camps in the Vilna region. Groups of doctors visited from time
to time to provide necessary assistance.

The German administration permitted ghetto inhabitants to
go out in organized groups to the bathing beach on the River
Viliya. Aproval in principle for these excursions was granted
at the beginning of June 1942, but the first groups left the
ghetto only at the beginning of August. The Sanitation-Epidemiological Unit was held responsible for these parties, as it was
classified as a health and cleanliness project.

A Medical Association was established in the ghetto for the
purpose of improving the state of health and strengthening the
professional ethics of the physicians.

Due to the intensive care and efficiency of the ghetto health
services, no epidemics of contagious diseases occurred within
the area of its competence. The mortality rate inside the ghetto
was much greater than during the pre-war epoch, but much
smaller than in the Warsaw ghetto. During 1942, the number
of deaths in the ghetto was 522, or 2.9 percent of the population, as compared with an average annual rate of 1.9 percent
among the Jews of Vilna during 1932–1937.[25]

Educational and Cultural Life in the Ghetto
A lively cultural life and extensive educational activities flourished in the ghetto. The first schools were opened immediately
after the enclosure of Vilna Jews, but teaching was disrupted
by the *Aktionen*. Regular teaching resumed only at the end of
November.

The two elementary schools in the ghetto had 700–900 pupils
ranging from ages five to twelve. There was also a religious
school with a few dozen children. Another primary school with

25 Dworzecki, *op. cit.*, pp. 295–299; Epstein's diary, pp. 52, 68–69;
Kruk, *op. cit.*, pp. 303–304; Balberyszski, *op. cit.*, pp. 370, 376–389.
During 1941, a total of 43,137 persons died in the Warsaw ghetto,
representing more than 10 percent of the ghetto population, in
contrast to a mortality rate of 1.2 percent among Warsaw Jewry
during the period of 1931–1935.

about 120 pupils functioned in the "Kailis" camp. The secondary school had four grades with about 100 students. Nursery schools and kindergartens for children whose both parents worked outside the ghetto were also opened. The Teachers' Association had over 100 members, and it held lectures on education, as well as on general topics.[26]

The ghetto faced the problem of caring for orphans whose parents had been murdered in the *Aktionen*. A boarding home for orphans of tender age was opened on March 8, 1942, but it failed to solve the problem of the scores of orphans aged nine to fifteen who roamed the ghetto and were prone to juvenile delinquency. These children were organized in gangs and stole from the houses and the Judenrat food stores. Thirteen children were in the ghetto jail at the beginning of March 1942, charged with various offenses, out of a total of forty youngsters who had been caught in acts of delinquency and whose identity was known to the ghetto police.

Education and judicial authorities met on March 7, 1942, to discuss the entire issue with a view to finding a way to come to grips with the problem of handling these delinquent youths. The police representative at the deliberations was Officer Joseph Muszkat.

It was decided to seek suitable employment for the youngsters. These orphans were organized by Police Officer Muszkat in the Transport Brigade in the ghetto in May 1942. Their job was to transport foodstuffs in handcarts from the Judenrat stores to distribution centers—the public kitchen and boarding houses. The children assumed charge of all domestic transport in the ghetto, operating dozens of wheelbarrows, and became a well-organized and competent group, useful to the ghetto. They were paid for their work in food and clothing. The boarding establishment in which the children of the Transport

26 Kruk, *op. cit.,* pp. 202, 210; Korczak, *op. cit.,* pp. 87, 89, excerpt from *Geto Yedies* which deals with the possibility of extending the school day at kindergartens until 5 P.M. to assist working parents; Kalmanovitch, p. 51.

Brigade were housed was put up on August 22, 1942. Muszkat, who was in charge of cleanliness in the ghetto on behalf of the police, placed children from the Transport Brigade in charge of hygiene and cleanliness in the homes and courtyards, and they reported on breaches of rules to the police.

In March 1942, Police Chief Gens established a central authority to deal with children up to the age of sixteen, to supervise them in their places of employment and in the homes and boarding establishments in which they dwelled. Orphans, children whose parents were in difficult economic straits, and children who were growing up in unsuitable moral surroundings or who were under ten years of age were admitted into the children's homes and boarding establishments.[27]

The public library was started during the initial period of ghetto life and had about 45,000 books. Approximately 2,500 permanent readers were registered in the library, and some 5,000 people paid monthly visits to the reading-hall in the summer of 1942. Small libraries were also opened in educational institutions and the youth club. On November 27, 1941, at the close of the mass murders, Fried published an order pertaining to the preservation of cultural treasures in the ghetto. By this order, ghetto residents were obliged to report to the secretariat of the public library on works of art, ritual articles, drawings and sculpture in their possession, and assemble them in the library for the public's perusal. Fried was also permitted by *Gebietskommissar* Hingst to take books for the ghetto library from the Y.I.V.O. building, which was controlled by the Rosenberg staff unit. The permit was issued on August 10, 1942.

On December 13, 1942, a festival was held at the theater to mark the lending of the 100,000th volume from the library. There was also a bookstore on the library premises. An archive and a scientific section, managed by Zalman Kalmanovitch were established by the library. Thousands of documents, including

27 Kruk, *op. cit.,* pp. 193–194, 196, 331, 474; Mushkat's testimony, p. 8; Kowalski, *op. cit.,* p. 164.

the orders issued by the German administration, instructions by the Judenrat and Jewish police, and testimony of survivors from Ponar and provincial townships, etc., were assembled in the ghetto archives. Gens appointed a team of writers in the early part of September 1942 to write the history of the ghetto.[28]

A symphony orchestra was organized in the ghetto, and its first concert for the public was given on January 18, 1942, under the sponsorship of Gens and the ghetto police. Deputy Police Chief Glazman opened the event with a memorial tribute to the Jewish victims. The artistic program for this first performance included *"S'g'lust zich mir vaynen"* ("I am moved to weep") by Chaim Nachman Bialik, excerpts from *Mirele Efros* by J. Gordon and from *Goldene Keyt* by Y.L. Peretz, a piano concerto by Chopin, *"Eli, Eli, lama azavtani"* ("O Lord, O Lord, why hast thou abandoned me") rendered by Cantor Idelson, and the song *Zamd in Shtern* ("Sand in the Stars") sung by the vocalist L. Levitska. The proceeds of the evening, which totaled 4,000 rubles, went for social welfare.

The ghetto police published an order on April 17, 1942 specifying that musical instruments must be registered so as to make them available to the orchestra. The Bund, Poa'lei Zion-Z.S., and other circles in the ghetto opposed holding concerts and shunned them. Leaflets headed, "Theatrical Performances Should Not be Held in Cemeteries," were circulated in the ghetto. But the political groups which at first were against concerts eventually reconciled themselves to these events and even came to accept them. Concerts became a popular social event and a spur to the growth of cultural and social life in the pent-up community.[29] Kruk, who had sharply criticized the first concert in the ghetto, was to write on March 8, 1942:

28 Balberyszski, *op. cit.*, pp. 437–440; Kalmanovitch, *op. cit.*, pp. 31, 34; Kruk, *op. cit.*, pp. 341, 418–419.
29 Kruk, *op. cit.*, pp. 136, 146–147, 195, 219, 221, 239; Moreshet Archives D.1.369 gives a summary of activities in the theater during 1942, showing that performances were given and audience attendance reached 38,000.

And yet life is stronger than anything else. The pulse of life begins to beat again in the Vilna ghetto ... The concerts, which were at first boycotted, have been accepted by the public; the halls are full. Literary evenings are crowded, and the hall cannot accommodate the throngs who turn out.

A music school was opened, and some 100 students enrolled. Two choirs, one in Yiddish and the other in Hebrew, were formed. An Association of Authors and Artists was established at the end of January 1942 for the purpose of encouraging literary and artistic endeavors, organizing performances, collecting works of art for the ghetto, and providing mutual help for members. An Association of Musicians was created on February 10, 1942. All of these associations consisted of people from variegated political and social walks of life; they were the initiators of a resurgence of cultural life within the ghetto.

Performances were also held in the schools. Such events marked the Jewish festivals and memorial days; children and adults alike participated. Unique cultural events were recitals or declamations of the authors' and artists' own works, or of compositions by others. Thousands of ghetto residents attended these performances.

The ghetto theater had its gala opening on April 26, 1942, with a performance of *Shlomo Molcho*. The audience included Judenrat members, the police, authors, artists, and of course a large public. The Judenrat Cultural Department was the sponsor of the theater inauguration. There was also a marionette theater in the ghetto. Workers who were employed outside the ghetto and returned late at night had special performances and lectures arranged for them in the ghetto theater at 10 A.M. on Sundays.

A Sports Club, with several hundred members, organized sundry sporting events in the ghetto; its playing field was inaugurated at a ceremony on June 10, 1942.

Educational activity and concerts were launched in the ghetto

by individuals and groups of public-minded persons even before the Judenrat created the specific departments to deal with
these enterprises. The Judenrat departments of Culture and of
Education were established in February 1942. When these were
in full operation the cultural activity considerably broadened,
encompassing lectures, theatrical performances, orchestral concerts, choirs in Yiddish and Hebrew, presentations by school
children, and scientific seminars on mathematics, physics, chem-
istry, nature, linguistics, philosophy, and social sciences.[30]

An assembly was held to mark the first anniversary of the
theater on January 15, 1943. Jaszunski, who headed the Department of Culture—and who along with his Bundist colleagues had at first opposed the theater—summed up, in his
opening address, the importance of having a theater in the
ghetto. Gens, in a speech expressing appreciation of ghetto cultural activity, declared:

> ...We wanted to give man the opportunity to free him-
> self from the ghetto for several hours, and this we
> achieved. We are passing through dark and difficult days.
> Our bodies are in the ghetto, but our spirit has not been
> enslaved...Before the first concert it was said that con-
> certs should not be held in graveyards. True, the state-
> ment is true, but all of life is now a graveyard. Our
> hands must not falter. We must be strong in body and
> soul...[31]

30 Dworzecki, *op. cit.,* pp. 223, 235–236; Balberyszski, *op. cit.,* p.
433; Kruk, *op. cit.,* pp. 139–140, 151, 159, 162, 345. The theater
continued to function throughout the existence of the ghetto, had
a repertoire consisting of such plays as *Korene yorn un waytsene
teg* ("Years of Corn and Days of Wheat"), *Men ken gornit wisn*
("One Can Never Know"), two revues by K. Broide, a series of
plays: *Grine felder* ("Green Fields") by P. Hirshbayn; *Der mench
untern brik* ("Man under the Bridge"), by O. Indy; *Der oyster*
("The Treasure") by D. Pinski; and *Der mabl* ("The Flood") by
Berger.
31 Moreshet Archives, D.1.363, stenographic transcript of speeches by
G. Jaszunski and Gens.

Religious Jews observed the *mitzvot* ("precepts of the Law") insofar as ghetto conditions permitted, for observant persons had to go to work on the Sabbath and festivals just as any other Jew. Prayer-services were held at the three ghetto synagogues, which were crowded with worshippers during the Jewish Holy Days. The religious elementary school and yeshiva held their classes in the synagogue. *Matzot* were baked for Passover; several booths were put up for *Succot,* "the Feast of Tabernacles"; and *Hakafot* ("circuits") were held in the synagogue on *Simchat Torah,* "the Rejoicing of the Law."

Several Vilna rabbis and others from townships in the vicinity lived in the ghetto.[32] No change in regard to religion occurred in the ghetto community in the wake of the new situation. Devout people did not lose their faith in the Almighty because of the massacres and continued to observe the religious commandments in the harsh conditions of ghetto life. The non-religious were not influenced by the exterminations to mend their secular ways and become pious. There was no separate department in the Judenrat to deal with religious affairs. Religious circles did not receive budgetary subventions, and the activity of the religious school and yeshiva were not financed by Judenrat sources. A certain amount of financial aid was given to the religious school by the Public Committee for Social Welfare.

The educational and cultural activities became focal points of the struggle for control in the ghetto during the period of stabilization. The principal contest for hegemony was waged between the Bund and the Zionists.

Judenrat member G. Guchman was the head of the Cultural Department, but in April 1942 Gens demanded that the Judenrat also associate him with its administration. His request was

32 Shur wrote in his diary that before Yom Kippur in September 1942, Gens published an announcement in the ghetto to the effect that all Jews without exception were to go to work outside the ghetto, or accept dire consequences [112]. Dworzecki, *op. cit.,* pp. 278–283; Kalmanovitch, *op. cit.,* pp. 36–39, 64; Epstein's diary, pp. 108–109; Kruk, *op. cit.,* pp. 349–350, 354, 520–521.

accepted, and the Judenrat ruled that the department be jointly administered by Guchman and Gens.

The Bundist G. Jaszunski, another Judenrat member, headed the Department of Education. A "public committee" to help the schools was established by the Bund on March 10, 1942. The Bund thus became a governing factor in the educational system of the ghetto.

The Zionist umbrella organization established the Brit Ivrit ("Hebrew Union") Society, with the object of organizing and carrying on the teaching of Hebrew and imparting a Zionist content to educational and cultural work. The Zionists opposed Bund control over the educational network and launched a struggle against it. The conflict centered around the purposes of education and its national character, the language of instruction—Yiddish or Hebrew—the number of teachers in each language, hours to be devoted to the teaching of Jewish history, the periods to be studied, heroic figures, etc.

Gens and his deputy Glazman opposed Bund control over the educational system—both because of their Zionist outlook and because it had become a focus of strength and influence inside the ghetto. At a Judenrat meeting on April 27, 1942, Gens demanded that Glazman be elected to serve with Jaszunski as head of the Department of Education. Gens invoked the precedent that the Department of Culture was administered by two persons, Guchman and himself. To emphasize the political character of his demand, which was directed against the Bund, he reported that the Bund had organized a "First of May" demonstration in the ghetto. Jaszunski threatened to resign if Gens' idea were accepted. The Judenrat decided, by a majority vote (Fried, Guchman, and Milkonovicki against the two Bundist members of the Judenrat, Jaszunski and Fishman) that Jaszunski remain director of the Education Department, but that he would have to consult with Glazman on all matters pertaining to education.

Jaszunski resigned from the post of director. Gens and the Zionists had won another important power-center in ghetto life.

The language of instruction in the schools continued to be Yiddish, but Hebrew language, Bible, and Jewish history were afforded several more hours weekly.[33]

However, the fight for control over the school system and its content had not ended. When Gens was appointed Ghetto Representative, he amalgamated the departments of Education and Culture, and Jaszunski was nominated to head the new, enlarged department. Gens apparently wanted to enlist Bund support for his appointment as Ghetto Representative and decided to win them over to his side by this device.

In view of the dissensions over the curriculum content, five committees of teachers were formed for redrafting the courses. They dealt with the following subjects: Yiddish and Hebrew teaching, religious instruction, Jewish and general history, mathematics, geography and nature. Gens was dissatisfied with the curriculum and convened a meeting of educators on March 1, 1943, to seek ways to enlarge the scope of national education in the schools and the possibility of incorporating religious studies into the syllabi. Gens clashed with Jaszunski on educational matters, and dismissed him on April 12, 1943. The Bund tried to activate various sectors of the ghetto population to prevent his dismissal, but to no avail.[34]

Dr. Leo Bernstein, a Zionist, was appointed to head the Department of Culture and Education. He introduced changes in the curriculum and added hours for the teaching of Hebrew and the geography and history of Eretz Israel. Emphasis was placed on Zionism and Hebrew in the theater and in literary recitals.

Leo Bernstein served in this capacity until June 1943, when he was dismissed by Gens, in the wake of the struggle between

33 *Ibid.,* pp. 200–202, 244, 246, 251; Dworzecki, *op. cit.,* pp. 216–217, 229; Korczak, *op. cit.,* pp. 87–88, 370.

34 Kalmanovitch, *op. cit.,* p. 58; Korczak, *op. cit.,* p. 362, article in *Geto Yedies* dealing with education for children, stressing the need for Jewish national education and teaching of Hebrew and Torah; Kruk, *op. cit.,* pp. 418, 470–471, 511, 516–517.

Gens and the ghetto underground, of which Bernstein was a member. Another Zionist, Israel Dimantman, was appointed in his stead, and served until the ghetto was liquidated.[35]

The struggle for control over culture and education continued throughout the entire existence of the ghetto. Control passed from the Bund to the Zionists, and when this was achieved, the cultural activities were given a greater Zionist orientation.

35 Leo Bernstein, member of the Zionist "umbrella" and among the initiators and founders of "Yechiel's Struggle Group"; I. Dimantman, teacher in the Hebrew School at Kovno and director of the Tarbut school in Vilna in 1940, met his death in Estonia in September 1944; Kruk, *op. cit.*, pp. 537–539, 546, 581.

Chapter 19

GENS: THE ABSOLUTE GHETTO RULER

Changes in Authority

Gebietskommissar Hingst, Murer, and Buragas arrived at the Judenrat offices on the morning of July 11, 1942, where Gens, Dessler and the Judenrat members awaited them.

Murer read a statement. Labor matters, he said, were of supreme importance in wartime. The Judenrat had not conducted itself with the requisite urgency but had held meetings, long deliberations, and balloting on these matters. Because of its methods and the lack of positive results, the Judenrat would be dissolved, and Gens was to be appointed the ruling authority in the ghetto, the "Ghetto Representative." Two deputies were assigned to him—A. Fried, for administrative affairs, and S. Dessler, for police matters. The changes were to be implemented beginning July 12.

The announcement stunned the Judenrat members, except for Gens and Dessler who had advance knowledge of it. Kruk wrote of the event under the headline: "The *Putsch* in the Ghetto." The report on the changes spread through the ghetto and aroused strong feelings, though not of surprise nor of resistance. Gens had been the acting suverain of the ghetto and had decisive influence over most sectors of life months before the official appointment.

The chief goal of the German administration in disbanding the Judenrat and the nomination of Gens as the "Ghetto Representative" was to enlarge the labor potential of the ghetto.

The German authorities took into account the fact that Gens was anyway in actual command of the ghetto and enjoyed more popularity than Fried, and thus it would be easier to implement their policy through his leadership.

Gens reorganized the ghetto administration and invited the Judenrat members to continue to work with him as directors of departments. They assented. The Bund decided not to oppose Gens and to continue to cooperate in the ghetto administration, though in the past they had resisted him on a number of issues.

Jaszunski, head of the Food Department in the preceding months, was appointed director of the Culture Department, which was broadened to include all educational areas in the ghetto—theater, schools, children's homes, library, archives, and sports. Braude continued as head of the Labor Department, a post he had held throughout the existence of the ghetto. Braude was also given the title of "Deputy to Gens for Labor Affairs." Guchman was transferred from managing the Housing Department to heading the Technical Department and taking charge of technical workshops. A. Fishman was made "Director of Small Industries"—tailoring, bootmaking, etc.—under Guchman. Milkonovicki continued as head of the Health Department. Fried was given the title of "Chief of Ghetto Administration," and was responsible for the General Department. Glazman, who resigned as Deputy Police Chief after Dessler was appointed his superior, accepted the post offered to him as Director of the Housing Department. The ruling consideration behind this decision was that this post would be very advantageous to the F.P.O. for pinpointing suitable places for use as secret arms caches and for arms drills. Gens also nominated a Court of Appeal—a function that had until then been discharged by the five Judenrat members.

Three days after being appointed "Ghetto Representative," Gens issued a manifesto to the ghetto inhabitants:

By the order of the *Gebietskommissar* of Vilna of July 12, 1942, I have assumed, as Ghetto Representative and Chief of Police, the entire responsibility for the ghetto. The basis of existence of the ghetto is Labor, Discipline, and Order. Every resident apt for work constitutes a pillar on which our existence is based. We must not have among us people who recoil from labor, behave improperly, or commit varied offenses. Confident that all inhabitants of the ghetto will understand this, I have ordered the release of all persons jailed in the ghetto, and I proclaim a general amnesty, thus affording to former criminals the opportunity to return to the proper path for their own good. But let no one doubt that, if it becomes necessary, I shall not shrink from taking the gravest measures against criminal elements, as soon as they appear. I believe that my present appeal will find unanimous support among all ghetto inhabitants and therefore I have ordered...

Gens proceeded to specify the categories of misdemeanors covered by the amnesty. These related mainly to offenses committed inside the ghetto itself—uncleanliness, non-wearing of the yellow badge, curfews, etc. Categories of offenses not covered by the amnesty were murder, causing grievous bodily harm, insulting or hitting a police officer, offenses against the administration, and disciplinary misdemeanors committed against Judenrat functionaries and policemen. The ghetto nicknamed the proclamation "Gens' Manifesto."[1]

The emphasis of the manifesto was on the new policy that Gens outlined in his call for labor, discipline, and order, viz., that every able-bodied person in the ghetto must work. He used threatening language toward criminal elements that might resist his policy so that the amnesty he would grant must not be interpreted as weakness. The manifesto also heralded to many who did not work, or whose livelihood was in trade, brokerage, or smuggling, that they would have to undertake manual labor. The amnesty for administrative misdemeanors,

1 Kruk, *op. cit.*, p. 309.

which affected many ghetto residents, was an attempt to win popularity.

Gens attached great importance to his bonds of communication with the ghetto community, and for that reason published a Yiddish weekly, *Geto Yedies* ("Ghetto News"), beginning in September 1942. Typed in several dozen copies, it was composed of six to sixteen pages and, in addition to being distributed among varied ghetto institutions, was posted on public billboards. Reports of ghetto events, news on places of employment, cultural life, housing matters, medicine, health, education, social welfare, and industrial development were included. Notices issued by the ghetto administration, orders, and prohibitions also appeared. Appeals by the ghetto directorate for maintenance of order were published during periods of unrest and to strengthen the confidence in the labor ideology. *Geto Yedies* was the only communications medium of importance in daily life. It continued to appear until the final phase of ghetto existence.[2]

The German administration, as a gesture to Gens, incorporated houses in Niemiecka, Oszmianska, and Jatkova streets into the ghetto. Thus, the area of the Jewish sector was extended about 40,000 sq. ft., and the transfer of about 1,500 inhabitants to these dwellings was planned. The approval was given on July 10, and the additional area was annexed to the ghetto at the beginning of September.

Council of the "Brigadiers"

The "Representative" had the assistance of the "brigadiers" in implementing the policy announced in his manifesto. He made it a practice to call meetings and conferences of the "brigadiers," at which he presented current problems and urged the workers to comply with his instructions. When occasions arose

2 The editor of the newspaper was Dr. Z. Feldshtein, of Lithuanian origin, writer and journalist, active in Brit Ivrit ("Hebrew Union") in the ghetto, who died in a concentration camp in Germany.

for Gens to communicate information to the community in matters that could not be printed in notices because of their sensitive nature vis-à-vis the German authorities, he summoned a meeting of the "brigadiers."

A meeting of "brigadiers" on October 13, 1942, heard a demand from Gens that they should not appeal to the Germans with whom they were in contact at work in cases of claims against the ghetto directorate or differences of opinion with it. Gens stressed to them that he would not tolerate the continuation of such a situation. He demanded that they establish a workers' council in each place of employment, to which they would report on their activities and with which they would consult, and that the council supervise the use of funds in each work-unit.[3]

To strengthen the link and cooperation with the workmen and foremen, Gens established, in November 1942, a Council of "Brigadiers," to which he appointed the members and its chairman—D. Kaplan-Kaplanski. The statutes of the council, which delineated its composition, functions, and methods was published on November 20. It stated that the council had been formed in accordance with Gens' instructions and was composed of seven members appointed by him from among candidates proposed at a general meeting of "brigadiers." It was stressed that the purpose of the council was to represent the "brigadiers" before the ghetto directorate, to provide them with guidelines, and to improve their standards.

The council discussed subjects relating to the functions and rights of "brigadiers," supervision of their activities, and matters relating to labor and labor discipline. The council submitted

3   YVA, JM/1195, Document No. 224, clauses 2, 4. Each labor unit collected money from its workers earmarked for use as gifts and bribes. Gens wished to be sure that some control would be exercised over these funds and that not every "brigadier" could do with them as he wished.

its proposals and decisions to Gens and the Labor Department.[4]

The Council of "Brigadiers" represented the working community and its problems before the ghetto administration. Matters relating to culture, use of the bath-houses, food, etc., were brought up and settled by them in conjunction with the "Ghetto Representative." Three "brigadiers" were elected to the Public Committee for Social Welfare on November 17 by order of Gens and became an influential group therein. With the Judenrat no longer in existence, the Council of "Brigadiers" developed into a public body that openly supported Gens and his policy.

The Productive Ghetto

The German authorities broadened the scope of their demands for Jewish manpower beginning in the spring of 1942, and the demands continued to increase throughout the existence of the ghetto. Ghetto Jews responded to the labor demands and opened workshops and small industries in order to convert the ghetto into the most productive center. Gens did his utmost to initiate a major production effort on the part of the ghetto craftsmen and artisans.

The growth of the ghetto's output proceeded along three main lines—the number of workmen and places of employment outside the ghetto, labor camps at forest and peat-digging sites outside Vilna, and crafts and industry inside the ghetto itself. The number of workers in the ghetto community was doubled in the first half of 1942, and in July reached a total of 8,000. The table on page 334 shows the number of work-places, number of workers, and the process of growth in the second half of 1942.[5]

The number of workmen in the ghetto community in April 1943 was recorded as 10,115. This figure rose progressively to

---

4 D. Kaplan-Kaplanski, born in Bialystok in 1899, was one of the leaders of YIVO in Vilna. He died in a concentration camp in December 1944; YVA, JM/1195, Document No. 223, copy of the original constitution of the Council of "Brigadiers."

5 Balberyszski, *op. cit.,* p. 340; Kruk, *op. cit.,* pp. 338, 363.

	July	August	September	October	November	December
No. work-places outside ghetto	234	255	255	255	273	346
No. workers outside ghetto	6,671	7,158	7,507	7,463	7,414	7,373
No. workers in plants and facilities inside ghetto	1,393	1,438	1,555	1,627	1,703	1,897
Total No. workers	8,064	8,596	9,062	9,090	9,117	9,270

14,000 by the end of June, of whom some 3,000 were employed in crafts and industry inside the ghetto.

Pursuant to the policy of productivity instituted under the Judenrat and strengthened by Gens when he became absolute ruler, the number of active workers continued to increase steadily, even though the aggregate number of ghetto residents showed no substantial rise. In May and June 1943 the rise in the total number of workers was caused by the arrival of people from the small ghettos near Vilna and from labor camps that had been closed down.

Gens aspired to achieve a total of 16,000 workers out of a population of over 21,000 during the summer months of 1943. He was also active in reducing the number of employees in the administration and ghetto services, except for those in children's institutions, in order to divert them into creative labor channels. The admission of more women, and children from thirteen and over, into the labor cycle enabled a further increase. Over one-third of those employed were females.[6]

Wages to be paid for Jewish labor were increased by the German administration at the end of November or beginning of December 1942:

6 Kruk, *op. cit.*, p. 524; Korczak, *op. cit.*, p. 275, excerpts from *Geto Yedies*, late June 1943.

Unskilled laborer — 30 pfennigs per hour
Skilled laborer — 44 pfennigs per hour
"Brigadier" — 50 pfennigs per hour
The Jewish workmen actually received only one-half of this pay. The other half was remitted to the *Gebietskommissar's* coffers. By the same order of the German administration, the working day was lengthened from eight to ten hours.[7]

Vilna Jews were taken away to labor camps where they were put to work as peat-diggers and lumberjacks. The peat-digging camps had been created at the beginning of the German occupation, and in the summer of 1942 they were increased and more Jews were removed from the ghetto to work there. The Labor Department encountered difficulties in recruiting men for these camps, and the ghetto police undertook searches for jobless inhabitants to be sent there. Workers from places of employment inside Vilna, apart from those engaged in army installations, were also taken to the camps.

The ghetto administration supplied provisions and medical aid for these camps, and ghetto police were posted there. Supervision was maintained by Lithuanian policemen. Difficult physical labor was involved, but from the standpoint of food, conditions were much easier than in the ghetto, as belongings could be exchanged for produce from the neighborhood farmers.

The lumber camps in the forests were built in June 1942, and there were 240 ghetto lumberjacks working in them. The dispatch of men to work in the forests was viewed suspiciously because of the fear that they might be sent to unknown places. But when the lumberjacks returned after a while, and others went out in their stead, the apprehensiveness subsided. These camps were at Kranovka, Gladcziszuk, Sorok-Tatar, and Vielkopolya. Part of the felled timber was earmarked for winter fuel for the ghetto. A special unit of the Ghetto Labor Department supervised these camps. The peat-extraction camps were at Bezdany (Beddonys), Riese, Biala-Vaka, Kena, and a

7 Kruk, *op. cit.*, pp. 415, 424.

number of other sites, all at a distance of 15 to 25 kilometers from Vilna, and each employing several hundred men.[8] Both peat-digging and timber-cutting were of economic importance to the German administration, and non-Jews were also obliged to take on this work.

The workshops affiliated with the Judenrat had been the basis for ghetto industry. These, and their personnel, had been designed in the beginning to undertake repairs and maintenance of ghetto houses—water pipes, sewerage and electricity. The demands of daily life pointed up the need for other workshops—tailoring, shoemaking, carpentry, smithies, and barbershops. The fact that the central management of ghetto manpower was vested in the Judenrat, and the fact that the Judenrat was responsible for housing maintenance and repairs in the ghetto, along with its role in providing clothing for workers and the needy, combined to turn the first workshops into Judenrat agencies, rather than private enterprises. The need for premises, tools, and raw materials also influenced this trend. Certain craftsmen and artisans pursued their trades independently in the Judenrat workshops after working hours and on rest-days. Small privately owned plants producing candies, soap, and cigarettes were also created.

The number of those employed in the ghetto workshops rose steadily during the second half of 1942: July—425, September—531, November—608, December—759.

The growth and expansion of the workshops were such that they began to supply the needs of the German administration, and production continued to increase. A special sales office was opened outside the ghetto to take orders for workshop products. It was located near the gate, in accordance with the *Gebietskommissar's* orders.[9] The increase from 759 hands in the workshops, recorded in December 1942, to 3,000 in May–June 1943, was the outcome of a deliberate policy on the part of Gens

8 *Ibid., op. cit.,* pp. 283, 285, 291, 339–340; Rolnik, *op. cit.,* pp. 70–71.
9 Lalberyszski, *op. cit.,* p. 312; Kruk, *op. cit.,* p. 440.

and the ghetto administration to expand ghetto industry for the purpose of supplying products to the German authorities. In an article published in *Geto Yedies*, issue No. 39, of May 16, 1943, it was stated:

> We are obliged to increase the percentage of productive workers among the ghetto population, which has grown. We must become a true working society, creative, productive, and earning, through its economic viability, the right to exist... Consequently, we have lowered the terminal age in the schools to thirteen years. We cut them off from their lessons, their teachers, and their childhood, and throw them into a hard life, so as to swell the ranks of the workers. We shall see to it that young girls, too, learn a trade. Our workshops are increasing. We already have industries in the ghetto, both light and heavy, furniture workshops, tin-smithies, forges, a turnery, and a locksmithy, fine mechanics, a syrup-producing plant, a pottery workshop, and a sewing workshop—large military and private orders...

Gens stated in a speech delivered in June 1943:

> ... The new and remarkable phenomenon in the life of the ghetto is the flowering of industry. Our industry, which was very small in scope last year, is now a foremost factor in ghetto labor. About 3,000 persons are now employed in the industrial field, and efforts are being made to raise the figure to 4,000, and after that even to 5,000. Both in our industrial sphere and in our work in the units, we must prove that, contrary to the accepted assumption that we shall not succeed in any craft, we are in fact most efficient, and no substitute for us can be found under present wartime conditions. Work in general, and work for the Wehrmacht in particular is the command of the hour...[10]

10 Korczak, *op. cit.*, p. 275, excerpt from *Geto Yedies*.

Ghetto industry was divided into two branches—light and heavy. Within the former category were workshops for tailoring, shoemaking, knitting, dyeing, ropemaking, watch-repairs, and barbershops. Heavy industry included timber and metal establishments. The Department of Industry had a section dealing with planning and another for vocational training.

A technical school for teaching locksmith and electrical trades was opened for the youth at the end of July or beginning of August 1942. The first class of nineteen pupils completed its studies on September 1, 1943; the second class had forty pupils; and in May 1943, 100 pupils enrolled. Courses in dyeing, carpentry, glaziery, building, and other vocations were begun at the outset of September 1942. The scope of vocational training was extended in December 1942, and approximately 250 pupils enrolled in the courses initiated during that month.[11]

The appointment of Gens as Ghetto Representative led to an acceleration in the number of ghetto workers employed in facilities on the outside and in the development of crafts and industry within the ghetto walls. The process of productivization in the confined community was optimal during the final months of its existence, when about 75 percent of over 20,000 inhabitants were employed in plants and establishments inside and outside the ghetto. This accomplishment had been made possible by four factors: the demand by the German administration for manpower and products, the belief of ghetto Jewry that their labor guaranteed them survival, the efficient organization of ghetto manpower by the administrative body headed by Jacob Gens, and the success in creating social conditions favorable to the utilization of that manpower.

Gens, as Ghetto Representative, fulfilled the expectations of the German administration in the critical sphere of exploitation of the Jewish labor force.

---

11   YVA, JM/1195, Document No. 280—diagram of the industrial structure of the ghetto, dated May 18, 1943; Kruk, *op. cit.*, pp. 337, 342–343, 393, 421, 547.

Chapter 20

THE SELECTIVE *AKTIONEN*

During the period of "relative stability," individuals and groups from among the Vilna ghetto community who had been convicted of various offenses were murdered at Ponar. Their "crimes" consisted of the acquisition and introduction of "illegal" provisions into the ghetto, attempts to save themselves by forged "Aryan" papers, and hiding outside the ghetto. Jewish women were arrested and shot at Ponar in September 1942 on the charge of maintaining sexual relations with Germans, despite the fact that they had been forced to enter into such relationships against their will.[1]

Aktionen *Against the Elderly*
An operation which was dubbed in the ghetto the "Old People's *Aktion*" was carried out on July 17, 1942, several days after Gens had been appointed Ghetto Representative. Jewish police went from house to house, taking into custody elderly people and chronic invalids. They were sent to Pospieszki, a former resort near Vilna, and placed in a building that had once been a rest-house. The party of ghetto police remained with the detainees and cared for them.

Rumors spread through the ghetto that another *Aktion*, directed against children, was about to be undertaken. Gens con-

<hr>

1 Kruk, *op. cit.*, pp. 351, 354, 356, 363; Epstein's diary, p. 73.

vened a meeting, in the theater hall, of all house superintendents
on July 22, 1942. In his address to them, he referred to the
"Old People's Operation" and affirmed that no *Aktion* would
be taken against children. Gens also said to a meeting of "brigadiers" that he had rejected a German demand to seize the
children, but that he had to obey their order to transfer the
old and ill who were unable to look after themselves.[2]

The ghetto police detained more elderly persons on the night
of July 23. The majority was released, but seven or eight were
taken to Pospieszki.

On the morning of July 26, eighty-four detainees were handed
over to Weiss and the Lithuanian police. They were placed on
trucks and taken to Ponar, where they were shot.[3]

Rumors of projected new *Aktionen* persisted in the ghetto.
Gens convened the ghetto police and announced that there was
no foundation to the reports of impending *Aktionen* and ordered
that rumor-mongers be arrested. Twenty people were taken into
custody and held in prison overnight. Things quieted down.[4]

The German administration implemented the "Old People's
Aktion" as part of its policy of extermination and to eliminate
non-productive elements in the ghetto. The operation also came
as a reminder to the Jews of the ghetto that they were allowed
to exist only by virtue of their labor, and that non-working
elements had no right to live.

Balberyszski recorded that Gens told him after the "Old People's *Aktion*": "I have no connection with the purge of the
elderly. It was an old debt which the Judenrat owed them.
They wanted several hundred people, and it was with difficulty
that the 'price' was reduced to 100 aged ..."[5]

Life in the ghetto continued as usual during the days that the
sick and elderly were detained at Pospieszki: the youth club,

2 Kruk, *op. cit.*, pp. 308, 310, 313, 315, 326; Epstein's diary, pp.
   67–68.
3 Kruk, *op. cit.*, p. 325; Rolnik, *op. cit.*, pp. 69–70.
4 Kruk, *op. cit.*, pp. 319, 326–327; Kalmanovitch, *op. cit.*, p. 27.
5 Balberyszski, *op. cit.*, pp. 451–452.

with its music, drama, and chess groups, was formally inaugurated on July 18; a literary evening was held on July 25 for a guest audience of about 200 artists and authors; Gens convened a meeting of intellectuals, and it was decided to establish an archive to perpetuate events, people and creative works; a prize for three works to be written on life in the ghetto, in Yiddish or Hebrew, was announced on July 26. The surrender to the Germans of the elderly and ill did not evoke bitter criticism; most of the Jews in the ghetto resigned themselves to the act, and perhaps even approved of Gens' policy and the method of its implementation.[6]

The Aktion *at Oshmyany (Oszmiana)*

Those sectors of the *Generalkommissariat* of Belorussia that were adjacent to the Lithuanian border were annexed to the *Generalkommissariat* of Lithuania in March 1942, and made subordinate to the *Gebietskommissar* of *"Vilna-Land,"* Wulff. These sectors included the small town of Oshmyany, as well as other townships in which there were small Jewish ghettos. Until then, these communities had escaped unscathed—apart from the assassination of groups of males perpetrated by the Einsatzgruppen in the summer and fall of 1941.

The German authorities decided to liquidate part of the ghetto and concentrate their inmates in four larger ghettos already in existence: Oshmyany, Swieciany (Svencionys), Mikhailishki (Mikaliskes), and Sol (Salos). Some of these small ghettos were completely liquidated. The ghetto at Kiemieliszki (Kiemeliskes) was liquidated on October 22, 1941, at which time all of its

6 Epstein's diary, p. 67; Kruk, *op. cit.,* pp. 319, 325–326, 328; Kalmanovitch, *op. cit.,* pp. 27–28.
   The diaries of Kruk, Kalmanovitch, Epstein, and Rolnik, which describe the murder of the elderly, neither accuse, nor criticize Gens or the police. Shur even expresses a rather positive attitude towards Gens [Frame 163] as he states "Gens handled the matter clear headedly, it is better to lose a few than to lose everyone..."

inhabitants were shot and killed on the outskirts of the town. A similar fate overtook the small ghetto at Bystrzyca.

In September or the beginning of October 1942, the German administration in Vilna assigned Gens the task of organizing the Jewish administration in the ghettos annexed to *Vilna-Land*. Officials and policemen from the Vilna ghetto were sent to these places to organize them according to the paradigm of Vilna. The ghetto police obtained permission from Murer to wear special dark-blue uniforms, peaked caps with the Shield of David emblem, and rank insignia on their caps and uniforms in preparation for their mission in the *Vilna-Land* ghettos.[7]

About 4,000 Jews were congregated in the Oshmyany ghetto. The German administration decided to liquidate some 1,500 members of the non-working ghetto population and assigned the selection of the victims to the Vilna Jewish police. The Jewish police left for Oshmyany on Monday, October 19, 1942, and returned to Vilna on the 25th. A total of 406 old and sick people from the Oshmyany ghetto were handed over to the Germans and Lithuanians by the Vilna policemen on Friday the 23rd, instead of the 1,500 that the Germans had asked for.

Gens convened a meeting of renowned Jewish personalities in Vilna on October 27, and gave them a report of the *Aktion* at Oshmyany and the events that had led up to it.

Protocol of the Meeting Devoted to the *Aktion* at Oshmyany,
October 27, 1942

Present: Ghetto Representative Gens; Commissar Dessler; Director of Health Department Milkonovicki; Deputy Ghetto Representative Fried; Fishman; Braude; Rabbi Jacobson; Kalmanovitch...

Gens: My friends, I have invited you here today in order to tell you one of the most terrible tragedies of Jewish life—when Jews lead Jews to death. This time I wish

7 Kruk, *op. cit.*, pp. 372–373, 377.

to speak openly. A week ago Weiss came and ordered us on behalf of the SD to proceed to Oshmyany. He said that there were about 4,000 Jews in the ghetto there and that it was impossible that such a number remain there, that the ghetto must be reduced, that people for whom the Germans had no need should be selected out and shot. First priority are women whose husbands had been caught last year by the abductors, and their children. Second priority, families with many children. When we received the order, we answered: "At your command" (*Zu Befehl*).

Dessler and the Jewish police left for Oshmyany. The Jewish police established and informed the *Gebietskommissar* in Vilna two or three days later that, first of all, it was impossible to send away those women whose husbands had been kidnapped, as they were working, and, secondly, there were no families with four or five children. I forgot to add: We had been ordered to select at least 1,500 people. We answered that we could not fill such a quota. We haggled, and when Mr. Dessler arrived with the report from Oshmyany, the figure was reduced to 800. After I had gone with Weiss to Oshmyany, the quota dropped once again, this time to 600 ... and the question of the women and children was removed from the agenda, and the matter revolved only around the elderly. The truth is that 406 elderly were collected at Oshmyany and were handed over.

When Weiss first came and demanded women and children, I told him that instead he should take old people. He replied: "The old ones will die off anyway during the winter, and we are obliged to reduce the ghetto population now." The Jewish police rescued all those who had to live. Those whose days were close to the end in any event had to go. And may these aged Jews forgive us, they were the sacrifice for our Jews and our future.

I do not want to speak about what our Jews from

Vilna went through in Oshmyany. I am only sorry today
that we were absent at the time of the *Aktion* in Kiemieliszki and Bystrzyca. All the Jews there, without any exception, were shot last week. Two Jews from Swienciany
came to see me today and asked me to save the Jews of
Swieciany, Vidzy, and other townships in the vicinity.
I ask myself again today: What will happen when we
have to conduct such a selection a second time?

It is my duty to tell you: Good Jews, go home! I
don't wish to dirty my hands and send my policemen
to do this contemptible work. But I say to you today, it
is my duty to sully my hands, as the Jewish people is
passing through its most terrible period now. At a moment when five million are no more, it is incumbent
upon us to save the strong and the young—not only
in age but also in spirit, and not to play with sentiments.
When the rabbi was told at Oshmyany that people were
missing for the quota and five aged people were hiding
in the *maline,* he said that the *maline* be opened. That
is a man with a strong and young spirit. I don't know if
all will understand and justify this, and if they will justify
it when we come out from the ghetto. But this is the
point of view of our police: to save what is possible,
without regard for our good name and our personal experiences.

All that I have told you is not pleasing to our souls
and our lives. There is no need that others know all this.
I have drawn you into a frightful secret which must remain in our heart. I want to show what the policemen
did, who carried out this dreadful work, who separated
people and said "left" and "right"...It is not a court
here. I want people to know what a ghetto is from the
other side, what a police force is, and what are the ways
that other Jews must go.

From you, my friends, I expect moral support. All of
us want to survive and to leave the ghetto. Many Jews

still don't comprehend the great danger in which we function, how many times daily we can be sent to Ponar...

As for myself, my fate brought me to the battlefield. I
was not afraid then, only afterwards, when I remembered
it. That is the situation now. We shall only feel the pain
of all this after we leave the ghetto. Today we want to
have strength. Those who believe should say: The Almighty will help us. The non-believer should say that the
Spirit of Society and Jewish patriotism will help him to
endure all this and, after the ghetto, to remain human,
for the sake of the great future of the Jewish people.

Rosenberg recently said that it was the duty of the
Germans to root out European Jewry. I don't know what
he means. Were he to come to our ghetto, he would be
afraid of us. People hunted in *malines,* murdered at
Ponar, cut off from their families have in the course of
a year built a new life, much more than the "Aryans"
have achieved. That is Jewry, a dauntless spirit, an ever-
lasting faith in life. And so, to foil Rosenberg's statement,
we shall fight today, and war sanctifies the means, even
though they are sometimes very terrible. Much to our
regret, we must fight with all our means, in order to
grapple with the enemy. Jewry has not seen blood for
2,000 years. It has seen many flames, but not blood. We
are seeing it today in the ghetto. Jews have returned
from Ponar wounded in arms and legs. Once five women
and a child who had arrived from Ponar lay in the hospital. Today, the Jewish people are well acquainted with
blood, and so sentiments are lost. I want to bring you
closer to life, to explain to you what life is in its naked
struggle. It is for that I called you—people—here,
you who are remote from the police.

Dessler: We received the order. It was terrible, but we
have become accustomed not to argue. I chose thirty of
the strongest police officers, and we drove by car to
Oshmyany...None of the men knew the purpose of the

journey. There was a Gestapo officer with me who told the Judenrat at Oshmyany that 1,200 women and children were required for work... I gave the order to register all the inhabitants, and, during two days, we began to distribute *shainen*... I couldn't tell the truth to the Judenrat either. I only asked them to prepare a list of the old ones, so that I could exchange them for the women and children who had been requested... On Friday we already had to hand over the people. We decided that all inhabitants would have to assemble in the square in groups according to their townships: Oshmyany, Olshany, etc. Their Judenrat and rabbi would be in front of each group... The order was given that children up to sixteen could remain home, if their parents wished. We did that so that the Jews would understand that the liquidation of the ghetto was not in the offing; if the children were left at home it meant that the ghetto would remain... I wanted to save the youth and the intelligentsia, which constitute our future...

Gens: I accept responsibility for the *Aktion*. I don't want discussions; no one is entitled to discuss things that I did or will do. I called you so that you can see what Jews are passing through and why a Jew dips his hand in blood. We've had these traumas in the ghetto more than once... If the time comes when the police have to go out again, and I see that it is for the general good, we shall go![8]

Weiss' consent to reduce the quota of victims from 1,500 to 600 persons was given after he had been bribed.[9]

---

8   Moreshet Archives, D.1.357, original minutes of the meeting comprising eight typewritten pages, recorded in Yiddish. Kalmanovitch, *op. cit.,* pp. 41–42.

9   Weiss' trial, TR–10/381, p. 27. It is therein stated that Weiss accepted bribes in the form of gold rubles and other valuable items given to him by the Ghetto Representative, i.e., Gens.

Gens and Dessler were the only ones who knew the true purpose of the journey of the Jewish police to Oshmyany. The officers and other personnel who went from the Vilna ghetto to that township knew nothing of its purpose until a day before the *Aktion* was carried out, on October 23.

M. Ganionski, who was a member of the F.P.O. employed as a secretary in the ghetto police and who went with the party of constables to Oshmyany, notified the F.P.O. Command before she left. They suspected that an extermination operation was due to be carried out at Oshmyany and sent one of the organization's members, L. Magun, to Oshmyany to warn the Jews there of the imminent *Aktion*. Magun arrived in Oshmyany as an "Aryan," succeeded in infiltrating the ghetto, and established contact with the inhabitants. They did not believe her.[10] L. Magun's mission was the first instance in which the F.P.O. attempted to upset the policy and activities of the ghetto administration.

When the policemen returned to the ghetto, the report rapidly spread that an *Aktion* had been carried out at Oshmyany and that the Jewish police had played an active role. The operation came as a shock to the ghetto community, but there was no general condemnation of the role played by Gens and the police. Kruk, who criticized the role of the police at Oshmyany, wrote: "The greatest tragedy was that public opinion largely acquiesced in Gens' stand..." Kalmanovitch wrote: "Had the foreigners (the Germans and Lithuanians) conducted the *Aktion*, the number of victims would have been larger." The ghetto community regarded the police action as a dictate of reality which had succeeded in saving as many as possible.[11]

After the Oshmyany *Aktion*, rumors circulated in the ghetto that another was due to take place shortly in Vilna. Many

10 Lazar, *op. cit.*, pp. 67–68, 76; Kruk, *op. cit.*, p. 374; Liza Magun, born in Vilna in 1920, was a member of Ha-Shomer ha-Za'ir and the FPO. She was arrested and murdered by the Security Police in Vilna in February 1943.
11 Kalmanovitch, *op. cit.*, p. 42.

people spent the night sleeping in *malines*. Gens fought these reports, and people were taken into custody for spreading them. *Geto Yedies* No. 15 of November 30, 1942, carried an article denouncing those who create panic in the ghetto.

Clash Between Gens and Glazman

In spite of the caustic statements he had declaimed at ghetto meetings, the Oshmyany *Aktion* weighed heavily upon Gens. He had attempted to justify himself by stating that the German administration had wanted to link him to the Kiemieliszki ghetto operation, but he had refused, and the outcome was that all 800 Jews there had been slaughtered. Had he participated in the *Aktion*, he stated, many Jews would have been spared. Gens was sensitive to the criticism leveled by intellectual circles, and, at a conference with the "brigadiers," he referred bitterly to the "stinking intelligentsia" which had risen against him.[12]

Gens was due to leave for Swieciany with a party of ghetto officials on November 1, 1942, in order to organize internal affairs according to the pattern of the Vilna ghetto. He instructed Glazman to join him in order to organize the Housing Department. Glazman suspected that the trip was connected with an *Aktion* and therefore refused. He was arrested upon Gens' order and taken to the ghetto jail on the night of October 31.

The F.P.O. Command decided that Witenberg and Borowska, both Communists, would apply to Gens to release Glazman. Gens and Dessler tried to maintain close ties with the Communist leadership, and it was believed that they did so in order to assure their future after the Soviet regime returned to Vilna. The F.P.O. was aware of the fact that intervention by Witenberg and Borowska (Communists) on behalf of Glazman (Zionist-Revisionist) could underscore the existence of a confederated underground organization. It was nonetheless decided to take action.

12 Kruk, *op. cit.*, pp. 391, 399–400; Kalmanovitch, *op. cit.*, p. 42.

Witenberg and Borowska met with Gens, and, as a result of this meeting, Glazman was released on November 5. He was dismissed from his post as director of the Housing Department and sent to the labor camp at Sorok-Tatar, 12 miles from Vilna.[13] Several of his friends among the Revisionists were arrested in the ghetto on November 16, among them Police Officer Auerbach and six others, some of them policemen. Glazman was brought back from the labor camp on November 18, and placed in the ghetto jail. Glazman and Auerbach were released in the beginning of December. The dispute between Gens and Glazman did not expand into a conflict between the former and the F.P.O., but remained confined to the personalities involved. Glazman enjoyed great repute with the ghetto community, and his refusal to go to Swieciany increased the feelings for him.[14]

The Ideology of Selective Cooperation
The "Old People's" and Oshmyany *Aktionen* marked an innovation in these operations. The murder of the victims in these actions had been implemented by the Germans and Lithuanians, but the selection of the people and their surrender to the Germans had been the work of the Jewish police.

According to Gens' ideology, that cooperation was justified. This belief was founded on the following postulates:

— The German authorities could have perpetrated the *Aktion* themselves and killed any number of Jews at any time, through the Security Police and Lithuanian units under their command, and had no real need to rely on the help of the Jewish police;

---

13 Kruk, *op. cit.*, p. 395; Kalmanovitch, *op. cit.*, pp. 43–44. Gens created the "Council of Brigadiers" a few days after Glazman's arrest in order to enlist public support for his policy and course of action.
14 Kruk, *op. cit.*, pp. 406, 408, 411–412, 416; Kalmanovitch, *op. cit.*, pp. 46–47, 49–50.

— If the selection of victims were to be handled by the Germans or Lithuanians, the first to be exterminated would be women and children, then the intelligentsia, who, from the standpoint of physical fitness, occupation, and age, were in part debarred from entering the productive labor cycle.

The conclusions that Gens reached from these premises were:

— To participate in the *Aktionen*, and, through the Jewish police, to offer the aged and chronic invalids as victims instead of women and children, in whom he saw the biological future of the people, and the intellectuals, whom he regarded as the spiritual future;
— To bargain with the Germans in regard to the number of victims and to limit their number to the minimum;
— To furnish the Germans with a smaller number of victims than agreed upon.

For its own reasons, the German administration wanted these selections implemented by the Jewish police, so as not to disrupt the work and production of the ghetto, to instill a sense of confidence within the ghetto community that the operation was a limited one, and to prevent agitation, resistance, and flight from the ghetto.

Selection by the German authorities would have required larger forces than those needed at the pits. An *Aktion* in which the selection would be performed by the Jewish police would require only a few dozen Germans, to transport the victims and have them executed. The desire to enlist the Judenrat and Jewish police and implicate them in the operations was also a factor in German preference of an *Aktion* perpetrated with the help of the Jews.

Concomitant with this approach by Gens and the vested interest of the German administration was the bribery of German officials by the ghetto bodies in an attempt to diminish the number of victims and influence the selection of the type of persons ensnared in the *Aktion*.

The Germans adopted the policy of selective murder operations during the period of "stability." Gens countered with a form of selective cooperation. This was in keeping with the "Work to Live" ideology founded on the hope that a number of Jews would remain alive, including women, children and intellectuals.

Part Five

THE TWILIGHT AND END OF VILNA JEWRY

Chapter 21

THE LIQUIDATION OF THE SMALL GHETTOS
AND LABOR CAMPS

The Situation Deteriorates

During the early months of 1943, the situation of the Jews in the Vilna ghetto and its affiliated labor camps, as well as in the ghettos in eastern Lithuania, deteriorated. This was primarily a result of events in Lithuania proper—the growth of Soviet partisan activity, the Jewish reaction to this activity, and the retaliatory German measures.

Anti-German tendencies mounted in Lithuania at the outset of 1943. The German defeats at Stalingrad and elsewhere, the attempts to recruit Lithuanians for the army, and the German efforts of colonizing the country were all factors that engendered increasing Lithuanian opposition. The Lithuanians did not respond to the orders to enlist in the German forces and demanded their country's autonomy.

The German administration took the retributive measure of closing the universities of Vilna and Kovno. Demonstrations, clashes, and mass arrests took place in Vilna, Kovno, and other cities. The rising political tension in Lithuania had no direct connection with the Jews, but the atmosphere of increasing German terror affected their policy toward the Jews in the ghettos.

The anti-German resistance on the part of the Lithuanian population was not indicative of any substantial change in their attitude to the Jews, which remained as hostile as in the past, but the Lithuanian underground nationalist press endeavored to wash its hands of Lithuanian complicity in the murder of Jews

[355]

and to place the blame on the Poles. An underground newspaper, *Laisve* ("Liberty"), issue No. 9 of May 25, stated: "Over 80 percent of the Jews of Lithuania have already been shot. The Germans conducted these executions, and they were carried out by Germans and all kinds of *Janeks* and *Jaseiks* (Poles) in Lithuanian uniform." This statement appeared in response to charges uttered over the Polish underground radio that the Lithuanians had not protested the murder of Jews.[1]

Anti-Semitism also increased within the Polish community in Vilna. There were reports in the German press and radio concerning a German discovery in the Katyn woods of mass graves of Polish officers who, since September 1939, had been Soviet prisoners. They accused the Soviets and Jews of having perpetrated these murders.

Soviet partisan activity extended in eastern Lithuania and in Belorussia beginning with the last months of 1942. The German administration associated this partisan activity, to a large extent, with the presence of Jews who had fled from the ghettos and organized themselves into partisan groups.[2]

The chief of the Security Police and SD in the *Ostland*, Rem, published a directive on November 16, 1942, stating: "The *Reichsführer* of the SS ordered, on November 3, 1942, that the entire working and surplus population, in the areas in which bands are active, be taken into custody ... and sent as laborers to Germany ... "[3]

---

1 *Archiwum Zakladu Historii Partii* — AZHP (Archives of the Polish Communist Party), Copy in YVA, 0-25/143, p. 7. The Lithuanian underground press of that period never published an appeal to Lithuanians to abstain from taking part in the extermination of Jews and to help them. This press voiced opposition to German appropriation of Jewish property, which they sought to appropriate for themselves. One of the underground organs stated: "What right have the Germans to confiscate Jewish property ... It is public property of the Lithuanian people and the Lithuanian state." See also Neshamit, *op. cit.*, p. 172.

2 YVA, 0-4/53-1, Documents Nos. 500, 531, 757.

3 *My Obvinyaem*, p. 237.

The object of the order was twofold: to prevent inhabitants of those sectors in which partisans operated from joining and helping them, and to augment the conscription of manpower for the war effort in Germany. The order was directed at the non-Jewish population, but its promulgation was also directed towards the Jewish inhabitants. The uprooting of the population, and especially of the Jews, in regions in which partisans were active, was a common German practice. The intensification of German countermeasures against the populace as a whole found redoubled expression in their anti-Jewish policy. A document issued by the *Reichskommissariat* for the *Ostland* on December 8, 1942, stated: "The solution of the Jewish problem in *Reichskommissariat Ostland* has been ceded exclusively to the Security Police."[4]

The "Work Cards" distributed by the German administration in April 1942 were replaced by numbers and identity cards in March 1943. These identity cards were printed on yellow paper and recorded first and last name, father's name, year and date of birth, family status, color of eyes and hair, and fingerprints. The numbers were on a round disc with a Shield of David at the center, and three Latin characters ("W" [Wilna], "G" [Ghetto], and "M" [Male] or "F" [Female]) were imprinted at the corners. Serial numbers for males and for females began separately from No. 1. The number had to be worn on a chain around the neck. The distribution of the new identity cards and the numerical discs served as a pretext for a census of ghetto manpower. The Labor Department in the ghetto was responsible for issuing them, and they were not given to people over sixty.

Liquidation of the Ghettos in Vilna-Land
Within the *Gebietskommissariat* of "Vilna-Land," close to the Lithuanian-Belorussia frontier, there were four small ghettos—Swieciany, Mikhailishki, Sol and Oshmyany—and several

4 YVA, 0–18/196.

labor camps in which there were Jewish workers from Vilna and the smaller ghettos. These four ghettos were within the jurisdiction of the Security Police in Vilna.

The German administration resolved to liquidate the four ghettos. Rumors of the intended liquidation circulated in the early days of March 1943 within the Vilna ghetto. Simultaneously, reports arrived of murder operations perpetrated in the Grodno ghetto during the distribution of the new identity cards and discs in the Vilna ghetto. The ghetto inhabitants were again seized with panic and alarm.

The ghetto administration attempted to pacify the inhabitants. An editorial in *Geto Yedies* No. 31 of March 21, 1943, stated:

> As regards the situation — Keep calm! More than once we have warned in *Geto Yedies* against panic... Last week our ghetto floundered in a mood of tension and, once again, without any foundation...
>
> To what does this refer—In accordance with the instructions of the German administration, published some time ago, Jews are forbidden to dwell along the Belorussian frontier, in an area 35 miles wide. It was on this basis that the evacuation of Jews began from the small ghettos situated in "Vilna-Land": Swieciany, Oshmyany, Mikhailishki, and Sol. Some of them would be transferred to the Vilna ghetto, and others to various labor camps. It should be emphasized that the transfer of these Jews is implemented with the help of, and under supervision by, the Jewish police of our ghetto...
>
> Nothing has changed in *the situation of our ghetto,* and no danger threatens it. Consequently, we advise — Do not lacerate your nerves with unfounded guesses. We must again demonstrate that everyone continues with his work, remain quiet and calm.

The rumor circulated in the Vilna ghetto that the evacuation of the 35-mile strip along the Belorussian border was the result of Soviet partisan activity in that region and the German fear that ghetto Jews might join these partisans.[5] The Germans informed the Judenrats in Vilna and in Kovno that the Jews from the small ghettos would be transferred to the ghettos of Vilna and Kovno and some labor camps. The Judenrat in the Kovno ghetto was told that it was obliged to furnish accommodations for the incoming Jews.

Garfunkel, a Kovno Judenrat member, writes:

> On March 3, 1943, Müller, who was in charge of ghetto affairs in the *Stadtkommissariat*, secretly informed the *Ältestenrat* that 3,000 Jews would be brought in from the outside and accommodated in the Kovno ghetto... *Stadtkommissar* Kramer himself told the *Ältestenrat* on March 31, 1943, that 5,000 (and not 3,000) Jews would be brought into the ghetto in a few days.[6]

The Vilna Jewish police was to escort the trains to Vilna and Kovno. Policemen from the Vilna ghetto arrived in the smaller ghettos to organize the evacuations. Gens visited Swienciany and Oshmyany and discussed the matter with the Judenrat there. The Vilna policemen decided, within the framework of German directives, who was to be sent to Vilna and who to Kovno. The Judenrat members, skilled workers and their families were selected to go to Vilna, the others to Kovno.

During the week of March 26 to April 2, 1943, 1,250 people came to the Vilna ghetto from Oshmyany, Mikhailishki, and Swieciany. The majority of these people were quartered in the synagogues, schools, and public institutions according to their ghettos of origin. Another 1,459 persons were sent from Oshmyany to labor camps in Zasliai, Ziezmariai, Kena, and Novo-Vileyka. The first stage of the liquidation of the small ghettos, including the removal of Jews to Vilna and the labor camps, was terminated on April 2.

5 Kruk, *op. cit.*, p. 472; Epstein's diary, p. 87; Kalmanovitch, *op. cit.*, p. 57; Korczak, *op. cit.*, pp. 161, 251.
6 Garfunkel, *op. cit.*, p. 139; Brown-Levin, *op. cit.*, p. 112; Kruk, *op. cit.*, pp. 483–484.

The second stage consisted of transferring to Kovno the Jews remaining in the small ghettos. Jews from Oshmyany, Sol, and Mikhailishki were brought to the railroad station at Sol on April 3 and 4. Those from Swieciany were taken to the station at Nowo-Swieciany on April 4. The Germans used freight cars, of which the apertures were bound with barbed wire. The Jewish police implemented the transfers to the railroad stations and supervised the boarding of the trains. Once on board the Jews were locked into the wagons from the outside by the Jewish police in accordance with German orders. Polish railroad workers who traveled on the trains received written transport orders on which the route was indicated: Sol-Kovno and Nowo-Swieciany-Kovno.[7]

Several days prior to April 5, 1943, a notice had been posted in the Vilna ghetto inviting Jews who had relatives in the Kovno ghetto and refugees from other ghettos to join the train of Jews from the smaller places when it passed through Vilna en route to Kovno. Rumors had circulated in the Vilna ghetto that the situation in Kovno was much better than their own. As a result, 340 people registered to proceed to Kovno. All of them were removed from the ghetto in the afternoon of April 4, led to the railroad station, and placed in six cars which were to be added to the train to Kovno.[8]

The train, which had left Sol in the evening of April 4, arrived in Vilna a few hours later, and the cars with the local ghetto passengers were attached. Gens boarded the train at Vilna to join the party of Jewish policemen who had escorted the train; they traveled in the first coach, which was not locked. The train left for Kovno before midnight.

After they had left Vilna, Gens learned from a Polish railroadman that they were in fact going to Ponar and not Kovno, which was in another direction entirely. The train halted at the

---

7 Kruk, *op. cit.*, pp. 486, 489, 497, 509, 537; *Sefer Zikkaron Swenzian*, Tel Aviv, 1965, pp. 551, 552, 1164, 1593, 1770.
8 Korczak, *op. cit.*, p. 162; Kruk, *op. cit.*, p. 498.

Ponar station; Gens and his men were taken off and brought to the Security Police office in Vilna by Lithuanian police. Gens then realized that the Security Police had in fact deceived him.[9]

The people locked in the wagons were unaware that they were in Ponar, surrounded by Lithuanian police units, and that the Jewish police was no longer with them. At dawn the cars were opened one after another. The passengers were taken out, marched to the edge of the pits and shot. Hundreds tried to escape, but they were shot dead at the station or in the surrounding fields. Only a few succeeded.

The train with the Swieciany people left the station at Nowo-Swienciany on the evening of April 4 and reached Vilna shortly before dawn the next day. Gens, who had been held until then by the Security Police, was taken the following morning to the station, met Dessler, who had arrived with the train from Novo–Swieciany and told him all that had happened. Five cars with people who were to be sent to the camp at Bezdany were uncoupled from the train and indeed taken there. Two cars, with members of the Swieciany Judenrat and their families were also detached and remained in Vilna. This reprieve was the result of Gens' last-minute efforts at the station. Gens also assisted several young men who had escaped the cars to reach the Vilna ghetto.[10]

The train with the Jews of Swieciany was detained at the Vilna depot for several hours. In the morning, after the people taken off the Sol train had been murdered, it too proceeded to Ponar. When the Swieciany Jews found themselves at Ponar, they realized they had been duped. They burst out of the wagons and began a mass flight, while others violently resisted the attacking Germans and Lithuanians with their fists, knives and revolvers that some of them carried. The Germans and Lithuanians fired indiscriminately into the crowd. They ordered the

9 *Ibid.*, pp. 500, 509; Dworzecki, *op. cit.*, p. 403.
10 Kruk, *op. cit.*, pp. 499–500, 509; *Sefer Zikkaron Swenzian*, pp. 1593–1594.

wagons to be moved, so that many who fell were crushed to death under the wheels. Some 600 people from the Swieciany and Oshmyany transports were slain during the attempted resistance and flight, and their bodies were strewn inside the railroad depot and on the adjacent fields. But there were also casualties among the Germans and Lithuanians who carried out the slaughter at Ponar.[11]

Some 4,000 people who arrived on the two trains were killed that day at Ponar. Several dozen managed to elude the slaughter and reached the Vilna ghetto.

The first reports that the Jews in the trains had been taken to Ponar and shot had already spread through the Vilna ghetto in the morning hours of April 5, while the *Aktion* was still in progress. Panic seized the ghetto. That evening the synagogue was filled with worshippers, and a "minor Yom Kippur" was proclaimed by the religious members of the community.

The Security Police learned that fugitives from Ponar had reached the ghetto, so the ghetto administration was ordered to register and report Jews who had arrived after April 5. The German administration revoked the order a few days later in order to pacify the simmering feelings in the ghetto, but this was only a temporary concession, and the demand was renewed in May. The ghetto authorities handed over seven elderly people and invalids instead of the Ponar fugitives.[12]

During the morning of April 6, the day after the Ponar massacre, Weiss arrived in the ghetto and demanded that twenty-five policemen accompany him to Ponar in order to bury the dead. The chief of Security Police in Vilna, Neugebauer, also came to the ghetto and assured Gens that no danger threatened the Jews of Vilna. The policemen accompanied Weiss to Ponar.

11 *Documents Accuse,* p. 272, Report of the Chief of Security Police and SD in Lithuania, in which it is stated that the Jews on the train resisted; one sergeant of the German Security Police was stabbed with a knife, and a Lithuanian Police Officer was shot by a Jew. Rolnik, *op. cit.,* pp. 85–86; Kruk, *op. cit.,* p. 514.
12 Kruk, *op. cit.,* pp. 506, 543; Korczak, *op. cit.,* pp. 163–164.

Before their departure Gens addressed them and explained the purpose of their journey. Fear in the ghetto spread, and the inhabitants did not believe that the policemen would return from their trip to Ponar.[13] One of the policemen gave an account of what transpired there:

When we left the ghetto, we believed that we were parting from it forever ... Just before Ponar, the car stopped, and we were ordered to continue on foot. We could see peasants hurrying to their homes, bent with loads on their backs: they had profited from the belongings of the murdered ... When we entered deeper into the woods, a horrifying spectacle was revealed to our eyes ... The whole area was strewn with bodies and human limbs ... Weiss took us to an enormous pit full of corpses and told us to cover them with earth ... One of the policemen stopped work and said the *Kaddish* [the prayer for the dead] ... After we had completed this work, Weiss led us to a second grave ... At the end of it all, he took us on a tour of the whole area and gave us explanations as though he were a guide at an exhibition: "Here are the graves of Jews kidnapped by abductors in 1941; here is a second grave of the "Provocation *Aktionen* ..." He then went on to the graves of the "Yellow Passes" and "Pink Passes" *Aktionen* ... He indicated a grave in which priests were buried and others of Russian prisoners of war ... At the conclusion of the tour, he ordered us to gather the bodies scattered over the area and throw them into a pit.[14]

The policemen returned to the ghetto at 9 P.M., after having

---

13 Kruk, *op. cit.*, pp. 501–502, 510. Gens stated that Weiss had demanded that people be assigned to him, but that Gens preferred policemen, on the assumption that the danger to the latter was less than to any people whom he would send to Weiss.

14 Lazar, *op. cit.*, pp. 98–100; Kruk, *op. cit.*, p. 512; Weiss' trial TR–10/29, pp. 3–4.

collected some 300–400 corpses of the escapees and burying them. It was the first instance in which the Germans showed Ponar to the Jews and told them what happened there, or that Jews were returned alive from that spot by the Germans. The Germans also photographed and filmed the burials as performed by the Jewish police. On April 6, the ghetto administration ordered that men and carts be sent to Ponar to collect the possessions and food that the murdered people had taken with them and to bring these goods to the ghetto. These articles were given to the social-welfare institutions for distribution.[15]

Gens assembled a meeting of "brigadiers," police officers, and public figures on April 10, 1943, and reported on developments in connection with the Kovno train. He said that when the German administration had decided on the liquidation of the ghettos in the province, Murer had not wished to admit a single Jew into the Vilna ghetto, but because of his [Gens'] intercession, he was able to obtain permission for 1,000 Jews to be brought there. The German authorities in Kovno should have received 5,000 people, but at the very last moment they refused to receive the Jews. The *Gebietskommissar* of Vilna also declined, whereupon the Security Police found the solution—Ponar. Gens declared that he had debated, for moral reasons, whether or not to accept the belongings of the murdered victims, but reached the conclusion that, due to the acute shortage of clothing in the ghetto and the hunger, he should accept the goods and food.[16]

The Kovno train *Aktion* undermined the feeling of security and confidence among the ghetto Jews. Thousands of physically fit people had been murdered for the first time since the mass exterminations in the Vilna ghetto at the end of 1941. The belief that the need for Jewish manpower would insure the ghetto's survival had been shattered by the Kovno train mas-

15 Kruk, *op. cit.,* pp. 503–505, 507; Lazar, *op. cit.,* pp. 100–101.
16 Kruk, *op. cit.,* pp. 509–510; Balberyszski, *op. cit.,* pp. 456–457.

sacre. Even the faith in Gens, and his power and influence with the German administration, had weakened. In April 1943, the report of the chief of Security Police and SD to the *Reich* Security H.Q. in Berlin on the situation in Lithuania, included the following passage:

4. *Jews*

During the month to which this report refers, areas of Belorussia annexed to Lithuania—Swieciany, Oshmyany... were cleared of Jews. These sectors, which are under constant partisan threat, were completely purged of Jews. The result is that we now have a frontier zone, 35–65 miles wide, in which there are no Jews.

The Jews who inhabited the aforementioned areas were assembled and classified into those fit for labor and those found unfit. About 4,000 received special treatment at Ponar on April 5, 1943...[17]

The report stated that a selection had taken place prior to the departure for Ponar, and the 4,000 Jews murdered there were considered to be "unfit" for labor. However, no selection had been made, and the murderers actually killed thousands who were physically fit.

The liquidation operations in the East Lithuanian ghettos had been scheduled for February 1943, but were postponed until the end of March or beginning of April. The Security Police and SD's progress report for February stated: "The purge of Jews from the frontier zone between Lithuania and Belorussia, in which the Jews transgressed the regulations confining them to the ghettos, has not yet been implemented."

The reasons for the postponement were apparently connected to the general unrest in Lithuania in March 1943, and the punitive *Aktionen* implemented in sectors of eastern Lithuania in February 1943, against farmers who did not relinquish crops to the Germans.[18] These operations necessitated large police

17 *Documents Accuse*, pp. 271–272.
18 *Ibid.*, pp. 267–269.

forces, thereby making it necessary to delay the liquidation of the ghettos until the end of March or the beginning of April.

Security Police and SD in Lithuania, which was responsible for exterminating the ghettos in eastern Lithuania, had apparently intended, during the planning stages of the February–March operations, to liquidate some of the Jews in the ghettos and to transfer those suitable for labor to the ghettos in Vilna and Kovno and to the labor camps. There was a demand for additional Jewish labor in Kovno, and the Security Police and SD report for March mentioned the need for 600 more ghetto Jews to fill urgent orders placed by the Wehrmacht with ghetto workshops, and the employment of women and children to meet these requirements. Requests for more Jewish workmen, especially for work at the airfield, had also been placed with the third Lithuanian ghetto, Shavli. Women and girls aged fourteen and up were incorporated into the labor cycle. The Labor Department in the Vilna ghetto was asked, several days after the murders at Ponar, to provide 100 workers for the *Vilna-Land Gebietskommissariat,* for the Jewish inhabitants there had been slaughtered in the Kovno train *Aktion.*[19]

The decision to liquidate the large majority of Jewish residents in the smaller ghettos was apparently taken towards the end of March. Garfunkel wrote that Kramer, the *Gebietskommissar* of Kovno, "agreed to the influx of Jews into the Kovno ghetto, but the Gestapo refused to tender its consent at the last moment because of information in its possession reporting the connection between these Jews and the Russian partisans, and therefore gave the order to liquidate them all." Kruk wrote that the chief of the Security Police and SD in Vilna, Neugebauer, stated that, had it not been for the connections maintained by the young men in the ghettos with the partisans, the incidents involving the Jews of Oshmyany and Swieciany would not have taken place.[20]

19 *Ibid.,* p. 268; Yerushalmi, *op. cit.,* pp. 178, 191, 194–195; Kruk, *op. cit.,* p. 518.
20 Garfunkel, *op. cit.,* p. 140; Kruk, *op. cit.,* pp. 547–548.

In the liquidated ghettos there indeed were groups of armed Jewish youths. One such group, numbering twenty-two combatants who were active in the underground in the Swieciany ghetto, left for the forests during the night of March 5/6, 1943, and began partisan activity. Other young men went out from the Oshmyany, Mikhailishki, and Sol ghettos to join partisan groups.[21] The Germans received reports of these flights into the forest and the partisan activities. But this information did not influence the decision to do away with the ghettos in the frontier zone, for that had been taken before March, before these young people left for the forests. It is possible, however, that the information did affect the *scope* of the exterminations in this *Aktion*, and the fact that thousands of potential laborers were also slaughtered.

The Security Police chiefs decided to assign the task of superintending the transfers to Gens in order to relieve themselves of the mission, but, above all, to dupe the Jews and prevent their flight into the forests. As a result, the lives of 2,500 Jews were saved, and they were brought to Vilna and some labor camps. Actually, this "reward" also benefitted the German demands for manpower.

Gens believed the German assertions that the Jews from the small ghettos were indeed to be sent to Kovno, and the fact that some Jews reached the labor camps and Vilna ghetto safely before the massacre reinforced his confidence.

Liquidation of the Labor Camps
Pursuant to the regulation prohibiting Jews from remaining in the frontier zone between Lithuania and Belorussia, the labor camps at Sorok-Tatar, Rzesza, and Biala-Vaka had been liquidated. The workers in Sorok-Tatar were returned to the ghetto on March 23, 1943. Approximately 700 laborers and their dependents were returned from Rzesza and Biala-Vaka between

21 *Sefer Zikkaron Swienzian*, pp. 1665, 1685, 1716; Kruk, *op. cit.*, pp. 492, 519.

April 5 and 7. Some 200 of the Biala-Vaka workers were returned there in mid-May at the request of the German administration. Vilna Jews were also sent back to the Rzesza camp.

There were 1,000 Jews from Vilna and Oshmyany in the Zezmariai camp who were employed there building the Vilna–Kovno highway, and fear for their safety mounted once the road was completed. They sought the aid of the Kovno Judenrat, and the latter approached the official in charge of Jewish labor in the local German *Arbeitsamt* and asked for the transfer of the Ziezmariai Jews to the Kovno ghetto on the grounds that it lacked workers. Approval was granted by the Security Police in Vilna, and a group of Jewish police from Kovno escorted 800 men of the camp and their families to the Kovno ghetto. About 140 skilled craftsmen were left in the Ziezmariai camp.[22]

Three labor camps were liquidated at the end of June and beginning of July 1943—Biala-Vaka, Kena, and Bezdany—by order of the Security Police office in Vilna. The liquidation operation was superintended by Kittel, who had arrived in Vilna in June 1943 to assume the post of officer-in-charge of Jewish affairs in the Security Police, succeeding Mayer, who was sent to the front-line.[23]

Some 300 Jews were employed in the Biala–Vaka camp, a short distance from the Rudniki forests. Six of the camp laborers stole rifles from the Lithuanian guards and joined a party from "Yechiel's Struggle Group," under the command of B. Friedman, which had left the Vilna ghetto on June 24, and passed through Biala-Vaka en route to the forests. Kittel and a party of Security Police came from Vilna to Biala–Vaka on

---

22 Garfunkel, *op. cit.*, pp. 140–141; Report of the *Kommandeur der Sicherheitspolizei und des SD* for Lithuania, July 31, 1943, YIVO Archives, Occ, E3b–96.

23 Kittel, born in Austria, had been a film actor and vocalist before the outbreak of the war. After joining the Security Police, he dealt with Jewish Affairs in France and Riga, and then went to Vilna. He was dubbed, *post facto*, "The Liquidator of the Vilna Ghetto." *Documents Accuse*, p. 290; Kalmanovitch, *op. cit.*, p. 67.

the 28th or 29th of the month, lined up all the camp laborers, and selected sixty-seven Jews to be shot as a reprisal for the escape of the six workers. The Biala–Vaka camp was later dissolved; some of the laborers escaped, while others were transferred to the Vilna ghetto.[24]

Kittel arrived at the Kena camp on July 8, convened all the laborers in one building, and addressed them. He stated that it was the duty of the camp inmates to work, not to be in touch with the "men of the forests," or engage in smuggling. During his address, scores of Security Police and Lithuanians cordoned off the building. When Kittel left the hall, fire was opened and grenades were thrown inside. Two hundred and forty Jews were killed.[25]

The day after the Kena massacre, on July 9, Kittel arrived at the Bezdany camp, which was still unaware of what had happened at Kena. Kittel ordered the men to assemble in a large warehouse, and, using the same method, the Lithuanians succeeded in killing 350 Jews on the spot. A few women and children, who were not in the camp when the attack took place, were saved. Local farmers were brought to the camp to bury the bodies.

There was an organized combat group with hidden arms at the Bezdany camp, but these people had had no time to reach the hiding-place due to the deceitful and surprise tactics which Kittel employed.

Hingst told Gens that the reason for liquidating these camps and their inmates was that they were in contact with the partisans and some of them had even gone out into the forests.[26]

24 YIVO Occ, E3b–96; Kalmanovitch, op. cit., p. 67; Kruk, op. cit., pp. 589–590. For Borka Friedman's group, see Chapter 22.
25 Kruk, op. cit., pp. 597, 601; Kaczerginski, Hurbn Vilne, op. cit., p. 69.
26 Kruk, op. cit., pp. 579, 601; Kalmanovitch, op. cit., p. 68; Testimony of A. Katz, YVA, 0–3/3959, p. 18; Yerushalmi, op. cit., p. 269, writes that reports reached the Shavli ghetto to the effect that Vilna ghetto inmates who had been to the peat-digging camps were shot because of their connections with the partisans.

The reports on the massacres at Kena and Bezdany reached the Jews in the Rzesza camp, and most of them fled and returned to the Vilna ghetto.

Several scores of Jews were employed in the camp at Zaczepki, which was under the control of the Todt organization. The Security Police came from Vilna to extirpate this camp as well. But the Todt personnel, who did not believe the Security Police assurances that the men would be returned to Vilna, drove them to the ghetto in their own trucks.

The last camp in the Vilna district was the one at Novo–Vileyka, and it was liquidated at the end of July. The Jewish workers were taken to Ponar and slain. Several days before this operation, fourteen laborers had fled and joined a group of F.P.O. combatants who had left the Vilna ghetto for the woods.[27] The liquidation of the camp at Novo–Vileyka was a result of the decision to expunge all labor camps in areas close to partisan activity, but the extermination of the camp workers was evidently in retribution for those who escaped to join the partisans.

These operations aroused apprehensions that the end of the ghetto in Vilna was approaching. Shur wrote in his diary for July 13 :

> Tension in the ghetto rose to a peak, it was thought that the liquidation was about to begin. Rumor had it that the Gestapo was demanding the liquidation of the Jews ... The official representatives of the ghetto did not lose their heads. They have appealed to the German military and civilian authorities for their help and asked for their intervention ... It had already become known, on the evening of July 13, that the danger had passed ... Gens and Dessler returned from a meeting with Hingst and repre-

27 Kruk, *op. cit.,* pp. 599–600; Shur's diary [2]. The reference was to a group of people from Novo-Vileyka who had joined the FPO group headed by J. Glazman. See also Kaczerginski, *Hurbn Vilne, op. cit.,* p. 159.

sentatives of German military units employing Jews, at which it had been stated that the decision was made not to exterminate the Jews of the Vilna ghetto.[28]

The issue of *Geto Yedies* published after the liquidation of the labor camps discussed these events. One announcement stated that, due to the flight of six Jews from Biala–Vaka, the Germans had condemned sixty Jews to death—ten persons for each one of the defectors—and in addition had killed seven children. The announcement stated that the German authorities had promised a similar penalty if further incidents occurred. The second announcement declared that the Kena and Bezdany camps were destroyed because of connections with the partisans. The editor of *Geto Yedies* added a warning of his own to these two notices. He said that Jews and their labor efforts had been taken into consideration until the moment the German administration had realized that the Jews were in contact with the partisans.[29]

The ghetto administration published an article in *Geto Yedies* No. 48 of mid-July 1943, entitled "The Only Way":

Once more, we went through terrible days during the events in the Vilna district (Kena, Bezdany, Biala-Vaka) ... But even now the truth, which we have not wearied of repeating, has been substantiated: only one reason guarantees our survival—our labor.

Even in the most dangerous moments, we must continue our work quietly, and not fall into the arms of despair. We must remain realistic and sane, cautious in deeds and words. We must not make it possible for anyone to assume that our ghetto may become a harmful or detrimental element. We are a working ghetto. We live between and among ourselves—Jews and Jews—and we have no contact with any extraneous factor. Day after

28 Shur's diary [1].
29 Kruk, *op. cit.*, pp. 602–603.

day we go off to work—punctually, disciplined and organized ... Although our life is difficult, we must rely solely on the power of wisdom and toil and tie our lot to the banner of labor. That is our only prop. It is our only way. We seek no other.[30]

This article expressed the pivotal ideas of the policy of the ghetto administration—Work to Live; avoid contact with the partisans and defection into the forests, so that the ghetto would not be regarded by the Germans as a dangerous element to be destroyed.

The labor camps at Biala–Vaka, Kena, Bezdany, and Novo–Vileyka were liquidated and their inmates murdered due to their connections with the partisans and the escape of some into the woods. Other camp workers were returned to the Vilna and Kovno ghettos.

The German administration in eastern Lithuania adopted a strong-arm policy during this period, including large-scale executions, also with respect to the non-Jewish population of the region. Punitive measures were invoked against villages and individuals for non-compliance with government orders on manpower enlistment, aid to army deserters, and assistance to partisans active in the area. The *Gebietskommissar* of *Vilna-Land*, Wulff, published an announcement addressed to the local population on August 12, 1943, in which he enumerated the reasons for the punitive steps taken and emphasized that the German administration would not tolerate sheltering partisans. The strict policy was pursued against Jews as well, and massacre was used as reprisal for any suspicion or report of affiliation with partisans and flight into the forests.

30 Moreshet Archives, D.485, the original manifesto.

Chapter 22

THE UNDERGROUND VERSUS THE GHETTO
ADMINISTRATION

Expansion of Underground Activity
The developments in the spring of 1943—the increase of partisan activity and the liquidation of the small ghettos and the labor camps—led to far-reaching changes in the ghetto underground and in its relationship with Gens and the ghetto administration. The ideology of the F.P.O. was put to a practical test in light of the new developments.

The massacres provoked an increase in underground activity and in the efforts to acquire arms. Hundreds of young men, some of them organized in groups, reached the Vilna ghetto from the small ghettos that had already been liquidated. These groups were in contact with their fellow-townsmen in the forests and in partisan units, and an exodus of organized groups from the Vilna ghetto to the forests began. The ghetto administration, as well as the underground, was forced to take a stand on the subject of these groups and their departure.

The reports of the Warsaw Ghetto uprising also strengthened the spirit of resistance. The F.P.O. drew great encouragement from the uprising and perceived it as a fulfillment and justification of its own ideology. The idea of armed resistance in the event of the liquidation of the ghetto, and the attempts to procure weapons, also spread to individuals not affiliated with the organized underground.

[373]

F.P.O.–"Yechiel's Struggle Group" Cooperation

The new situation came to the fore in the relationship between the F.P.O. and "Yechiel's Struggle Group." Negotiations for a merger of the two bodies began in April–May 1943. Their differences of opinion focused on two principal issues—first the manner of affiliation; and, secondly, the arms problem. The F.P.O. leaders wanted the members of "Yechiel's Struggle Group" to join its ranks as individuals, after appropriate personal examinations. They also requested that all the armories of "Yechiel's Struggle Group" be turned over to the F.P.O. and that separate arms purchases cease. The practical significance of these demands was the disbandment of "Yechiel's Struggle Group."

The representatives of "The Group" rejected these demands and presented their own terms: "Yechiel's Struggle Group" was to affiliate with the F.P.O. as an independent unit, and remain as such within the F.P.O.; and they would retain all arms in their possession.

The F.P.O. negotiators acceded to most of "Yechiel's Struggle Group's" demands, and in the agreement reached in May 1943 the following terms were included:

— "Yechiel's Struggle Group" would affiliate with the F.P.O. as a unit with autonomous rights as to admission of members and possession of arms;

— The F.P.O. staff command would receive reports on new members admitted, and the two groups would cooperate in all that pertained to arms acquisition;

— Yechiel Scheinbaum was appointed representative of "Yechiel's Struggle Group" on the F.P.O. Staff Command.[1]

Ideological matters, in regard to combat inside the ghetto or withdrawal into the forests, were not covered by the agreement. Each side remained autonomous in these respects. "Yechiel's Struggle Group" displayed readiness to take part in

1 Dworzecki, *op. cit.*, pp. 378–379; *Sefer ha-Partizanim*, pp. 34–35.

ghetto fighting, if the situation so demanded, prior to their departure for the forests. Pursuant to the agreement, "Yechiel's Struggle Group" was integrated into the plan for ghetto combat.[2] The agreement did not lead to the fusion and unification of the two organizations, but it did serve to increase coordination and cooperation between them.

A further important development was the establishment of close ties between the F.P.O. and the non-Jewish Communist underground in the city of Vilna. J. Vitas-Valunas, who was head of the City Council in Vilna until the German invasion, returned to that city at the beginning of 1943. Vitas had been in the underground since the Nazi invasion and, upon returning to Vilna, established a Lithuanian Communist underground group called Lietuvos islaisvinimo Sojunga ("Union for the Liberation of Lithuania") on February 24, 1943.

The Communist Party in the ghetto established contact with Vitas through W. Kozlowski, a member of the "Union for the Liberation of Lithuania." The outcome of these contacts was the creation of the "City Underground Committee of the Lithuanian Communist Party" under Vitas' leadership. Its membership was composed of J. Przewalski and M. Karablikow of the Polish Communist Z.W.C., I. Witenberg and B. Szeresznyevski of the ghetto Communist Party, and Kozlowski.

The structural framework of the City Underground Committee embraced only Communist organizations. The contact between Vitas and the F.P.O. was established through the ghetto Communists. It resulted in the constitution, on May 8, 1943, of an umbrella organization for the three groups—the Jewish F.P.O., the Polish Z.W.C. and the Lithuanian "Union for the Liberation of Lithuania"—called the "Vilna Anti-Fascist Committee." It comprised both Communists and non-Communists. The head of the joint committee was Vitas, and Witenberg represented the F.P.O. The "Vilna Anti-Fascist Committee" served

---

2 Reznik's testimony, 0–33/419, p. 26; Collective Interview, Yechiel Group, pp. 53–54.

as a framework for common action and coordination, not as a united organization. The liaison between the F.P.O. within the ghetto and the "Anti-Fascist Committee" outside was maintained through ghetto couriers.[3]

The Vilna Anti-Fascist Committee and the "City Underground Committee" had no contacts with the U.S.S.R. or with Soviet partisans operating in the forests at that time.

The F.P.O. leaders, with the exception of the Communists, had no knowledge of the existence of a Communist "City Underground Committee" or of the fact that Witenberg was a member of that Committee.

Kovner comments:

> From the day the Communist remnants organized in the city, they needed a nexus with the ghetto more than we with them, in order to strengthen themselves in manpower, arms, printing material . . . We knew this and were glad of it . . . Part of it was overt and we on the staff knew about it, but from that moment on, the Communist cell in the ghetto operated on two levels . . . Witenberg reported to us about those aspects which concerned us, but not about all of their connections. Had we known that Witenberg was a member of the "City Committee," we would not have agreed that the Chief of the F.P.O. Command also be a member of the Communist Committee; we would have said there ought to be another Communist, but not him.[4]

The F.P.O. was the largest and most organized of the three organizations that constituted the Vilna Anti-Fascist Committee.[5] The F.P.O. retained its complete independence within the

---

3 *Gitlerovskaya okupatsiya*, pp. 209–210; Juchniewicz, *op. cit.*, pp. 59–60.

4 Collective Interview—FPO. p. 32.

5 The FPO totaled some 300 organized members during the period in which the anti-Fascist committee was created. The ZWZ and the

Committee in all spheres—enlistment of members, arms' acquisition, and policy vis-à-vis the Judenrat. At a later date, the F.P.O. was to maintain direct contact with the partisan units in the forests and send men to join them, though not through the Vilna Anti-Fascist Committee.

Within the context of F.P.O.–"Anti-Fascist Committee" relations, the demand was voiced that "anti-Fascist combat groups" be organized outside the ghetto in order to assist in the event of fighting within it. It was also proposed that a partisan base be created in the forests adjoining Vilna to which F.P.O. fighters could retreat and find refuge after fighting inside the ghetto. The Committee was asked to prepare hiding-places inside the city for F.P.O. personnel and to help the F.P.O. in procuring arms. Funds were deposited with Vitas for arms purchases for the F.P.O.[6]

Clash Between Gens and the F.P.O.

Until the spring of 1943, there had been no direct clash between the ghetto administration and the F.P.O. The F.P.O. agreed that it was vital to ensure the continued existence of the ghetto and therefore did not denigrate the measures pursued by the ghetto administration regarding labor and the organization of daily life in the ghetto. It did not strive to dominate the ghetto in place of the Judenrat, except at the time when the ghetto might be faced with the threat of annihilation. The existence of the ghetto during the period of stability enabled the F.P.O. to organize and build up strength for the uprising on the day of the liquidation. On the other hand, it denied the illusions and hopes of survival that the ghetto authorities fostered among the inhabitants as part of the "Work to Live" ideology.[7]

Union for the Liberation of Lithuania numbered a few dozen members each.

6 Korczak, *op. cit.*, pp. 181, 182; *Sefer ha-Partizanim*, p. 37.
7 Kovner, "Nissayon Rishon," *op. cit.*, pp. 10–11, 13. Kovner states: "The underground had no ambition to take power except at the moment it became active — until then its response was to create

Gens and the ghetto administration were aware of the existence of the F.P.O., but took no counter-measures against that body and its leadership. Gens did not take issue with the existence of the F.P.O. as long as its activities were not counterproductive and did not endanger the basic elements of ghetto survival, as he saw them.

On a number of occasions Gens had expressed the view that, when the time for annihilation of the ghetto came, he personally would present himself as a combatant and would even lead the fighting. He maintained personal ties with Witenberg and other Communists and F.P.O. leaders, and went so far as to invite them to the Political Club in his home. These relations had begun before the F.P.O. was created and continued throughout its existence. Some of the F.P.O. members, and the Communists in particular, believed that their ties with Gens would be advantageous to their underground activities and hoped to extract from him information on imminent *Aktionen*.[8]

This peaceful coexistence terminated in the spring of 1943, when a violent political clash developed between Gens and the underground. The direct cause of this development was the increased efforts to acquire arms and the departure of groups of young men for the forest. Several cases occurred during May in which ghetto Jews were detained by Security Police for possession of weapons, and a number of Lithuanians and Poles informed against Jews who tried to obtain arms from them.[9]

The Security Police cautioned Gens against the consequences likely to befall the ghetto if the Jews continued to acquire fire-

---

a body that would exercise influence on the public..." Collective Interview—FPO, p. 7.

8 Kovner, "Nissayon Rishon," *op. cit.,* pp. 12–13; Collective Interview—FPO, pp. 8, 11–13, 16; Reznik's testimony, 0–33/1238, pp. 13–14; Collective Interview, Yechiel Group, pp. 70, 71; Mushkat's testimony, p. 36.

9 Kruk, *op. cit.,* pp. 532, 534, 549, 563, speaks of the Jews arrested while in possession of arms. They were executed along with their families in several cases.

arms. Gens regarded this development as a potential danger to the existence of the ghetto and undertook measures directed against this practice and against the underground leaders. On May 15, 1943, he convened a meeting of the "brigadiers" and police and told them:

> I have asked you to come here, ladies and gentlemen, to explain the following: I have lately been at Gestapo headquarters, and talked with the head of the SD. He spoke with me about guns. And I am bound to tell you that he is by no means a fool. He said: "The ghetto is vital from an economic standpoint, but if you run risks like stupid people and if security is involved, then I'll wipe you out. And even if you have thirty, forty or fifty revolvers, even then you won't be able to save yourselves, you'll only bring the catastrophe nearer.
>
> "Why have I called you here? Because today again a Jew has been arrested while trying to buy a pistol. I still don't know how things will end ... Maybe all the elderly will be taken ... or the children ... Think it over and decide if all this is really worth it! For those of sound mind, there is only one answer: It is not worthwhile!
>
> "It's not worthwhile dealing with *Poles* ... Take heed and see what's happening among the Poles—how one man sells his brother, and how many Jews have gone to Ponar because of the Poles ..."
>
> As long as the ghetto is a ghetto, we who bear the responsibility for it will do everything in our power to guard the ghetto from evil. Today every Jew bears the responsibility for his own family, and if this isn't enough, I shall place responsibility on every room, and if this is insufficient, I'll place the responsibility on every apartment, or on the whole building.
>
> Each one of you must look after the other, and if you find any hotheads, it is your duty to tell the police. This is no question of "informing." "Informing" will be the case

if you keep quiet and people suffer ... I demand that the
"brigadiers" get to know their people. An officer must
know his men. The "brigadiers" don't know their people,
they think they only have to carry transit permits and
bring food in through the gate ...

Don't provoke! If we're not provoked, let's not be provocative, because we'll be asked to pay the price for it!

Think of what your path should be, and see where we're
standing! Good night.[10]

The police began to conduct searches for arms caches, but
without success. Searches were made of everyone passing
through the ghetto gate. The F.P.O. reacted to these combings
by moving the caches to safer places and placing them under
guard.[11]

Pursuant to a demand by the German administration, at the
end of May 1943, to send fifty workers to the town of Ponevezh,
the ghetto administration decided to get rid of several of the
F.P.O. leaders and to send A. Kovner, C. Lazar, and B. Schnei-
der. The F.P.O. learned of this plan, and all three hid until
after the group of workers had left for Ponevezh. The ghetto
police searched for the hideaways, but did not find them. Witenberg urged the ghetto administration to forgo the idea of de-
porting F.P.O. members, and the controversy ended with the
accession of the ghetto administration.[12]

The ghetto police took steps against groups of youths that had
been brought to Vilna from the small ghettos as a consequence
of a tragic incident at the ghetto gate. Chaim Levin of Swieciany

---

10 Korczak, *op. cit.*, pp. 286-287; Kruk, *op. cit.*, p. 548. This speech
    already contained a threat concerning the collective responsibility
    of family members and all house-tenants.

11 Kruk, *op. cit.*, pp. 542, 549–551, writes that the searches bore an
    educational character, the aim of which was to warn those who
    acquired arms that "when arms are purchased, they must be well
    concealed."

12 Korczak, *op. cit.*, p. 179; Lazar, *op. cit.*, pp. 112–113; Kruk, *op. cit.*,
    pp. 59, 561, 569.

was detained by the Jewish police while trying to leave the ghetto. Levin pleaded that they let him go, but the police guard refused and forcibly dragged him into the guardroom. Levin whipped out a pistol, fired, and killed the Jewish constable. Gens was summoned to the gate, demanded that Levin hand over the weapon, and, when he refused, shot and killed him on the spot. This occurred on June 12, 1943.[13]

The ghetto police reacted to Levin's fatal resistance by implementing searches and arrests among the youngsters of Swienciany, Grodno, and other townships. Ghetto-administration spokesmen inveighed sharply against those who had recently come to Vilna, "enjoyed the hospitality of the Vilna ghetto and want to plunge it into disaster."

The F.P.O. commanders decided that, in view of the iron-fist policy Gens had launched, if the ghetto administration were to make any attempt to dissolve the F.P.O. or initiate steps against its leaders, they would react with force, and—if the necessity arose—even employ firearms. This decision aroused a bitter dispute within the Bund. Some committee members opposed the F.P.O. attitude, justified the Judenrat, and demanded that Bund members within the F.P.O. rise against the decision. The Bund held a number of discussions on the matter, but finally resolved by a majority vote not to take any action against the F.P.O.[14]

The Ghetto and the Forests

A two-way traffic between the ghetto and the forests began in the spring of 1943, and expanded during the summer. Couriers and guides arrived from the forests, and organized groups of youths left the ghetto to join the partisans.

Two messengers from a group of Jewish partisans of the former Swieciany ghetto, which had been operating in the

---

13 Kruk, *op. cit.*, pp. 565–568; Kalmanovitch, *op. cit.*, p. 164. The murdered policeman was Moshe Gingold.
14 Kruk, *op. cit.*, pp. 564, 568–570, 572–574.

woods, arrived in Vilna at the beginning of April 1943. These two men, Yitzhak Rudnicki and Yashke Gertman, had come to establish contact with the F.P.O. Command. They conferred with the F.P.O., proposing that members of that organization join them in the forests. The F.P.O. countered with a proposal that the entire group of partisans from Swienciany come to the Vilna ghetto and join the F.P.O. The negotiations had no practical outcome, each side holding to its own position, and the emissaries returned to the forest.[15]

Four more members of the Swieciany group, which had in the meantime joined with a Soviet partisan group led by Fiodor Markov, arrived in the Vilna ghetto at the beginning of June 1943. These youngsters had told their commanders of the existence of an armed Jewish underground in the Vilna ghetto and suggested they might go there to bring back fighters. The first to reach Vilna were M. Shutan and I. Porush, carrying a letter from Sidyakin, who commanded the "Czapayew" partisan unit in Markov's brigade. They met I. Witenberg, gave him the letter, and made a verbal request that F.P.O. detail men to the forest.

A few days later two more couriers came from the forest, bringing a letter to the F.P.O. from Markov. The letter, which included an invitation to send men to the forest, was relayed to the F.P.O. Staff Command. The F.P.O. responded negatively to the proposal, stating that its purpose was to fight inside the ghetto. The partisan envoys then began to organize a group of youths from their home town in order to take them into the woods.[16]

M. Shutan was arrested by the ghetto police and found to be in possession of a list of people preparing to leave. Shutan was brought before Gens and Dessler for interrogation. Gens said to him:

15 *Sefer ha-Partizanim*, p. 36; *Sefer Zikkaron Swenzian*, p. 1717 (Yitzhak Rudnicki is the author, Yitzhak Arad).
16 *Sefer Zikkaron Swenzian*, pp. 1667, 1697. The two couriers with the letter from Markov were Y. Gutman and I. Wolfson.

[382]

You want to save Jews by taking them into the forests? Tell me, how many Jews will you be able to rescue this way, 100, 200, or let's suppose even 500? These people will all be the physically fit, those who insure the ghetto's survival. You want to take out just these and leave to the mercy of God only the aged, the sick, and the children whom the Germans will liquidate at once. I shall not allow it... The situation on all the fronts is changing... It may be that the Germans will be compelled to retreat and won't have time to liquidate the ghetto... We must not shorten its existence, even by one day. I shall fight for every day, and history will judge me for this in future... I am interested that brave, armed young men remain in the ghetto so that when the time comes, we shall be able to resist. I know of the existence of the F.P.O. and all its arms' caches. I know the time will come when I'll need them... When the time for destruction of the ghetto comes, we shall need all the armed boys. We'll all fight then.

Shutan told Gens that he had come to the ghetto as a partisan to take men back with him to the forest, and he would have to return and inform Markov that Gens had prevented him from accomplishing his mission. Gens agreed that Shutan should take his fellow townsmen into the forest and even release those who had been imprisoned in the ghetto jail. He ordered that the departure through the gate of twenty-five young men with Shutan be permitted, and the group left the ghetto on June 12, 1943.[17]

Ten men of "Yechiel's Struggle Group," led by B. Friedman, who was a police officer, left the Vilna ghetto on June 24, 1943, in the direction of the Nacza Forests about 80 miles south of Vilna. This group had connections with the Soviet partisans active in that region. These contacts had been made through several men who did not belong to the ghetto underground and

17 *Ibid.*, pp. 1668–1670; Kruk, *op. cit.*, pp. 571–572.

had left Vilna for the Nacza woodlands in April 1943, to join the guerrillas. Couriers had been sent into the Vilna ghetto from the Nacza group, and they guided Friedman's party back to the forests. This vanguard from "Yechiel's Struggle Group" had the task of preparing a base inside the forests for more detachments. En route to its destination, the party passed through the Biala-Vaka camp, where they were joined by the six laborers mentioned in the previous chapter. It was the first organized outfit from the Vilna underground that left for the forests.[18]

The departure of this group, which included police officers, had strong repercussions in the ghetto. Gens gathered the police together and raised this point:

> We are faced with the question of leaving for the forest ...
> Why should I not go? Because the question now arises —
> 1 or 20,000! The ghetto exists by virtue of 2,500 strong
> young men. The rest dance around them ... Just imagine
> if 500 men went out, what would happen then? ... I put
> myself in Neuegebauer's place ... I would wipe out the
> entire ghetto, because a man must be an idiot to allow a
> nest of partisans to develop under his nose ... My in-
> terest is to preserve a loyal ghetto so long as it maintains
> itself, so that no one can come to me with the charges
> that ... those who went were from the police ... Freede
> and Friedman betrayed us ...[19]

Gens reacted bitterly to the defection by Friedman's group, in contrast to the attitude he had adopted when sanctioning the departure of Shutan and his friends for the forest. He had agreed to this because Shutan's group were youngsters of the eastern Lithuanian ghettos who had only remained in Vilna for

18 *Ibid.*, pp. 580–581; Testimony of N. Rogovski, ICJ (12) 78, p. 15. The liquidation of the Biala-Vaka camp was connected with this departure to the partisans in the forests.

19 Korczak, *op. cit.*, pp. 199–200. The complete speech by Gens appears in Kruk, *op. cit.*, p. 581. Freede, like Friedman, was a police officer.

a short while, had not been absorbed into the labor cycle, and were a security nuisance. He was also impressed by the fact that Shutan had approached him on behalf of the Commander of the Soviet partisans. He wanted to maintain good relations with the Communists in the ghetto and the Soviet partisans, as a precautionary measure, to protect himself after the victory over Germany.[20]

The Friedman group was different: it was composed of "Vilnaites," among them officers and policemen upon whom his policy and power relied. Gens was also afraid that this desertion might serve as a precedent for others, in which case his policy to preserve the existence of the ghetto would collapse. He therefore decided to act against those suspected of having connections with the defecting group and which might organize others for departure. The action was directed against Glazman of the F.P.O. and Bernstein of "Yechiel's Struggle Group."

Glazman was taken into custody at his home on the Sabbath, June 25, 1943, and taken to police headquarters in the ghetto. The F.P.O. Command immediately learned of his arrest, and several dozen of its members were called up and posted in the courtyards of houses on Rudnicka Street near the place where Glazman was being held.

Glazman was removed from the police building at 4 P.M., handcuffed and escorted by policemen, and led in the direction of the ghetto gate. He was to be sent to the Rzesza labor camp. En route, the F.P.O. men attacked the police escort and freed their captive. Among those who freed Glazman were also policemen.

Gens decided not to employ force, and called in the members of the F.P.O. Command for a conference. He told them that in order to maintain his prestige and that of the ghetto police Glazman was obliged to proceed to Rzesza. He promised that Glazman would not be harmed and would be allowed to

20 Reznik's testimony 0–33/1238, p. 146; Korczak, *op. cit.,* p. 146;
    Testimony of A. Bogen, Moreshet Archives, A. 54.

return to the ghetto within a short time. Gens threatened that, if Glazman did not go, he and Dessler would no longer administer ghetto affairs. The F.P.O. command surrendered, and Glazman left that day for Rzesza.

The same evening Gens delivered a speech to an audience gathered in the theater and referred to the clash with the F.P.O. Gens said that he was ready to transfer the administration of ghetto affairs, but as long as he remained responsible, he would conduct matters to the best of his ability. Gens made it clear that his purpose was "to preserve the lives of the majority of the Jews in the ghetto, and not of a small bunch of heroes."

Another meeting between Gens and F.P.O. leaders took place during the night of June 26, several hours after Glazman left for Rzesza. The relations between the ghetto directorate and the underground organization, which had deteriorated during that period, was reviewed, but nothing tangible resulted.[21]

When Gens and Dessler learned that the assailants who had freed Glazman included policemen who were F.P.O. members and that there were many within the ghetto police who backed the organization, they decided to purge the police of these elements. On June 27, 1943, Dessler dismissed eleven officers and policemen who were F.P.O. adherents or supporters. A number were sent to hard labor on the airfield at Porobanek. Leo Bernstein, director of the Cultural Affairs' Department in the ghetto, was relieved of his post because of his active involvement in "Yechiel's Struggle Group" and his relations with Friedman's party, which had gone into the forests.

The clash that freed Glazman from police custody was the first instance of violence between the F.P.O. and the police. For the first time, ghetto inhabitants witnessed a group of organized young men using force against the police; it was in fact the first time that the existence of an underground organization inside the ghetto had been openly demonstrated. Public opinion in the ghetto, in this case, was behind the men who had freed

21 Kruk, *op. cit.*, pp. 582–583, 585; Lazar, *op. cit.*, pp. 108–110.

Glazman.[22] The F.P.O.'s concession in regard to his going to Rzesza was made to prevent a further deterioration in their relationship with the Judenrat.

Glazman remained at Rzesza for about two weeks, and returned to Vilna after the labor camp there was dissolved. While at Rzesza, Glazman met a young man named Hirsh Glik, who wrote the famed partisan song: *Zog nit kayn mol, az du geyst dem letstn veg* ("Let us not say that this is the last road"). Glick gave Glazman the lyrics, and he brought them back to the ghetto.

The Witenberg Affair
An open and large-scale clash between the F.P.O. and the ghetto administration, which was later called "the Witenberg Affair," took place in the middle of July 1943. Its outcome was decisive for the F.P.O.

The first chapter of the affair began in Vilna, outside the ghetto walls. The German Security Police had uncovered the City Underground Committee of the Communist Party through a Lithuanian agent, J. Vaitkevicius, who had infiltrated the organization. The secretary of the committee, J. Vitas, and committee member Kozlowski, were arrested at the end of June 1943. Vitas and Kozlowski were killed after interrogation and torture by the Security Police. During his interrogation Kozlowski revealed that he had maintained contact with a Jewish Communist named Itzhak Witenberg.[23]

Kittel of the Security Police arrived at the ghetto on July 8, and demanded that Witenberg be surrendered. The latter had gone into hiding when the Communists in the ghetto learned that members of the City Underground Committee had been arrested, and the ghetto police was unable to trace his where-

---

22 Balberyszski, *op. cit.,* pp. 432–433; Kruk, *op. cit.,* pp. 586–587; Dworzecki, *op. cit.,* p. 382.
23 *Gitlerovskaya okupatsiya,* pp. 213–214; Juchniewicz, *op. cit.,* pp. 61–62; S. Palewski, "Zikhroynes," *YIVO Bleter,* Vol. XXX, No. 2, 1947, p. 203; Rolnik, *op. cit.,* p. 89.

abouts. Kittel detained Auerbach, a former police officer, whom Kozlowski admitted knowing, and took him to the Security Police offices in the city, but he was released the next day and returned to the ghetto.[24]

The F.P.O. Command, with the exception of the Communist members, had no idea of the arrests among the Communists in the city, as the ghetto Communists had not reported to the F.P.O. leaders. The F.P.O.'s information came from Auerbach, after his release. Gens invited the F.P.O. leaders to his home on July 15, at 9 P.M. The invitation aroused no suspicion. On this subject Kovner relates: "... A messenger came and said something had happened and Gens wanted to meet with us ... These meetings had taken place more than once or twice ... The command was unaware that the present meeting was connected with Witenberg, otherwise Witenberg would not have gone ..."[25]

The meeting was delayed and began close to midnight. Witenberg, Chwojnik, Borowska, and Kovner attended. Glazman did not participate because of his strained relations with Gens.

When the F.P.O. Command had assembled in Gens' home, Dessler left in the direction of the ghetto gate. This aroused the suspicion of a policeman who belonged to the F.P.O., and he reported to Kaplinsky and a group of F.P.O. members gathered at F.P.O. headquarters. Kaplinsky, with a group of men, arrived at 7 Rudnicka street in time to see Dessler, accompanied by two Lithuanian policemen, entering No. 6 Rudnicka, where their F.P.O. colleagues were seated with Gens.

Dessler and the Lithuanian security men entered Gens' apartment, arrested Witenberg, and led him in the direction of the gate. The Kaplinsky group, which was lying in ambush, fell on the Lithuanians and the Jewish police and wrenched Witenberg from their clutches. Witenberg and his F.P.O. rescuers went into the carpentry workshop at No. 3 Oszmianska and barri-

---

24 Sutzkewer, *op. cit.*, p. 161; Korczak, *op. cit.*, p. 182. The reasons for the arrest and subsequent release of Auerbach have still not been clarified.
25 Collective Interview—FPO, pp. 29–32.

caded themselves there. Witenberg ordered a general call-up of the F.P.O.[26]

In the meantime, Gens informed the F.P.O. leaders gathered in his apartment that it was Kozlowski who had informed the Security Police about Witenberg. After a heated exchange, the F.P.O. leaders left and met with Witenberg at No. 3. Oszmianska. They decided that he should go into hiding and that the F.P.O. would resist his arrest, with force if necessary.

Disguised as a woman, Witenberg went into hiding in a small room at 15 Straszuna Street. By the morning hours, the F.P.O. had mobilized its members and concentrated them in two houses at Nos. 3 and 8 Oszmianska.

Gens urgently summoned a meeting of the police, the "brigadiers," and a group of the *shtarke*,[27] which was held at 3 A.M. in the courtyard of the Judenrat building. He informed them that the Security Police had arrested a Communist named Kozlowski, who had disclosed, under interrogation, that he maintained contacts with a ghetto Jew named Witenberg and that there was a clandestine printing press in the ghetto, which printed circulars for the Communist Party. Gens stated that the Security Police insisted on taking Witenberg into custody, that otherwise they would liquidate the entire ghetto.

The general feeling of those present at the meeting was that Witenberg should be surrendered. The group of *shtarke* left the meeting for the place where the F.P.O. men were assembled, attacked them with stones and sticks, and demanded Witenberg's surrender. The F.P.O. Command gave orders not to use arms, repelled the attackers, and prevented them from breaking into the houses. The *shtarke* were joined by crowds of workers rallied by the "brigadiers." [28]

---

26 Korczak, *op. cit.*, pp. 182–184; Rolnik, *op. cit.*, p. 89; "Der Wittenberg Tog," *op. cit.*, pp. 195–196.

27 The *Shtarke* ("Strong ones") were porters and some underworld figures upon whom Gens and Dessler relied during emergencies in the ghetto.

28 Korczak, *op. cit.*, pp. 186–187; "Der Witenberg tog," *op. cit.*, p.

The consensus among the ghetto residents was that a ghetto of 20,000 people should not be imperiled for the sake of one man whose activity was connected with Communists outside the ghetto, and that he had jeopardized the ghetto by these activities, which were incompatible with the situation of the Jews within it. Dessler, who had been at Security Police H.Q. that morning, telephoned the ghetto administration and reported on behalf of the Security Police that, unless Witenberg was surrendered alive, German forces would enter the ghetto. The report, which spread throughout the ghetto, was interpreted as a threat of liquidation, and there was a general demand to surrender him.

Gens knew that he had neither the force nor the necessary means to take Witenberg into custody and surrender him to the Security Police without the consent of the F.P.O., which was armed. He therefore decided to pursue another course of action.

A delegation from the ghetto directorate, including public figures, communicated the Security Police announcement to the F.P.O. command. The latter faced a difficult choice—civil strife, with the entire ghetto ranged against them, and arms obtained to do battle with the Germans being used against Jews, or the surrender of Witenberg. They came to the decision that Witenberg must surrender himself. A similar decision had been adopted earlier by the Communist group within the ghetto. Witenberg was told about this in his hideout, but he refused and left the room in which he was concealed to take cover in an attic. The F.P.O. leaders lost touch with him.[29]

197; Lazar, *op. cit.*, p. 125. Collective Interview — FPO, p. 33, Kovner states: "Before morning, we printed an appeal to the Jews of the ghetto calling for an uprising, as Witenberg's arrest was nothing but a pretext for the subsequent liquidation of the ghetto." This appeal, however, was not circulated in the ghetto, and Kovner explains this on the ground that "inside myself, I knew that for the first time I was not telling the truth..."

29 Korczak, *op. cit.*, p. 187; Dworzecki, *op. cit.*, pp. 387–388; Lazar, *op. cit.*, p. 126; "Der Witenberg tog," *op. cit.*, pp. 209–210, Genia Barkan, in whose room Witenberg hid, explains that the report of the decision by the Staff Command that he give himself up

The Jewish police and ghetto inhabitants began to search feverishly throughout the ghetto. In the afternoon Witenberg was caught by a number of ghetto residents, but he succeeded in escaping and reached 6 Oszmianska, which was guarded by F.P.O. men. The F.P.O. leaders went to him there, presented him with the facts and proposed that he surrender himself. He argued that the ghetto faced liquidation anyway and that the Germans were seeking, as a preliminary measure, to liquidate the underground leaders; his attitude was that armed resistance should begin immediately. The leaders, on the other hand, explained that the ghetto population did not believe this was the case, and if the F.P.O. started fighting, it would first have to use its weapons against the Jews of the ghetto who demanded his surrender. In reply, Witenberg offered to commit suicide and that his body be handed to the Germans, but the ghetto administration stated that the German Security Police wanted him alive.[30]

Kovner describes the meeting with Witenberg in the garret at No. 6 Oszmianska:

> We came to Witenberg after having contacts with Gens, to clarify possibilities other than surrender. We wanted to examine [with Gens] what would happen if we smuggled him out ... There was a suggestion that someone else would surrender himself instead of Witenberg ... It became evident from the replies that it must be Witenberg, that he was known to them, that someone would check there (at the Security Police) his identity ... Witenberg claimed to our surprise that it was not only he himself who was being spoken of. I then said to him, and Glazman supported me: "If that is so—give the order,

was brought by the courier, B. Krapnicki, who informed him of it, and she took Witenberg out of her room and hid him in an attic.

30 Lazar, *op. cit.*, pp. 126–127; "Der Witenberg tog," *op. cit.*, p. 211; Korczak, *op. cit.*, pp. 187–188.

everything is ready, everyone is at his post, there is a proclamation (for the ghetto population). Give the order and we'll fight." He did not give the order. Witenberg asked that Krizowsky go to Gens and find out if he could do anything for him after he was surrendered... He received a reply with a big promise... Then, some of his Communist comrades came to the attic. Sonia Madeysker, Berl Szeresznyevski came, and that was very significant. Witenberg asked everyone of us: "What do you say?" Everyone answered: "You must decide." Then he asked Sonia and Berl: "What should I do?" And they said: "You must go" (to the police). Witenberg asked if that was the opinion of the (Communist) comrades, and they told him, "Yes." I don't know when their colleagues met to discuss this...[31]

Witenberg decided to surrender himself to the Security Police after he heard about the feelings rife among the ghetto population and the attitude of the F.P.O. Command and his party comrades. The final decision was Witenberg's. He asked that a meeting be arranged for him, alone with Gens, before he was surrendered to the Germans. He parted from his associates and named Kovner commander of the organization. Kovner describes Witenberg's last moments with his comrades: "Then a moving and dramatic event occurred, that had nothing to do with the underground, between him and his girlfriend. She cried out that we were betraying him and sending him to his death... She also said some harsh things about all of us, that we were sacrificing him."[32]

F.P.O. members gathered in Oszmianska Street silently took leave of their commander, who went in the direction of the ghetto administration building to meet Gens. He was accompanied by Krizowski and the Jewish policemen. Dessler and

31 Collective Interview — FPO, pp. 33-34.
32 Collective Interview — FPO, pp. 35-36; Lazar, op. cit., pp. 127, 129.

Krizowski were present at the encounter between Witenberg and Gens. Krizowsky later related that Gens swore to Witenberg that he was not to blame for all that had happened, that he had been "informed" upon by people outside the ghetto. Gens promised that if Witenberg did not break during the first interrogation, he would activate his contacts to release him.[33]

Witenberg was taken out of the ghetto and handed over to the Security Police who were waiting outside. On the evening of July 16, 1943, he was taken to the Security Police headquarters. The next morning he was found dead in his cell. He had poisoned himself with cyanide of potassium, which he had brought from the ghetto. It had been given to him by Gens at their last meeting, before he was surrendered. The F.P.O. command had also wanted to equip him with cyanide of potassium in case he could not stand up to the interrogation, but had been unable to procure it before Witenberg went to Gens.[34] Witenberg apparently decided to take his life when he realized that he would not leave German hands alive, and out of fear that he would not be able to endure the interrogations and torture, would break and give the names of his underground comrades. He gave no information to the Security Police before he committed suicide, and none of his friends in the ghetto underground or outside was arrested in the wake of his detention.

The ghetto community as a whole supported Gens' actions in regard to Witenberg's surrender and opposed the F.P.O. They were not ready to endanger the existence of the ghetto and its entire population for the sake of one man, and they indeed believed that the Germans would have liquidated the ghetto, or a part of it, had Witenberg not been surrendered.[35] This inci-

---

33 Collective Interview — FPO, p. 36. Krizowsky was a Communist and close to Dessler, and this enabled him to act as messenger between the FPO and Gens and Dessler.

34 Rolnik, *op. cit.*, p. 91; Mushkat's testimony, p. 13; Collective Interview — FPO, p. 36.

35 Kalmanovitch, *op. cit.*, pp. 73-74, wrote: "... The Organization

dent occurred a few days after the liquidation of the labor camps at Bezdany and Kena, which resulted in the murder of many hundreds of youngsters of working age. This event was probably uppermost in their minds. At the same time, they lived in great hope of imminent rescue in view of the reports of tremendous victories by the Red Army on the Eastern Front and the German defeat in Italy. The attitude of the ghetto community, and its demand to surrender Witenberg, influenced the decision of the F.P.O. Command that he surrender.

The initial reaction of the F.P.O.—Witenberg's forcible release and a general call-up—had been spontaneous. This reaction stemmed from an instinctive assessment that Witenberg's arrest foreshadowed the dissolution of the F.P.O. and probably was a first stage in the final liquidation of the ghetto. However, during discussions with Gens later in the day, it became evident to them that the request to hand over Witenberg was directed at him personally, as a member of the "Communist City Underground Committee," without any connection to his role as F.P.O. commander. They also learned that the statement by Gens referring to a wave of arrests of Communists in the city and Kozlowski's report on Witenberg were correct and that their Communist associates in the F.P.O. had been aware of this and had kept it secret from them. There was no immediate danger to F.P.O.; they were not facing an alternative between armed resistance or liquidation of their group, but between surrendering Witenberg to the Security Police or fighting— which meant using their arms first against the Jews of the ghetto and then against the German armed forces. Had the situation reached this point, it would no doubt have precipi-

---

(FPO) was liable to plunge the entire community into disaster even before it began to operate. For the time being, the organization was active inside [the ghetto], disturbing the Commander's (Gens') activities ... The youths, who undertook to preserve the damaged honor of their people, disgraced the name of God ... Self-defense (FPO) has a false direction ... "; Rolnik, *op. cit.*, p. 91.

tated the destruction of the ghetto, including that of the F.P.O. itself.

Prior to the Witenberg Affair, the F.P.O. had decided in their explanations to the "Regulations of Combat," that they would initiate combat only if there were a threat to the whole ghetto and not in defense of individuals.[36] Therefore, waging armed combat over the Witenberg Affair was contrary to its ideology and policy. The F.P.O. Command took into account that Witenberg might break under interrogation and torture and reveal its existence, but believed in his ability to withstand it. Gens and Dessler harbored similar fears and knew the entire ghetto would be jeopardized should Witenberg break under questioning. This is how Gens' statement to Witenberg before he was transferred to the German police is to be understood; if he held out he would be released. The cyanide of potassium was the alternate way out.

Ghetto inhabitants were relieved when the affair ended with only one victim. Witenberg won appreciation and general sympathy in the ghetto for his gallant behavior and tragic death.

The First F.P.O. Group Goes Into the Forest
Following the Witenberg Affair, the F.P.O. was placed in a quandary. It had come to realize that the ghetto community was not on its side, and even took an inimical attitude in its confrontation with the Jewish ghetto administration. The question now arose whether, on the day the ghetto was doomed to be annihilated, the population would respond to the call to revolt, since without such a response the uprising would be devoid of all significance.

Consequently, the F.P.O. was faced with the choice of persisting with their decision to remain in the ghetto and fight, or abandon the idea and leave for the forests. Glazman supported leaving the ghetto for the forests. He and many others among the F.P.O. rank and file did not believe that the populace would

36 See Chapter 15.

respond to a call for uprising on the day the ghetto was liquidated.[37]

A day before the Witenberg Affair the two partisans Shutan and
Gertman returned once more to the ghetto. Both had met in the
forests with the partisan brigade commander Markov and reported to him about the F.P.O. and the two Communist organizations in Vilna—the Lithuanian and the Polish. Markov had
sent them back to Vilna to meet Witenberg and request that
he send armed men into the forests, and transmit a message
to the Communist groups outside the ghetto to establish a
regular communications' link with them. Shutan and Gertman
met the F.P.O. staff in the ghetto and transmitted Markov's
request.

It was Markov's second approach to the F.P.O. concerning
the dispatch of men to the forests, but this time the demand
was for armed males. It was a serious dilemma, as not all of
the F.P.O. members had weapons, and the ratio of women in
the ranks was a large one. On this subject Kovner says: "The
meaning of it was that we would have to take the few weapons
we had, take out the best of our men, and leave behind in the
ghetto a small group without arms, and without a solution."[38]

The decision that was accepted was a compromise between
the ideology which had until then ruled the F.P.O. and the
demand to opt for the forest. The command adopted the stance
that it was necessary to remain in the ghetto in order to rise
up when the ghetto would be liquidated, on the assumption
that the people would join in the uprising at that time. At the
same time, it was resolved to send into the forests a group of
people who were in personal danger, such as Glazman, Sze-
reznyevski and others. They should establish a partisan base
that would extend help to the ghetto fighters and serve as a
refuge after the uprising. It was decided to call those leaving
"the Leon Group," after Witenberg's code name.

37 Korczak, *op. cit.*, pp. 189–190; Treger's testimony, pp. 15–16. 18–19.
38 *Sefer Zikkaron Swenzian*, pp. 1670–1671; *Sefer ha-Partizanim*, p. 35;
Kovner's testimony, ICJ (12) 83, p. 33.

Abba Kovner published an "Order of the Day" with the departure of the "Leon Group":

As a result of the tragic situation in which we are placed, the organization's commander, Witenberg, gave himself up to the Gestapo with his, and our assent. It is likely that history will blame us for it. It is likely that no one will know exactly what our situation was, for a long time, and that our act stemmed from the great responsibility that we have towards the ghetto, the masses, with whom *we could not—dared not—fight.* The shock within our organization has been tremendous. Witenberg's image will be tied to the life of our people, and for us he will always serve as a noble symbol of heroism. The first company of fighters going out into the forests will be named after him. We shall honor the memory of our Commander in the fight with the enemy.

The organization will remain in the ghetto and, under conditions of indescribable difficulties, will persevere in its activity. No conditions of any kind can shatter our spirit; we will multiply our efforts.[39]

The "Leon Group," numbering twenty-one men, went out of the ghetto at dawn on July 24. They went as a wood-cutting group and were escorted by a uniformed policeman who was a F.P.O. member. The group hid their weapons in their clothing. Y. Gertman served as guide. Shutan writes that he met with Gens, with the consent of the F.P.O., and told him of the purpose of his errand, and that Gens knew and agreed to the departure of the "Leon Group" from the ghetto. As a result of

---

39 Korczak, *op. cit.,* pp. 190–192; Treger's testimony, YVA, 0–3/ 3670, p. 16; *Sefer ha-Partizanim,* p. 38. The departure of Szerezs-nyevski and his wife Rosa, both of whom were active communists, was apparently connected with the uncovering of the Underground Urban Committee of the Communist Party and Witenberg's discovery, and the fear that the Security Police was likely to uncover Szerezsnyevski, who was in contact with the Communists outside the ghetto. Collective Interview — FPO, p. 38.

this meeting, another took place between Gens, Kovner, Borowska, and Kaplan, during which Gens promised not to hinder the F.P.O. men from leaving for the forests.[40]

The "Leon Group" passed through the labor camp at Novo-Vileyka, where it was joined by fourteen young men and women employed there. There was some hesitation about accepting them because of the difficulties of the route, the dangers inherent in the movements of large groups, and because these newcomers were not armed. But the Novo-Vileyka party insisted, and the "Leon Group" leaders had to agree. Now totaling thirty-five, the party pushed on in the direction of the Narocz forests.

Near the bridge over the river Vileyka, about 20 miles north of Vilna, they fell into an ambush. In the ensuing battle, nine F.P.O. men in the "Leon Group" lost their lives, and the rest scattered into the adjacent forest. This engagement took place on the eve of the Sabbath, July 24, 1943. Several of the nine who fell were evidently wounded and were executed by the Security Police only after having been interrogated. Glazman gathered thirteen men of his group, which had dispersed, and continued the trek until they reached the Narocz forests, a distance of about 90 miles from Vilna, four days later.[41]

Collective Responsibility

German Security Police arrived in the ghetto on the Sabbath, July 25, at noon, and demanded the arrest of the family-members of the "Leon Group" and the "brigadiers" at the work-sites where the defectors had been employed prior to their flight. Identity discs had been found on the bodies of the nine men who perished or were caught, and the German Police was able to identify them and their families from the card-index of ghetto residents at the Jewish Police H.Q. These peo-

40 Lazar, *op. cit.*, pp. 130–131; *Sefer Zikkaron Swenzian*, p. 1672. Jacob Kaplan was elected to the FPO Staff Command as the Communist representative to succeed Witenberg.
41 Lazar, *op. cit.*, pp. 131–134; Korczak, *op. cit.*, p. 193.

ple, altogether thirty-two, were taken to Ponar and executed on July 27, 1943. The labor camp at Novo-Vileyka, through which the "Leon Group" had passed, was liquidated on July 28. The inmates were taken to Ponar and shot. This apparently was in retaliation for permitting the passage of the "Leon Group" and the fourteen workers who joined it.

A general meeting of "brigadiers" and ghetto inhabitants was held on the evening of July 27. Kittel announced the execution of the thirty-two men and threatened that the system of collective punishment would continue. A statement on collective responsibility was published in the ghetto: the family of everyone who escaped into the forest would be executed; if no family was found, those responsible would be the escapee's roommates; and if these, too, were not found, the responsibility would rest upon the tenants of his apartment, or, in their absence, the tenants of the entire building. Units of laborers employed outside the ghetto had been divided into tens. In the event that one of the ten did not return to the ghetto, the remaining nine would be executed.

Gens called a meeting of the "brigadiers" after the executions. He spoke out against those who organized the defection to the forests and stressed that they were placing the ghetto in jeopardy. He dwelt on the responsibility of the group foremen and stated that each unit of ten was to choose one person who would be responsible for it. He urged that every instance in which someone was suspected of planning to escape be reported.[42] Gens and the ghetto administration altered the policy of tacit consent to the flights into the forests and decided to pursue a tough line against them and also against the F.P.O.

The following article was published in *Geto Yedies* on August 1, 1943:

Tens of thousands of flowering lives have been torn from our midst ... In each one of these cases, we were con-

42 Rolnik, *op. cit.*, pp. 93–96; Kalmanovitch, *op. cit.*, pp. 77–78; Korczak, *op. cit.*, pp. 134–135.

fronted by outside forces over which we had no control ...
Such was not the case with the thirty-two souls uprooted
from our midst last Monday ... It is clear that the sacri-
fices were unnecessary, their deaths lie on the consciences
of those who, by their irresponsible behavior, made inno-
cent people pay with their lives for a crime not of their
making ... May the blood that has been spilled be a last
warning to us all, that we have but one way—the way
of labor ... May the spilled blood be a warning to the
"brigadiers," column-leaders, group leaders and every individual Jew, to immediately report cases of people missing from the work units, from home, from the room.
This is no time for sentiments and family feelings ...
Such a report is not talebearing, as many believe ... It is
the duty of every inhabitant of the ghetto.[43]

The order concerning collective responsibility rendered the
inhabitants of the ghetto guardians over one another. People
feared that they would pay with their lives for the flight of
a family member, a tenant, or a work-mate. The ghetto authorities redoubled their surveillance over the F.P.O. members, and
searches for arms were intensified. The disaster that had overcome the "Leon Group," the death-in-action of nine leading
members of the underground organization, and the statement
on collective responsibility brought about a temporary suspension of defections to the forest by F.P.O. members.

The ghetto authorities convened the F.P.O. Staff Command
and told them that the Security Police knew of the existence of
an armed organization in the ghetto. Gens demanded that all
arms be surrendered to him, promising to hide them until the
time came for their use. The F.P.O. agreed to negotiate on the
matter, hoping in this way to gain time, for they anticipated
that new developments would radically change the situation.[44]

43 Korczak, *op. cit.*, pp. 195–197; *Sefer Zikkaron Swenzian*, p. 1677.
44 Korczak, *op. cit.*, p. 189; Lazar, *op. cit.*, p. 138.

Chapter 23

THE DEPORTATIONS TO ESTONIA

Himmler's Order to Liquidate the Ghettos
The fate of the ghettos in *Ostland* was determined by an order
issued by Heinrich Himmler on June 21, 1943:

The *Reichsführer* SS   Field Command Headquarters,
RF/Bn. 38195143 g   June 21, 1943

1) To the Higher SS and Police Leader, *Ostland*
2) To the Chief of the SS Economic and Administrative
   Main Office.

———————

1. I order that all the Jews still remaining in the ghettos
   in the *Ostland* area have to be closed in concentration
   camps.
2. I prohibit to bring out the Jews from concentration
   camps for outside work, beginning August 1, 1943.
3. A concentration camp must be erected in the vicinity
   of Riga, to which must be transferred all the manufacturing of clothing and equipment that the Wehrmacht is doing now outside. All private firms must be
   eliminated. The workshops are to become plain con-
   centration-camp workshops. The Chief of the SS Economic and Administrative Main Office is requested to
   take care that this reorganization does not cause any
   reduction in the necessary production for the Wehrmacht.
4. The greatest possible part of the male Jews must be

brought to the concentration camp in the oilshale area for the mining of oilshale.

5. Non-essential inhabitants of the Jewish ghettos are to be evacuated to the East.

6. August 1, 1943, is set as the day for the reorganization of the concentration camp.

(Signed) H. Himmler

This decree was the continuation of Himmler's policy, adopted in the General Government of Poland in the fall of 1942 and the beginning of 1943, to increase the tempo of the exterminations and to concentrate the Jews apt for labor in concentration camps for exploitation by the SS, out of the bounds of the civil administration and army interference.[1]

A. Rosenberg held a conference in his office in Berlin on July 13, 1943, concerning the demands for manpower in the Eastern Territories and the dispatch of workers to Germany. The execution of Himmler's order regarding the liquidation of the Jewish ghettos was also discussed. Rosenberg's deputy, Mayer, emphasized that there were 72,000 Jews in the *Ostland* ghettos, of whom 22,000 were earmarked for "evacuation to the East" (i.e., extermination), and the remainder were to be confined in concentration camps.[2]

---

1 Nuremberg Document, NO-2403; G. Reitlinger, *The Final Solution*, London, 1968, pp. 300–301, views Himmler's order against the background of the revolt in the Warsaw ghetto. Within six months of that revolt, the large remaining ghettos were completely liquidated—Lwow, Sosnowiec, Bialystok, Minsk, Vilna, and Riga; *My Obvinyaem*, p. 74, n. 2, states that the destruction of the Riga ghetto was implemented as part of Himmler's order for the liquidation of ghettos in the East following the Warsaw ghetto uprising. See Mark Dworzecki, *Mahanot ha-Yehudim be-Estonia 1942–1944*, Jerusalem, 1970, pp. 64, 102.

2 Nuremberg Document, NO–1831. The 72,000 Jews in the *Ostland* to whom Mayer refers were concentrated as follows:

Vilna	20,000	Riga	15,000
Kovno	17,000	Minsk	8,500
Shavli	5,000	Lida	7,500

The German administration in the *Ostland* provided its own interpretation of Himmler's decree. Clause 3 stated that reorganization must not cause a reduction in the volume of products designated for the army. This created a loophole enabling the civilian administration to allow Jews to remain where their labor was required. A document issued by Dr. Karl Vialon, director of the Finance Department of the *Reichskommissariat Ostland*, on July 31, 1943, stated:

> ... Workshops which cannot continue their production in large concentration camps shall be centralized in small camps. Thus, for example, a small section of the former Riga ghetto shall be turned into a concentration camp ... The *Generalkommissar* of Riga shall assume charge of the camp at my request. Naturally, the security-police functions will be the responsibility of the police. Proceeds will accrue to our budget, as has been the case hitherto, but there is still no final agreement in the matter ...[3]

The civil administration in the *Ostland* had no desire to yield all the Jewish manpower for confinement in large concentration camps, which were controlled by the *Wirtschaftsverwaltungshauptamt* (WVHA, SS Economic and Administrative Main Office), and it was therefore decided to establish small branch-camps, some of which would remain in the same area in which the ghettos had been located and would continue to be affected to the civil administration. This decision countermanded Himmler's order both in context and in spirit. The attitude adopted by the civil administration was influenced by financial considerations. The ghettos and their Jewish labor were a source of substantial income for the civil authorities, and they were not ready to dispense with it. Their budget in the Eastern regions depended upon local revenues, and any decline in these would, of course, impinge upon the budget in its totality. The argument between the civil administration and Security Police offi-

3 YVA, 0–4/53–2, Document No. 810.

cials on the income derived from Jewish labor lasted until the end of German administration in the *Ostland*.[4]

First Transport to Estonia and Mass Resistance — August 6, 1943

On August 1, 1943, about 3,000 Jewish workers were dismissed from 100 work-sites outside the ghetto. On the other hand, the number of men employed by the Todt organization on the railroad and at the Porobanek airfield was increased. A rumor circulated in the ghetto on August 5 that thousands of workers and their families were to be sent to work in Riga. Many people did not leave the ghetto for work that morning because they feared being caught and sent to Riga. Gens addressed a crowd that had congregated outside the Judenrat offices in the evening and urged the people to go to work, claiming there was no danger for the ghetto. He did not deny the rumors concerning the demand that thousands of workers be sent to Riga.

During that night, hundreds of people who had not gone to work were arrested and taken to the ghetto prison. Many of the relatives of those in custody gathered outside the prison and threatened to break in and release the detained men. To avoid a violent clash, they were all freed, but were warned that they must report to work.[5]

The following morning, July 6, 1943, thousands of men and women left the ghetto for their places of employment. When

4 YVA, 0–/53–2, Document No. 826; Nuremberg Document, NO–2074, letter from the Ministry for the Eastern Territories to the SS Economic and Administrative Main Office, dated May 10, 1944. The letter notes that the conversion of the ghettos into concentration camps under SS control created a budgetary deficit in the civilian administration. It requested a transmission of income from Jewish laborers in the concentration camps to the civilian administration and states the necessity for a reexamination of those who benefit from the income of Jewish labor.

5 Kalmanovitch, *op. cit.*, pp. 78–80; Dworzecki, *op. cit.*, pp. 361-362.

the Jewish workers reached Porobanek airfield, they were suddenly surrounded by Estonian troops. The thousand workers in this unit began to jump over the barbed-wire fences and attack the troops. About twenty were killed on the spot. Many were wounded. And while some succeeded in fleeing, most were apprehended and taken to the railroad station, where they were loaded onto freight cars.

About 100 workers at the Borbiszki armaments base were seized by German soldiers while on their way to work. Some of them succeeded in escaping. There were also escape attempts from the railroad station to which the people were taken. Many were killed and wounded in these clashes and in the mass-escape attempts. Approximately, 1,000 people were collected and sent to Estonia.

Gens arrived at the station before the train left, brought food and water, and assured the captive laborers that they were being taken to Estonia. Since the Kovno train massacre, the Jews of Vilna had ceased believing in German announcements that people were being transported to work. They were convinced they were being sent to their death, and, therefore, they resisted and tried to escape. Most of those who escaped reached the vicinity of the ghetto, but German and Estonian patrols were waiting for them at the gate, and some were caught.[6]

News of the workers' abduction became known in the ghetto during the morning, when the first of the fugitives returned. The ghetto turned into a seething cauldron. The general feeling was that the end had come. Gens returned to the ghetto around noon and announced that the people had been taken to Estonia. He told the assembled crowds that the Germans had requested him to provide people for Estonia and Riga, but that he had rejected their demand, and in retaliation the workers outside the ghetto had been seized. He said that the "brigadiers" had

---

6 Kalmanovitch, *op. cit.*, pp. 80–81, 83; Korczak, *op. cit.*, p. 202; Dworzecki, *Mahanot be-Estonia, op. cit.*, pp. 73–84; Rolnik, *op. cit.*, p. 101.

also gone with the transport and would return in a few days
with a report on the situation of the deportees.

The next day Gens was asked by the German authorities to
send substitute workers to the work-sites where the deportees
had been employed, but people were afraid to leave the ghetto,
and Gens was forced to send 250 Judenrat employees and
policemen. Neuegebauer and a Security Police party came to
the ghetto during the evening of August 9 and spoke to the
"brigadiers." He promised that their colleagues, the foremen
who had been sent to Estonia, would return in a few days and
bring letters from the workers there. In the meantime, he urged,
the ghetto workers should go to the city work-sites, pointing out
that war needs necessitated the existence of a Jewish labor force
and promising there would be no further seizures. His statement
somewhat calmed the people, and the number of those who
left the ghetto for work increased.[7]

The day after Neuegebauer's visit to the ghetto, Gens issued
the following order to the ghetto inhabitants:

Order No. 128   August 10, 1943
From the Chief of the Ghetto and the Police
    Relying on the assurances of the Chief of the German
Security Police and SS of yesterday, I hereby announce:
    1. The Jews who fled from the transport to Estonia
will not be punished;
    2. This method of sending people from work-sites will
not be repeated.
    Upon the assumption that there must be no unemployed
persons in the ghetto, I demand that all of you who are
not working report for employment at once.
    A census of the unemployed, men and women, aged 16
to 60, will be held today, Tuesday, August 10, 1943, from
11 A.M. to 8 P.M. without intermission.
    Those who fail to comply with this order concerning

---

7 Balberyszski, *op. cit.*, pp. 466–468; Kalmanovitch, *op. cit.*, pp.
81–83.

the census and labor obligations will be punished in the most severe manner by the German administration.

(signed) Chief of the Ghetto[8]

The census was necessary in order to obtain an estimate of the number of unemployed and to respond to the demand by the German administration for workers to replace those deported to Estonia.

"Brigadier" Heymann, who had accompanied the workers to Estonia, returned to the ghetto on August 11, and reported that they were in a labor camp at Vaivara. He brought letters in which most of the men requested that their relatives send warm clothing and food. Several letters hinted that the labor camps were close to the front-lines, which aroused hopes of imminent liberation or the possibility of escaping and crossing through the lines. Neuegebauer's speech, the "brigadiers" who returned with the letters and Gens' appeal to the ghetto population were all meant to persuade the ghetto inmates that the others had been sent to work and not to be liquidated. This credibility was necessary to facilitate additional human consignments to Estonia. The ghetto inhabitants were convinced that their relatives and friends had indeed been sent to the labor camps and not to their deaths.

In its August 6 *Aktion*, the German administration succeeded once again in surprising the Jews, but this success was only partial. The number of those seized and sent to Estonia was much smaller than had been anticipated. Jewish resistance and mass flight had somewhat disturbed the German plans.

The Second Transport to Estonia; Reactions in the Ghetto
The German administration demanded another 4–5,000 people for work in Estonia, and Gens was promised that there would be no seizures at work-sites if he himself were to provide the requisite number. He began the registration of people for this purpose and gave priority to members of the families who had

8 Moreshet Archives D.1.344, original document.

been taken away on August 6. Some of these relatives volun-
teered to go in order to join those already in Estonia. People
who had come from the ghettos in the Vilna province at the
beginning of 1943 and the unemployed were also included. The
ghetto police, which was in charge of the preparations, told
people who had been listed that if they did not report for departure, they would be taken forcibly. When people went into
hiding their neighbors were seized in their stead, until they revealed the hiding-places.

The assembly was carried out on August 19–23, and the
second consignment, which left for Estonia on the 24th, consisted of 1,400–1,500 men, women, and children, instead of the
4–5,000 whom the Germans had requested.

Unrest and fear prevailed among the ghetto community, which
was being depleted of its labor force, and there was growing
anxiety over what the future might bring. The ghetto administration expanded the workshops, and additional workers were
absorbed into the tailoring and knitting establishments, which
were engaged on army-contract orders and worked in three
shifts. Gens addressed the ghetto inhabitants on August 29,
stating that the deportations to Estonia had ceased, and if further manpower were needed, persons non-essential to the ghetto
would be sent. He called for patience and declared that an end
to the suffering was approaching. Gens wanted to gain time by
cooperating in the deportations to Estonia—furnishing as
small a number as possible of people for deportation and retaining most of the residents in the ghetto, thus continuing his
past policy.

Meanwhile, news was heard of German defeats on various
fronts, and hopes rose among the ghetto community that the
collapse of Nazi Germany was close at hand. The general feeling was that the liberation was near.[9]

9 Dworzecki, *Mahanot be-Estonia, op. cit.,* pp. 75–76, 136 and 92n;
Balberyszski, *op. cit.,* p. 470; Kalmanovitch, *op. cit.,* pp. 84–87;
Rolnik, *op. cit.,* pp. 101–103.

The F.P.O. did not regard the two transports to Estonia in August as the liquidation of the ghetto and apparently accepted the assessment made by Gens in this respect. Consequently, it did not react by calling for an uprising or *en masse* withdrawal to the forests. But the F.P.O. did help groups from the smaller ghettos escape. These were likely to be marked for deportation to Estonia and therefore singled out. Five groups with 150–200 people left for the Narocz forests during August 1943; some with F.P.O. help, others on their own. Three other groups, with a few dozen persons, left for the forests in August on the initiative of "Yechiel's Struggle Group."[10]

The order concerning collective responsibility had lost much of its significance after the deportations, the dismissals from work-sites outside the ghetto, and the disturbances and changes in the addresses of ghetto residents. The "tens" at work-sites, which had been an obstacle, were no longer effective, and the imposition of collective responsibility on families had little validity, since in the altered conditions it was difficult to locate them. Nonetheless, most of those who left the ghetto were those originating from the provincial ghettos, because of the ideological stand taken by the F.P.O. against leaving for the forests.

The Communist underground in Vilna resumed its operations, and the City Underground Committee was reorganized on August 10, 1943. Sonia Madeysker represented the ghetto Communists on the new underground committee. The F.P.O. renewed its contact with the Communist underground, after a lapse of several weeks, following the discovery of the former city underground committee by the Security Police and the death of Vitas.

"Albina" (Gessia Glezer), a Jewess and longtime Communist, who had been sent from Moscow to Lithuania in June 1943, arrived in Vilna to aid in the reorganization of the Communist underground. She entered the ghetto and conferred with the F.P.O. Staff Command, presenting the Communist point of view— that it was necessary to leave the ghetto for the forests and

10 Korczak, *op. cit.*, pp. 198–199.

join the partisan fighters. She negated the existence of a separate Jewish underground in the ghetto and claimed it was necessary to organize the underground on an urban, and not an ethnic, basis. The F.P.O. command did not acquiesce and continued to support the plan for an uprising in the ghetto.[11]

The Aktion *of September 1–4; The F.P.O. Clash with the German Forces*

At 5 A.M. on Wednesday, September 1, 1943, German and Estonian police forces surrounded the ghetto, and workers employed outside were not permitted to leave. Estonian soldiers entered the ghetto and began to seize inmates. The German administration demanded that the Chief of the Ghetto dispatch 3,000 males and 2,000 females to Estonia.

The report that the ghetto had been closed and people kidnapped spread rapidly through the streets. People began to head for the *malines.*

The F.P.O. command, though at first taken aback by the German *Aktion,* quickly organized and issued a general call-up order to all its men. The couriers spread the password *Liza ruf* ("Liza calls") through the ghetto. The first battalion gathered at 6 Straszuna and the second at 6 Szpitalna, near the organization's armory. Selected groups went to bring the arms from the various caches to central points. The second battalion, consisting of about 100 combatants, was suddenly surrounded by Germans and Estonians, before it was able to obtain its weapons. The Commander, G. Zipelevits, gave the order to scatter, and some twenty-five men succeeded in crossing through and reaching the first battalion. But the majority of the second battalion was seized and removed from the ghetto.

The capture of the second battalion constituted a most serious blow to the F.P.O. Its encirclement by the Germans had been the result of denunciation. The German security forces had

---

11 *Gitlerovskaya okupatsiya,* pp. 223–224, 244; Prszewalska's testimony, p. 25; Brown-Levin, *op. cit.,* p. 125.

been brought to the assembly place by "Brigadier" Heymann and a Jewish policeman.[12] The purpose was apparently to have the fighters overcome before they were able to arm themselves, and thus to forestall a violent clash, and at the same time to fill the quota of men needed for the shipment to Estonia with F.P.O. members.

The F.P.O. Command decided to muster its entire remaining strength in Straszuna Street and constitute a defense area there. Men from "Yechiel's Struggle Group" joined the F.P.O. in accordance with their agreement, and they operated as a joint force. The F.P.O. plan of defense was to converge at the main bastion at 6 Straszuna, which was on the boundary of the ghetto. A small force took over the houses at 7 and 8 Straszuna and covered the approaches to the main position at No. 6, thus establishing a closed, defended area. A group of F.P.O. combatants brought the weapons from the 2nd Battalion armory to the main stronghold at 6 Straszuna. By 9.00 A.M. the F.P.O. was prepared to fight. Y. Scheinbaum was appointed to command the force at the forward position at 12 Straszuna, which consisted of several scores of fighters.[12]

At noon the F.P.O. issued a manifesto to all inhabitants calling for armed resistance to deportation.

> Jews! Defend yourselves with arms! The German and Lithuanian hangmen have arrived at the gates of the ghetto. They have come to murder us! Within a short while, they will lead us group after group through the gate. Thus they led out hundreds on the Day of Atonement! Thus they led us out on the night of the White, the Yellow and the Pink Passes. Thus they led our brethren and sisters, our mothers and fathers, our children. Thus were

12 See the diary of Hermann Kruk in Estonia (testimony of Moshe Vein) included in Korczak, 3rd edition, p. 376; Auerbach's testimony, p. 10; Auerbach was in the 2nd Battalion and among those who succeeded in escaping when they were surrounded by the Germans; Collective Interview — FPO, pp. 44–45.

tens of thousands taken out to their death! But we shall not go! We shall not stretch our necks like sheep for the slaughter! Jews! Defend yourselves with arms! Do not believe the reassuring prevarications of the murderers. Do not believe the statements of the traitors. Anyone who goes out of the ghetto gate has only one route—to Ponar. And Ponar means death! Jews! We have nothing to lose, death will snatch us up in any event. And who still believes he will remain alive when the assassin is obliterating us with systematic consistency? The hand of the hangman will fall upon every person. Flight and cowardice will not save life! Only armed resistance can save our lives and honor. Brothers! Better to fall in battle in the ghetto than to be led as sheep to Ponar. And know ye: There is an organized Jewish force within the walls of the ghetto that will rise up with arms. Lend a hand to the revolt! Do not cower in hideouts and *malines*. Your end will be to die as rats in the grip of the murderers.

Jewish masses! Go out into the street! Whoever has no weapons, take up a hatchet; and whoever has no hatchet, take steel and cudgel and stick! For our fathers. For our murdered children! To revenge Ponar, hit the murderers! In every street, in every courtyard, in every room. Inside the ghetto and outside it. Hit at the dogs! Jews! We have nothing to lose! We shall save our lives only if we wipe out our murderers. Long live freedom! Long live armed defense, death to the murderers!

September 1, 1943, Vilna Ghetto

The Command of the F.P.O.

With the exception of a party of youngsters who joined the F.P.O. positions in Straszuna Street, the inhabitants did not respond to the call for an uprising. The F.P.O. maintained its defensive positions on Straszuna Street.[13]

13 Korczak, *op. cit.*, pp. 200, 208–209, 293, 295; Lazar, *op. cit.*, pp.

The German and Estonian soldiers and policemen, accompanied by Jewish police, continued the searches and arrests of males. Gens ordered the detention of males up to the age of twenty, from forty years upward, and those who had no small children. At one stage of the searches and arrests, he urged the Security Police officers to withdraw their forces from the ghetto and promised that the Jewish police would supply the requisite number of people. Gens knew of the F.P.O. deployment on Straszuna Street and was apprehensive lest the German and Estonian presence in the ghetto lead to a bloody clash with the F.P.O., a contingency which in his view could plunge the entire ghetto into disaster. He also wanted to preserve the labor force and essential craftsmen in the ghetto, which would be possible only if the ghetto police made the arrests. The Security Police agreed to his pleas to halt the searches and seizures and withdraw from the ghetto.[14]

By late afternoon, however, only some 600 males had been taken. The Germans and Estonians were again brought into the ghetto toward evening, in order to extend the scope of the hunt. A group of Germans reached 15 Straszuna. The occupants were ordered by loudspeaker to come out of the *malines*, and, when they did not respond, the Germans blew up the building. The F.P.O. fighters under the command of Scheinbaum, who were in the forward position at 12 Straszuna, opened fire on the Germans, who returned the fire with automatic weapons. Scheinbaum was killed instantly, and the other combatants retreated to the main post at 6 Straszuna. The Germans blew up the house at No. 12 and left the ghetto at nightfall. On that day the Germans blew up houses in Straszuna and Disna streets. Many dozens of people who were inside the *malines* met their end under the rubble.[15] The Germans with-

160–161; Collective Interview — FPO, p. 41; Treger's testimony, p. 20.

14 Korczak, *op. cit.,* pp. 208, 210, 212, excerpt from *Geto Yedies;* Rolnik, *op. cit.,* p. 164; Auerbach, p. 11.

15 Rolnik, *op. cit.,* pp. 105–106; Auerbach's testimony, pp. 11–13; Collective Interview — FPO, p. 43.

drew out of fear of being trapped in the ghetto alleyways at night. A total of 1,300–1,500 males were taken on September 1, for deportation to Estonia.

The clash between the underground and German security units at 12 Straszuna did not develop into a full-scale battle due to the late hour at which the incident flared up and the withdrawal of the German forces toward nightfall. Gens feared that, if the German security forces continued their searches the next day, they might reach Straszuna Street again, clash with the underground squads, and bring about open battle in the ghetto—an eventuality he wished to avoid.

On Thursday evening, September 1, Gens reached an agreement with the Security Police that the Jewish police would provide the required quota without the participation and presence of German forces in the ghetto. *Geto Yedies,* which reported the events of September 1–5, commented: "... To our joy the head of the ghetto, Gens, and the chief of police, Dessler, succeeded in persuading the representatives of the German administration to withdraw their troops from the ghetto and to assign the conscription of labor forces for Estonia to the Jewish police."[16]

The task that Gens took upon himself—the concentration of thousands of people for deportation to Estonia—was a heavy one. Gens established an auxiliary Jewish police force in order to assist the regular Jewish police in snaring people for deportation and as a reserve unit capable of action in the event of a clash with the F.P.O., without the need to call in the German security troops. The volunteers wore armbands inscribed *Hilfspolizei* ("Auxiliary Police") and were provided with special papers. They began service on September 2, 1943.[17]

On Thursday and Friday, September 2 and 3, the ghetto police and the auxiliaries continued to round up men for de-

---

16 Korczak, *op. cit.,* p. 212; Balberyszski, *op. cit.,* p. 470.
17 Rolnik, *op. cit.,* p. 107; Lazar, *op. cit.,* p. 168.

portation. A crowded meeting was held in the Judenrat courtyard on Friday morning, and Gens appealed to the public to
volunteer for Estonia, warning that those who hid would be
discovered by the police. Hundreds of males answered the call,
but a large number again went into the *malines*. The recruitment of women for Estonia began on Sabbath morning, September 4. Gens convened a meeting of women in the Judenrat
courtyard and called upon those women whose husbands had
been sent to Estonia to volunteer for the journey. Most of the
women whose husbands had been deported to Estonia came
of their own free will. Altogether, 2,200 women left for Estonia.[18]

Nonetheless, several hundred males were still required to
complete the quota. During the afternoon of September 4,
Gens convened the ghetto police and auxiliaries in the Judenrat courtyard. The auxiliary police, by now numbering hundreds
of men, was brought to the ghetto gate and handed over to
the Lithuanian police, in order to complete the quota. Gens
was aided in this action by a group of the *Shtarke* who were
part of the auxiliary police but remained in the ghetto.[19]

At nightfall on September 1, the F.P.O. Command was faced
with the need to decide upon its future course of action. The
ghetto had not risen to the call for insurrection. During the
discussion that night, Kovner presented two options—to
break out through the ghetto walls and fight to reach the
forest, for which the prospects were vague, or, to bide their
time in the ghetto until the completion of the present operation, and then to leave in an organized manner, for which
there were good prospects of success.

The Staff Command chose the second alternative. They pro-

18 Korczak, *op. cit.*, pp. 212–213; Auerbach's testimony, p. 14, writes
    that he and twenty-five of his comrades voluntarily presented
    themselves for transport to Estonia; Testimony of S. Harten,
    YVA, 0-3/2262, p. 11, describing her voluntary departure for
    Estonia to be with her husband.
19 Lazar, *op. cit.*, p. 169; Balberyszski, *op. cit.*, p. 473.

ceeded on the assumption that they could maintain a foothold in the ghetto until the end of the *Aktion*.[20]

The F.P.O. combatants spent September 3 and 4 concentrated at 6 Straszuna Street on the alert, their strength unimpaired. The ghetto police did not enter this area. Close contact was maintained between Gens and the F.P.O. leaders throughout the days of the *Aktion*, and he sent them information through messengers that the ghetto was not about to be liquidated and that the operation was a limited one designed to send labor to Estonia. By these reports, Gens wanted to forestall any initiative by the F.P.O., which could only bring about a violent collision with the Germans.[21] Lazar writes that, by agreement with the ghetto administration, the F.P.O. undertook not to launch any action on its own and that the former agreed to try to deter the German forces from reaching the F.P.O. positions in order to avoid large-scale armed conflict within the ghetto.[22]

Gens succeeded in obviating a battle inside the ghetto by agreeing to supply the necessary labor force to be sent to Estonia; and, as a result, the Germans did not enter the ghetto until the close of the operation.

Why the Uprising Did Not Take Place
It was the first time since the beginning of November 1941 that the ghetto in Vilna had been cordoned off and surrounded by

---

20 Dworzecki, *op. cit.*, pp. 412–413; Korczak, *op. cit.*, p. 213.

21 Lazar, *op. cit.*, pp. 172–174, writes that some of the FPO members who brought their families and other Jews from the ghetto also found refuge in this building. Gens learned of this and insisted that the FPO staff, with whom he communicated through Krizowski, who served as courier between him and the FPO, remove all persons not belonging to the FPO from the premises at 6 Straszuna. The FPO did not comply, and Gens was compelled to yield; Collective Interview — FPO, p. 46.

22 Lazar, *op. cit.*, pp. 161, 166–167; Reznik's testimony, 0-33/1238, pp. 27–28, denies the existence of an agreement between the FPO and Gens.

troops, and thousands of people had been snatched from their houses and the streets and deported. The F.P.O. regarded the situation on the morning of September 1 as sufficient cause for uprising, and published a manifesto in which it called the people to rise immediately. There was no response. The public believed Gens that those being taken were to be sent to Estonia and not—as stated in the F.P.O. call—that "anyone going out of the ghetto gate has only one route, to Ponar."

It was not the alternative of death at Ponar or rebellion and death in a fighting ghetto that the ghetto inhabitants faced; rather, their option was being sent to a labor camp, where the chance of life existed, or insurrection and certain death in the ghetto. The F.P.O. could have tried to begin a revolt, to face the inhabitants with the *fait accompli* of a ghetto battle in the hope that they would join the insurrection, but it did not pursue this course for moral and practical reasons. Writing of the moral reasons, Kovner says:

> As regards revolt, we cogitated more than anything else over the moral aspect. Were we entitled to do this, and when? Were we entitled to offer people up in flames? Most of them were unarmed—what would happen to all of them? And if in the meantime it turned out that this was not liquidation? We were terribly perplexed as to what right we had to determine their fate...[23]

Additional factors attenuated the ability of the F.P.O. to begin the rebellion. The capture of the 2nd Battalion, which reduced its fighting cadres, severely impaired its strength and fighting competence and also the morale of the men. The German *Aktion* on September 1 came as a surprise. The F.P.O. was unprepared for a move that discombobulated its plans and compelled it to take a defensive position in a narrow section inside the ghetto. Korczak writes of how things appeared to the F.P.O. on September 1.

23 Kovner's testimony, ICJ (12)83, pp. 11–13; Reznik's testimony, 0–33/419, p. 28.

All its plans, all its expectations, all its prayers went up in smoke... There is no longer any hope that the battle, which a handful of fighters, limited in number, would initiate, could turn into a mass defense...The rebellion, should it break out, would be nothing but an act of individuals alone, of no wide-national value, and would not open the door to mass rescue...[24]

Hence, the events on September 1 caused a radical change in the plans of the F.P.O.—renunciation of the idea of a ghetto revolt and, in its place, the decision to leave for the forests and engage in partisan warfare.

An entirely different situation might have arisen had the German security troops reached Straszuna Street and met the F.P.O. there, thus precipitating large-scale combat. The Germans knew of the presence of armed groups in the ghetto as a result of the Witenberg case, the "Leon Group," and arms' acquisitions by ghetto Jews. The armed encounter at 12 Straszuna also lent authenticity to the reports concerning armed ghetto bands.

But the Vilna Security Police appears to have wanted to avoid a far-ranging violent encounter inside the ghetto. It may have feared being saddled with the responsibility for having failed to prevent the organization of an armed force in the ghetto under its control. The Warsaw Ghetto revolt and the blame laid on local SS officials was undoubtedly well known to their Vilna counterparts.[25] These considerations evidently moti-

24 Sefer ha-Partizanim, pp. 44–45, 47; Treger's testimony, p. 43, on the capture of the 2nd Battalion: "...We felt as though we had been beaten. At first we were filled with the desire to enter into battle, and prepared for it. We were already tensed up for it, and it seemed that our wings had been clipped..."

25 The Chief of the SS and Police for the Warsaw district, Von Zammern-Franknag, was ousted from his post in the first days of the Warsaw uprising, tried by court martial, and found guilty of having abetted the Jews in the organization of the uprising in the Warsaw ghetto, and letting them fortify strong points and collect arms. "...The court regarded this as criminal negligence,

vated the Security Police in agreeing to Gens' suggestion that he supply the required labor quota and that they withdraw from the ghetto. Thus, the measures taken by Gens during September 1–4 prevented a bloody clash between the Germans and the F.P.O.

inactivity, and contempt for German authority..." See J. Kermish, *Mered Getto Varshah be-Einei ha-Oyev*, Jerusalem, 1959, p. 99.

Chapter 24

THE LIQUIDATION OF THE VILNA GHETTO

Creation of Labor Camps

Approximately 11–12,000 inhabitants remained inside the ghetto after the three transports to Estonia between August 6 and September 5, 1943. Some 7,130 persons had been deported.[1]

The German authorities in Vilna continued to implement the instructions found in Himmler's decree of June 21, 1943. The ghetto administration received the new orders concerning the cancellation of employment outside the ghetto. On September 5, Gens issued the following announcement:

> The transport of people for work in Estonia has been completed. Tranquil life and normal work will be instituted in the ghetto along these lines:
>
> (a) Outside employment has been cancelled ... henceforth Jews will work only in the ghetto workshops;
>
> (b) All persons of physical ability will be incorporated into the labor cycle;
>
> (c) I call upon all ghetto inhabitants to return quietly to their homes, maintain order and carry out all my instructions.

---

1 An excerpt from *Geto Yedies* (Korczak, *op. cit.*, p. 213) shows that 10,200 Jews remained there, evidently people who had registered in the census taken on September 6. One to two thousand people had not registered for fear of being sent to Estonia. This figure does not include the people at "Kailis."

Warning! Those guilty of stealing property will be punished by death.[2]

A severe shortage of food was the immediate result of the elimination of employment outside the ghetto and the prohibition on leaving. Prices soared, and people were left jobless.

The ghetto administration began to reorganize life in the depleted ghetto. Gens published a notice to the public on September 6 about taking a population census in order to ascertain how many remained in the ghetto. He wanted to expand the workshops—which had become the sole creative factor following the dismissal of those employed outside the ghetto—by bringing in another 2,000 people to replace those sent to Estonia.

Ghetto inhabitants were warned not to take up residence in the homes vacated after the deportations to Estonia. The ghetto authorities further announced an additional food distribution in the public canteens in view of the shortages and warned against speculation.[3]

A group of 350 Jewish workers in the HKP workshops, and their families, numbering together some 800 persons, were transferred to two building blocks at 37 Suboch Street. Their removal from the ghetto took two weeks (until September 18). Some of the "Kailis" workers who had resided until then in the ghetto were moved into the camp attached to the factory, and the total there rose to 1,250 persons. The military-hospital employees, some seventy persons with their families, went to live in a camp in Antokol (Antakalnio) Street, near the hospital. Artisans and service hands employed by the Security Police, about sixty persons with their relatives, were removed from the ghetto in the last days of August and housed in a small prison

---

2 Korczak, *op. cit.*, p. 213; the third paragraph was apparently directed against the FPO members who remained concentrated at 6 Straszuna.
3 Korczak, *op. cit.*, pp. 214–215; YVA, JM/1195, Document No. 41.

building in Rossa (Rasu) Street.[4] This Jewish labor camp, under Security Police auspices, was the only one in Vilna not employed by the German Army, and its retention in Vilna was contrary to the spirit of Himmler's decree of June 21, 1943.

The transfer of workers and their families to four camps outside the ghetto—HKP, "Kailis," the military hospital, and Security Police—was completed in mid-September. Over 9,000 Jews remained in the enclosed ghetto.

The Underground Groups Leave for the Forests

A general exodus of underground members from the ghetto to the forests began after the September 1–4 *Aktion*. Three Jewish partisans who had come on a mission for the guerrilla commanders Markov and "Yurgis" (S. Zimanas) arrived at the Vilna ghetto on September 7. The trio was led by A. Bogen, who had suggested to Markov that he go to Vilna to bring back a group of ghetto youths. Markov agreed but stressed that they would have to come with their own weapons and include physicians, who were especially needed by the partisans. "Yurgis," who was in charge of the Communist underground in Vilna, sent a letter to the Jewish Communist underground in the ghetto through Bogen, and a second note to the underground in the city.

Bogen and his colleagues conferred with the F.P.O. Staff Command, transmitted Markov's request and also Glazman's demand to the F.P.O. to leave for the forests quickly—a step which, in his opinion, would enable the creation of a Jewish combat unit there. It was agreed that the three partisan emissaries should serve as guides for the groups going out. Bogen met with members of the City Communist Committee outside the ghetto and relayed the letter from "Yurgis." [5]

The departure from the ghetto was difficult because there were no longer groups of workers who left the ghetto. Exit was

4 Balberyszski, *op. cit.*, pp. 476–477; Katz's testimony, pp. 19–20; Kaczerginski, *Hurbn Vilne, op. cit.*, p. 100, evidence of Dr. Boraks.
5 Bogen's testimony, pp. 2–3, 5–9; Lazar, *op. cit.*, p. 177.

permitted only on those days when the *Chevra Kadisha* morticians removed the dead for interment in the cemetery outside the walls. A F.P.O. member therefore became assistant grave digger, and arms were smuggled out in coffins to the cemetery, where they were buried. The F.P.O. men departed stealthily from the ghetto during the night, crossed the city to the cemetery, dug up their weapons, and proceeded in the direction of the Narocz forests. They made their exit through a side-gate in Jatkowa Street. Although Gens knew about the defections, he made no attempt to prevent them.

Five F.P.O. combat groups, totaling about 150 men, departed for the Narocz woods between September 8 and 13. Each party consisted of about thirty men.[6] Between seventy and ninety F.P.O. fighters still remained in the ghetto, including the majority of the Staff Command.

During the course of preparations for this last group to leave, the F.P.O. Staff Command received an order from "Yurgis" to proceed to the Rudniki forests, about 35 miles south of Vilna, instead of to the Narocz forests, which were located some 150 miles northeast of Vilna.

Vilna and the underground urban organizations were within the jurisdiction of the Soviet-Lithuanian partisan movement. Lithuania was divided into two zones of action during the reorganization of the movement at the end of August and beginning of September 1943. The northernmost zone was under the responsibility of an operational group led by M. Sumauskas ("Kazimir"), while the main base remained in the Narocz forests in Belorussia. The southern zone, which comprised the district of Vilna, was under the command of the "Yurgis" operational group, which had established its base in the Rudniki forests in Lithuania.[7] As a result of the reorganization, "Yurgis'" order had been sent to the F.P.O. Command, as organizational

6 Korczak, *op. cit.*, pp. 218–219; *Sefer ha-Partizanim*, p. 48; Treger's testimony, pp. 17–18. The female guides between the ghetto and the cemetery were FPO members Treger and Kempner.

7 *Gitlerovskaya okupatsiya*, p. 223. The instructions to the FPO

ties between the Vilna underground groups and Markov had been severed, since his brigade belonged to the Soviet-Belorussian partisan command.

The F.P.O. commanders faced a difficult decision in light of "Yurgis'" order. The greater part of the F.P.O. organization was at Narocz, and the effect of diverting the remaining members to Rudniki would be to further divide the F.P.O. and prevent the establishment of a united Jewish partisan unit composed mainly of F.P.O. members. On the other hand, the Rudniki forests had the advantage of proximity to Vilna, thus facilitating communications between the forest and the city.

The F.P.O. staff decided to obey "Yurgis'" instruction. Two F.P.O. couriers were sent to reconnoiter a route from Vilna to the Rudniki woodlands. The two scouts fell into a German ambush. One of them was killed, but the second succeeded in escaping and reached the Rudniki forests. As a result the F.P.O. remained without guides.[8]

"Yechiel's Struggle Group" decided to take its men out into the forests after the deportations of September 1–4, without consulting the F.P.O. command. The cooperation between the two organizations, agreed upon in May 1943, had stood up until Scheinbaum's death in action. After that loss, and the September 1–4 deportations, the bond broke.

Three groups of "Yechiel's Struggle Group," numbering over seventy men, left the Vilna ghetto for the Rudniki forests on September 11, 13, and 15. Their departure for the Rudniki forests had been prompted by their ties with a Soviet partisan group based in the region, but was not related in any way to "Yurgis'" order.[9]

were apparently included in a letter from Zimanas ("Yurgis") that Bogen brought to the Underground City Committee.

8 Korczak, *op. cit.*, p. 224; *Sefer ha-Partizanim*, pp. 48–50.

9 *Sefer ha-Partizanim*, p. 46; Dworzecki, *op. cit.*, pp. 406–407. The link with this Soviet partisan group was established by C. Sulc, who knew "Batya," a commander of the group, from pre-war days.

The Death of Gens

During the afternoon of September 14, 1943, Gens was called to Security Police H.Q. with Dessler. He had already received a warning during the morning, from a German or Lithuanian source, that the Security Police intended to execute him, and he was advised to flee. Gens replied that his flight was likely to bring calamity to the entire ghetto, and he therefore decided to appear at the Security Police H.Q. in spite of the danger. He parted from his brother Solomon at the ghetto gate and told him that if he were not back by 8 o'clock that evening, it was a sign that he would never return.

Gens and Dessler arrived at the Security Police building in Miczkiewicza Street. Dessler was sent back to the ghetto, but Gens was taken to the small jail in Rossa Street by *Obersturmführer* Neuegebauer and by Weiss, under escort of a Lithuanian policeman. A grave had already been dug in the courtyard of the prison. Gens was taken into the yard, blindfolded, shot by Neuegebauer, and buried on the spot. It was 6 P.M.[10]

The report of the murder spread rapidly through the ghetto several hours after the event. The general feeling was that the elimination of Gens signaled the total liquidation of the remaining ghetto population. Shur writes in his diary:

> The report on the killing of Gens spread like lightning throughout the ghetto and hit the inhabitants like a thunderbolt. If there had ever been two opinions about Gens, if Gens had supporters and opponents—there were no longer two opinions nor any who hated him. All, virtually all, understood that the ghetto had lost in the person of Commander Jacob Gens one who was important

10 Balberyszski, *op. cit.*, p. 474; Lazar, *op. cit.*, p. 180; Weiss' trial, TR-10/29—evidence by Danziger at the trial of Weiss, pp. 2, 4, evidence of Weiss, p. 14. Danziger was in the Rossa jail and saw how Gens was brought there and heard the shots when he was killed.

to them all, a man of wide vision and great understanding of historical moments ... [11]

Lazar, a leading F.P.O. member, writes:

> The hearts of the Jews mourn the tragedy of Gens. It may be charged that his course was harmful, but everyone knows he was never a traitor. All that he did during his tenure as Chief of the Ghetto was for his people... Everyone knows that Gens had many opportunities to save himself... but he renounced his personal safety to devote himself to the ghetto. He believed in his ability, and was convinced to the last moment that he would be able to save the remnants [of the ghetto].[12]

Kittel, who was in charge on behalf of the Security Police, entered the ghetto in the morning hours of September 15, convened the policemen, and said that Gens had been shot the day before because of non-compliance with the directives of the German administration. He also stated that Dessler would take the place of Gens as Chief of the Ghetto.[13]

Dessler, who had returned to the ghetto after the arrest of his superior officer, said that Neuegebauer had told Gens in his presence: "There is a nest of Jewish partisans in the ghetto who fought us. You, as Chief of the Ghetto, did not turn them over to us. I arrest you for that..."

The ghetto inmates connected the murder of the ghetto chief with the fact that the Security Police had learned that, during the last deportation to Estonia, he knew of the existence of an armed underground in the ghetto and deliberately assumed the responsibility of supplying people for deportation in order to force the German Security Police out of the ghetto and prevent

11 Shur's diary [6].
12 Lazar, *op. cit.,* p. 181; Reznik's testimony 0–33/419, pp. 13–14, also expressed his positive opinion of Gens.
13 Balberyszski, *op. cit.,* p. 475; Lazar, *op. cit.,* pp. 182–183; Rolnik, *op. cit.,* p. 110.

a clash between the German forces and the Jewish underground.[14]

To the very last, Gens believed that he would maintain the Vilna Ghetto and save at least part of its population until the victory over Germany. Several weeks before his murder, after the first two deportations to Estonia, at the end of August 1943, he stated:

> ... I want to postpone the *Aktion* so as to gain time, which is so valuable for us. Time is on our side. I am convinced that the Soviet Army will reach Vilna by December of this year, and if at that time the ghetto still survives, even though a few will be left in it, I shall know that I completed my task. I can then announce with a quiet heart and pure conscience that I did my duty to my people and to the future. Jews, try to hold on until the end and believe that we shall win a better life.[15]

Gens erred in his fundamental conception—that the German administration regarded the existence of the ghetto and its inhabitants vital for economic reasons, above all other considerations. This illusion was shattered with his murder.

The Security Police murdered Gens because they no longer needed his services in a ghetto doomed to extinction, and because they learned that Gens had helped the ghetto underground move most of its members to the forests in the period following the deportations to Estonia.

---

14 Korczak, *op. cit.*, p. 219; Dworzecki, *op. cit.*, p. 404, writes that in the ghetto "it was said that Gens had been accused by the Gestapo of having maintained connections with the partisan movement and of having given them assistance" and that he was shot for that reason. Lazar, *op. cit.*, p. 182, writes that Gens' assassination was directly related to the capture of several Jews who had escaped from the ghetto into the forests and who had confessed under interrogation that Gens had aided them in their flight.

15 Lazar, *op. cit.*, p. 157.

Dessler's Flight

On Sunday morning, September 18, German security forces surrounded the ghetto, and its inhabitants sought shelter in *malines*. Kittel arrived in the ghetto and demanded that Dessler round up several hundred males for labor. Dessler gathered a group of policemen and ordered them to go through the ghetto calling for artisans to register in the Judenrat building in order to be moved to housing outside the ghetto. Hundreds of artisans registered as requested and returned home.

During the afternoon, Dessler, his family, and several relatives, fled to a hiding-place they had prepared outside the ghetto. The defection of Dessler came as a heavy blow. The ghetto remained without leadership, and it was apparent that the end was near. Kittel ordered the ghetto police to collect the registered artisans, but they now chose to hide in *malines*. Kittel then directed the police to seize the men, and sent a German force into the ghetto. The search and seizures were unsuccessful, and during the afternoon only several dozen males were captured. Disappointed with the scanty results of the operation, Kittel gave orders to release the captured men and left the ghetto with the German force.[16]

Those F.P.O. members who were still in the ghetto gathered at 6 Straszuna from the morning hours of September 18 and took up defensive positions, but the Germans withdrew from the ghetto without entering into combat with the F.P.O.[17]

Kittel appointed Oberhart to command the police, and on the initiative of the ghetto police, a new ghetto council was set up under B. Biniakonski, a Kovno Jew, manager of the workshops

16 Balberyszski, *op. cit.*, pp. 476–478; Rolnik, *op. cit.*, pp. 110–111; Dessler and his associates remained in hiding outside the ghetto for several months until they were arrested by the Germans. Dessler apparently worked for the Security Police for a while after he was arrested and then was murdered by them. Weiss' trial, TR-10/29, p. 6, states that Dessler was sent by the Security Police to Kovno or Riga after his arrest.

17 Lazar, *op. cit.*, pp. 185–186; Sutzkewer, *op. cit.*, p. 168.

in the ghetto. The new council included A. Fried, Milkonovicki, Guchman, Fishman—former members of the Judenrat and department directors in the ghetto administration—and Solomon Gens, Jacob Gens' brother.

The Last Days

On Thursday morning, September 23, 1943, the German Security Police informed the new head of the ghetto administration, Biniakonski, that the ghetto was being liquidated, and all its inhabitants were to be sent to labor camps in Estonia.

German and Ukrainian security forces surrounded the ghetto. Kittel and officials from the *Gebietskommissariat* arrived during the morning and ordered Biniakonski to summon the inhabitants to an assembly in the Judenrat courtyard. Several hundred people gathered there. One of the *Gebietskommissariat* officials read the following notice in German:

> In the name of the *Reichskommissar* of the *Ostland*, I order that the Vilna Ghetto, which has been in existence for the past two years, be liquidated. The inhabitants of the ghetto will be removed today, partly to Estonia and partly to Latvia. The population is urged, for its own good, to obey the order quietly, to pack its belongings before 12 noon, and to leave the ghetto gates in an orderly manner.

Biniakonski repeated the announcement in Yiddish. Kittel was the last speaker. He said: "By this order all of you must leave the ghetto. If any people remain in the houses, they will be blown up."

Officials of the *Gebietskommissariat* took over the ghetto coffers, the workshops with their equipment, and other property from the ghetto administration.

Most of the people obeyed the German order and went to the gate, believing that they were being sent to labor camps.

and not to their death. Hundreds entered the *malines*.[18] During the afternoon, thousands of people started to move towards the gate with pitiful few possessions tied together in bundles. Kittel and a number of Germans stood at the gate and counted those leaving. They were sent from the gate towards Rossa Square, along a route that was lined on both sides by German security police. A German inspection point had been set up near Rossa Square, from which the males were sent in one direction and the women and children in another. The separation of men, women and children was carried out swiftly. The men were shepherded into an alleyway, and the women ordered into the monastery courtyard and then to a nearby ravine. Blows and cries accompanied the separation. Thousands of people were held there throughout the night, in the open, with rain pelting down, and the entire area was strictly guarded by Ukrainian patrols.[19]

Ukrainians entered the ghetto during the afternoon and took out all the inmates of hospitals, the orphanage, and children's home, loaded them on lorries to the accompaniment of blows and invectives, and sent them to Rossa Square, where they joined the women and children. The Ukrainians then burst into the houses and began to search for people in hiding. They even set off explosive charges in order to force out those in the *malines*. German lorries started to remove the equipment from the workshops and other places in the ghetto. At nightfall they left the ghetto along with the Jews who had been captured.

During the night of September 23–24, the only ones remaining in the ghetto were those secreted in *malines* and hundreds of policemen and ghetto administration personnel and their families, who had gathered at Police H.Q., at 11 Szpitalna. Altogether there were about 2,000 people.

18 Balberyszski, *op. cit.*, pp. 479–481; Rolnik, *op. cit.*, pp. 111–113; Zeidel, *op. cit.*, p. 64.
19 Rolnik, *op. cit.*, pp. 113–116; Shur's diary.

German security forces returned to the ghetto on the morning of September 24. Ukrainian soldiers took everyone, including the police and their families, to Rossa Square. Several people who tried to escape were shot on the spot. Men were separated from women and children, and the people were thrust together with those that had been brought there the previous day. The Ukrainian soldiers robbed the Jews of their watches, money, and clothing, under a rain of blows and invectives.

The people were divided into groups of seventy, put on freight cars, and in the evening of September 24, began the trip to Estonia. The trainload of males arrived there on September 29. As the train passed through Shavli, on the 25th of the month, people threw out notes, which some Lithuanians brought to the Shavli ghetto. The missives stated that the Vilna ghetto had been liquidated; 1,600 people were on the train; and behind them were trucks carrying 6,000 women and children—all bound for Estonia.[20]

The treatment of the women and children was far more savage. At noon on September 24, they were all ordered to proceed towards the monastery, where Germans and Lithuanians carried out a selection. The younger, healthier women were sent to one side; the others and the children to the other side. The women divined that the separation meant life or death, and terrifying scenes ensued. Many mothers pleaded with the Germans to let them go with their children to the "non-essential" side; there were others who tried to appear younger so as to be directed to the side earmarked for working women; and mothers tried to hide their infants in the bundles they carried. That evening some 1,400–1,700 young women were transported to the Kaiserwald camp outside Riga, in Latvia.

20 B. Epstein, "Di likvidatsye fun vilner geto," *YIVO Bleter*, Vol. XXX, 1947, pp. 125–126; Balberyszski, *op. cit.*, pp. 482–485, 489–491, 507; Zeidel, *op. cit.*, p. 66; Yerushalmi, *op. cit.*, pp. 273–274; testimony of I. Segal, YVA, 0–3/2669, p. 2.

The Vilna Jews who were banished from the ghetto on September 23–24 believed they were to be sent to labor camps as complete family units and had no inkling of the planned massacre. The precedent of three deportations to camps in Estonia, in which the people were indeed sent to the labor camps, had nourished this illusion. The German administration had deceived the last surviving Jews of Vilna. Had they not believed they were being sent to labor camps, there is no doubt that thousands would have taken refuge in the *malines,* as during the *Aktionen* in October and November 1941.

There had been some 10,000 Jews in the ghetto on the eve of the liquidation swoop on September 23, 1943. Some 8,000 were taken to Rossa Square, and 2,000 remained in the ghetto *malines.* About 1,600–2,000 of the males assembled at Rossa Square were dispatched to camps in Estonia, and 1,400–1,700 women to Latvia, totaling 3,000–3,700 persons. Another 4,300–5,000 women and children were sent to the Maidanek gas chambers, and several hundred elderly and sick people were shot at Ponar.[21]

The Vilna ghetto, which had been established in September 1941, was finally and completely liquidated on September 23–24, 1943. Four labor camps occupied by Jews remained in Vilna—"Kailis," HKP, the military hospital, and the Security Police.

The Last F.P.O. Party Leaves for the Forests

When the ghetto was encircled on September 23, the F.P.O. members were concentrated at 6 Straszuna. Several days earlier the Command had begun preparations to leave for the Rudniki forests and awaited the return of the guides they had sent out to reconnoiter. The Command had considered escaping from the ghetto through the urban sewer system. S. Kaplinski, who was acquainted with the sewer routes because he had smug-

---

21 Rolnik, *op. cit.,* pp. 117–122; Epstein's diary, pp. 127–129; Balberyszski, *op. cit.,* pp. 492–493.

gled arms through them into the ghetto, was sent to test the likelihood of such an exit. He returned from his mission at about 10 A.M. and reported that it was possible to leave the ghetto through the sewers—in spite of the danger in the event of rain, at which time the channels and sewers would fill with water. The F.P.O. commanders decided to leave the ghetto by this route.

Kovner sent Vitka Kempner and Zelda Treger out of the ghetto to contact Sonia Madeysker, then living on the outside, and inform her of the plan. The three women, with the help of members of the city Communist underground, were to await the F.P.O. party at the exit from the tunnels at 5 Ignatowska Street and direct them to hiding-places in the city until their departure for the forest. Treger and Kempner found Madeysker, and they made the necessary preparations to receive their comrades from the ghetto.

Close to midday, when the ghetto inhabitants were on their way to the gate and to Rossa Square, the F.P.O. group filtered out, individually, in two's and three's, from 6 Straszuna to the mechanical workshops at the corner of Rudnicka and Niemiecka Streets, where the manhole of the urban sewer system was located. One by one they descended into the sewers with Kaplinski in the lead. There were between 80 and 100 persons. The F.P.O. Command had ordered that persons not belonging to the organization would not be taken. This was in response to a few dozen young men who wanted to join those leaving the city and to family members.[22]

Movement through the tunnels was slow and extremely difficult. Korczak writes:

> Darkness prevails in the tunnel...The pale light of a lamp illuminates the way and we advance. My shoulders rub against the narrow pipe, I cannot move my hand...

22 *Sefer ha-Partizanim*, p. 50; Kowalski, *op. cit.*, p. 262; Collective Interview — FPO, pp. 53, 55, 57; Treger's testimony, pp. 23–24; Zeidel, *op. cit.*, pp. 64–65.

A single thought occupies my mind—not to get my weapon wet and not to fall behind ... The pipe, which is over 1 meter in diameter ends suddenly, to become a smooth, round tunnel of only ½ meter. I crawl. The muddy water covers my garments ... The file halts. The report comes back that someone has fainted, he is lying in the middle and blocking the passage ... He is put on one side ... I lose all sense of time ... The order is whispered back: Make ready for exit.[23]

The F.P.O. fighters who had entered the sewage tunnels at about 12 noon emerged at 5 Ignatowska Street at 7 P.M., after darkness had fallen. Madeysker, Kempner, Treger, and two Lithuanian constables who were in the Communist underground awaited them. The F.P.O. party divided into two groups and went to separate hideouts, one in a cellar in the Pushkin Palace in Subocz Street, the other in the "Kailis" camp.

At dark, the F.P.O. members went out in pairs at spaced intervals from the courtyard, traversed the city streets in the direction of the hiding-places, and arrived at their destinations according to schedule—except for one group. A party of four, among them Abraham Chwojnik and Jacob Kaplan, both members of the Staff Command, were stopped by a German patrol which demanded that they identify themselves. The group fired at the patrol and killed a German security policeman. The four were caught, taken to Rossa Square, and hanged by Kittel in full view of the Jews gathered there.[24]

The main group, numbering fifty persons, including Kovner, Borowska, and Kaplinski, stayed in the Pushkin Palace cellar for two days, awaiting the arrival of the guides who had been

23 *Sefer ha-Partizanim*, pp. 50–51.
24 Treger's testimony, pp. 24–25; Collective Interview — FPO, pp. 55–56; *Sefer ha-Partizanim*, p. 52; Kaczerginski, *Hurbn Vilne,* *op. cit.*, pp. 73–74, writes therein that among those caught was also Itzhak Witenberg's son, Hirsh, a boy of sixteen. The German killed was named Max Gross.

sent to reconnoiter the route to Rudniki. The trio of F.P.O. women—Kempner, Treger, and Madeysker—maintained the link between the dispersed parties and the urban underground and also provided food.

On September 25, the report was received from a courier of the urban underground that the guides had been ambushed and killed and no guide could come from the forest. It was pointless to continue their sojourn in the cellar, and the janitor insisted that the group leave, so Kovner decided to proceed in the direction of the Rudniki forest without a guide. The group left on the night of September 26, drifted along the city streets in small groups, and gathered outside the city. After midnight, the whole group resumed their march in the direction of Rudniki and arrived there on September 27. The second party, which had hidden in the "Kailis" factory camp and numbered a few dozen persons, left for the Rudniki forests on the night of September 27. They also included F.P.O. members who lived in "Kailis." They arrived in the forests a day or so later and joined Kovner's group.[25]

The F.P.O. had been taken by surprise on September 23, when the ghetto was encircled and the liquidation commenced, despite the fact that the events of the preceding weeks and days provided adequate information to demonstrate that the ghetto was on the brink of a disaster. The escape through the sewer system and the arrangements to hide in the city were improvised at the last moment. It demonstrated great initiative and resourcefulness, but its success was based largely on luck.

The F.P.O. demurral against allowing non-members to join in the escape through the sewers must be seen against the background of events on the morning of September 23—the surprise German *Aktion*, the absence of any clear information on the tunnel route, their fate upon emerging from the sewers, where they could hide outside, and how they would proceed

25 *Sefer ha-Partizanim*, pp. 52–56; Collective Interview — FPO, p. 57; Treger's testimony, pp. 31–32; Kowalski, *op. cit.*, pp. 263–265.

to the forests. Apart from these factors, which influenced the refusal to accept non-members, there were also the instructions that had come from the partisan commanders that only armed combatants would be accepted in the partisan units.

Causes of the Dissolution of the Vilna Ghetto

There were three ghettos in the *Generalkommissariat* for Lithuania—Vilna, Kovno, and Shavli—that Himmler's order of June 21, 1943 marked for complete liquidation. The Vilna ghetto, which at the beginning of August 1943 contained 18,500– 19,000 inmates, was completely destroyed.

The fate of the Kovno and Shavli ghettos was different. They had been transferred from the jurisdiction of the civilian administration to that of the SS authorities and had officially become concentration camps in September 1943. Thousands of people had been taken out of these two ghettos and placed in camps attached to employment sites in the two cities and the adjacent areas. On October 26, 1943, 2,800 people were sent from Kovno to camps in Estonia. The position of the Jewish communities in the two cities deteriorated considerably when the ghettos passed into Security Police control, and *Aktionen* were implemented against children and the elderly. Nevertheless, most of the people in these two ghettos remained there until the final weeks before the liberation of these cities by the Soviet Army in July 1944, and were only then forcibly evacuated to Germany.[26]

Himmler's decree of June 21, 1943, prescribed the general lines for the dissolution of the ghettos, the creation of concen-

26 Yerushalmi, *op. cit.*, pp. 302–306. In Shavli, eight hundred children and elderly people were removed on November 5 and murdered. Garfunkel, *op. cit.*, pp. 177–178, writes that in Kovno, 1,300 children and elderly people were removed on March 27 and 28, 1944, and murdered. The Jews of Kovno were evacuated on July 7–12, 1944. The city was liberated on August 1, 1944. The Jews of Shavli were evacuated during the week of July 15–22, 1944. The city was liberated on July 27, 1944.

tration camps, the dispatch of people to the camps in Estonia, and the extermination of Jews not required for labor purposes. The officialdom in the *Reichskommissariat Ostland* transmitted and clarified this decree. The German administration in Lithuania had the authority to determine the method of execution of these orders in that region.

Himmler's order was implemented in Vilna with utmost severity—the ghetto was utterly destroyed, and only a small part of the total ghetto population remained in labor camps to serve army needs. All able-bodied persons were transported to camps in Estonia and Latvia, and thousands of people, mainly women and children, were annihilated. The question is: Why did the fate of the Jews of the Vilna ghetto differ from that of the Jews of the Kovno and Shavli ghettos in the summer of 1943? Economic considerations did not rule in this case. The Vilna ghetto community was no less essential or important to the German Army and the war effort than the other two ghettos. The German administrative officials in Lithuania could have selected the quota of persons required for deportation to Estonia and Latvia from all three ghettos by closing less-essential places of employment and thus reducing the size of the ghettos in a balanced fashion. A solution of this kind would have been more reasonable from the economic standpoint.

There were other factors that determined the tragic fate of the Vilna ghetto during this period. The following monthly reports from the Chief of the Security Police and SD in Lithuania give the reason for them. The report dated July 31, 1943, stated:

... *Jews*
In the month under consideration enemy propaganda dealt with the Jews to an increased degree. Rumors were spread in the various ghettos that *Grossaktionen* would take place within a short period in which not only children, old people and the unfit would be shot by the Security Police, but all the occupants of the ghettos without exception. As

a result there was something like panic in the various ghettos, particularly in the Vilna ghetto. In two peat-cutting camps near Vilna the Jews tried to escape and to join a group of bandits [partisans]. In a third peat camp an atonement measure* was carried out ... The exposed situation of the Vilna area, with respect to the neighboring area of partisans and the activities of the PW** necessitate the withdrawal of the Jews from the Vilna area and their continued placement in concentration camps elsewhere. An incident that took place on July 25, 1943, near Vilna demonstrates that such measures are essential: On this day a group of about 30 Jews succeeded for the first time in leaving the city and acquiring arms in order to join the bandits. The group was stopped by a Commando of a Partisan-fighting unit of the German and Lithuanian Sipo (Security Police) and the Lithuanian Order Police, and most of them were shot ...[27]

This report relates to the liquidatioin of the Biala-Vaka, Kana, and Bezdany labor camps at the end of June–mid July 1943, because of their inmates having joined the partisans and having contacts with them (see chapter 21, pp. 368–369), and the fleeing of the Glazman group from Vilna to the forests (see chapter 22, pp. 398–400). This report stresses the urgent need for the removal of the Jews of Vilna and its surroundings to concentration camps because of the partisan activities in the area and the contacts the Jews of the ghetto had with them.

A report dated September 1, 1943, stated:

4. *Jews.* It was not possible last month to implement the new arrangements for the fullest utilization of Jews for

* Murder
** The reference is apparently to the *Polnische Widerstandsbewegung* — Polish Resistance Movement, units of the AK which operated in the neighborhood of Vilna.
27 YIVO Archives, Berlin collection, OccE3b & 96.

labor purposes ... because there is no concentration camp ready ... To prevent rising panic among the Jews from reaching a peak, which might provoke resistance and particularly mass flight, it was agreed with the SS WVHA that first of all the Jews of Vilna should be removed ... The Jews learned long ago of the planned measures, and this created panic since they believed they were going to be executed. As a result, hundreds of Vilna Jews tried to escape. Some of them were shot together with their families, but the larger part was caught. Others returned of their own free will. About 30–40 Jews succeeded in escaping. There were also difficulties during the separation of families. To carry out the planned measures, it is necessary to have considerable police manpower and guard forces.[28]

This report referred to August 1943, when two transports were taken from the Vilna ghetto to the concentration camps of Estonia and explained why the first groups of people were taken from Vilna. The Security Police chiefs wanted to exploit the element of surprise, since they feared resistance and mass flight if the Vilna Jews were to have advance knowledge of what awaited them. After the Witenberg affair, the German ambush of the "Leon Group" en route to the forests, and the arrest of armed Jews a short while after the first transportation to Estonia, the Security Police became aware of the existence of centers of resistance inside the ghetto.

The report of the Chief of Security Police and SD in Lithuania, dated October 1, reaffirmed the reason for liquidating the Vilna Jews:

4. *Jews.* Only one change occurred in the solution to the Jewish question last month—the handling of matters related to the utilization of Jews for labor was taken over

---

28 *Masinės zudynes Lietuvoje, 1941–1945,* Vilna, 1965, Vol. I, pp. 243–244.

by the Director of the SS WVHA. Taking into account the considerable demand for labor in the places where minerals are being mined, and due to certain difficulties in the Vilna Ghetto, the ghetto was completely evacuated. The need arose a number of times here to crush the serious resistance of the Jews. Our establishment suffered losses in the last *Aktion*. One *Unterführer* was killed and one wounded.[29]

Two of the above-mentioned factors determined the fate of the Vilna ghetto—the demand for *manpower in Estonia* and *certain difficulties in the ghetto,* i.e., the centers of resistance there. The German administration in Lithuania sought to achieve two goals by liquidating the ghetto: first, to fulfill the numerical demand for manpower in Estonia; second, to liquidate the Vilna ghetto as a core of resistance and a source of reinforcements for the partisans.

Thus the Vilna ghetto was issued its death warrant. Thousands were sent to concentration camps, thousands more to extermination. But the German administration failed, in spite of its surprise tactics and siege methods, to prevent hundreds of armed and unarmed youth from leaving the ghetto to fight in the forests.

29 *Ibid.,* pp. 244–245. In this report, p. 243, the Soviet editors also interpret the German reference to "certain difficulties in the Vilna ghetto" as meaning the resistance movements in the ghetto and the departure to the forests to join the partisans.

Chapter 25

THE FATE OF THE REMNANT

After the ghetto in Vilna had been liquidated, the survivors continued to struggle for their lives in three regions, separated one from the other by thousands of miles: the forests of Narocz and Rudniki, the labor camps and *malines* in Vilna, and the concentration camps in Estonia and Latvia.

Labor Camps
Some 2,300 people were left in the two large camps, "Kailis" and HKP, and some 150 others lived in the two small camps attached to the military hospital and Security Police. The camp inmates were the responsibility of the Security Police, not of the civil administration. The regime and way of life in these camps resembled ghettos rather than concentration camps. Family members were not separated, clothing was ordinary, each family provided for itself, and no daily roll-calls were held. Police supervision and control over movement was less strictly enforced than in the concentration camp. The inmates worked as craftsmen and in services. The camps were like solitary islands in the midst of the city, and their inhabitants lived in fear from day to day.

An *Aktion* involving children under fifteen in the "Kailis" and HKP camps took place on March 27, 1944: the people in "Kailis" were given word that they would have to take their children to the clinic near the camp to receive anti-typhoid shots. The mothers brought their young to the clinic. Suddenly, Weiss of the Security Police and Lithuanian policemen arrived, grabbed the children from their astonished mothers, and loaded them onto trucks. The mothers resisted, and several of them were put on the vehicles, too. Weiss and the Lithuanians then entered the "Kailis" camp and began searching for children whose parents had succeeded in hiding them. Several were found and seized.

During the early morning hours of the same day, after the men left for work, Germans and Lithuanians surrounded the HKP camp and began to remove the children amidst scuffles and resistance by the women. One woman who shouted "Murderer!" to Weiss was shot on the spot.

Approximately 200 children were taken that day from "Kailis" and HKP. They were driven to the railroad station and put on trains for the death camps in the General Government. A group of the elderly was also removed for extermination. Dozens of children who succeeded in surviving this *Aktion* were obliged to remain in hiding for months on end.[1]

Malines and the Quest for Refuge

Some 2,000 Vilna ghetto Jews did not obey the German order of September 23 to proceed to Rossa Square. For the most part they hid within the ghetto or in the sewers, and a few found refuge with Christian acquaintances. Most of these hideouts were discovered by the police, or the inhabitants were forced to emerge due to lack of food and water, after the German authorities cut off the water supplies of the area. German security patrols regularly searched the former ghetto area. Those who came out of hiding in order to forage for food and water were apprehended, and in many cases forced by the police to guide them to the cubbyholes in which they had been living. Several of these were discovered by non-Jewish inhabitants, who came into the ghetto area to look for abandoned property, and were reported to the police.

1 Kaczerginski, *Hurbn Vilne, op. cit.,* pp. 81–83, 87–89, 91–92; Weiss' trial, TR–10/381, p. 14.

The people discovered in *malines* were taken to the Security Police. They were detained there until groups of 100 were collected, and then they were to sent Ponar. Some 100 males who were caught in *malines* were classified as skilled workers and removed to the HKP camp at the beginning of October 1943, at the insistence of the Wehrmacht officer in charge of the camp.[2]

Several hideouts for small groups of people were located outside the ghetto. One *maline* of this sort was in the cellar of the Benedictine monastery on Ignatova Street.

The "Kailis" camp served as a haven and transit point for hundreds of Jews who had been in hiding in *malines* or in the sewers and had been compelled to leave them. "Kailis" was guarded by Jewish police, and it was comparatively easy to infiltrate. During the early weeks of October 1943, some 600 "illegal" Jews were able to hide there or pass through. Some of them succeeded in registering as dependents of the "Kailis" workers and gained legal status. On October 16, 1943, German security chief Kittel conducted a search there and arrested sixteen "illegals," who were sent to Ponar. There were no "illegal" residents at the HKP workshop camp, as the conditions there eliminated the possibility of *malines*. People who had fled from the ghetto area found only temporary refuge at HKP and were compelled to seek more permanent havens elsewhere.[3]

Places of refuge on the "Aryan" side were possible only with the goodwill of the local population. The Polish underground, expressing the sentiments of the Polish people in the occupied areas, reported to the Polish Government-in-Exile in London that the destruction of the ghetto in September 1943

2 Kaczerginski, pp. 28, 68, 74–75, 76–80; testimony of Dr. Boraks in Kaczerginski, *Hurbn Vilne, op. cit.,* states that 2,000 Jews were shot at Ponar in October 1943: they had been caught in *malines* and other hiding places; E. Gerszatter, "Oyf yener zayt geto," *Bleter vegn Vilne,* 1947, p. 43.

3 Testimony of Dr. Boraks in Kaczerginski, *Hurbn Vilne, op. cit.,* pp. 100–101; testimony of S. Yashuner, YVA, 0–3/1830, p. 19.

had "caused to a large extent the paralysis of the Communist Underground in Vilna."[4] It emerged from this report that the Polish underground conceived the liquidation of the ghetto as a positive step in the campaign against their Communist adversaries. This frame of mind among the Poles, who were in the large majority in Vilna, obviously failed to create auspicious conditions for sheltering the hundreds or thousands of Jews requiring refuge. There were, however, among the Poles some who extended a helping hand to the persecuted Jews of Vilna.

The attitude of the Lithuanians, including the anti-German underground of the Center parties, was hostile, even after their attitude toward the Germans changed at the outset of 1943. The Lithuanian populace in Vilna did not provide refuge for the Jews. Many hundreds of Jews who had disobeyed German orders and did not come out of hiding on September 23 and 24, were therefore unable to find shelter and refuge in that atmosphere of apathy and animosity. During the ten months between the liquidation of the ghetto in September 1943, and the liberation of the city in July 1944, the majority of them fell into German hands and were killed at Ponar. Few of them survived.[5]

Cremations at Ponar

In order to obliterate all traces of the mass graves and leave no sign of Nazi crimes, Himmler set up a special unit, Commando 1005, under the leadership of Paul Blobel.

A special unit was established in Vilna at the end of September 1943 to dig up the graves at Ponar, exhume the remains and burn them. The unit included about seventy Jews caught after the liquidation of the ghetto and ten Soviet prison-

---

4 AZHP — 202/II–8, p. 22.
5 Testimony of S. Jaffe, YVA, 0–3/2803, pp. 33–40; Gerszatter, *op. cit.*, pp. 42–43; Kaczerginski, *Hurbn Vilne, op. cit.*, pp. 55–57, speaks of a *maline* in which there were fifty-four persons. It was discovered two weeks before the liberation and all of its occupants were taken to Ponar and shot.

ers of war suspected of being Jewish. These men were kept in an underground bunker, a deep pit to which the only access was by a ladder that was hauled up after the slave-laborers descended. The bunker was surrounded by an electrified barbed-wire fence. They were brought up for their gruesome work in the mornings and returned to the pit at night. They were fettered at the ankles, with chains long enough to allow them to take ordinary steps but not to run. German SS guards maintained strict watch over them throughout the day and night. Their work consisted of opening the mass graves, extracting the disintegrating corpses, piling them up in huge heaps, and setting fire to them.

It was obvious to these unfortunates that the Germans would murder them after they completed their grisly labors, and so they sought ways of escape. They dug a tunnel, some 35–40 yards long, which led from the pit along a line under the barbed-wire and the mined fences around the pit and came out on the other side. They did their digging at night, by hand and with spoons. The earth that was removed was dropped between the cubicles in the pit, raised the level of the floor, and was also scattered in other places. The digging lasted about three months, and the escape from the bunker took place on the night of April 15, 1944. They removed the fetters around their feet with the aid of a file they had found. About forty of the prisoners made their way out of the tunnel before the guards discovered the escape and opened fire. Twenty-five of them were caught or killed, and about fifteen managed to elude their pursuers. Eleven of them reached the Rudniki forests and joined the partisans.

On April 20, 1944, seventy people were taken from the "Kailis" camp to continue cremating the corpses. They were murdered before the Germans retreated from Vilna. Commando 1005 cremated between 56–68,000 bodies at Ponar.[6]

6 Kaczerginski, *Hurbn Vilne, op. cit.*, pp. 37–38, 40–41, 49–54; Sutzkewer, *op. cit.*, pp. 188–190, 193–195, 197–199; *Gitlerovskaya okupatsiya*, pp. 177–178; Weiss' trial, TR–10/381, pp. 13–14.

Liquidation of the Labor Camps: July 2-3, 1944

On June 23, 1944, the Soviet armies opened a general offensive along the Belorussian front about 260 miles east of Vilna, broke through and advanced rapidly towards Vilna. The central front of the Wehrmacht collapsed, and the German forces were in full and confused retreat.

The labor camps in Vilna were liquidated on July 2 and 3. A total of 2-2,300 Jews were taken away from "Kailis," HKP, and the military hospital to Ponar and murdered. Hundreds of people went into hideouts in "Kailis" and HKP, but SS troops searched them on the following days and threw grenades into suspicious places. Most of the people in hiding were killed where they lay concealed, or were caught and taken out to be shot. There were several armed groups at the HKP camp, and one of them, hidden in a *maline*, attacked an SS patrol on the night of July 4, killed two of the Germans, and broke out of the camp. Some 150–200 Jews were saved in the *malines* at HKP or succeeded in fleeing.[7]

The Soviet Army liberated Vilna on July 13, 1944. Several hundred Jews of Vilna lived to see the liberation. They were the survivors of *malines* and other hideouts.

Camps in Estonia and Latvia

During the liquidation of the Vilna ghetto, some 8,500–9,500 Jews had been deported to the concentration camps in Estonia, and 1,400–1,700 women to the Kaiserwald camp outside Riga, in Latvia.

The camps in Estonia were subordinate to the SS WVHA. The economic exploitation of the prisoners outside the camps was the responsibility of the German Todt labor organization. The central camp in Estonia was at Vaivara, the headquarters of the SS which had jurisdiction over twenty camps throughout

---

7 *Sefer ha-Partizanim*, pp. 153–154; Kaczerginski, *Hurbn Vilne*, *op. cit.*, pp. 92–105, containing testimonies of people rescued from Kailis and HKP.

Estonia. The largest of them, Vaivara, Klooga, and Lagedi each housed 1,000 to 2,000 prisoners. The smaller ones had several hundred inmates.

From among the camp inmates, the Germans chose an "Elder of the camp" (*Lagerälteste*), who had several assistants. Their duties were limited to internal camp life, such as organizing the work in the smithies, fumigation chambers, laundries, etc. These men had no punitive powers, as was the case with those holding similar posts in concentration camps in Germany, but these men enjoyed certain work and food privileges.

Men and women lived in separate divisions of the camp, with barbed-wire partitioning them, and any communication or contact between them was forbidden. The people dwelt in dilapidated huts under conditions of extreme congestion—in many cases hundreds of them in one room. Upon arrival in the camp, the heads of the men and women were shorn. The quantity of food doled out hardly afforded minimum subsistence level. Conditions were much harder than life in the Vilna ghetto.

Hundreds of children, mostly from among those who came to Estonia in the second transport from Vilna on August 24, 1943, were also among the inmates. The Vaivara and Ereda camps had approximately 200 children in each. Smaller groups were incarcerated in other camps. Most of the children over thirteen succeeded in finding work along with the adult inmates. Younger children were employed in various capacities in the workshops and camp services. About 800 children, elderly and sick people were sent from the camps in Estonia to one of the death-camps in Poland in mid-February 1944. The majority of children under thirteen were also included in this transport.

The camp inmates worked for the army: building fortifications, road and railroad construction, felling trees in the forests, and the like. They also worked in the raw-materials mines manufacturing oil-shale. A work-day lasted twelve hours. The backbreaking labor, the scarcity of food, and the poor sanitary conditions caused much illness and an enormous mortality rate. "Selections" were held from time to time, and the more sick and enfeebled were taken out and executed.[8]

The fate of the women sent from the Vilna ghetto to the Kaiserwald camp near Riga—the working conditions and life in the camp, the "selections" of the weaker ones and the weeding-out of the very young and elderly—was no different from that of the inmates in the camps in Estonia.[9]

Underground groups were created in several of the camps in Estonia. Their initiators and active elements were drawn from men of the 2nd Battalion of the F.P.O., who had been taken during the deportation *Aktion* on September 1, 1943. A group of F.P.O. men in the camp at Soski organized a clandestine cell of about twenty men. This unit established contact through Estonian guards at the camp with Soviet partisans who were operating east of the Narva River. The group planned to escape and join the partisans in February 1944, but because of the Soviet Army advance, the camp was evacuated and the flight plan was never implemented. Underground groups were formed also in Klooga and other camps.

The difficult camp conditions, the stringent German surveillance, the lack of communication and acquaintance with the local population made it impossible to organize extensive underground activities. Consequently, there were no concrete results of the clandestine undertakings, except for the successful flights of individuals and small groups.[10]

With the approach of the Soviet armies toward Estonia and Latvia, the last and most tragic period in the lives of the Jewish inmates began. "Selections" were conducted in the camps

8 Dworzecki, *Mahanot be-Estonia, op. cit.*, pp. 125–129, 135, 137, 215–218; Balberyszki, *op. cit.*, p. 510; Yerushalmi, *op. cit.*, pp. 354–355.

9 Rolnik, *op. cit.*, pp. 122–123, 151, 162–164.

10 R. Korczak, *Lehavot ba-Efer*, third edition, 1965, pp. 377–378; Dworzecki, *Mahanot be-Estonia, op. cit.*, pp. 304–305; Zeidel, *op. cit.*, pp. 73–79.

at the end of July 1944, and prisoners who appeared to be ill or weak were taken out and executed. This action was nicknamed by the Jews "the 10% *Aktion*," as that was the percentage of people murdered in most of the camps.

The evacuation of the camps began at the end of July, and the inmates were sent to the camp at Stutthof, in East Prussia. They were transportated via the Baltic Sea, as the Soviet Army had penetrated Lithuania and Latvia and cut off the landways. Conditions on the vessels were the worst possible, and many of the prisoners died en route.

In January 1945, with the advance of the Soviet Army to Stutthof, thousands of people were marched westward for hundreds of miles, without food, under severe winter conditions. Many who fell by the wayside were shot by the SS guards— this on the eve of the liberation. Some of the people succeeded in eluding their guards and hid for several days; they were liberated by the Soviet forces.[11]

In the Narocz Forests

The Narocz forest region, which lies about 90 miles east of Vilna, covers thousands of square miles south of the large Narocz Lake. Some 35 miles north of the lake there is a second expanse of forests known as Koziany. The population in these forest areas is Belorussian. The Soviet partisans under the command of F. Markov began to operate there as early as 1942. A Lithuanian operational group led by M. Sumauskas, codenamed "Kazimir," and Zimanas, known as "Yurgis," arrived in the Narocz sector from the U.S.S.R. at the beginning of the summer of 1943.

Hundreds of Jews—including families and children who had arrived there in 1942 and the first half of 1943—were

11 Balberyszski, *op. cit.,* pp. 555–572. He was eye-witness to the murders at Lagedi and Klooga; Dworzecki, *Mahanot be-Estonia, op. cit.,* pp. 338–340. At Lagedi, 426 Jews were murdered on September 18; and at Klooga, 2,500 on September 19; Rolnik, *op. cit.,* pp. 168, 194–203.

in the Narocz forests, having fled when the ghettos in the district were liquidated. Some of the armed young men had been accepted into the partisan formations; the others organized family camps. The inhabitants of the family camps lived in the harshest conditions. They suffered food shortages, harassment by the partisans, and sweeps by German army units. The condition of the Jews in the partisan formations was also none too easy, and in some of them the Jews suffered from anti-Semitism and discrimination.

The first group of F.P.O. that reached Markov's brigade in the Narocz forests was the "Leon Group" commanded by Glazman. This unit left the ghetto on July 24, 1943 (see chapter 22, pp. 398–400).

Markov decided to accede to Glazman's request and form a separate Jewish partisan detachment within his brigade. It was called Mestj ("Revenge"), and a Lithuanian Jew, Z. Ragovski, who had arrived from the U.S.S.R., was appointed commander. Glazman was named Chief of Staff of Mestj. Glazman and his colleagues hoped to preserve the F.P.O. organization through the creation of an independent Jewish partisan unit in the forests.

Markov's assent, supported by "Yurgis," to establish a Jewish unit, apparently stemmed from the assumption that it would integrate all those Jews who were in the forests and did not belong to other outfits. These Jews were a nuisance as well as a human problem that the Soviet partisan command could not ignore. Markov was also interested in establishing a framework that would absorb additional parties of F.P.O. men who would come into the forests from the ghetto. It could also be that personal considerations influenced the decision—Markov was married to a Jewess, and "Yurgis" was a Jew.

Mestj consisted of seventy men at the time of its creation at the beginning of August 1943. It accepted into its ranks men who had trickled in from the ghetto between September 8 and 13, and increased to 250 men. Only part of the force was armed, mainly with pistols, which were not suited for guerrilla warfare. Hopes of obtaining weapons from the brigade were dashed. In contrast to other partisan regiments, Mestj included many women, who were mainly F.P.O. members.

Daily life and acclimatization to forest conditions were exceedingly difficult for the former urbanites. The people slept on the ground without blankets; overcoats were the only protection against the piercing night cold. Food was meager and procuring it hazardous. Some of the men were assigned to "economic action"—simply, to obtain food. Mestj took part in the sorties carried out by the Markov Brigade and fought in the attack on the township of Miadziol and in other attacks. These activities raised the morale of the unit.

Klimov, the secretary of the Communist Party Council in the Vileyka district, opposed the existence of a separate Jewish unit because the Soviet partisan movement was organized on a territorial, not a national, basis. Consequently, there were Belorussian, Lithuanian, and other such partisan movements, but there was no place for disparate national units. Klimov and Markov therefore decided to dissolve the Jewish unit.

Anti-Semitism, rife among parts of the Soviet partisans, also probably contributed to this decision. The partisan command also feared that separate Jewish partisan activity would serve to increase the opposition of the local population and enable German propaganda to present the partisan movement as a Jewish one.

Before Mestj was disbanded, Glazman found out that "Yurgis" was to move to the Rudniki forests to organize a Lithuanian partisan brigade there and that the F.P.O. members who were still in the Vilna ghetto had been ordered to go there. Glazman and about twenty of his men left Mestj and went over to "Yurgis."

On September 23, 1943, the day on which the Vilna ghetto was liquidated, the Mestj was called to appear before the brigade commander, who announced that it was being disbanded. Markov explained that there were men in the group who had no military experience or training in the use of weapons, while, on the other hand, partisans in other units possessed such military expertise, but lacked arms. He must make certain, he stated, that the arms be placed in the hands of those who knew how to use them properly. He declared that the weapons would be confiscated from some of the fighters, particularly the young women, and others who had weapons would be incorporated into another unit of the brigade; the remainder would form the brigade's "maintenance unit."

In accordance with this announcement, a group of combatants with arms, including the Jewish commanding officer of Mestj, was sent to the Komsomolski unit, and the remainder were disarmed. The majority of the Mestj outfit was organized into a maintenance unit and given a few weapons for self-defense and for obtaining food.[12]

The disbandment of Mestj was accomplished several days before the great German hunt through the Narocz forests. The partisan command learned of the concentration of the German forces and decided not to enter into combat with the numerically superior enemy, but to withdraw from the threatened zone before the Germans cordoned it off. This was the customary partisan tactic in the face of superior enemy forces. The withdrawal was directed toward the Koziany forests.

The siege came as a heavy blow to the Mestj combatants, whose unit had been dissolved and were as yet unable to reorganize. The F.P.O. members, who were newcomers to the forests and still insufficiently acquainted with the conditions and the locality, suffered greatly. About 200 Jews from the "maintenance" personnel and other Jews of the family camps gathered in the vicinity of the Komsomolski camp and beseeched its Russian commander to take them along, and not leave them to the mercy of the Germans. He refused, and even fired

---

12 Korczak, *op. cit.*, pp. 226, 229–232, 236–239; Lazar, *op. cit.*, pp. 214–216; A. Keren-Paz, "Derekh ha-Yissurim shel Partizan Yehudi," *Pirsumei Muze'on ha-Lohamim ve-ha-Partizanim*, Tel Aviv, September 1973, Vol. II, No. 5(20), pp. 11–13.

warning shots to frighten those who tried to follow the tracks of the unit.

The Komsomolski unit advanced in the direction of the Koziany forests, but in the meantime the Germans had closed this route. It was therefore necessary to split up into several smaller groups, with each group trying to make its own way through the German lines. In this way the Jews were segregated from the other fighters and left on their own.

The brigade command ordered the maintenance unit to clear the hospital of the wounded and carry them to safety in the marshes. They were then instructed to leave and seek another place of refuge. The Jewish partisans and families who remained in the Narocz forests found refuge in the marshy area, which the Germans found difficult to comb thoroughly. Yet, approximately 130 Jews were killed in the German siege.

Glazman and thirty-five of his Jewish fighters were instructed by "Yurgis" to make their way through to the Koziany forests, where the Lithuanian partisan brigade, Zalgiris, commanded by "Casimir," was located. Upon reaching the Koziany forests, they discovered that a German operation had begun there as well. "Casimir" ordered Glazman to retreat in the direction of Narocz and then to proceed southwest to the Rudniki forests. On the morning of October 8, Glazman and his group were surrounded by German troops, and after a fierce battle all of the Jewish partisans fell, with the exception of a young girl who succeeded in escaping.

Within a few months, during October 1943, the partisan units that had retreated returned to the Narocz forests. During the winter of 1943–44, the position of the Jews in the Narocz woodlands took a turn for the better. The internal organization of the partisan force grew stronger, and discipline more firmly consolidated. The position with regard to weapons greatly improved as a result of the parachuting of arms from the U.S.S.R. Jews without weapons were admitted into some of the units. A group of F.P.O. members was incorporated into the "Istrebitel" ("Destroyer") brigade, and others into the Kalinin brigade. The Jewish maintenance group was reestablished as part of the Markov Brigade Command. Another party of F.P.O. members joined the Zalgiris brigade and went into the forests of Koziany.

The disbanding of Mestj eliminated the possibility of concentrating the F.P.O. members into a Jewish fighting force in the Narocz woods. Those of its men who operated in the Narocz and Koziany areas found their place as fighters in various partisan formations, but only after great vicissitudes. Many of them excelled as courageous guerrillas while blowing up trains, attacking garrison troops, conducting ambushes and other actions. Scores were killed in clashes with the enemy.[13]

In the Rudniki Forests

The Rudniki forests lay at a distance of some 35 miles south of Vilna, covering about 1,800 sq. miles, through which the main highway between Vilna and Grodno passed. The population in this region was both Lithuanian and Polish.

Soviet partisans began activity in the Rudniki forests in the summer of 1943 when a party of parachutists set up a base in the area. Their commanding officer was Captain "Alko." A vanguard of the Soviet-Lithuanian partisans arrived in the Rudniki forests from the Narocz woodlands at the beginning of September 1943, and its objective was to prepare for the southern command of the Soviet-Lithuanian guerrillas, whose commanding officer was "Yurgis."

The first to arrive in the forests from the Vilna ghetto were men from "Yechiel's Struggle Group." Several days after the *Aktion* of September 1–4, 1943, about seventy men of the organization, part of whom were armed, left the ghetto in three separate parties and reunited in the Rudniki woods near the base created by Captain "Alko." The organization had connections with one of the partisans in "Alko's" unit, "Batya."[14]

13 Lazar, *op. cit.,* pp. 218–221; Korczak, *op. cit.,* 3rd edition, pp. 240, 245, 248–251.
14 "Batya's" name was Groilowski. During the Soviet regime, he

"Yechiel's Struggle Group" was now commanded by Magid, Brand, and Ring.

The "Yechiel's Struggle" men wanted to join Captain "Alko's" group, but the latter refused to accept them on the grounds that he was unable to accept unarmed men and women who lacked military experience and training. He was ready to enlist twenty armed men and suggested that the others establish a separate family camp. The "Yechiel's Struggle" people rejected the offer on the grounds that they were not prepared to leave the bulk of their members without weapons. They organized their base about 1½ miles from "Alko's" camp.

The F.P.O. members who had left the ghetto on the day of its liquidation arrived in the forest in two groups: the first comprised some fifty persons, who came on September 27, 1943; and the second, about twenty to thirty persons, arrived several days later. The groups were commanded by A. Kovner and C. Borowska. With the advent of the F.P.O. members, the Jewish base totaled about 150, equally divided between the two groups.

The primary question was whether to preserve the independence of the Jewish formation and maintain close ties with Captain "Alko's" unit, or to integrate and operate under the aegis of the Soviet-Lithuanian partisan movement, with which the F.P.O. had maintained contact while still in the ghetto, and in accordance with whose instructions they had come to the Rudniki forest. The F.P.O. supported the link with the Soviet-Lithuanian partisan movement, whereas "Yechiel's" men were in favor of an alliance with Captain "Alko's" unit. Finally, the decision was made to join the Soviet-Lithuanian partisans. Abba Kovner was appointed as the Commanding Officer of the entire Jewish base, and Borowska the Political Commissar.

commanded the militia at Olkieniki (Valkininkai) near the Rudniki forests. After the arrival of the Germans, he went underground and in 1942 commanded a small group of partisans that operated in the Rudniki area.

The change in the command of the formation and its acceptance as a regular partisan battalion, complete with the requisite military discipline, aroused resentment and objections particularly among the Yechiel group members and the commanders who had been replaced. The latter regarded themselves as the veterans in the forest and felt they had previous military training superior to that of the new command. The antagonism between the two organizations, which stemmed from ghetto days, had not disappeared.

The new command transferred the camp deeper into the woods, to a small island in the marshy area. Logs laid in the marshes formed a footway to the camp, in which huts made of boughs and branches were put up. Their first step was to establish contact with Sonia Madeysker, who had continued her underground activity in Vilna,[15] and to focus on bringing groups of people from the labor camps in the city out into the woods. The courier Zelda Treger, a F.P.O. member, traveled the route between Rudniki and Vilna many times.

Another two groups of forty persons each were brought out of the "Kailis" camp in Vilna in the course of a month. More Jews from Vilna and other hiding-places had joined the forest camp, and their number now topped 250. To enable the effective enforcement of discipline and control, the camp was divided into two battalions, and, subsequently, as the number of people increased, a third battalion was formed. The battalions, according to the order of their formation, were: the Mstitel ("Avenger") battalion under A. Kovner, Za pobedu ("To Victory") battalion led by S. Kaplinsky, and the Smert Fashizmu ("Death to Fascism") battalion commanded by Jacob Brawer. Each had its own political commissar as well.

The growth in numbers of people and the link with the Li-

15 Sonia Madeysker was active in the leadership of the Communist underground in Vilna until the eve of the liberation of the city, when she was caught by the German Security Police. She attempted to commit suicide, but was only injured, and was taken to a hospital where she died a short while later.

thuanian group brought no substantial improvement in the quantity of arms, and the majority remained unarmed, which hindered the implementation of military operations. Nonetheless, the Jewish partisans went out on their first mission—the cutting of telephone lines on the main highway to Vilna. Four Jewish partisans, among them Vitka Kempner, left for Vilna to blow up transformers and the water supply. They penetrated the city, reached the "Kailis" camp, established contact with Madeysker, and carried out their mission in full cooperation with the Communist underground. The urban electricity and water supply systems were damaged. The operation was carried out in the middle of October 1943. When they returned, the group took back sixty unarmed persons from the "Kailis" camp to the forests. Their arrival increased the total in the camp to 350. A fourth battalion called Borba ("Struggle") was formed under the command of a former F.P.O. member, A. Aharonowicz.

Difficult food problems arose with the swelling of the ranks, necessitating the assignment of large forces to "economic operations," in the course of which the first casualties were sustained. "Economic operations" in the Rudniki region were more hazardous than in the Narocz locality. Partisan activity in this neighborhood was in its infancy, and the German administration had full control over the area outside the forest. Communications were easier, and the woodlands were traversed by roads, which made swift military movement possible. The Lithuanian and Polish populations were hostile toward the Soviets and also anti-Semitic. When partisan activity mounted, several villages organized self-defense groups, which were armed by the Germans.

The Jewish partisans in Rudniki often encountered resistance from the farmers during their "economic" raids. German ambushes on the return routes, when the raiders were laden with provisions, were a particular danger.

The Jewish companies began to coalesce and acquire combat experience. They sabotaged highways, bridges, and other objectives, blew up electric and telephone lines, and appropriated arms in the villages.

In mid-October 1943, "Yurgis" arrived from Narocz with his staff and took over the command of the Soviet-Lithuanian guerrilla movement in all of southern Lithuania. The Lithuanian partisan units in Rudniki were formed into a brigade. "Yurgis" issued an order to the command of the Jewish units to desist from bringing more Jewish groups into the forests. This came as a severe blow.[16]

"Yurgis" wanted to avoid a situation in which the overwhelming majority of the partisans in Rudniki would be Jews, thereby exercising a nefarious effect on the attitude of the local populace to the entire partisan movement, which they would tend to regard as an exclusively Jewish camp. It may also be assumed that the Soviet-Lithuanian partisan movement had no desire to see a Jewish majority in its ranks for Lithuanian-national reasons. Furthermore, the difficulties in obtaining food and the fact that the people streaming into the forest brought no weapons certainly influenced the decision to some extent.

The Brigade Command decided, at the outset of November 1943, to establish a Lithuanian guerrilla base in the Nacza forests in order to expand the scope of partisan activity in the south of Lithuania. "Yurgis" ordered two Jewish battalions, which included over 100 fighters, to proceed to Nacza and establish their base there. They were given few arms—eleven rifles and two submachine-guns. Berl Szeresznyevski was appointed Commanding Officer of the force.

When the contingent reached the Nacza forests, it found itself in a most difficult position. The entire area was populated by Poles who were hostile to Jews and Soviet partisans. Lacking sufficient arms, protracted partisan experience, and enough food, the group found it impossible to carry out its task. The

16 Lazar, *op. cit.*, pp. 244–245, 254–255; Korczak, *op. cit.*, 3rd edition, pp. 208–210.

Nacza plan ended in failure, and the combatants returned to the Rudniki forests in mid-December 1943.

The partisan command decided that the four battalions should not remain entirely Jewish, and at the beginning of 1944 some non-Jewish partisans were added to their ranks. The Jewish commanders were also replaced, although most of the deputy commanders were Jews. Yet, in spite of the changes and the fact that the Jews felt these circumstances spelled discrimination, all four battalions remained Jewish in character.

Anti-Semitism was rife in other formations in the Rudniki forests. In several cases Jews were taken out and shot for offenses for which non-Jewish offenders were given lenient punishment.[17]

Men of the combat organization in the Kovno ghetto began to arrive in the Rudniki forests from the end of November 1943, and by the end of May 1944 they had reached a total of about 200. The Kovno Jews were grouped in three battalions of the Kovno Brigade. Ties were established, and friendly encounters ensued between the Vilna ghetto forest veterans and the Kovno ghetto newcomers.

Polish partisans of the Armia Krajowa arrived in the vicinity of the Rudniki forests in the spring of 1944. These Poles tried to expel the Soviet partisans from the region, regarding it as Polish in character and a part of the independent Poland that was to rise after the war. Clashes and conflicts broke out between the Polish and Soviet partisans. The Jewish partisans in Rudniki took part in these clashes and suffered losses in the fighting with the Poles. Scores of Jews who hid with the villagers in these forests were murdered by Polish partisans.[18]

After the receipt of the parachuted arms in the spring of 1944, a far-reaching change for the better occurred in the posi-

17 D. Levin, *Lohamim ve-Omdim al Nafsham*, Jerusalem, 1974, p. 210; Korczak, *op. cit.*, pp. 258, 260–262, 275, 279–281.

18 Juchniewicz, *op. cit.*, pp. 96, 100, 111; Lazar, *op. cit.*, p. 285; Levin, *op. cit.*, p. 188; Korczak, *op. cit.*, 3rd edition, p. 278. Testimony of N. Bazilian, YVA, 0–3/2335, pp. 28–30.

tion of the Soviet partisans in the Rudniki region. They could now increase their strength and make possible the expansion of their military activity and the mining of railroads. The Jewish battalions also benefitted from an increase in arms and sabotage material and amassed considerable partisan experience. Groups of Jewish guerrillas under Jewish command carried out many combat actions—swoops, ambushes, punitive raids against hostile villages, and the blowing up of railroad tracks. Partisan activities continued to mount in scope and quantity during the early summer months. Scores of Jewish partisans fell in these encounters

The great offensive by the Soviet armed forces began on June 23, 1944, and, within weeks, they covered 220 miles and reached the entrance to Vilna. The Vilna partisan units joined the Soviet army units. Soviet forces cut off Vilna on July 7 and 8, 1944. Attempts by the surrounded German troops to break out of the iron ring were defeated, and 8,000 German soldiers were killed and 5,000 taken prisoner in the battle for Vilna.

Jewish partisans from the Rudniki forests followed the Soviet Army into the city. Members of the Jewish underground who had left the ghetto in September 1943 and had gone out to fight the German enemy now returned to Vilna as its liberators.

Chapter 26

IN SUMMARY: A DOOMED STRUGGLE

The Vilna Jews' struggle for existence in the face of Nazi forces bent upon their extermination lasted three years—from June 24, 1941, until July 13, 1944. From the outset there was no question as to who held the balance of power. On the one side was the ruthless German machinery of destruction. It was strong, well organized and could rely on the aid of thousands of Lithuanian volunteers. It also had a clear and well-defined aim: the extermination of Jews. Throughout, the Germans retained the initiative in choosing the time, place, and method of extermination; they were experienced in deluding their victims, deploying the arts of duplicity, and were capable of mustering forces and utilizing the element of surprise to launch their death-dealing *Aktionen*. On the other side, the Jewish community of Vilna was isolated from other Jewish communities, a minority in a hostile or indifferent environment, without foreknowledge of German intentions. The Jews were helpless and lacked guidance from any external factor. These conditions pre-determined the results of the struggle.

The policy of the German administration in Vilna was dictated by the general objective of total extermination. Poised against this end were the local interests and requirements for manpower, which necessitated the retention of a part of the victims. The ruling hierarchy in the Eastern Territories was not centralized, and it was therefore possible for the lower echelons of German administration, in the *Gebietskommissariat* and *Generalkommissariat*, to provide their own interpretations of the general objectives of Jewish annihilation, to influence, and sometimes even to determine, their scope and timetable.

From July until the beginning of November 1941, the administration pursued a policy of exterminating Jews irrespective of age, sex, and ability to work. Due to the large number of Jews in Vilna, it was impossible to liquidate them in one fell swoop, as was the case in the small townships in which the Jewish inhabitants totaled only several thousand. The extermination of Vilna Jewry, therefore, was implemented in a series of separate *Aktionen*, during each of which some thousands of persons were put to death over a period of several months. Concurrently, thousands of Jews were employed in various establishments belonging to the administration, some of which were important for the war economy. There was neither sufficient time nor enough skilled workers to replace Jewish labor.

The German authorities coordinated both processes—extermination and the discharging of Jews from employment—and also prescribed the schedule of the annihilation measures. First to be murdered were unemployed Jews, then those who worked in places from which they could be taken without disrupting production. Last were the skilled craftsmen and others who were engaged in plants vital to the war effort, who would have to be replaced by non-Jews. The various passes distributed to the Jews by the authorities were meant to regulate the pace of the extermination and to assist in identifying the victims at each stage.

The purpose of the concentration of the Jews of Vilna and their enclosure in the ghettos was twofold: as a form of persecution and as a stage of extermination. As long as Jews were dispersed among the non-Jewish populace in all parts of the city, it was easier for them to hide from or elude their oppressors. The *Aktionen* required large forces to seal off areas of the city, to facilitate the identification and seizure of the Jews.

A DOOMED STRUGGLE

Immuring them in the ghetto enabled a considerable saving of German and Lithuanian manpower and released these men to implement *Aktionen* on a larger scale. The creation of two separate ghettos was part of the technique of extermination. It enabled convenient classification of victims, deceived the Jews with regard to German intentions, and created illusions among large numbers of them.

Due to the needs of the German Army in the latter part of 1941, they insisted upon sparing Jewish skilled hands and labor employed in certain German establishments from extermination. Several sectors of the civil administration supported this approach. A struggle ensued among the civil administration, the army, and the SS elements. As a result of this struggle, in the *Reichskommissariat Ostland* it was decided to temporarily suspend the extermination of Jews employed in military and economic enterprises.

When the extermination was discontinued, some 33,000 Jews had already been murdered in Vilna, and 20,000 remained enclosed in the ghetto, among them more than one-third unemployed "illegals."

The mass extermination was resumed in April 1943. As a result of increased partisan activity in eastern Lithuania, the German administration adopted a stricter policy towards the entire civilian population in the region. With regard to the Jews, this policy was expressed by large-scale massacre, including the labor forces in places where there was suspicion of a connection with the partisans. The massacre of the Jews of the ghettos of eastern Lithuania on the Kovno-bound train and of workers in the labor camps of Biala-Vaka, Kena, Bezdany, and Novo-Vileyka was the result of this policy.

Himmler's decree of June 21, 1943, covering all ghettos in the *Ostland,* determined the fate of the Vilna Ghetto. Nevertheless, it was applied in Vilna with particular severity, for in Vilna the ghetto was completely liquidated.

The decision to liquidate the Vilna ghetto, and thus fulfill the demand for manpower in Estonia, and to employ less dras-

tic measures in the Kovno and Shavli ghettos was made because the Vilna ghetto was suspected of being a nest of resistance and partisans, as compared with the ghettos of Kovno and
Shavli.

The Local Population

The attitude of the local population greatly influenced the
possibilities and scope of the rescue of the Vilna Jews. Large
sections of the general population were overtly anti-Semitic and
benefitted from German policy toward the Jews in that they
succeeded in expropriating their property.

The Lithuanian population in Vilna generally cooperated with
the German authorities and took an active part in killing the
Jews. The incorporation of thousands of Lithuanian auxiliaries
in the extermination operations made it possible for these massacres to be implemented on such a wide scale during the initial
months of German administration, before this practice was
applied elsewhere. Even later, when the Lithuanians became
disappointed with the Germans after their expectations of independence were dashed, no substantial change was apparent
in their attitude toward the Jews.

The Polish population, which constituted the majority in
Vilna, did not cooperate with the Germans, but neither were
they helpful to the Jews nor did they give them shelter. The
Polish underground operating in Vilna and the Communist underground that was organized later on took no share at all
in aiding and rescuing the Jews.

Jews who fled from the ghetto or from extermination and
sought aid from the local population encountered refusal for
the most part, and were even handed over to the German
police; although there were some "Righteous Gentiles" who
jeopardized themselves by sheltering the fugitives. The Germans imposed severe penalties, including the death sentence,
on those helping or harboring Jews, thus intimidating and in-
fluencing the local citizens. The hostile and indifferent attitude
of the overwhelming majority of the local population, strength-

ened by the German terror, denied the Jews of Vilna the opportunity for large-scale rescue.

Jewish Reaction

The Jews of Vilna, as the Jews in all of Lithuania, were the
first in Europe against whom the German policy of mass extermination was applied. They had no prior knowledge or
warning of their fate, nor were they prepared for the blow
administered to them. The suddenness of the German invasion
and the flight of the Soviets, coupled with the violence directed
against them by the non-Jewish population, shocked the Jews.
The disappearance of the thousands of men abducted in July
1941, and the mass *Aktionen* during the period of September-
December 1941, implemented with utmost brutality and on such
a scale, increased the shock. So in the fall of 1941, when the
Jews could have known the real meaning of Ponar, most of
them had already been murdered.

They struggled for survival. Two outlets were available to
them during that period—hiding out inside the ghetto, or
fleeing and seeking refuge among the Jews of Belorussia. During the last quarter of 1941, about 11–12,000 Jews were thus
rescued, in addition to the 12,000 Jews that the German administration left in Vilna as "legal" residents.

The first Judenrat was elected by the former leading members of the Jewish community. Its membership comprised a
broad spectrum of political forces that had functioned in the
past in "the Jewish Street" and constituted a continuation of
the traditional leadership. The liquidation of the first Judenrat
and the seizure of other leaders in the various *Aktionen* depleted
the ranks of the traditional leadership. The second Judenrat
that was established in the ghetto was not even elected. The
chairman, A. Fried, was appointed by the Germans, and it was
he who chose the other members—who were, for the most
part, public figures from the vestiges of the first Judenrat.

The appointment of Gens as the "Ghetto Representative,"
and the dissolution of the second Judenrat on July 12, 1942,

put an end to the traditional leadership. Gens was a newcomer who had risen to his post because of the conditions and demands of ghetto life. The German administration saw fit to appoint him to this powerful post solely in order to increase the exploitation of Jewish labor, on the assumption, which proved to be warranted, that through him they would successfully fulfill their objectives.

The policy of the two Judenrats and of Gens was based on an attempt to rescue the Jews of Vilna, or at least part of them. This policy was founded on the assumption that within the German administration there were factors interested in maintaining a Jewish labor force for their exploitation. Consequently, by increasing the number of workers and productivity of the ghetto, it would be possible to prolong its existence. This assumption had a foothold in reality, as there were indeed those within the German administration who sought to retain the Jewish working element in the ghetto. The continuity of their existence afforded hopes that, in the event of the sudden collapse of Germany, the Nazis would not have sufficient time to liquidate the ghetto inhabitants.

During Gens' tenure, ghetto productivity reached its peak. Gens instilled the ideology of "Work to Live" and made it a motto for daily life. His policy made the ghetto a working and productive unit, and some 75 percent of the 20,000 inhabitants were employed in establishments outside the ghetto or workshops inside. This was no small achievement for the administration and Gens' competent leadership. A lively cultural life flourished, schools functioned, social-aid projects were organized, and health services prevented the spread of contagious diseases. The ghetto administration was the principal initiator of these activities.

Gens regarded cooperation with the German authorities as essential, to the point of participating in the *Aktionen*. He believed that, with his cooperation, he would be able to reduce the number of victims and limit them to elderly people. Gens stood firmly against handing over women and children for

[466]

extermination, even though the Germans deemed them superfluous, and he succeeded in protecting them in the selective
Aktionen that he implemented.

The Judenrat and, to a greater degree, the ghetto administration run by Gens were not institutions that implemented the
instructions of the German authorities to the letter nor in their
intended spirit. It was a leadership that endeavored, while
fulfilling the orders of the German administration and avoiding
direct confrontation with it, to extend maximum aid to the
Jewish ghetto community, to save Jews, and to initiate activities
to increase the prospects of ghetto survival. Yet, despite their
good intentions, the Judenrat and ghetto administration headed
by Gens served as tools in helping to execute the policy conducted by the German authorities.

The parties that had been dismantled during the Soviet regime reappeared in the form of active groups in ghetto life.
Party leaders served in Judenrat institutions and were active
in the public life of the ghetto. As a rule they supported the
actions of the Judenrat and of Gens and did not constitute an
opposition.

The underground organization F.P.O. was established in the
ghetto at the end of January 1942. It was the first Jewish
group in Europe that prepared for armed resistance against
the enemy. From the standpoint of size, coherent internal
organization, quantity and categories of firearms at its disposal,
connections with other underground elements, its operational
and partisan activity, there was no comparison between the
F.P.O. and other Jewish underground organizations in Europe.

The underground in the ghetto did not oppose Gens and his
doctrine of "Work to Live," but denigrated the illusions and
hope that by pursuing that course the Jews of the ghetto would
be permitted to survive. The F.P.O. clearly saw the liquidation
of the ghetto approaching and prepared itself for that eventuality by promoting the idea of an uprising to which most of
the ghetto inhabitants would rally. Gens also foresaw a situation in which the ghetto would be liquidated and, for a fairly

long time, did not oppose, and even aided to some extent, the formation of an armed underground that would sally forth to fight on the day of final liquidation. Gens hoped that he would be able to direct this force so that it would not collide with the overriding policy of productivity and the image of a ghetto loyal to the German administration. Reality proved that both these objectives were unachievable. There was an inherent contradiction between a productive ghetto and the image of loyalty, on the one hand, and the acquisition and smuggling-in of arms and departure of ghetto inhabitants for the forests, on the other. These activities could not be implemented without being discovered by the German administration and without jeopardizing the policy on which Gens had founded the existence of the ghetto. During the final months of the existence of the ghetto, a bitter and violent struggle ensued between Gens and his administration on one side and underground elements on the other. The ghetto community at large also participated in the clash.

The ghetto inhabitants as a whole supported Gens' policy of ensuring the survival of their community through their labor, yet at the same time took a sympathetic attitude toward the clandestine forces whose presence in the ghetto restored their debased honor—and perhaps also inspired undefined hopes for the future. But when the ghetto inhabitants felt that underground activity was likely to endanger their existence, they allied themselves with Gens and acted forcibly against the dissenters, as in the Witenberg Affair.

When the F.P.O. called upon the ghetto inhabitants to join in an uprising against the Germans on September 1, 1943, the Jews did not respond to their call. They were not faced on that day with the alternative of ghetto revolt or of being marched to Ponar for immediate liquidation. The alternative was between ghetto revolt or deportation to labor camps in Estonia. A ghetto revolt at that point could not offer a way to life, but only to death—albeit different from that which the Germans planned for them. The majority of the ghetto

Jews could not even fight and die in combat, as they had no weapons. This alternative was reserved for only several hundred armed members of the underground. For the 20,000 inmates, the ghetto revolt meant hiding in *malines* and meeting death when the house was blown up or burned down. Therefore they preferred the alternative of Estonia; this at least granted them a longer lease on life and the hopes implicit in that prolongation.

The F.P.O. did not launch a revolt not only because the people failed to respond to their call, but because they also had an alternative—leaving the ghetto for the forests. This alternative gave more chances of survival and more possibilities for fighting the enemy, and most F.P.O. members preferred this to the one-time fight within the ghetto walls, which would have faint prospects of rescue. Confronted by the failure of the ghetto inhabitants to respond to the call for an uprising and the alternative of leaving for the forests, the F.P.O. Command decided on the latter course.

The Vilna ghetto underground partially succeeded in its aims. It succeeded in taking the majority of its members into the forests and organizing them into partisan units that fought gallantly against the enemy. The withdrawal to the forests did not proceed as the F.P.O. had planned. They conceived the resort to the forests for partisan warfare only after a ghetto revolt, when as many inhabitants as possible would join them. Because the fighters adhered to this idea until the last possible moment, their secession to the forests was much more difficult to undertake. An earlier decision to leave would have made it possible to take not only F.P.O. followers, but also more young men out of the ghetto.

The option of the forests and the *partizanka* as a means of rescue and struggle were available only to armed young men. The couriers who came to the ghetto from the woods brought with them the message that only those with combat ability and arms would be accepted in partisan units. The forest was no place for Jewish masses from the ghetto. Moreover, the distance between Vilna and the forests and the intervening hostile environment deterred mass flight. Seven hundred underground members reached the forests from the Vilna ghetto, and, in spite of the many difficulties and hindrances, they became partisans and fought heroically against the Nazis.

The Jews of Vilna behaved and reacted in consonance with the conditions dictated by the realities of life; these realities permitted no other reaction. In the prevailing conditions, the policy laid down by Jacob Gens was the only one that afforded hope and some prospect of survival. But even this failed, and the fact that the ghetto was productive did not spare it from liquidation.

The fate of the Jews of Vilna after the liquidation of the ghetto was tragic. The greater majority of those deported to Estonia and Latvia, those who remained in the labor camps in Vilna, and others who sought rescue in hiding-places were eventually murdered by the Germans.

Jewish Vilna had its origins in the late fifteenth century. Over many generations, the Jewish community of Vilna grew and prospered, and by dint of its writers, scholars, rabbis, and in- stitutions devoted to the Torah and the intellectual content of its existence, that community won a central and enduring place in the spiritual life of the Jewish people the world over. Such was Jewish Vilna until its annihilation by the German Nazis and their Lithuanian collaborators. The period of the Holocaust was, for the Jewish citizen of Vilna, one of struggle without prospect; the forces of extermination that were arrayed against him were simply too overwhelming. Out of a total of approx- imately 57,000 Vilna Jews subjected to the Nazi regime, only some 2-3,000 survived, one-third of them in the forests—a pitiful remnant of the terrible destruction of "Jerusalem of Lithuania."

Most survivors did not come back to Vilna. Those who did at first, later left, for they could not—and did not want to— rebuild their lives on the ruins of Jewish Vilna. Most left for Palestine, to find personal resurrection alongside national re- vival in the State of Israel.

APPENDIX A

PROVISIONAL DIRECTIVES FOR THE TREATMENT OF JEWS IN *REICHSKOMMISSARIAT OSTLAND*

For the ultimate solution* of the Jewish problem in the territory of the *Reichskommissariat Ostland,* my directions contained in my speech in Kaunas on July 27, 1941, are to be implicitly followed.

If in the course of implementation of my oral directions further measures are taken, especially by the Security Police, they are not affected by the following provisional directives. The aim of the *provisional* directives is only to guarantee the minimum measures taken by Commissars General and *Gebietskommissare* there, and only for so long as extensive measures for the ultimate solution of the Jewish problem are impossible.

Ia The present directives cover to begin with only the Jews who are subjects of the German Reich, the Protectorate of Bohemia & Moravia, former republics of Poland, Lithuania, Latvia, Estonia, the U.S.S.R., or their member states, or who are stateless.

Ib Other alien Jews, various half-breeds and partners of Jews who do not want to share the fate of their Jewish partners, are not to be given an exit permit to leave the *Reichskommissariat,* as it is a war-zone. They are to be watched. With this end in view, the following can be imposed on them: daily compulsory registra-

---

* Read: the extermination of all Jews.

[471]

tion, prohibition of changing their domicile, assignation of specified domicile, prohibition of leaving the town or city area, confinement to domicile. If necessary they are to be taken in custody until further decision.

II A Jew or Jewess is he or she who is descended at least from three racially pure Hebrew grandparents. Moreover, a Jew or Jewess is he or she who is descended from one or two racially pure Hebrew grandparents and either

a) is or was a member of the Judaic religious community, or

b) was married on June 20, 1941, or later, to a person who is a Jew or Jewess in the meaning of the present directives, or lived, lives now, or will live in the future, in conjugal community with such a person.

III In case of doubt, the *Gebiet* ("City") Commissar decides, as he is duty bound, who is a Jew in the meaning of the present directives.

IV The General Commissars must at once undertake the following measures, provided that civil administration has been set up in their areas:

a) Through compulsory registration, all Jews must be registered with indication of name, sex, age, and residence. Full coverage is also secured by using the lists of Jewish communities and the evidence of reliable local people;

b) The Jews are to be ordered to wear a distinctive mark—a yellow six-pointed star not less than 10 cm. across—on the left side of the chest and on the middle of the back;

c) Jews are to be forbidden:

(1) to change their place of permanent residence and their domicile without the permission of the *Gebiet* ("City") Commissar.

(2) to use the pavement (sidewalk), means of public conveyance (railway, trams, buses, steamers, cabs, etc.) and motor-cars,

(3) to use public rest and recreation areas, e.g., bathing places, parks, sports and play grounds, etc.,

(4) to visit theaters, cinemas, libraries, and museums,

(5) to attend schools whatsoever,

(6) to own cars and radio sets,

(7) to butcher according to Jewish rites;

d) Jewish physicians and dentists are allowed to treat Jews only.

If ghettos or camps are set up, Jewish physicians and dentists are to be dispersed there for care of the inmates. Jewish apothecaries are to be allowed to practice their trade only in ghettos or camps. Apothecary shops hitherto managed by Jews are to be turned over to Aryan management. Jewish veterinaries are prohibited their trade.

e) Jews are barred from the following professions and occupations :

(1) solictor, lawyer, barrister,

(2) notary public, counsel, legal adviser,

(3) banker, money-changer, pawnbroker,

(4) agent, middleman, broker,

(5) real-estage agent,

(6) any itinerant trade;

f) For the handling of Jewish property the following is to be ordered:

(1) *General*
Jewish property is to be seized and secured. From the moment of seizure, the former Jewish proprietor loses all rights to his property. Trans-

actions violating the present regulations are invalid and are hereby declared null and void.

(2) *Compulsory Registration*

All Jewish property is to be registered at once. The manner of registration is to be set by General Commissars or by *Gebietskommissare*. Everyone who is in possession or in charge of Jewish property, or who without being owner, possessor, caretaker, or custodian, dispose of Jewish property, is obliged to register that property. Thus, compulsory registration affects not only Jewish owners, but also all those who manage Jewish property, or have taken it in safe-keeping, or have gained possession of it in any other way.

Jewish property is to be registered on special blanks, a specimen of which is appended.

The General Commissars order the procedure of registration with regard to local conditions and name the office that is to accept the completed registration sheets. If possible the registration should take place at the offices of the *Gebietskommissare*. But the *Gebietskommissare* should also be empowered to authorize non-German offices to issue and accept registration blanks. These offices have to forward the handed-in registration sheets to the *Gebietskommissare*.

(3) *Compulsory Handing-over*

The Jewish property is to be handed over at first notice. The handing-over notification can be made by way of a public appeal or by personal order to individuals. The General Commissars must order, by a public appeal, the

immediate handing-over of the following objects:
a. local and foreign currency,

b. bonds, securities, effects and evidence documents of any kind (e.g., shares, debentures, IOU, promissory notes, bank books and savings-bank books),

c. valuables and jewellery (e.g., coined and uncoined gold and silver, other noble metals, jewels, gems, etc.).

The objects handed over are to be registered in a continuously numbered acceptance ledger in duplicate (copy) according to appended sample. The registration entry is to be signed by the person delivering the objects and by the office accepting them. The copy of the entry is to be forwarded by the accepting office to the *Gebietskommissar* without any delay. The objects handed over are to be sent to the pay-office of the *Gebietskommissar* and secured there. Special directions will be issued concerning the realization of the objects in question.

(4) *To meet living expenses* the Jewish population is allowed to keep:

a. the part of their household articles needed for bare subsistence (e.g., furniture, clothes, and linen);

b. a daily sum of money of .20 *Reichsmark* (2 rubles) for every Jewish family member. The monthly sum is to be released in advance;

V   The following additional measures with regard to local conditions, especially economic ones, are to be vigorously aimed at:

a) The countryside is to be cleared of Jews;

b) Jews are to be ousted from al trades, especially from trading with agricultural produce and other food-stuffs;

c) Jews are to be banned from places that are important from the economic, military, or ideological point of view, or are resorts and spas;

d) The Jews are to be concentrated in towns or quarters of big cities with a predominantly Jewish population, where ghettos are to be set up. Jews are to be prohibited from leaving the ghettos.

In their ghettos they are to be given only such an amount of foodstuffs which the population at large can do without, but not more than is needed for scanty feeding of the ghetto inmates. The same applies to other necessities of life.

The ghetto inmates are to arrange their internal affairs by self-government, to be supervised by the *Gebiet* or City Commissar or his deputy. For the maintenance of public order in the ghettos, one may select a force from among the Jewish inmates themselves. They can be armed with rubber truncheons or with sticks at best and must wear on the right upper arm a white armlet with a yellow six-pointed star on it.

For sealing off the ghettos hermetically from without, it is expedient to use auxiliary police from among the local population. Entering the ghetto is to be made subject to permission by the *Gebietskommissar*.

Able-bodied Jews are to be put to forced labor in accordance with the demand for labor. The economic interests of local people worthy of futherance may not be impaired through Jewish forced labor. The forced labor can be performed by Jewish teams in ghettos, outside of ghettos, or by individual Jews outside of ghettos where such had not yet been set up (e.g., in the workshop of the Jew). The remuneration has not to correspond to the work performed; it has only to serve for the bare subsistence of the forced laborer and his disabled family members, taking into account his other ready money (cf. IV f 4 b). The private enterprises and persons for whose benefit the forced labor is performed pay an adequate sum of money at the pay-office of the *Gebietskommissar*, which in its turn pays out an adequate remuneration to the forced laborers. Special directions will be issued as to the balancing of the incoming sums of money.

It is left to the discretion of the General Commissars to uniformly introduce the measures enumerated under Number V in their respective territories or to authorize their *Gebietskommissars* to introduce them individually. The General Commissars are also empowered to give more detailed directions in keeping with the present directives or to authorize their *Gebietskommissare* to do so.

APPENDIX B

EXPLANATIONS TO THE REGULATION

When the Regulation was being reviewed, questions of important principles arose in several units. Some of the questions stemmed from misgivings, founded on weakness and insufficient readiness to accept combat realities. For that reason, the Command felt itself bound, without reference to which of the groups confronted these problems, to furnish a full reply to these questions:

1. How should the organization behave in the event of partial liquidation of the ghetto?
2. What was a fighter to do if left alone, without any prospects to continue fighting against a superior enemy force?
3. Why not go to the forests immediately?
   What is the ultimate combat objective?
4. Is it permissible to hide in a *maline*?

ANSWERS

A. *How should the organization behave in the event of partial liquidation of the ghetto?*
1. The F.P.O. will begin to fight when danger threatens the ghetto in its entirety.
2. It is possible that partial *Aktionen* of a local character may be implemented in the ghetto at the cost of dozens or hundreds of lives.

3. Our attitude is that the life of every Jew is worth defending, and it is forbidden to abandon them to enemy hands.
4. But the F.P.O., which is not a large military force capable of launching open war on the enemy, will not undertake action in the defense of the life of each individual Jew.
5. The F.P.O., which is the vanguard of the surviving Jewish population (not only in Vilna), can—by its annihilation—leave the ghetto defenseless.
6. Such tactics would be regarded as quixotic and suicidal. Moreover, the Jewish public would condemn us as *provocateurs*, and we would have to fight our own brothers.
7. But a premature action is tantamount to frivolity; an action taken too late—a crime.
8. The F.P.O. will begin to fight at the time of an *Aktion* that they deem to be the beginning of the end.
9. The time for action will be determined by the Central Command by an evaluation of the situation and in accordance with reliable information at its disposal.
10. Our inadequate armament supply justifies the premise that the F.P.O. cannot be activated at any time. But this cannot justify withholding combat at a time when danger threatens the general existence of the ghetto. It is our duty at such time to fight with every available weapon, and even without weapons—with our bare hands.

B. *What was a fighter to do if left alone, without any prospects to continue fighting against a superior enemy force?*
11. If placed in such a position as a result of battle, the individual fighter must retreat.
12. If there are still active combat groups, the fighter must forge his way to join them at any cost.
13. If there are no such combat groups left, the fighter may seek rescue.
14. Despite the readiness of the F.P.O. fighter to fall in battle, it is not his ultimate goal to fall in battle on the last foothold of the ghetto.

[479]

15. The purpose of the F.P.O. is not defense of the ghetto but defense for its own sake.
16. The purpose of the F.P.O. is resistance and rescue.
17. This is not to say that a man who sees himself outnumbered and outgunned should, in advance, give up the fight.
18. Avoidance of action in the hour of battle for any reason (inadequate arms, lack of opportunity, etc.) are tantamount to treason.

C. *Why not go to the forests immediately?*
19. No. The desire to go into the forests immediately shows a lack of understanding of the basic tenets of the F.P.O.
20. The concept of a Jewish Partisans' Organization is both national and social: to organize the struggle of the Jews to defend their life and honor.
21. Immediate withdrawal into the forests at this juncture would be interpreted as seeking personal refuge and rescue, just as hiding out in a *maline* means seeking individual rescue.
22. We shall go into the forests only in the afternoon of battle. After having carried out our mission, we shall take with us as large a number of Jews as possible and forge our way into the forests, where we can continue our struggle against the murderous conqueror as an integral part of the general partisan movement.
23. Only through combat and resistance can the Jewish masses be saved with us.

D. *Is it permissible to hide in a* maline?
24. No! The reply to this question has already been clarified in the Regulation. Going into a *maline* is, under all conditions, treasonous.

4 April, in the Vilna Ghetto

The Commander

[480]

APPENDIX C

INSTITUTE OF STATISTICS IN THE VILNA GHETTO DEPARTMENT OF ACCOUNTS

Income of Ghetto Administration in First Half of 1942

	Income (in Thousands of Reichsmarks)								
	Food Dept.	Labor Tax	Internal Tax	Housing Dept.	Health Dept.	Industry	Burials	Miscl.	Total
January	16.7	10.5	—	13.3	4.2	1.0	1.5	10.4	57.6
February	30.4	11.8	—	13.7	4.7	2.2	2.1	8.2	73.1
March	48.8	19.2	1.3	17.0	8.4	1.9	1.9	6.1	104.6
April	48.8	20.1	2.0	22.0	12.5	2.5	1.1	5.0	114.0
May	61.7	20.8	6.5	21.4	19.7	2.1	0.8	5.4	138.4
June	86.0	26.3	6.2	23.0	19.6	2.1	0.6	7.1	170.9
Total	292.4	108.7	16.0	110.4	69.1	11.8	48.0	42.2	658.6

Expenditure of Ghetto Administration in First Half of 1942

	Expenditure (in Thousands of Reichsmarks)				
	Wages	Social Welfare	Maintenance	Miscl.	Total
January	32.5	7.8	—	7.6	47.9
February	46.4	15.5	6.1	11.2	79.2
March	59.4	23.2	2.8	4.5	89.9
April	52.0	23.8	11.6	2.7	90.1
May	71.1	34.2	10.2	1.0	116.5
June	74.1	38.0	7.0	1.2	120.3
Total	335.5	142.5	37.7	28.2	543.9

Food Distribution (in Tons) — Judenrat Cooperative
(January–June 1942)

Commodity	Method of Distribution	January	Feb.	March	April	May	June
Bread	Food cards	65.4	57.2	52.7	58.0	58.0	64.0
	Cooperative	2.6	2.9	20.4	11.6	8.5	16.4
Flour	Food cards	7.5	7.5	9.0	7.5	5.0	11.0
	Cooperative	1.8	11.9	2.3	0.3	0.1	0.4
Vegetables	Food cards	16.3	16.5	24.8	26.8	6.7	18.8
	Cooperative	9.6	13.5	40.1	22.5	34.0	35.6

Distribution by Public Kitchen (January–June 1942)

	January	February	March	April	May	June
Total No. of Lunches	86,227	93,557	94,933	73,580	86,983	93,449
Free meals of this total	42,829	55,242	60,730	58,718	65,468	74,766
Percentage of free meals	49.7	59.0	64.0	79.8	75.3	80.0
Daily average of meals	2,782	3,341	3,062	2,453	2,806	3,115
Total No. Evening meals	8,754	9,395	9,382	9,083	14,754	21,831

BIBLIOGRAPHY

BOOKS

Ajzensztain, B. *Ruch podziemny w ghettach i obozach; Materialy i dokumenty.* Warsaw: Centralna Zydowska Komisja Historyczna w Polsce, 1946.

Appeal (An) ed., Lithuanian American Information Center, New York: 1944.

Balberyszski, M. *Shtarker fun ayzn.* Tel Aviv: Hamenorah, 1967.

Bartoszewski, W. *Ten jest z ojczyzny mojej; Polacy z pomoca Zydom, 1939–1945.* Cracow: Wydawnictwo ZNAK, 1966.

Black Book (The). ed., Jewish Black Book Committee. New York: 1946.

Blumenthal, N. and Kermish, J. *Ha-Meri ve-ha-Mered be-Getto Varshah.* Jerusalem: Yad Vashem, 1965.

Brown, Z. and Levin, D. *Toldoteha shel Mahteret.* Jerusalem: Yad Vashem, 1962.

Catastrophe of European Jewry (The). eds., Y. Gutman and L. Rothkirchen. Jerusalem: Yad Vashem, 1976.

Cohen, I. *Vilna.* Philadelphia: Jewish Publication Society of America, 1943.

Dallin, A. *The German Rule in Russia 1941–1945.* London: Macmillan, 1957.

Documents Accuse. ed., E. Rozauskas. Vilna: Gintaras, 1970.

Documents of German Foreign Policy, 1918–1945. Vol. VIII. Washington: U.S. Government Printing Office, 1954.

Dworzecki, M. *Yerushalayim de-Lita ba-Meri u-va-Sho'a.* Tel Aviv: Mifleget Po'alei Eretz-Yisrael, 1951.

———, *Mahanot ha-Yehudim be-Estonia, 1942–1944.* Jerusalem: Yad Vashem, 1970.

Engelshtern, L. *In getos un velder; Fun Vilne biz di Naliboker vildenishn.* Tel Aviv: Ha-Kibbutz ha-Me'uhad, 1972.

Gar, J. *Azoy iz es geshen in Lite; Tsu der geshikhte fun der sovetisher memshole 1940–1941.* Tel Aviv: Hamenorah, 1965.

Garfunkel, L. *Kovnah ha-Yehudit be-Hurbanah.* Jerusalem: Yad Vashem, 1959.

Gilboa, Y. *Lishmor la-Nezah.* Tel Aviv: Masada, 1963.

Gitlerovskaya okupatsiya v Litve; Sbornik statyey. Vilna: Mintis, 1966.

Grossman, C. *Anshei ha-Mahteret.* Tel Aviv-Merhavia: Sifriat Po'alim, 1965.

Gutman, Y. *Mered ha-Nezurim.* 2nd ed. Tel Aviv: Sifriat Po'alim, 1963.

Haupt, W. *Heeresgruppe Mitte 1941–1945.* Bad Nauheim: H. H. Podzum, 1968.

Hilberg, R. *The Destruction of the European Jews.* Chicago: Quadrangle Books, 1967.

Höhne, H. *The Order of the Death's Head.* London: Secker-Warburg, 1970.

Hoth, H. *Panzer-Operationen.* Heidelberg: R. Vowinckel, 1956.

Istoriya Velikoy Otechestvennoy Voyny Sovetskovo Soyuza 1941–1945. Vol. II. Moscow: Voyennoye Izdatelstvo Ministerstva Oborony SSSR, 1961.

Kaczerginski, S. *Partizaner geyen!* 2nd ed. Munich: Oyf der vakh, 1948.

———, *Hurbn Vilne.* New York: Tsiko, 1947.

Kalinin, P. *Partizanskaya respublika.* Minsk: Bielarus, 1968.

Kermish, J. *Mered Getto Varshah be-Einei ha-Oyev.* Jerusalem: Yad Vashem, 1959.

Korczak, R. *Lehavot ba-Efer.* Tel Aviv: Sifriat Po'alim, 1946.

Kowalski, I. *A Secret Press in Nazi Europe.* New York: Central Guide Publishers, 1969.

Kruk, H. *Togbuch fun vilner geto.* New York: YIVO, 1961.

Lazar, H. *Hurban u-Mered.* Tel Aviv: Massu'ot, 1950.

Levin, D. *Lohamim ve-Omdim al Nafsham.* Jerusalem: Yad Vashem, 1974.

Masines zudnes Lietuvoje, 1941–1945. Vol. I. Vilna: Mintis, 1965.

Muzey in Paneriai (Der): Revolutsye-muzey fun der Litvisher SSR. Vilna: Mintis, 1966.

My Obvinyaem. Dokumenty i materialy o zlodeyaniyakh gitlerovskikh okupantov i latyshskikh burzhuaznykh natsionalistov v Latviskoy Sovetskoy Sotsialisticheskoy Respublike 1941–1945. Riga: Liesma, 1967.

Nazi-Soviet Relations, 1939–1941; Documents from the Archives of German Foreign Office. Washington: U.S. Printing Office, 1944.

Neustadt, M. *Hurban u-Mered shel Yehudei Varshah.* Tel Aviv: Hahistadrut Haklalit, 1946.

Prestupnye tseli — prestupnye sredstva; Dokumenty ob okupatsionnoy politike fashistskoy Germanii na teritorii SSSR (1941–1944). Moscow: Gospolitizdat, 1968.

Rann, L. *Ash fun Yerushalayim de-Lite.* New York: Vilner Farlag, 1959.

Reitlinger, G. *The Final Solution.* 2nd ed. London: Mitchell, 1968.

Rolnik, M. *Ani Hayevet le-Sapper.* Jerusalem: Ahiever, 1965.

Rudashevski, Y. *The Diary of the Vilna Ghetto.* Tel Aviv: Lohamei Hagetta'ot and Ha-Kibbutz ha-Me'uhad, 1973.

Sefer Dror. Ein Harod: Ha-Kibbutz ha-Me'uhad, 1947.

Sefer ha-Partizanim ha-Yehudim. Vol. I. Tel Aviv: Sifriat Po'alim, 1958.

Sefer ha-Shomer ha-Za'ir. Vol. I. Merhavia: Sifriat Po'alim, 1956.

Sefer Milhamot ha-Getta'ot. Tel Aviv: Ha-Kibbutz ha-Me'uhad, 1954.

Sefer Zikkaron le-Ezor Swenzian. ed., S. Kanc. Tel Aviv: Irgun Yoz'ei Ezor Swenziany b'Israel, 1965.

Sheib, I. *Ma'aser Rishon.* Tel Aviv: Hamatmid, 1950.

Shutan, M. *Geto un vald.* Tel Aviv: 1971.

Sudarski, M. and Katsenelnbogn, A. *Lite.* New York: Kultur-gezelshaft fun litvishe yidn, 1951.

Sutzkewer, A. *Getto Vilna.* Tel Aviv: Shavi, 1947.

Tenenbaum, J. *Race and Reich.* New York: Twayne, 1956.

Tenenbaum-Tamaroff, M. *Dappim min ha-Delekah.* Tel Aviv: Ha-Kibbutz ha-Me'uhad, 1948.

Tennenbaum-Backer, N. *Ha-Adam ve-ha-Lohem.* Jerusalem: Yad Vashem, 1974.

Trunk, I. *Judenrat.* New York: Macmillan, 1972.

United States 83rd Congress, House of Representatives: Third Interim Report of the Select Committee to Investigate Communist Aggression and the Forced Incorporation of the Baltic States into the U.S.S.R. Washington: U.S. Government Printing Office, 1954.

Vsenarodnoye partizanskoye dvizheniye v Belorusi v gody Velikoy Otechestvennoy Voyny. Minsk: Bielarus, 1967.

Warlimont, W. *Im Hauptquartier der deutschen Wehrmacht 1939–1945.* Frankfurt am Main - Bonn: Athenäum Verlag, 1965.

Yahadut Lita. Vol. III. Tel Aviv: Ha-Agudda le-Ezra Hadadit le-Yoz'ei Lita be-Israel, 1967.

Yerushalayim de-Lita; Illustrated and Documented Album. ed., L. Rann. New York: Laureate Press, 1974.

Yerushalmi, E. *Pinkas Shavli.* Jerusalem: Mossad Bialik and Yad Vashem, 1958.

Zeidel, H. *Adam be-Mivhan; Pirkei Sho'ah.* Tel Aviv: 1971.

ARTICLES

Barlas, H. "Mivza Aliyat Lita," *Dappim le-Heker ha-Sho'ah ve-ha-Mered*, 2nd Series, Vol. I, 1970.

Bauer, Y. "Rescue Operations through Vilna," *Yad Vashem Studies*, Vol. IX, 1973.

"Der Witenberg tog in vilner geto," *YIVO Bleter*, Vol. XXX, 1947.

Dworzecki, M. "Anton Schmidt; Feldwebel Anti-Nazi be-Getto Vilna," *Yad Vashem Bulletin*, XIX–XX, 1959.

Epstein, B. "Di likvidatsye fun vilner geto," *YIVO Bleter*, Vol. XXX, 1947.

Friedman, P. "Tsi iz in der Nazi-tsayt geven an 'Ander Daytshland'? Dokument fun der yidisher untererdisher organizatsye vegn Anton Schmidt," *YIVO Bleter*, Vol. XXXIX, 1955.

Gar, J. "Baltishe lender," *Algemayne entsiklopedye — Yidn*, Vol. VI, 1963.

Garlinski, J. "Polskie panstwo podziemne (1939-1945)," *Zeszyty Historyczne*, Instytut Literacki, Paris, 1974.

Gerszatter, E. "Oyf yener zayt geto," *Bleter vegn Vilne*, ed., Farband fun vilner yidn in Poyln, Lodz, 1947.

Helman, Y. "Le-Reshita shel ha-Mahteret ha-Haluzit be-Polin ha-Kvusha," *Dappim le-Heker ha-Sho'ah ve-ha-Mered*, 2nd Series, Vol. I, 1970.

Idelstein, Y. "Masa u-Mattan im Shiltonot Brit ha-Mo'azot al Yezi'at Yehudim," *Gesher*, Vol. I, No. 42, 1965.

Juchniewicz, M. "Udzial Polakow w litewskim ruchu oporu w latach 1941–1944," *Wojskowy Przeglad Historyczny*, 1968.

Kalmanowitch, Z. "A togbuch in vilner geto," *YIVO Bleter*, Vol. XXXV, 1951.

Keren-Paz, A. "Derekh ha-Yissurim shel Partizan Yehudi," *Pirsumei Muze'on ha-Yohamim ve-ha-Partizanim*, Tel Aviv, September 1973, Vol. II, No. 5(20), pp. 11-13.

Kermish, J. "Nigudim Ma'amadiyim be-Getto Varshah," *Enziklopedya shel Galuyyot*, Vol. II, 1959.

Klibanski, B. "The Underground Archives of the Bialystok Ghetto," *Yad Vashem Studies*, Vol. II, 1958.

Kovner, A. "Nissayon Rishon le-Haggid," *Yalkut Moreshet*, No. 16, 1973.

Libo, A. "Vos mayne oygn hobn in Vilne gezen...", *Bleter vegn Vilne*, 1947.

Neshamit, S. "Ben Shituf Pe'ulah le-Meri," *Dappim le-Heker ha-Sho'ah ve-ha-Mered*, 2nd Series, Vol. I, 1970.

BIBLIOGRAPHY

Oren, O. "Me-Vilna Derekh Yappan el ha-Olam ha-Hofshi," *Yalkut Moreshet,* No. XI, 1969.

Palewski, S. "Zikhroynes," *YIVO Bleter,* Vol. XXX, 1947.

Perlis, Y. "He-Halutz bi-Yme ha-Hurban be-Polin," *Mi-bifnim,* Vol. VI, 1940.

Reznik, N. "Ha-Tenuah be-Getto Vilnah u-be-Ya'arot Lita," *Massu'ah,* Vol. I, 1973.

Shohat, A. "The Beginnings of Anti-Semitism in Independent Lithuania," *Yad Vashem Studies,* Vol. II, 1958.

Segal, I. "Der ershter kontsert in vilner geto," *fun letstn khurbn,* Vol. I, 1946.

Skolski, S. "Betar be-Mahteret Rusyah," *Ha-Medinah,* 1944.

Soloveichik, A. "Dray fertl yor unter di daytshn in Vilna," *YIVO Bleter,* Vol. XXX, 1947.

Sudarski, M. "Yidn in der umophengiker Lite," *Kultur-gezelshaft fun litvishe yidn,* 1951.

Zabiello, S. "Ksztaltowanie sie koncepcji 'Burzy,'" *Wojskowy Przeglad Historyczny,* 1968.

ARCHIVAL MATERIAL OF SPECIAL INTEREST

YAD VASHEM ARCHIVES

1) *Isaac Stone Collection of NS Documents 0–18*
— *Einsatzgruppe A*
Complete Report of October 15, 1941, operations and experience against the Partisans, Nuremberg Doc. L–180.
— From *Reichskommissar Ostland* II a 4, Provisional Directives for the Handling of the Jewish Questions in *Reichskommissariat Ostland*, Nuremberg Doc. PS–1138.
— Notice of September 3, 1941, signed Gewecke, on the liquidation of Jews in Shavli. Nuremberg Doc. PS–3660.
— Letter from the *Gebietskommissar* in Shavli to the *Reichskommissar Ostland* in Riga concerning SS-*Standartenführer* Jäger, pertaining to encroachment of SS in the confiscation of Jewish Property, signed Gewecke, September 8, 1941. Nuremberg Doc. PS–3661.
— Letter from the *Gebietskommissar* in Shavli to the *Generalkommissar* in Kovno about Jewish affairs in Shavli, signed Gewecke, September 10, 1941. YVA, 0–18/142.
— Letter from the *Gebietskommissar* in Shavli to the *Reichskommissar Ostland, Gauleiter* Lohse, Riga, on differences with the SS (Hamann and Jäger) in connection with the handling of Jewish affairs, signed Gewecke, September 11, 1941. YVA, 0–18/144.
— Letter from the *Generalkommissar* in Kovno to the *Reichskommissar Ostland* in Riga, pertaining to report IIa4 of August 18, 1941, about ghettos, September 12, 1941. YVA, 0–18/146.
— Note about confiscation of Jewish property in Vilna. Signed Wysocki, Riga, September 23, 1941. YVA, 0–18/148.
— Copy of a letter concerning confiscation of Jewish property by SS in Kovno, September 24, 1941. YVA, 0–18/149.
— *Reichskommissar Ostland* to the *Höhere SS-und Polizeiführer* at the *Reichskommissariat Ostland* in Riga on Police measures and handling

of Jewish property, signed Lohse, September 25, 1941. YVA, 0-18/151.

— *Reichskommissar Ostland* to the *Generalkommissar* in Riga, Kovno, Minsk on Police measures and handling of Jewish property, signed Lohse, September 25, 1941. YVA, 0-18/151.

— Letter from the *Generalkommissar* in Riga, Department II to the *Reichskommissar Ostland* concerning arrangement of ghettos, Jewish forced labor camps, obligation to register and relinquish Jewish property and also measures applied to *Mischlinge*, signed Hürmann, October 20, 1941. YVA, 0-18/154.

— Letter from *Reichskommissar* for Occupied Territories, Berlin, concerned departments, to *Reichskommissar Ostland* in Riga on executions of Jews in Libau, signed Dr. Leibbrandt. October 31, 1941. Nuremberg Doc. PS-3663.

— Telex from *Reichskommissar Ostland,* to the *Gebietskommissar* of Vilna about Jewish manpower for the Wehrmacht. YVA, 0-18/157. November 7, 1941.

— Letter from *Reichskommissar Ostland* to SS-*und Polizeiführer* at *Reichskommissariat Ostland* on liquidation of Jews, and training of native professional replacements, November 8, 1941. YVA, 0-18/165.

Notice by Trampedach on a complaint of the Wehrmacht, concerning Jewish manpower.

— *Reichskommissar Ostland* Department II political, to Department I personnel concerning *"Referat Judentum,"* August 10, 1941. YVA, 0-18/184.

— The *Generalkommissar* in Kovno to the *Gebietskommissare* in Kovno, Vilna and Shavli on the establishment of the ghettos, signed Dr. von Renteln, August 26, 1942. Nuremberg Doc. PS-3659.

— *Reichskommissar Ostland* to the *Höhere* SS-*und Polizeiführer* in Tallin, Riga, Kovno, Minsk on Jewish professionals working for the Wehrmacht, December 2, 1941. YVA, 0-18/203.

2) *Sutzkewer-Kaczerginski, Vilna Collection*
    JM/1951 (microfilm)

— 1-7, Maps of:
    Ghettos I & II, Ponar, Plastics' Plant, etc.

— 223, Regulations concerning "Brigadiers" Council, November 28, 1942.

— 224, Speech by Gens at a meeting of the Brigadiers, October 13, 1942.

— 233, Internal Memorandum of April 30, 1942, from the Labor Department to the Judenrat about taking women instead of men, for work within the ghetto, to permit the men to work outside as prescribed by German order.

— 280, Diagram of the industrial structure of the ghetto, May 18, 1943.
— 649, N. Reznik's account of the activities of the FPO.
— 651, Proclamation: "Lomir zikh nisht lozn firn vi shof tsu der shkite," January 1942.
— 687, 15 Documents on Jewish possessions appropriated by Lithuanians and Germans.
— 688, A. Sutzkewer's account of the liquidation of the ghetto and flight to the forests (1942).
3) *Unpublished Diaries* (on Vilna)
— Epstein, Lazar, JM/2822.
— Shur, Grisha, JM/2786.
4) *Trials and Other War Crimes Materials*
— Trial of Filbert, Alfred Karl: Yad Vashem, TR–10/388 and TR–10/388a.
— Trial of Gewecke: YVA, TR–10/657, TR–10/670, TR–10/683.
— Trial of Murer, Franz: YVA, TR–11/233.
— Trial of Weiss, Martin: YVA, TR–10/29, TR–10/381.
— Trial of Werner, Windisch: YVA, TR–10/646, TR–10/665.
— Group trial — SS personnel, Pinsk Area: TR–10/786.
— Report of Soviet Commission on investigation of Nazi War Crimes in Vilna: Yad Vashem, 0–53/430.
— Einsatzgruppen Case N–IX: (Nuremberg Document)
    a) — *Ereignismeldungen UdSSR*, 1–195.
    b) — *Meldungen aus den besetzten Ostgebieten.*
Summation Report of Einsatzkommando 3, December 1, 1941 (Jäger Report) 0–18/245.

MORESHET ARCHIVES

No.

D.1.485 : Notice by the *Gebietskommissar* of Vilna district, Wulff, to the local population announcing punitive measures against those resisting the Germans, August 12, 1943.

D.1.343 : Announcement by Chairman of Judenrat, A. Fried, of April 16, 1942, concerning the replacement of permits.

D.1.344 : Order by Gens, of August 10, 1943, concerning registration of manpower in the ghetto.

D.1.346 : Announcement by Gens, of August 22, 1943, concerning obligation to report for work.

ARCHIVAL MATERIAL

D.1.347 : Announcement referring to cultural activities in the ghetto, June 21, 1943.

D.1.354 : Report on activity of the Ghetto Police in first half of 1942.

D.1.355 : Speech by Gens at meeting of "Brigadiers" and police chiefs, on March 5, 1943, concerning acquisition of arms from Poles.

D.1.357 : Minutes of meeting of October 27, 1942, devoted to hearing report of the *Aktion* at Oshmyany.

D.1.361 : Excerpts from the *Geto Yedies.*

D.1.362 : Excerpts from newspaper.

D.1.409 : Historical survey of the Old Ghetto in Vilna (1633-1869) and the ghetto during the Nazi regime — prepared by Dr. Heller in the Vilna Ghetto, at the request of representatives of Alfred Rosenberg Institute functioning in Vilna.

D.1.4634 : Announcement by Gens of July 6, 1943, prohibiting possession of silver, gold, etc.

D.1.4638 : Announcement by Gens of the murder of two Jews caught buying food outside the ghetto.

D.2.102 : Short annotated diary by Abba Kovner.

TESTIMONIES

YAD VASHEM ARCHIVES (YVA)

1.	Adamowicz, Irena —	0-33/415
2.	Arkin, Pnina —	0-3/2048
3.	Auerbach, Arieh —	0-3/2733
4.	Bazilian, Natan —	0-3/2335
5.	Bergmann, S. —	0-3/3043
6.	Bram, Joshua —	0-3/3045
7.	Bronowski, Shlomo —	0-3/2335
8.	Hazan, (Ya'ari) Bella —	0-33/298
9.	Hazan, Bella (additional testimony has not been cataloged)	
10.	Collective Interview, FPO (Abba Kovner, Reizel Korczak, Vitka Kempner)	0-3/3882
11.	Harten, Shoshana —	0-3/2262
12.	Haubensztok, Emma —	0-3/1286
13.	Jaffe, Sarah —	0-3/2803
14.	Yashuner, Shlomo —	0-3/1830
15.	Karni, N. —	0-33/1274

16.	Katz, Abba —	0–3/3959
17.	Kovner, Abba (A) —	0–33/353
18.	Kovner, Abba (B) —	0–33/1239
19.	Misulowin, Michael —	0–3/1781
20.	Mushkat, Joseph —	0–3/3748
21.	Przewalska, Josepha —	0–3/3027
22.	Reznik, Nissan (A) —	0–33/1238
23.	Reznik, Nissan (B) —	0–33/419
24.	Segal, Israel —	0–3/2669
25.	Sneh, Moshe —	0–33/1237
26.	Steiman, Leon —	0–3/1782
27.	Treger, Zelda —	0–3/3670
28.	Wolkoviski-Shilmaver, Feiga —	0–3/1783
29.	Zelinska, Hadassah —	0–3/1827

INSTITUTE OF CONTEMPORARY JEWRY (ICJ)

1. Basuk, Chaim (12) 70
2. Harmatz, Joseph (12) 124
3. Collective Interview, "Yechiel's Struggle Organization" (12) 88
4. Kovner, Abba (4) 2
5. Kovner, Abba (12) 83
6. Kuperberg, Zippora (12) 161
7. Rogowski, Nyuma (12) 78
8. Telrant, Elhanan (12) 180

MORESHET

1. Bogen, Alexander — A. 54
2. Rindziunski, Alexander — A. 381
3. Trotzki, Samuel — D. 2.55

BEIT LOHAMEI HA-GETTA'OT
Rindzionski, Alexander — (on tape only)

INDEXES

A. INDEX OF PLACES

B. INDEX OF PERSONS